MASTERS OF THE UNIVERSE,
SLAVES OF THE MARKET

MASTERS OF THE UNIVERSE,
SLAVES OF THE MARKET

Stephen Bell & Andrew Hindmoor

Harvard University Press
Cambridge, Massachusetts
London, England
2015

Printed in the United States of America

First printing

Library of Congress Cataloging-in-Publication Data

Bell, Stephen, 1954–
Masters of the universe, slaves of the market / Stephen Bell, Andrew Hindmoor.
pages cm
Includes bibliographical references and index.
ISBN 978-0-674-74388-5 (alk. paper)
1. Banks and banking. 2. Financial crises. 3. Global Financial Crisis, 2008–2009.
4. International finance. I. Hindmoor, Andrew. II. Title.
HB3725.B45 2015
332.109'0511—dc23 2014028185

In memory of Robert Harold Bell and Fan Austin

Contents

Abbreviations

ABS	asset-backed security
ANZ	Australia and New Zealand Banking Group
APRA	Australian Prudential Regulation Authority
BCBS	Basel Committee for Banking Supervision
BMO	Bank of Montreal
BNS	Bank of Nova Scotia
CBA	Commonwealth Bank of Australia
CDO	collateralized debt obligation
CDS	credit default swap
CEO	chief executive officer
CIBC	Canadian Imperial Bank of Commerce
CLO	collateralized loan obligation
CMBS	commercial mortgage-backed security
CRO	chief risk officer
ED	executive director
FCIC	Financial Crisis Inquiry Commission
FDIC	Federal Deposit Insurance Corporation
FICC	fixed income, currency, and commodities
FPC	Financial Policy Committee
FSA	Financial Services Authority
FSOC	Financial Stability Oversight Council
HI	historical institutionalism
HUD	Department of Housing and Urban Development

ICB	Independent Commission on Banking
IIF	Institute for International Finance
IMF	International Monetary Fund
LBG	Lloyds Banking Group
MBS	mortgage-backed security
NAB	National Australia Bank
NED	nonexecutive director
OCC	Office of the Comptroller of the Currency
OFHO	Office of Federal Housing Oversight
OSFI	Office of the Superintendent of Financial Institutions
OTC	over the counter
OTS	Office of Thrift Supervision
PAIRS	Probability and Impact Rating System
PRA	Prudential Regulatory Authority
RBA	Reserve Bank of Australia
RBC	Royal Bank of Canada
RBS	Royal Bank of Scotland
RMBS	residential mortgage-backed security
ROE	return on equity
SEC	Securities and Exchange Commission
SIV	structured investment vehicle
TD	Toronto-Dominion
VaR	value at risk

Introduction

The banking and financial crisis that peaked in 2008 and that engulfed many of the major US, UK, and European commercial and investment banks in the New York and London markets was "arguably the greatest crisis in the history of financial capitalism" (Turner 2009b, 5). Very few bankers fully understood the scale and complexity of the new financial markets they had created, with their vulnerabilities and huge "systemic risks" and their capacity to inflict economic carnage on a vast scale. This book seeks to establish a clear account of what happened during the crisis, why it happened, and what can be done to prevent another crisis from occurring.

We argue that the *origins* of the crisis can be gleaned from answering an obvious but rarely posed question—Why did the financial and banking systems in the core economies of the United States and the United Kingdom implode, while the banking systems in other countries, such as Australia and Canada, did not? Such comparisons provide a vital clue: banking crises, or their absence, we argue, are largely driven by the nature of the banking markets found in each country. We provide a detailed comparative analysis showing how, even within an apparently globalized banking system, the behavior of individual banks was shaped by nationally specific market contexts. We find that banking markets with high levels of competition and low returns from traditional lending are likely to pursue risky forms of trading activities and are prone to financial crises. In the United States and the United Kingdom, highly competitive banking markets placed bankers under intense pressure to reengineer their balance sheets in the search for additional profits, largely in highly leveraged mortgage-backed securities (MBSs) trading. It was the collapse of these markets that triggered the banking crisis in 2007. Such pressures were strong in the United States and the United Kingdom, but weak in the Australian and Canadian markets. National market conditions in banking thus emerge as the key explanation of the *origins* of the crisis.

We also show that structural forces embodied in so-called systemic risk within financial markets were central in driving the *scale* of the banking and credit crisis. Systemic risk was manifested in the high leverage or debt relationships between major banks and wholesale funding markets in the United States and the United Kingdom. When the value of MBSs collapsed, bankers and credit markets became uncertain about which banks were facing what losses. The result was a market panic that saw credit markets freeze. This was the proximate cause of the *scale* of the crisis.

Unlike during the 1930s, the financial crisis that began in 2007 and peaked in 2008 did not stem from a collapse in the real economy. Nor was it on the whole an old-fashioned banking crisis caused by poor lending decisions to corporate borrowers with inferior credit standards. True, some banks, such as HBOS in the United Kingdom and Wachovia in the United States, were compromised by the legacy of poor corporate and property lending decisions, but for most banks, as we show in Chapter 3, loan default rates were relatively low. For example, Lloyds Bank and Barclays Bank in the United Kingdom had loan impairment rates of only 2.5% and 2.7%, respectively, in 2007, while in the United States, Bank of America had just 0.6% of gross loans recorded as impaired in 2007, while Citigroup and JP Morgan Chase had impaired loans at just 0.25% and 0.15%, respectively.*

The origins of the financial crisis can instead be traced back to losses in subprime MBS markets in the United States. However, the subsequent scale and severity of the crisis stemmed not simply from these losses, which were, when measured against the size of the overall financial system, relatively small, but from a more general fall in the value of the assets held on bank balance sheets and especially by the freezing of wholesale funding mar-

*Unless otherwise attributed, data relating to bank balance sheets in this and subsequent chapters is drawn from the OSIRIS database.

kets on which banks relied. Much of this was driven by market overreaction and panic in response to the initial subprime and MBS losses and by uncertainty about which banks were sitting on what losses as the crisis unfolded. It was the fragile nature of the financial structures that had been created and the systemic risk thus generated that was the core problem.

Most accounts of the crisis offer either exposés of greedy, reckless bankers and financiers, or long lists of factors that contributed to the crisis: from low interest rates that fueled housing and financial asset bubbles, to weak financial regulation, to the collapse of the US subprime real estate market, to the subsequent unraveling of the complex financial instruments built on subprime mortgages. The former accounts are usually written by journalists or bank insiders and offer detailed descriptions of what happened inside banks but often fail to adequately place banks in wider contexts of influence (W. Cohan 2009, 2011; Sorkin 2009). The latter accounts are usually offered by economists, but the "list" approach makes it hard to tell what really matters or how contributing factors fit together (Davies 2010; Stiglitz 2010; Blinder 2013).

This book offers a different approach, one that allows us to isolate *key* drivers of the origins and scale of the crisis from the long list of causal factors produced in many accounts. It is true that the factors just noted were a part of the story. But these were not the primary factors that actually drove banks and the behavior of bankers. Regulation, for example, was focused mainly on capital levels in individual banks and lacked a perspective on the system as a whole. Nor did regulation seriously probe or question the rise of trader banks, the growth of the so-called shadow banking system, or the buildup of trading or leverage in the core markets. Indeed, in some ways, regulation encouraged such trends. Regulation, then, was permissive. It interacted with markets, but it did not fundamentally drive bankers in the direction they took, especially in pursuing trading and massive leverage structures. Indeed, in the United States and the United Kingdom, powerful bankers were highly influential in obtaining the regulation they required. Our analysis thus distinguishes between more fundamental causal factors such as market structure and those that were merely permissive. Our institutional and structural analysis of the crisis points primarily to the impacts of liberalization and "financialization," especially intense market competition; new, attractive trading opportunities; and the buildup of system complexity and risk in the core markets. In Australia and Canada we also show how the absence or diminished nature of such factors produced quite different outcomes.

We thus argue that the economic and financial crisis was essentially a banking crisis driven by bankers interacting with institutional and wider structural contexts that strongly shaped behavior and outcomes. Starting in the 1970s, bankers and state leaders in the heartlands of global finance in the United States and the United Kingdom presided over the liberalization of financial markets. This was a major institutional change that radically expanded the domain of markets, market forces, and competition in contemporary capitalism and in finance. Liberalization was partly a reaction to the strong financial regulation of the postwar decades: a period in which banking and finance were restrained by the capital controls and fixed exchange rates of the postwar Bretton Woods international financial architecture and by domestic interest rate and credit regulations. These regulations were put in place as a response to the financial and banking calamities of the 1930s and as part of postwar efforts to stabilize the financial system. Financial liberalization from the 1970s lifted these shackles and resulted in what is now often called financialization: a structural change in capitalism marked by the huge and growing scale of the financial sector.

The incentives and pressures embodied in banking markets are central to our story. In the crisis-hit countries, market incentives built around remuneration systems offered huge rewards for those willing to take risks in the growing financial markets. Competitive market pressures and the fear and market penalties of being left behind by competitors drove many banks to take extraordinary risks, especially with the new financial instruments associated with the securitization bonanza that took off in the first decade of the twenty-first century (hereafter referred to as the 2000s). This saw formerly illiquid assets such as mortgages and other forms of debt repackaged into complex tradable securities such as collateralized debt obligations (CDOs) or collateralized loan obligations (CLOs). These were assembled and traded on an industrial scale, and, as noted, their collapsing values in 2007 and 2008 sparked the crisis. Such trading was pumped up by a huge increase in bank debt or leverage, the latter defined as bank debt relative to capital. To rapidly expand their trading and asset portfolios, banks borrowed more and more money, which meant a huge increase in exposure to short-term wholesale funding markets. The growth of financial trading and leverage within interconnected banking and financial markets amplified systemic risk, a structural feature of financial markets that made the system more fragile and prone to chain reaction effects, panics, and financial collapse (Haldane and May 2011).

Bankers, while authoritative within their own proximate institutions (and in relation to the state), were in fact constrained, and in many cases they appeared as almost "enslaved" by these wider institutional and structural pressures. In the United States and the United Kingdom, liberalization had freed bankers and financiers from earlier forms of regulation, but it had subsequently constrained them in highly competitive markets that generated strong pressures to engage in high-risk banking practices that increased systemic risk and set the stage for the collapse of the entire system. Nevertheless, not all bankers, even in the United States and the United Kingdom, succumbed to these pressures. As we show in later chapters, the ideas held by senior bankers were also central to how they read the situation and how they acted. Those who were sanguine about market developments and who truly believed in the financial boom were the ones who became "enslaved" by it. They did not much question the market and institutional pressures they confronted and instead joined the herd and rode the boom.

Important here too was the fact that liberalization did not result in the retreat of the state from financial markets. Deregulation created opportunities for banks to reengineer their balance sheets, but governments continued to support the growth of the financial sector through deposit-protection schemes and explicit guarantees in the United States and implicit guarantees in the United Kingdom that banks that were deemed "too big to fail" would, if necessary, be bailed out in a crisis. This form of state support constituted a type of moral hazard that encouraged further risk taking. Moreover, other financial regulations, especially the design of capital controls, further encouraged the growth of the shadow banking sector composed of nonbank financial entities and the securitization of financial assets. Our key argument, then, is that bankers (and supportive state elites) in the core, interlinked Wall Street and London financial markets created but were then overwhelmed by the market institutions and financial structures they had built.

We use the methods of political science to study the behavior of bankers in these institutional and structural contexts. We draw on institutional theory, especially historical institutionalism, to help us understand how bankers shaped and were shaped by the banks and wider institutions and structures in which they operated. Agents and the contexts in which they operate are mutually shaping. This key insight will help us explain banking behavior and outcomes. Studying such "agency-structure" interaction has long been a staple of political science analysis. In this perspective, institutions, such as banks, are best seen as mediating the relations between agents and wider contexts. The ideas held by agents are also an important mediator, shaping how agents perceive the world and operate within it. Furthermore, as Streeck (2009) argues, we need to locate institutional analysis, particularly in political economy, within an account of broader systemic or structural transformations, especially in relation to major transformations in capitalism in recent decades, such as financialization. This is a more realistic and encompassing approach than the current mainstay of comparative political economy, the varieties of capitalism approach (Hall and Soskice 2001), which tries to explain the behavior of firms as rational efficiency seekers shaped by relatively narrow sets of institutional parameters.

Most strands of institutional theory argue that institutions heavily shape and constrain agents. Yet senior bankers were (and remain) authoritative within their own institutions, especially in the core markets of the United States and the United Kingdom. In the 1990s and 2000s these Masters of the Universe—a phrase popularized by Tom Wolfe's account of a Wall Street tycoon in *The Bonfire of the Vanities*—reshaped their institutions and revolutionized banking and finance. During this period, a new kind of "trader bank" (Erturk and Solari 2007) emerged, characterized less by traditional lending to businesses and house buyers, and more by securitization and large-scale financial trading supported by highly leveraged wholesale borrowing and massive balance sheet expansion. Such activities explain why between 2004 and 2007 the balance sheets of the world's ten largest banks more than doubled in size, while the balance sheets of banks in the United Kingdom grew to five times GDP (Acharya, Cooley, et al. 2009, 286). As we demonstrate through a detailed analysis of bank balance sheets in Chapter 3, however, the largest UK and US banks reengineered their balance sheets in different ways and to differing degrees. In the United

Kingdom, the Royal Bank of Scotland (RBS) and Barclays massively expanded their investment bank operations. HBOS largely avoided financial trading but became overcommitted in mortgage and commercial property lending. JP Morgan Chase entered but then wound back its exposure to the securitization market. Citigroup, Merrill Lynch, Bear Stearns, and Lehman Brothers demonstrated no such reticence. Between January 2006 and August 2007, for example, Citigroup issued $18 billion in CDOs, which, rather than being sold to third-party investors, were retained on the bank's own balance sheet (FCIC 2011, 196). By December 2007 Citigroup had accumulated $37 billion of "sub-prime related direct exposures," $43 billion of "highly leveraged loans and financing commitments," $22 billion of Alt-A mortgage securities (Citigroup 2008, 10), and $114 billion in off–balance sheet guarantees. While the individual details of bank balance sheets differed, the largest banks in the United States and the United Kingdom appeared collectively to have fashioned new kinds of immensely profitable financial products, mastered risk, and launched a "platinum age" for the global economy.

Bankers and cooperative state elites, especially in the United States and the United Kingdom, built this new liberalized financial system. The majority of bankers and financiers were driven by sanguine beliefs about the safety of the new markets and products they had created and by the huge material rewards these markets offered. Liberalization and financialization also had important political spillovers. They helped create a power structure that bewitched most political and regulatory leaders, who saw financial sector growth as a valuable source of innovation, taxes, jobs, and national prestige. In turn, states provided subsidies that cheapened credit for big banks, as well as low official interest rates and permissive forms of financial regulation.

Then came the crash. Our account of how this unfolded is contained in Chapters 1 and 2, which emphasize the way in which agents became trapped within the financial structures they had created. The turmoil began with the collapse of the real estate bubble in the United States and the associated losses in the subprime mortgage securitization markets, starting in 2007. These collapsing markets then produced losses on the balance sheets of exposed banks. Importantly, these declared losses were not huge, yet they were sufficient to trigger the crisis. This is because the banking system that had evolved during the financial boom was highly vulnerable to systemic risk fueled by chain reactions and market panics. MBS trading turned out to be risky, partly due to the complexity and opacity of the securities that were being traded. The myriad and largely opaque debt and trading interconnections among banks worldwide made it very hard to calculate counterparty risk. Exactly who was holding what and who was going to lose how much as a result of falling asset prices became impossible to determine. Sentiments in this context were important. As the crisis gathered, fear and eventually panic engulfed the system. Banks and other financial institutions stopped lending to each other, and interbank credit evaporated. This soon led to a general liquidity crisis that destroyed banks and damaged whole economies. Leverage, opacity, complex interdependencies between financial institutions, and dependence upon short-term wholesale funding were the sources of systemic risk that were the proximate causes of the implosion of Northern Rock, Bear Stearns, Lehman Brothers, HBOS, and RBS.

Bankers and financiers had created this fragile asset and debt structure in the decades prior to the crisis. And in a classic two-way agency-structure interaction, it was the structure of systemic risk that would eventually be their undoing. Our Masters of the Universe had unwittingly sealed their own fate. Prior to the crisis, bankers appeared to be in complete control. Yet they were in fact operating in a highly fragile structure they had created. Liberalization empowered the Masters of the Universe, but it also trapped them within institutions and structures they did not fully understand and could not control. Bankers were overwhelmed and were revealed as almost slaves of the markets they had helped create. The story here is also analogous to the fate of the brilliant creator of the Frankenstein monster that eventually turns on its master.

We know that the nature of banking markets and the intensity of competition among the largest banks were important causes of the crisis because different types of market context shaped different forms of banking behavior across countries. The 2007–2008 meltdown is often described as a "global" financial crisis. Yet outcomes varied markedly across countries, something that is often overlooked within previous accounts of the crisis (although see J. Friedman 2009, 152–155). Banks in Australia and Canada, for example, largely avoided trading the kinds of securities based on US subprime mortgages that sparked the crisis. Much the same applies to banks in Japan, Israel, France, and Spain (Howarth 2012; Royo 2012). The main reason why so many bankers behaved differently in these countries is that the banks were operating in different kinds of markets, especially in relation to the level of competitive pressure and the nature of profit opportunities. Banks in Canada and Australia, on which we focus in Chapters 4 and 8, could make high profits through traditional lending practices and did not confront the same pressures to reinvent themselves as trader banks. They thus avoided the fate of most of the bankers in the core US and UK markets.

While we emphasize the impact of institutions and structures on agents, our account is not deterministic. As noted above, although institutions and structures exerted strong pressures, what also stands out is a small but nevertheless significant level of *within-country* banking variation in the United States and the United Kingdom. The particular character of agents and their ideas, as well as corporate cultures, thus matters. Different agents and bank cultures can interpret the same context differently and potentially act with at least some degree of discretion. Despite the findings of behavioral finance theory, which we detail in Chapter 1, not all bankers in the core markets became irrationally exuberant or rushed to follow the herd. The particular and variable patterns of discretion and insight forged by agents, even in similar institutional contexts, are thus an important part of our story, reflecting the variability of agents' ideas and discrete micro-institutional capacities. As we show in Chapter 7, a number of banks in the core markets largely avoided the meltdown. Banks such as HSBC and Lloyds TSB (prior to its takeover of HBOS) in the United Kingdom and JP Morgan, Wells Fargo, and Goldman Sachs in the United States avoided the worst of the carnage. They were not swayed by the euphoria of their rivals and managed either to resist intense market pressures to copy the apparently successful strategies of their immediate rivals, or, in the case of Goldman Sachs, having accumulated significant exposures, managed to reverse their positions. We show how and why they did this, underlining the fact that sometimes some agents can resist or sidestep wider pressures.

There are two other features of this book. First, having set out the institutional and structural pressures that shaped bankers in broad terms in Chapters 1 and 2, we then focus on bankers in the United States and the

United Kingdom at a finer level of detail. In Chapter 3, we get inside the major banks in these countries through a meticulous analysis of their balance sheets, specifying their trading and leverage exposures. Here, we draw extensively upon annual reports and financial statements as well as standardized data on company performance. In Chapter 5 on the United States and in Chapter 6 on the United Kingdom, we also get inside these banks through interviews and other accounts of how bankers thought and acted at the micro level. While we emphasize institutional and structural pressures and constraints on bankers, it is also necessary to explore how bankers themselves interpreted, shaped, and responded to such pressures. Only by reconstructing such an account of agency and the contexts in which bankers operated can we explain why bankers behaved as they did. This approach will allow us to understand why bankers at banks such as Bear Stearns, Citigroup, or RBS so badly misread their positions and eventually succumbed to systemic pressures and collapse. It will also allow us to understand why bankers at JP Morgan or Wells Fargo read their situation differently and avoided the worst trading excesses and avoided a meltdown. This approach will also help us understand why Canadian and Australian bankers did not reengineer their balance sheets and become trader banks despite multiple entreaties to do so. In aiming to reconstruct the mind-set and strategy of bankers and show how this shaped and was in turn shaped by the contexts in which they operated, we utilize insider accounts of what bankers did and how they thought. We use testimony on crisis inquiries in the United States and the United Kingdom and the transcripts of interviews we conducted in 2012 and 2013 with bankers, regulators, and other informed observers.

Second, our book directly links its causal analysis of the crisis to a diagnosis of contemporary reform measures. The two key drivers of the crisis were risky securities trading in the context of massive leverage and mounting systemic risk. Trading and systemic risk thus need to be addressed through major reforms. As we argue, however, this is not what is happening. Bank lobbying and reticent governments have instead produced relatively small increases in bank capital and have attempted to shield commercial banking from the excesses of trader banking. Neither reform goes far enough or squarely addresses the root causes of the crisis. Moreover, governments in the United States and the United Kingdom still appear to favor large, complex financial sectors. They also persist in believing that highly competitive banking markets are inherently valuable, without recognizing that competitive market pressures were one of the structural roots of the crisis. The deeper problem limiting reform is that bankers and financial interests remain powerful in the United States and the United Kingdom and in wider settings. This is not just due to their famed lobbying capacity. Their power also derives from the structures that liberalization and financialization have created. The centrality of finance in the core economies has produced a high degree of state dependence on finance, particularly as a source of jobs, tax revenue, and credit, as well as campaign contributions. In the United Kingdom, this has been distilled as the "British Dilemma" by Chancellor George Osborne (2010): the need to "preserve the stability and prosperity of the nation's entire economy" while also protecting London's status as a "global financial centre that generates hundreds of thousands of jobs." State elites on both sides of the Atlantic still believe in "big finance." We argue that despite the crisis and attempts at reform since, the underlying nexus between finance and the state still persists, limiting more fundamental reform.

The Chapters

In Chapter 1 we unpack the theoretical tools we will use to explain the behavior of bankers in the four countries we study—the United States, the United Kingdom, Canada, and Australia. At the level of agency, we show how findings from behavioral finance research help us understand behavioral pathologies such as market overshooting and herding behavior among bankers. However, we need to place agents in wider shaping contexts. We employ a historical institutionalist approach because we believe this offers the best way to understand the mutually shaping interactions between our key agents (bankers) and the institutional and wider structural contexts in which they operated. We focus on bankers and emphasize how the contexts in which they operated partly shaped their beliefs, preferences, and behavior, their institutional discretion, and the resources and opportunities available to them.

In Chapter 2 we show in more detail how bankers in the financial heartlands of the United States and the United Kingdom revolutionized banking in the 1990s and 2000s and how this resulted in the massive growth of bank balance sheets, securitization, financial trading, leverage, and wholesale borrowing. We explain the complexities of the new financial engineering and innovation that led to an explosion in financial trading through processes such as securitization and the creation of financial instruments and derivatives such as CDOs. We also trace how this process was funded and how banks radically expanded their balance sheets by taking on massive leverage. In the second part of the chapter we then describe how the financial crisis unfolded in 2007–2008—how the downturn in the US subprime market sparked a far larger crisis in the banking system: firstly, through balance sheet losses from collapsing prices in MBSs and other trading assets and, secondly, via the systemic risk created through the extension of leverage and wholesale funding in increasingly opaque, complex, and fragile markets.

In Chapters 3 and 4 we analyze the banks in the four countries we study. We provide a detailed analysis of bank balance sheets that shows how the largest banks in the United Kingdom and the United States (Chapter 3) and Australia and Canada (Chapter 4) behaved in the years prior to the crisis. These chapters describe what the major banks in each of these countries actually did and show how variable bank behavior actually was, both across countries and within them.

In Chapters 5 and 6 we examine how bankers and regulators in, respectively, the United States and the United Kingdom thought and behaved in the years prior to the financial crisis. Institutional incentives and increased competition encouraged many banks to extend their leverage, trading, and dependence upon wholesale funding, leading to the growth of an extremely fragile banking system characterized by the presence of huge systemic risks. Did bankers and regulators recognize these risks? We argue that, in most cases, they did not. The prevailing ideas held by most bankers did not question the institutional pressures and incentives that drove them on. Bank executives believed that their internal risk management technologies allowed them to carefully calibrate risks; that securitization had led to a dispersal of risk; that the use of derivatives such as credit default swaps (CDSs) had allowed them to effectively insure risks; and that continued economic growth would create further profit opportunities. Executives were also reassured by the sanguine risk assessments of credit rating agencies, boards of directors, regulators, and politicians, who expressed few concerns about whether the financial boom was sustainable and, in many cases, actively encouraged risk taking. We use interview material and documentary evidence to show how most bankers understood the financial world prior to the crisis. We show how they reconstructed their banks and shaped wider institutional arrangements, such as regulation and risk management, in pursuit of their strategies. In this way, these two chapters complement and extend the detailed balance sheet analysis of individual bank performance in Chapters 3 and 4 and the broader and more general argument about institutional change and the accumulation of systemic risk in Chapters 1 and 2.

In Chapter 7 we explain how some of the more prudent UK and US banks mentioned earlier managed to largely avoid the crisis. We explore why these banks resisted pressures to become trader banks and why others that did, such as Goldman Sachs, outwitted the market and reversed or offset their exposures prior to the crisis. Given the pressures on the banks in these markets, this is a story about agency and about swimming against the tide. It is about the different ways in which executives in these banks saw and understood the world prior to the crisis and about the different ways in which these banks operated, often exploiting particular market niches and capacities. Despite institutional and structural pressures, these more prudent banks show that agents can sometimes confront wider forces and carve out distinctive strategies. One of the great unanswered questions, however, is how long some of these banks could have held out if the boom had continued for several more years.

In Chapter 8 we show how and why the major Canadian and Australian banks similarly avoided joining the herd. We argue that government regulation of the market, particularly of capital and leverage, was stronger in these countries and that this partly explains the conservatism of these banks. We also argue that in both countries earlier banking crises had a chastening effect on behavior. Bank behavior was, however, also strongly shaped by market forces. In both countries competitive pressures were less intense, and high profits could also be made from traditional business and mortgage lending within buoyant economies. This reduced the incentive banks had to reengineer their balance sheets and empowered agents within the banks who perceived the risks inherent in adopting new trading strategies.

Finally, Chapter 9 addresses questions about bank reform. It argues that this needs to focus on market pressures that drove risky trading and the excessive buildup of leverage within banking systems. Current reforms to boost the capital base of banks and to try to shield commercial banks from risky trading are a start but do not go far enough. Bolder moves are required to reduce the market pressures that drive risky trading and leverage. Canada and Australia show what a model of sound banking and finance looks like, so there are lessons here about how to build more resilient banking systems, especially in terms of market structures that incentivize more conservative and stable forms of banking. The Conclusion provides an overview of our key arguments.

1

Masters of the Universe

Why did so many bankers in the core US and UK markets reinvent their banking strategies and use high leverage to pursue what turned out to be risky securities trading, and why did losses in these markets spark such a huge financial crisis? In contrast, why did Australian and Canadian bankers largely eschew such practices and broadly pursue a traditional banking approach? Further, why did some bankers even in the United States and the United Kingdom resist following the herd and instead pursue safer strategies? This chapter and Chapter 2 provide a broad explanation of such bank behavior and banking outcomes.

To explain bankers' behavior we need to understand how bankers thought and acted, focusing first on their ideas and basic cognitive processes. Beyond this, we also need to examine how bankers and financiers shaped and were shaped by the contexts in which they acted. To do this we use various approaches, including behavioral finance theory and an expanded version of historical institutionalism (HI), a theory drawn from political science (Steinmo and Thelen 1992; Hall and Taylor 1996; Lowndes 2010; Bell 2011). Institutional theories in political science and in other disciplines such as sociology and economics argue that people create institutions but are subsequently shaped by them. Institutions are the rules, norms, and role expectations that shape agents' agendas and preferences and that constrain or enable institutionally situated behavior. This approach can help us explain the behavior of bankers within banks.

A limitation, however, is that such an approach tends to overplay institutional constraint and underplay just how authoritative and assertive institutional agents such as bank chief executive officers (CEOs) can be in shaping institutions. Another limitation is that institutional approaches have not given sufficient attention to the interactions among agents, institutions, and wider structures (Bell and Feng 2013). Institutions are essentially about rules and norms, but structural factors, such as population growth or the structure of markets or the economy, are much broader. Structural factors matter in our account, especially regarding the collapse of the US housing market, the nature of profit opportunities with financial markets, and the systemic risk embodied in financial markets that amplified specific losses in leveraged securities markets into a full-blown financial crisis. It is therefore necessary to analyze how institutions shape and are shaped by broader structural transformations in capitalism, such as financialization (Streeck 2009).

In this chapter we first explore banker agency and how bankers thought and acted, drawing on theories of behavioral finance. These accounts, however, also need to locate agents within wider contexts to fully explain behavior and outcomes. To this end, we review HI theory, arguing that it needs to extend its focus on institutions to wider structures and also to questions of political power. In the second part of the chapter we focus on the power of bankers and financiers in relation to the state and show how, in the United States and the United Kingdom, an alliance between finance and state leaders led to the liberalization of the financial sector from the 1970s. This was a process of institutional change that liberated bankers and financiers and promoted structural change in the form of financialization. In Chapter 2 we show how bankers and financiers were, however, heavily shaped—indeed, almost "enslaved"—by the institutional and structural dynamics of markets that had constituted the revolution in banking and that would eventually lead to their demise.

How Bankers Think

Looking back with the benefit of hindsight, it seems painfully obvious that the trading and leverage models used by so many banks in the financial centers of New York and London in the years prior to the crisis were unsustainable. How could an estimated 64,000 securities have been issued with an AAA credit rating in 2005–2006 when only slightly more than a dozen publicly listed companies in the United States were considered equally creditworthy (Dash 2011)? How could banks in the United Kingdom have been allowed to wind down their cash reserves to less than 1% of liabilities (King 2009a)? How could credit rating agencies have been allowed to compete to advise on packaging the securities they also rated? And how is it that a California strawberry picker earning $14,000 a year was lent $720,000 to buy a house without even paying a deposit (M. Lewis 2010, 97)? To help us answer such questions we need to understand how our key agents and those in authority thought and made sense of the world.

Institutions and structures only exert an effect when mediated through the activities of people (Archer 2000). This suggests that the ideas and basic behavioral biases of people shape how they interact with institutions and wider structural forces. An agency-based HI approach can easily integrate constructivist notions of interpretive agency and give full recognition to the fact that ideas, language, and intersubjective discursive processes provide the crucial building blocks for establishing meaning and understanding and thus of purposeful action in politics and institutional life (Bell 2011). As we show in later chapters, the different ideas held by bankers about the housing market or the safety of mortgage-backed securities (MBSs) helps explain the markedly different banking strategies we encounter, both across countries and also within the United States and the United Kingdom. Therefore, in order to understand why bankers behaved as they did prior to the crisis we need to understand how they understood the financial world and the risks they thought they were taking.

Most of the participants in the financial system were not simply responding to skewed incentive structures such as bank remuneration schemes that rewarded risk taking; they were also on the whole "true believers." The assumption made within many banks was that their trading activity and leverage were largely riskless. Ideas we now regard as flawed survived because traders, CEOs, regulators, investors, and politicians were not rational but "boundedly rational" (H. Simon 1957). Bankers and financiers operated on the basis of incomplete information and were susceptible to myopia, overoptimism, and bandwagon effects. A virulent form of market euphoria came to dominate the thinking of many bankers. This led them to discount or neglect complex or inconvenient information and warning signals (Hindmoor and McConnell 2013). At the height of the boom many bankers were willing to take huge bets based on hunches and imitative strategies. Such ideas and motives mattered because in an uncertain environment the assumptions key actors made about how markets worked, how other actors would behave, and how governments would respond shaped their perceptions and actions. Post the crisis, the former chairman of the Federal Reserve, Alan Greenspan (2009), pointed out that "once a bubble emerges out of an exceptionally positive economic environment, an inbred propensity of human nature fosters speculative fever that builds on itself, seeking new unexplored, leveraged areas of profit . . . Speculative fever creates new avenues of excess until the house of cards collapses."

All this can be traced back to more basic cognitive and behavioral drivers that have been extensively explored within behavioral economics and behavioral finance, fields of research that have emerged in recent decades to correct the lack of realism about human behavior found in many standard economic models (R. McMahon 2005, 4). Most fundamentally, these approaches reject rational actor accounts of agency and focus instead on "bounded rationality" and simplifying interpretive and decision-making procedures such as the use of heuristics, as well as important cognitive and behavioral biases, including "irrational exuberance" (Shiller 2000). Studies of bounded rationality find that actors do not assess all choice options in a fully informed way when making decisions but instead take shortcuts to economize on search and deliberation costs, evaluating only some options, often with limited information. Simon (1957) argues that agents "satisfice" by opting for an "acceptable" solution under conditions of uncertainty and "constrained optimization." Agents use heuristics, simplifying assumptions or rules of thumb when making decisions under conditions of uncertainty (Tversky and Kahneman 1974; Kahneman and Tversky 1984). They also display a wide array of cognitive biases (Conlisk 1996). For example, most bankers did not respond to warning signals in the run-up to the crisis because, like most other actors, they did not routinely update their beliefs or assumptions on the basis of new evidence. Instead, they exhibited "confirmation bias," highlighting evidence that confirmed their existing prejudices while filtering out or dismissing conflicting evidence as implausible (Jervis 1976; Hermann and Preston 2004). In *Thinking, Fast and Slow,* Kahneman

(2011, 248) points more generally to people's willingness to jump quickly to conclusions on the basis of limited evidence, often ignoring the possibility that there are "unknown unknowns."

A further important finding from behavioral studies comes in the form of prospect theory, which argues that agents subjectively define value in terms of gains or losses from a given (often current) position rather than in terms of final gains or overall wealth positions. A related finding is that individuals tend to worry more about losses and will take bigger risks to avoid losses than to secure a gain. In other words, people tend to be loss averse and will worry about downside risks generally about twice as much as they value gains (Kahneman and Tversky 1979; Tversky and Kahneman 1992). At a first glance, this does not look like a useful theory of banking behavior prior to the crisis, where great risks were being taken to secure gains rather than avoid losses. The apparent paradox can be resolved by pointing out that most of the agents in question did not perceive their behavior to be particularly risky and did not link their activities to large potential losses. Instead, they were optimistic about their behavior and were determined not to lose out on profits being made by their immediate rivals.

Behavioral studies also point to the effects of problem specification or "framing." Agents tend to frame decisions narrowly, dealing with individual decisions in a piecemeal fashion without necessarily looking for alternative or broader perspectives. People also tend to be optimistic about the outcomes of their decisions and systematically underestimate risk and the probability of an unfavorable outcome. They also tend to discount to zero the likelihood of low-probability events (Kahneman and Tversky 1979). They are thus prone to "disaster myopia." They are often unaware of the limits of their knowledge, tend to treat assumptions as facts, and tend to rely on recent information or experience when making decisions. They often overemphasize their ability to read and control events, and attribute success to their own abilities and efforts rather than to luck. They also tend to become overly committed to original courses of action and do not like to renege on a stated course of action or plan. Furthermore, they accept and highlight information that supports current courses of action. Individuals also tend to follow trends and fashions; they are reassured when others make similar decisions and hence are subject to herding behavior (Thaler 1993, 2000; Schleifer 1999). Such perspectives complement an agent-centered HI account of institutional life by offering a more rounded account of agency.

Transposing all this into financial markets means that "not only do investors make mistakes, but they do so in a predictable fashion" (Montier 2002, 1). As we shall see in subsequent chapters, all of the biases and traits just noted are good illustrations of the behavior of many of the CEOs and other senior executives who dominated Wall Street and the City of London during the financial boom that preceded the crisis. Limited rationality within financial markets also means that emotions such as optimism or fear come to play a large role in coping with uncertainty and in shaping behavior and outcomes (Pixley 2004). Behavioral studies thus help us understand the cognitive and emotional roots of widely observed market phenomena such as the mispricing of risk, herding behavior, and cycles of irrational exuberance and euphoria followed by fear and panic leading to market collapses. These are exactly the types of dynamics that have been analyzed historically by scholars of financial market volatility and that form the behavioral base of systemic risk and market collapses (Kindleberger 1978; Minsky 1982). As Alan Greenspan (2013, 6) has argued, "Our propensities related to fear, euphoria, and culture . . . virtually define finance." Furthermore, and as we show in subsequent chapters, the existence of these biases and traits was compounded by bonus payment schemes that encouraged risk taking.

An important caveat, however, is that not all bankers behaved like this in the run-up to the crisis. For example, as we show in Chapter 7, even in the financial heartlands of the United States and the United Kingdom, a minority of prominent bankers heeded warning signals, were risk averse, and did not succumb to irrational exuberance or herding behavior. In banks such as Goldman Sachs, for example, substantial efforts were made to gather detailed information on market trends and to monitor daily market positions in an effort to avoid potential losses, especially on the eve of the crisis. There was thus a willingness among a minority of bankers to avoid the worst excesses of the boom, to question widely accepted views, and to interrogate and challenge data and arguments rather than simply follow the herd. It is also the case that bankers in different market systems, in countries like Australia and Canada, did not display irrational exuberance and ran relatively conservative balance sheets.

Clearly, then, the generalizations made by behavioral finance theory are just that: they explain many but not all cases of behavior, as we show in more detail in Chapters 7 and 8. Behavioral finance theory tends to focus primarily on agents and does not probe fully enough the wider institutional or structural contexts in which agents operate. The strength of our comparative institutional approach is that it shows that agents operating in different types of markets and wider contexts tended to behave differently. The tenets of behavioral finance theory are thus not universals but are contingent on wider conditions. The variability of individual agency and varying institutional and structural pressures clearly matter in explaining banking behavior.

Expanding the Envelope of Historical Institutionalism

Agents do not operate in a vacuum but shape and are shaped by the institutional and wider structural contexts in which they operate. As Karl Marx once famously observed, "Men make their own history, but they do not make it as they please; they do not make it under self-selected circumstances, but under circumstances existing, already given and transmitted from the past" (quoted in Tucker 1978, 575). Institutions are primarily about the rules and norms (formal or informal) that shape actor behavior. Institutions matter because they shape actor identities, interpretations and preferences, the norm and rule-based scope of agents' discretion, and the resources and opportunities available to agents within institutions. As Scharpf (1997, 41–42) argues, "Once we know the institutional setting of interaction, we know a good deal about the actors involved, about their options, and about their perceptions and preferences." Nevertheless, various strands of institutional theory, including earlier strands of HI, have tended to emphasize highly constraining notions of institutions. Prominent theorists such as North (1990, 3) even define institutions as "humanly devised constraints that shape human interaction." This is a "sticky" form of institutional theory with a limited account of agency, which has been better at explaining institutional stasis and continuity than change. Blyth (1997, 230) is among many critics who argue that institutional theory, including earlier versions of HI, see institutions as "constraining rather than enabling political action." Weyland (2008, 281) similarly argues that "institutionalism has emphasised inertia and persistence," offering a "static" view of institutional life. Schmidt (2008a, 314) also sees the established institutionalisms as "subordinating agency to structure," while Crouch and Keune (2005, 83) argue that "institutional configurations are often presented as a straitjacket from which endogenous actors cannot escape." We are sympathetic to such arguments and wary of overly "sticky" versions of HI theory (Bell 2011). The sweeping institutional changes that constituted the banking revolution during the 1990s and 2000s in the United States and the United Kingdom suggest there is something wrong with such accounts.

In recent years there have been a number of revisions and improvements to HI, shifting it toward a more agency-centered, "post-determinist" (Crouch 2007) form of analysis that recognizes that institutions are mutable and that mutually shaping interactions between agents and institutions are important in driving change (see Steinmo and Thelen 1992; Campbell 2004, 2011; Crouch 2005; Bell 2011; Bell and Feng 2013). A major step forward was Thelen's work with various colleagues pointing to sources of agency-based discretion as a basis for incremental institutional innovation and change (Streeck and Thelen 2005; Mahoney and Thelen 2010). Recent work by constructivist institutionalists also argues that agents can reinterpret institutional rules and norms, again creating space for agency (Blyth 2007; Hay, 2007; Schmidt 2010). Bell (2011) has cautioned, however, that ideational accounts need to ground agents squarely within institutional and wider settings.

A further weakness of existing institutional analysis can also be identified. Dominant institutional approaches have often neglected how institutions interact with wider structures, suggesting that institutional theory may have an excessively narrow account of the forces that shape actors and institutional change. Theorists often conflate institutions and structures or use the terms interchangeably (for example, Cortell and Peterson 1999). This conceptual muddling is not helpful because it prevents us from distinguishing between institutions and structures and examining how agents within institutions dialectically interact with wider structures. Bell and Feng (2013) have thus argued for an "agents in context" approach that expands the range of contexts with which agents dialectically interact. They use this approach to show how economic transition and changing power structures in the Chinese party state helped shape institutional change, underpinning the rising authority of the People's Bank of China in recent decades. If institutions are about how rules and norms shape behavior, structural effects are a broader phenomenon. For example, a traffic light at a local intersection (an institution) may have been installed largely as a result of wider structural changes, especially population growth and the nature of the road system. Structures are often materially defined: a demographic structure or the structure of an economy. Broader political phenomena might also be seen in structural terms, for example, the structural power of business or the power of the state. More abstractly, structures can be defined as "strategically selective" terrains, including power configurations, material incentives or disincentives, or other rationales or pressures that may lead agents to favor certain developments or choices over others (Hay 2002; Jessop 2007). Because structural factors are typically the result of embedded historical processes, they arguably form a broader background context in which specific institutions operate and change. Although "structuralist" accounts in political analysis are often handled in a way that implies deterministic patterns of *constraint*, in reality, structures can help both constrain and empower agents. Institutions are best seen as mediating the relations between agents and wider structures (Bell 2011). From the perspective of given agents, the impact and indeed the meaning of structural forces will be shaped by the institution in which they are located.

Existing institutionalist literature has not entirely neglected structures. Leading scholars such as Steinmo and Thelen (1992) originally distinguished between institutions and structures, but focused largely on the former, essentially bracketing off the influence of structures. Subsequently, Thelen (1999, 383) argued that "institutional arrangements cannot be understood in isolation from the political and social setting in which they are embedded," while Pontussen (1998) has criticized HI for focusing too narrowly on "intermediate level institutions" and ignoring wider "structural" environments." More recently, Thelen (2011, 55) has argued that "prevailing structures influence the kinds of change-agents and change strategies that are likely to emerge and succeed in specific institutional contexts." Although these observations are not extensively theorized, these scholars do point the way toward a more encompassing form of analysis.

We need to tease out distinctions among agents, institutions, and changing structural contexts and study their mutually shaping interactions through time in order to explain banking behavior and outcomes. The banking crisis reveals just how important institutions and structures were (and are) in shaping behavior and outcomes. As with institutions, agents engage in mutually shaping interactions with wider structures that also have institution-like effects in terms of constraining and enabling agents. In this manner, the essential insight of institutional theory is confirmed but broadened beyond the institutional domain. Our dialectical method here is based on Margaret Archer's (1995, 2000, 2003) approach and (1) models agents, institutions, and structures as being analytically distinct in the sense that each has properties that are not simply reducible to the other at any given point in time; (2) models agents as operating in institutional and structural contexts that are pregiven at any particular point in time; (3) models agents, institutions, and structures as operating in a dialectical, mutually constitutive relationship over time; and (4) sees institutional and structural effects as ultimately mediated and actualized by agency. As Archer (2000, 465) puts it, "Structures only exert an effect when mediated through the activities of people." This implies that the ideas and interpretations of situated agents also matter.

We argue that at one level bankers were empowered by proximate institutions and by the evolving structures of finance: they were authoritative and reshaped their institutions and revolutionized banking. Once these institutions were created, however, bankers became almost enslaved by institutional incentives and competitive pressures, as we show in Chapter 2. Bankers responded to such pressures with financial innovation in pursuit of new market opportunities. It is these market pressures and dynamics that largely explain the different patterns of banking across the different countries in our study. After reengineering their balance sheets, bankers in the United States and the United Kingdom were then blindsided by structural change in the form of the housing collapse in the United States and falling mortgage-backed asset prices. Further structural effects were manifested in the form of systemic risk amid contagion and cascading failures in financial markets more broadly.

A further step in our analysis is to join Streeck (2009) in arguing for an approach that embeds analysis in a broader account of major contemporary structural transformations in capitalism. As he suggests, "Why institutional change in today's capitalist political economies proceeds the way it does rather than some other way, cannot, I suggest, be explained in terms of an institutional theory as such but only in terms of a theory of *capitalism* as a substantive, that is, historical social order" (Streeck 2009, 3). From this perspective Streeck (2009, 13) bemoans "the self-imposed agnosticism of comparative institutionalism with respect to the big questions." He also argues that the theoretical purview of nineteenth- and early twentieth-century social theorists on the broad sweep of history and in studying institutions amid transformations in capitalism has given way to the narrower concerns of many of today's institutionalist approaches. In the present analysis, we argue that institutional change in the shape of the liberalization of financial markets in the United States and the United Kingdom fostered financialization, a major structural change in capitalism that saw the growing scale and complexity of financial activity and markets.

Broadening HI's canvass will help deal with two further problems in institutional theory identified by Lieberman (2002, 698): institutional "reductionism," as well as "the exogeneity of certain fundamental elements of political life." We deal with the former and the latter by locating institutions within wider settings, emphasizing the effects of structures and political power. Finally, while our account emphasizes market constraints and structural impacts, we should not lose sight of agency. Indeed, in later chapters we test the limits of our seemingly "structuralist" argument by examining several cases where banks in the United States and the United Kingdom resisted structural pressures, indicating the importance of not losing sight of agency in such situations or in more general theorizing.

Liberating the Masters of the Universe

At the height of the boom, amid surging profits, huge remuneration packages, and dizzying new forms of financial innovation, bankers and financiers in the United States and the United Kingdom appeared as Masters of the Universe. Authoritative bankers and state leaders in these countries refashioned financial capitalism in the decades prior to the crisis, producing a series of interrelated institutional and structural changes that would reshape banking and finance.

Liberating the Masters of the Universe involved the deregulation and liberalization of finance in the United States and the United Kingdom, starting in the 1970s. The subsequent growth in the scale and scope of financial markets reflected a process of financialization (Epstein 2005; Dore 2008; Krippner 2011). This was an outgrowth of liberalization and reflects a structural shift in the center of gravity of contemporary capitalism and economic exchange into the financial orbit. Financialization is marked by the rapid growth of the financial sector relative to the real economy and by the growth of financial innovation, led especially in the 2000s by securitization and other forms of derivatives trading (Crotty 2009; Gowan 2009), which we explain and discuss in the following chapter. Financialization was also marked by the growth of corporate and household debt. In 1997 household debt as a proportion of GDP was 70% in the United States, 75% in the United Kingdom, and 42% across the European Union. By 2007 debt had risen to 100% in the United States, 110% in the United Kingdom, and 60% in Europe (Turner 2009b, 13). Crouch (2009) argues that household borrowing supercharged otherwise stagnant economies (including a stagnating median wage in the United States) and acted as a form of "privatised Keynesianism." Financialization also witnessed the growing globalization and interconnectedness of financial markets. Financialization was a structural change that promoted systemic risk: the enhanced prospect of chain reaction effects in markets that would rapidly escalate into crises. Financialization thus made the financial system much more fragile. Focusing on the United States, Krippner (2011) traces the origins of financialization to deregulatory moves in credit markets as well as increased international capital inflows that led to an explosion of household, business, and public sector debt from the 1980s onward. Cheap credit, especially in the 2000s, rapidly rising debt levels, and lax regulation would see the subsequent rise of equity, property, and financial asset price bubbles.

Liberalization and financialization were not processes that occurred independently of the state, nor did they imply the simple retreat of the state. As banking and finance grew, bankers and financiers gained greater power, further reinforcing the push for liberalization and financialization. Financialization, then, was not just about economic change; it also reflected changes in the structure of political power.

The changing structural position of bankers in the economy and the economic resources and credit they increasingly controlled within the United States and the United Kingdom gradually gave (and continue to give) substantial structural power to bankers. This is in line with standard structural power arguments that reveal how control over economic resources creates an important platform for political power due to the structural dependence of the state on economic performance that is largely controlled by private sector investors (Lindblom 1977; Bell and Hindmoor 2013). In both the United States and the United Kingdom, banking and finance became major economic sectors in the decades prior to the crisis. Banks contributed substantially to tax revenues, accounting for almost 25% of corporation tax revenue in the United Kingdom (CityUK 2008). Governments also came to increasingly rely on credit supplied by the financial system to fund ever-growing structural deficits, an outcome reflecting a more fundamental failure to control budgets in the face of mounting distributional tensions and, more recently, in the face of financial crises (Krippner 2011; Streeck 2011). Governments also came to regard banks as a pillar of national comparative advantage in which the interlinked London and New York markets were dominant. Although there was a debate about the potential dangers of rising asset price inflation within central banks and technocratic circles, governments, it seemed, were happy to ride the asset price booms of the 1990s and 2000s (Hay 2013). Indeed, in analyzing the US situation, McCarty et al. (2013, 14) argue that successive governments have been compliant in fostering "political bubbles," which they define as "policy biases which foster and amplify market behaviors that generate financial crises." As these scholars argue, politicians have been lured by the prosperity associated with financial sector growth and have been seduced by the same forms of irrational exuberance that have gripped financial market participants.

Expanding financial empires thus acted as a power structure, materially and ideationally, that drew in state leaders who came to believe in and support the growth of finance and financial innovation. As we argue in Chapter 9, this state-finance nexus in the United States and the United Kingdom now inhibits fundamental reform of finance (see also Bell and Hindmoor 2014).

Structures, however, do not come with an "instruction sheet" (Blyth 2002), implying that the meaning and ramifications of structural power need to be interpreted and worked out on the ground by key agents. Various scholars have shown how ideas can mediate structural power relations, either increasing or decreasing the salience of such power (Hay and Rosamond 2002; Bell 2013). Structural power thus works through the real or potential benefits or costs of real or threatened business or financial activities in relation to state actors who must *perceive* such benefits, costs, or threats as significant and meaningful. Barnett and Duvall (2005, 53) argue that structural forms of power that "distribute asymmetric privileges also affect the interests of actors, often leaving them willing to accept their role in the existing order of things." Subservience might be one manifestation of power relationships, but power can also reflect the ability to create an ideational or discursive order that helps align the interests of others to one's goals by encouraging them to see the situation in sanguine terms or as one that is beneficial to them. It is certainly true that government and state leaders in the United States and the United Kingdom came to strongly identify with the goals of the financial sector. Barnett and Duvall (2005, 55) refer to this as a form of "productive power," the "constitution of subjects . . . through systems of knowledge and discursive practices." Lukes's (1974) concept of power through ideational hegemony and Foucault's (1991) notions about disciplinary power present similar types of argument. As Woll (2014) points out, the capacity of financial interests to draw in the state was not so much about coercive forms of "capture" but was more about willing support and compliance due to material incentives and ideational convergence.

The arcane nature of high finance in the run-up to the great crash also lent the sector a certain aura and mystique. Bankers, but also state leaders, thought that the booming financial markets had been made resilient and safe and that risk had been tamed through advanced risk management techniques and by the wide distribution of risk through the securitization process. Prior to the crisis, Alan Greenspan (2004) thought that "not only have individual financial institutions become less vulnerable to shocks from underlying risk factors, but also the financial system as a whole has become more resilient." Mervyn King (2007), the former governor of the Bank of England, was also sanguine, pointing out that "risks are no longer so concentrated in a small number of regulated institutions but are spread across the financial system . . . That is a positive development." The International Monetary Fund (IMF) and other key institutions also believed this. Bankers believed that risk had been effectively managed and that the "super-senior" securitized assets that they were holding on their own balance sheets were extremely unlikely to lose value, especially given the perceived stability of the US housing market. In reaching this assessment, bankers and regulators were further reassured by the positive assessments provided by private credit rating agencies such as Moody's, Standard and Poor's, and Fitch—who, it should be noted, were being paid by issuers to rate financial instruments. As we show in Chapter 5, credit rating agencies played a key role in reassuring potential investors that assets were extremely safe.

Ultimately, writes Simon Johnson, the "financial industry gained political power by amassing a kind of cultural capital." In the United States, "the attitude took hold that what was good for Wall Street was good for the country . . . and that large financial institutions and free-flowing capital markets were crucial to America's position in the world" (Johnson 2009). In the United Kingdom, the typical starting point of policy deliberations was the question asked by Economic Secretary Ed Balls (2006): "What more can I do . . . to support and enhance the critical role that the banking industry plays in our economy?" The structural position of banking and finance in the United States and the United Kingdom meant that the sector's interests were paramount in the minds of state policy makers. Interactions between these agents also took place in the cloistered world of "quiet" politics (Culpepper 2011), marked by low public visibility and informality. Here, the supposedly expert judgments and technical acumen of bankers were largely accepted by the authorities, with the latter trusting the former to be prudent. Governments in the United States and the United Kingdom also received substantial campaign contributions from the financial sector, and powerful congressional committees and lax campaign funding rules within the United States rendered the political system vulnerable to rent-seeking pressure. Also important was the political influence of banks that stemmed from their ability to exploit their structural position in the economy and a widespread faith in the dynamism of financial markets. For all of these reasons the authorities supported the banks and finance through policies of market liberalization and permissive regulation, which helped propel the boom in the US and UK financial markets.

Some writers have laid the blame for the crisis squarely on regulation and the role of government (Taylor 2009; Wallison 2009). Low interest rates, lax regulation, and perverse regulatory incentives were problems, to be sure. But the problem with solely blaming government is that this ignores the fact that bankers were powerful and influential enough to get the forms of regulation they required (Hindmoor and McGeechan 2013). Liberalization and financialization were a project forged by an alliance of financial and state leaders in the United States and the United Kingdom. Regulatory arrangements bore the clear imprint of the power of bankers as well as compliant governments, offering little resistance to the forward rush of booming markets spurred by market competition and the quest for high returns.

Institutional change thus resulted from the efforts of bankers, business leaders, and neoliberal state elites to expand the domain of markets, market forces, and competition in financial markets and more broadly in contemporary capitalism. The macroeconomic stability of the "great moderation" of the late 1990s and 2000s was taken as evidence that this approach worked. And despite serial financial crises, liberalization was also supported by fundamental doctrines of financial economics, such as the "efficient markets hypothesis," which became the "working ideology" of both Wall Street and the City of London (Kwak and Johnson 2010, 5). This claimed that free financial markets priced financial assets correctly, thus supposedly eliminating the possibility of financial bubbles (for a critique see Quiggin 2010, chapter 2).

Liberalization also reflected the neoliberal faith in the efficacy of market competition and the promotion by the state of active competition policies, which were increasingly seen by authorities in the United States and the United Kingdom as an alternative to prescriptive banking and credit regulation. Starting in the 1970s, an increasingly influential view held that postwar bank regulation had protected the interests of the largest banks. In particular, regulators believed that large banks could attract deposits at low interest rates, so enhancing their profitability, because of the existence of deposit insurance schemes and, among investors, a belief that the banks were "too big to fail" and would be bailed out in the event of a financial crisis. The lesson drawn from this analysis was that more competition was needed to safeguard the interests of consumers. In pursuing this agenda, regulators and state elites generally believed that markets were in general self-correcting, that competition was the most effective check on poor management or excessive risk taking, and that, therefore, the primary responsibility for the effective management of risk ought to belong not to regulators but to the private sector (Turner 2009b, 87). The view also formed that banks had developed superior risk management practices. Regulators in the United States and the United Kingdom did not believe that markets were perfect and that banks always and everywhere optimally allocated resources. What they did believe was that banks that took poor decisions would be disciplined by the market.

Such faith in banking markets had not always been apparent. In the aftermath of the banking collapses of the Great Depression, politicians restructured the banking industry and introduced far-reaching reforms to reduce the likelihood of any future banking catastrophes. At the domestic level, in the United States for example, financial regulation was embodied in various banking acts of the Depression era that sought to control bank interest rates and to segment the banking market, in part to deal with the "ruinous competition" that had been a problem leading to banking fragility in the 1930s (Bhide 2010, 228). At the international level, there were also reforms after the financial turmoil of the 1930s that saw the imposition of capital controls and managed exchange rates under the Bretton Woods system of international financial architecture introduced in 1944. Overall, the postwar era was one in which banking and finance were heavily regulated by the state.

Liberalization gradually jettisoned these controls. Streeck (2009, 25) sees liberalization as "re-forming" capitalism after "its temporary . . . artificial confinement in an elaborate set of market-breaking institutions after the Second World War." International capital controls and regulated exchange rates were jettisoned by the United States in the early 1970s amid growing pressure on the dollar and the growth of the unregulated Eurodollar market. As we detail in Chapter 2, domestic banking controls in both the United States and the United Kingdom were also relaxed, in part because they had become difficult to manage under inflationary pressures and the fluctuating exchange rates of the 1970 and 1980s, and in part because of intense pressure for liberalization by bankers and financiers who were keen to shake off the constraints of postwar regulation and amid broader concerns that the US and UK banking sectors were becoming less competitive internationally (Suárez and Kolodny 2011). Financial liberalization also saw a shift toward market allocation of credit, combined with efforts to combat inflation, which saw a big jump in official interest rates in the early 1980s. Yet the higher interest rates generated by the market failed to impose restraint on credit growth, which soon exploded in the public and private sectors (Krippner 2011).

The limitations of national-level regulatory arrangements in the United States and the United Kingdom were exacerbated by the perverse incentives created by the international Basel capital regulations. Basel was the first internationally agreed attempt to regulate and harmonize the amount of capital banks hold on their balance sheets as a buffer against risk and economic downturns. It was negotiated through the auspices of the Bank for International Settlements' Basel Committee on Banking Supervision in 1988 and subsequently adopted by over one hundred countries. The impetus for its creation came from regulators in developed countries who feared that banks in developing countries were holding insufficient capital and that there could develop a regulatory "race to the bottom." The Basel rules required a number of banks to raise their levels of capital. Yet Basel I also resulted in a fall in *average* capital holdings across all banks in developed countries. This occurred because banks that held more than the approved minimum saw Basel as giving them an approved opportunity to reduce their level of capital. Turner (2009b, 55) argues that the Basel accord was "not based on any clear theory of optimal capital levels, but rather represented a pragmatic compromise" between different banks and between the banks and regulators.

As a result of careful lobbying by the banks and because of poor regulatory design, Basel created a number of loopholes that gave banks an incentive to expand their subprime lending, securitize their loans, and move assets off their balance sheets and into the "shadow" banking system (Blundell-Wignall and Atkinson 2008). The subprime incentive arose because the Basel capital levels were calibrated around risk-weighted assets. Traditionally, business lending has proved riskier for the banks than domestic mortgage lending. Therefore, Basel required the banks to hold more capital for business loans than for mortgages. Because the prime mortgage market was already at near-saturation, especially in the United States, the banks found it profitable to aggressively enter the more risky but potentially more profitable subprime market, which, in terms of the risks of default, Basel I treated no differently from the rest of the mortgage market (J. Friedman 2009, 144).

The Basel rules also created a catalyst for securitization, the process of turning relatively illiquid financial assets such as mortgages into marketable financial products. As the banks discovered, all kinds of assets can be securitized: mortgage payments, credit card loans, student loans, car loans, and lease payments. Securitization was attractive to the banks because it meant that they could reduce the risks to which they were exposed. Moreover, Basel I made such securitization practices even more attractive not only because the banks avoided having to hold capital against assets that had been securitized and sold but because the banks did not have to hold as much capital on securitized assets that they bought from others. In this respect, the Basel rules encouraged regulatory evasion and attempts to find loopholes in the rules, an activity usually referred to as regulatory arbitrage. In this instance a key response to the Basel rules was to give banks an incentive to shift assets off their balance sheets. The loophole here was that while banks were required to hold capital where they were dependent on funding from deposits or long-term loans, bank-sponsored structured investment vehicles (SIVs), which funded the purchase of securitized assets using short-term, sometimes overnight funding, did not hold deposits and were, nominally at least, legally independent of a parent bank. This meant that they did not have to hold capital because the banks' stake in them was counted as an asset (Acharya and Richardson, 2009, 201; Acharya and Schnabl 2009, 89). Using a model pioneered by JP Morgan in 1997, banks rushed to create SIVs that either bought their securitized assets or the assets of other banks using borrowed short-term funds. The catch is that, while nominally independent, the banks had either guaranteed the SIVs' borrowing or were viewed, by traders in the market, to be willing to stand behind their SIVs in order to protect their reputational capital.

The Basel Committee on Banking Supervision has been strongly influenced by bank lobbying (Tsingou 2008; Hellwig 2009; Lall 2012). The regulatory work of the Basel Committee has been conducted during an era of great change in the banking sector. The banks argued that they should be allowed to use their own internal risk assessments for determining risk-weighted capital buffers. These arguments were accepted, in a process

Hellwig (2009, 190) describes as "regulatory capture by sophistication" in which "the quality of professional risk modeling in sophisticated banking institutions seems to have been taken for granted." The result was amendments to the Basel I rules in 1996 that allowed banks to assess their own risk exposures and weightings, which in turn affected how much capital they were expected to hold. This amendment to Basel I was further embedded in the new Basel II rules that were released in 2004. Basel II was notable for its commitment to self-regulation. Rather than impose particular risk weightings on particular categories of assets, Basel II allowed banks that could satisfy regulators that they had rigorous internal risk management processes in place to set their own risk weightings. Sheila Blair, the former chair of the Federal Deposit Insurance Corporation (FDIC) in the United States, cites studies that indicated that Basel II would see a "dramatic" decline in bank capital, in most cases reducing capital by over 60%. The US banks had argued that their improved risk management systems as well as competiveness issues sanctioned lower capital. However, the FDIC fought against the implementation of Basel II in the United States. As Blair (2012, 30) argues, "The FDIC fought and delayed US implementation, and we were even more determined to stop it as we watched capital levels decline among the big European banks as they moved forward with Basel II adoption."

Conclusion

In this chapter we have introduced a framework for analyzing how bankers behaved and how, with the support of state leaders in the core markets, they reshaped banking and finance in the decades prior to the crisis. A key argument is that besides analyzing the bounded rationality and idiosyncrasies of bankers, we also need to locate our key agents in the broader contexts that they shaped but that also shaped their behavior. In this chapter we have shown how financial market liberalization starting in the 1970s was an important form of institutional change that liberated and empowered bankers and financiers, leading to a more profound form of structural change: financialization. On the eve of the crisis, leading bankers in the United States and the United Kingdom appeared as Masters of the Universe in control of vast financial empires who were also highly influential in relation to the state. These agents managed to restructure the institutions and rules of the regulatory apparatus that controlled banking and finance in the United States and the United Kingdom. These interlinked markets would become the site of a financial boom in the 2000s supported and propelled by a nexus of prevailing ideas and material interests. Vast fortunes could be made by riding the boom, and governments too were willing to join in. However, as we show in Chapter 2, although bankers had helped create this new financial edifice, it in turn began to exert powerful pressures on bankers, to a point where most of them almost became virtual slaves to the gathering market and structural forces that would lead to their undoing.

2

"Slaves" of Markets and Structures

The banking crisis is often blamed on the reckless behavior of bankers. But just as important, if not more so, to an understanding of the causes of the crisis is the institutional and structural context in which bankers and financiers operated. We saw in Chapter 1 how financial liberalization was championed by bankers and state elites in the United States and the United Kingdom, producing the rise of "trader" banks amid a banking and securitization revolution and associated structural change in capitalism marked by the shift to financialization (Erturk and Solari 2007). In this chapter we show how bankers and financiers in the crisis-hit markets, especially those who became "true believers" in the securitization boom, became almost "slaves" to the markets and wider structural forces thus created. Liberalization produced intense levels of competition and pressures for higher returns, an exacting form of market discipline. In this pressure cooker environment most market actors responded to changing incentives and market opportunities through radical institutional and financial innovation, channeling activity into casino-like financial trading pumped up by stratospheric levels of leverage. As we show here, although bankers and supportive state elites created this system, most of these agents and their successors were eventually overwhelmed by it, especially by wider structural forces embodied in systemic risk that can see a trigger event (such as losses in subprime securities) rapidly escalate into cascading failures across complex and highly interlinked financial markets.

The financial crisis that climaxed in 2008 began with a downturn in the US housing market in late 2006, which led to the collapse in the market for subprime mortgage-backed securities (MBSs) and related assets. This chapter explains how these losses became the key trigger for a much larger crisis in the dominant US and UK financial markets, featuring a complete loss of confidence in MBSs, the subsequent collapse of interbank lending, and the freezing of the international credit system that led to the destruction or near destruction of many banks.

The Banking Revolution

Banks have traditionally performed three key economic functions: they administer the payments system by executing customers' payment instructions and transferring funds between accounts; they provide an apparently safe home for deposits, thus encouraging saving; and they use their deposit base to fund longer-term loans to customers and businesses, so making possible mass investment in the economy. Traditionally, the profits from mainstream or commercial banks came from charging a higher interest rate on loans than was paid on deposits. This was the so-called 3–6–3 model of banking—pay 3% on deposits, charge 6% on loans, and be on the golf course by 3:00 p.m. (DeYoung and Rice 2004, 34). This kind of banking activity was not riskless. Bank failures have been a recurring feature of economic history (Borio, Furfine, and Lowe 2001; Reinhart and Rogoff 2009). Banks have failed when loans defaulted through poor lending practices or as a result of a major economic downturn (as happened in the Depression of the 1930s). Banks are threatened if depositors lose confidence and withdraw their deposits, causing a bank run and the possible collapse of a bank (F. Allen, Babus, and Carletti 2009). Banks can also fail if short-term wholesale lenders in money markets lose confidence and conduct a run on a bank, which is essentially what happened in the 2008 crisis. These dynamics reflect an important structural problem in banking known as the maturity mismatch: banks borrow short and hold deposits on demand but lend or hold far less liquid assets on a longer-term basis, thus exposing them to risk. In the recent crisis this maturity mismatch was exacerbated by high levels of leverage. Leading financial theorists such as Hyman Minsky (1982) have pointed to the long-standing tendency within financial markets to speculate on rising prices using borrowed money and the resulting periods of financial failure that occur when investors are forced to sell their speculative investments in a falling market to try to repay their loans, which again is what happened in 2008.

Starting in the 1970s the traditional 3–6–3 banking model came under increasing pressure as governments, particularly in the United States and the United Kingdom, sought to promote competition within the banking sector as a part of a wider deregulation agenda, described in Chapter 1. One consequence of increased competition was the growth of the nonbank financial sector centered upon pension and mutual funds, hedge funds, and private equity firms. A second consequence was the emergence of former regional banks as major national competitors. In the United Kingdom, for example, the market share of the Newcastle-based Northern Rock, measured in net lending, rose from 7.7% in 2003 to 13.4% in 2006 (Northern Rock 2006, 36). As banks were forced to compete for customers, interest rate margins—that is, the difference between the interest rate banks could lend at compared to the rate they had to pay to depositors or creditors—began to fall. This was a third consequence of greater competition. Matthews and Thompson (2005, 10) show that in the United Kingdom the interest rate margin fell from 3.9% in 1979 to 1.1% in 2006. Increased competition, falling interest rate margins on traditional mortgage and business lending activity, and the threat this posed to profits became a part of the structural environment in which banks found themselves operating in the decades prior to the crisis. The environment was also marked by low interest rates in the first part of the 2000s. Low interest rates meant that for investors such as pension funds, the rates of return available from investing in government and corporate debt were now relatively low. This gave these investors and the banks and hedge funds seeking their business an incentive to seek other, more profitable, investment opportunities (Caballero and Krishnamurthy 2009).

High levels of competition often follow in the wake of financial market liberalization, and such periods often drive financial market crises (Hellwig 2009, 152). In this instance, deregulation of capital markets was accompanied by the rise of large institutional investors that pressured markets for "shareholder value," featuring highly mobile investors and short-term capital placements, the threat of hostile takeover, and intense pressures for high short-term returns. As we show in Chapters 5 and 6, where we examine in more detail how bankers operated in the United States and the United Kingdom, there were strong market pressures to grow balance sheets and dramatically elevate profits through leveraged trading. Managers and executives operated in a fishbowl of market scrutiny by financial analysts, institutional investors, and the financial media. For individual bankers, competitive market criteria were directly tied to remuneration packages, promotion criteria, and peer pressure within organizations. The lead bankers and traders set the pace with huge remuneration packages and rapid promotion. In such a context, those who did not perform adequately or who raised concerns about risk were usually ostracized or sacked. Alan Greenspan characterized management as "caught in a terrible dilemma." "They could protect their shareholders and they could be sitting there for years with a good balance sheet. But their status in the marketplace would be going down, down, down as would the value of their stock" (quoted in Faber 2010, 168). A combination of high rewards and fear thus drove behavior. We often think of investment excesses as driven by overoptimism or "irrational exuberance," but as Hellwig (2009, 164) notes, "One should appreciate that fear can be just as powerful" in motivating risk taking.

Williams (2010, 42) describes the market environment as one in which "a firm's stock price was . . . the market's referendum on the company's financial health." The Bank of England's executive director of financial stability, Andrew Haldane (2012a, 4), argues that the intensity of market competition forced banks to pursue higher profits, producing a "financial arms race" as banks struggled for competitive advantage. He reports that a key metric of profitability, return on equity (ROE), was 1% in UK banks in 1989 but had increased to 38% by 2007. Returns at this level implied not just market acumen but risk taking as well. In such a context "market discipline" was not about carefully assessing bank risk in relation to returns but instead became biased toward high returns and risk taking (Hellwig 2009, 163). Competition thus produced "markets in vice" (J. Braithwaite 2005) as bankers were pushed into desperate efforts to reduce equity buffers and boost trading and leverage in ways that eventually produced disastrous outcomes.

Markets also mattered in a second way, especially by opening up new profit opportunities in trading, which increasingly led to structural change in financial markets. Traditionally, commercial banks had been banned from trading, whereas investment banks had focused on limited trading for clients, not on proprietary trading using their own or borrowed funds. However, from the 1980s trading became more widespread, first in the newly liberated foreign exchange markets and by the 1990s and 2000s in increasingly liberated domestic financial markets. As profits on traditional lending and deposit taking were increasingly squeezed, many commercial banks sought to reengineer their balance sheets in a desperate search for ways to boost yield. Investment banks too were looking for new ways to make money. Increasingly, profit pressures saw banks reengineer their balance sheets to secure profit through securitization and other forms of derivatives trading (as explained below) (Crotty 2009; Gowan 2009). These new forms of activity saw a blurring of earlier distinctions between commercial and investment banking, producing the rise of "trader" banks that were central to the derivatives trading and securitization bubble whose collapse sparked the crisis (Dore 2008; Crotty 2009; Gowan 2009; Krippner 2011).

Securitization and trading in MBSs and other derivatives proved immensely profitable for banks at a time when overall market prices were rising. Banks could package securitized assets and pass them on for a fee; hold such assets on their balance sheet and receive interest payments; or sell such assets to other investors or other banks at a profit. Furthermore, as asset prices increased, banks took on more leverage to help fund increasing volumes of securities trading. The promise was of a never-ending virtuous circle in which asset prices continued to increase, so allowing banks to increase their leverage and profits and buy more assets, further inflating the market. The banks believed that they could achieve this while insulating themselves from potential losses through credit default swaps (CDSs) or other forms of hedging.

In the United States and the United Kingdom the markets in which bankers operated were also highly distorted, full of perverse incentives. Streeck (2009, 158) sees liberalization as involving "a retreat of public institutions, including the state, in favor of private ones." Vogel (1996) has a different view that sees liberalized markets often being associated with new regulatory rules imposed by the state. In banking and finance there was a different outcome again. Here there was a substantial degree of regulatory retreat that gave more market freedom to bankers. Not only were regulations abolished, but state leaders handed over important regulatory authority to banks and private agents. For example, as we saw in Chapter 1, instead of external regulatory risk auditing, banks were instead allowed to use in-house risk methodologies to determine the amount of capital they needed to maintain. Private ratings agencies were also allowed to play a crucial role in risk assessment.

Despite handing over substantial authority to markets, liberalization was nevertheless accompanied by continuing state support and a range of distorting market interventions. Continued forms of state support came in the form of deposit insurance schemes that cheapened the cost of funds to large banks, encouraging trading and leverage. The state also provided ongoing bailout or lender of last resort functions in case of a general liquidity crisis, again providing a backstop. Andy Haldane (2012c, 4) has calculated the taxpayer subsidy to the world's largest banks at $70 billion every year between 2002 and 2007—roughly half of the average posttax profits enjoyed by these banks over that period.

In a normally functioning market, the prospect of bankruptcy encourages managers to carefully balance the risks entailed in the pursuit of additional profit against the prospect of failure. Instead, distorted financial markets generated moral hazard and risk taking. Indeed, in the wake of the financial crisis, amid financial inefficiency and market failure, the scale of state support for the sector was ramped up in the form of massive bailout measures that essentially substituted public resources for private financial resources. Haldane (2012b, 5) suggests that "support to the financial sector amounted to perhaps as much as two-thirds of annual GDP in the UK and US."

In recent decades in the both the United States and the United Kingdom, liberalization has produced a series of financial crises followed by bailouts or other forms of state support in a self-perpetuating cycle. In the United States, the belief that the Federal Reserve would cut interest rates to support collapsing markets became known as the "Greenspan put." As Roubini and Mihm (2010, 73) observe, "Market traders believed the Fed would always ride to the rescue of reckless traders ruined after a bubble collapsed." Regulators and Wall Street came to believe that busts were manageable.

A similar view formed in the United Kingdom. Mervyn King (2009b, 3) has commented that "one of the key reasons—mentioned by market participants in conversations before the crisis hit—is that the incentives to manage risk and to increase leverage were distorted by the implicit support or guarantee provided by government to creditors of banks that were seen as 'too important to fail.'" The "too big to fail" syndrome became a major source of market distortion and moral hazard, creating a rational incentive in highly competitive markets on the part of managers and other stakeholders to take additional risks knowing that if they won they would reap huge benefits and that if they lost they would be bailed out.

Securitization

The process of securitization is central to an understanding of both the causes and course of the 2007–2008 crisis. Securitization was a major financial innovation that saw previously illiquid forms of debt such as mortgages repackaged into tradable residential mortgage backed securities (RMBSs). The process of securitization was pioneered by a senior trader, Lew Ranieri, at the investment bank Salomon Brothers in the 1980s. By the 2000s securitization had become a financial commonplace. A large part of the securitization market was composed of so-called agency RMBSs issued by the US government–sponsored mortgage giants Fannie Mae and Freddie Mac. Out of the total structured credit market in the United States of around $11 trillion, the agency RMBSs totaled almost $6 trillion (Milne 2009, 64). The second-largest market was asset-backed securities (ABSs), consisting of securities composed of other assets including vehicle loans, student loans, credit card debt, and other forms of nonmortgage debt. This market was about $2 trillion in size. Commercial mortgage-backed securities (CMBSs) accounted for another $1trillion. There was also the sector of the RMBS market that was based on riskier subprime mortgages originated in the US market. The subprime mortgage market had grown rapidly and had doubled every year through the 2000s. By 2006 subprime mortgages accounted for about 40% of new mortgages in that year. It was the huge and growing demand for subprime mortgages that helped fuel the US housing boom. The decline in the quality of mortgages was a further outcome. By late 2007 the securitization market based on subprime mortgages was in the order of $800 billion. This was a large market, though still only a fraction of the entire structured credit market and only a fraction of the RMBS market (Milne 2009, 64).

Securitization began as a method of increasing mortgage lending, pioneered by Fannie Mae and Freddie Mac in the 1960s. Traditionally, banks lent money to a homeowner and was then repaid over a scheduled period along with interest. Until the loan is repaid the bank stands to lose money if the borrower defaults. At its simplest, securitization involves the packaging and selling of debt to an outside investor who receives payments from borrowers, assuming they do not default on their loans. In theory, it would be possible to securitize a *single* mortgage debt by selling it to an investor. In practice, however, Fannie and Freddie bought large numbers of mortgages, often from different parts of the US market, parceled these together, and sold the rights to secure a slice of the income from the resulting security to outside investors. In this way, Fannie and Freddie made investments in mortgage securities *less* risky. In a normal year, a usually predictable proportion of mortgage holders will default as a result of unemployment, divorce, or some other personal calamity. Investing in a security composed of a large number of mortgages is therefore safer than purchasing the right to the income stream from a single mortgage, which might default. There was a further safeguard in place. Mortgage securities could be constructed from a pool of mortgages taken from different parts of the country, thus further spreading risk.

One reason why the value of securitized loans grew so rapidly was that consumers were acquiring more debt, as noted in Chapter 1. At a time of historically low interest rates in the early to mid-2000s, debt was extremely cheap. Investment in property also seemed to offer the prospect of high returns. Between 1997 and 2006 the average house price in America rose by more than 120%. By 2005 more than 40% of homes in the United States were being purchased as either second homes or with the intention of reselling them as prices rose (Williams 2010, 118). Hellwig (2009, 158) comments that "it is probably not a coincidence that real-estate appreciation accelerated at roughly the same time in 2003 when investment banks moved aggressively into mortgage securitisation."

The pace of securitization also accelerated because of the invention of new structured instruments. In the 1990s banks realized that they could, in theory at least, further reduce the risk attached to buying a security, and so make it more attractive to investors by turning securitized mortgage investments into collateralized debt obligations (CDOs). Here, a parcel of mortgages was divided into different layers or tranches: senior, mezzanine, and junior. Purchasing the senior tranche of a CDO RMBS entitled an investor to the first set of payments from mortgage holders. If investors purchased the mezzanine tranche they received any mortgage repayments once the senior holders had been paid. If they purchased the junior tranche they received the remaining payments once everyone else had been paid. This meant that the senior tranche of a CDO was safer than an RMBS that had not been divided in this way. Indeed, the senior tranches of CDOs were presented as being effectively riskless because it was assumed that there was simply no possibility of more than a relatively small fraction of the mortgage borrowers whose repayments flowed into an RMBS defaulting on their loans simultaneously. Securitization in the form of CDOs was a significant and profitable innovation because pension and mutual funds were required by their trustees and by regulation to invest only in the safest of financial products, which had been given a high credit rating by agencies like Moody's and Standard and Poor's. In 2006 the agencies gave AAA ratings on $505 million of the $698 million of structured securities issued by Goldman Sachs, for example (W. Cohan 2011, 484). At this time, only a handful of US companies, including household names such as Johnson and Johnson, ExxonMobil, Berkshire Hathaway, and Microsoft, were considered worthy of the same AAA credit rating on their corporate debt. Investors and fund managers could generate a higher return on structured credit than on Treasury bonds, the latter being the industry benchmark for secure investment.

Between 2000 and 2007 the global pool of money seeking fixed-income investment returns increased from $31 trillion to $67 trillion (Williams 2010, 119). Securitization created a new source of supply for investors and a new source of demand for the banks. As the group executive of the National Australian Bank (NAB), Rick Sawers, explained to us in an interview, "If you could give someone a risk that was equivalent to a government bond—a AAA risk—and give them 10 to 15 basis points in yield more than they'd get on a government bond, then that's what they wanted" (8 May 2012). Furthermore, and as the banks realized, the logic of dividing securities into different tranches could be applied not only to residential mortgages but to business loans, credit card debts, auto loans, commercial mortgages, music royalties, student loans, time share loans, and small-business loans.

The creation of CDOs also provided a fillip for the subprime housing market. Subprime mortgages were those issued to borrowers with poor or nonexistent credit ratings or inadequate documentation. Lenders always recognized that subprime borrowers were less likely to meet their repayments, and this has traditionally inhibited the growth of this market. The manufacture of investment securities from groups of mortgages did not in itself change this situation. A securitized bundle of subprime mortgages would not necessarily be any more attractive to a risk-averse borrower than a single subprime mortgage. But through securitization and the construction of CDOs, bankers could create AAA-rated "super-senior" tranched securities by either placing a small number of subprime mortgages within a larger bundle of prime mortgages or, more ambitiously, constructing a security composed entirely of subprime mortgages from which the senior holders were entitled to the first set of repayments. As long as losses were not catastrophic (an erroneous view, as it turned out), only the lower tranches should lose money in a downturn. This was a new form of financial alchemy. A pool of what otherwise would have been low-rated BBB securities could be transformed into a new security that was mostly rated AAA. It was a form of "slicing and dicing that enabled supposedly rock solid securities to be extracted from highly risky subprime mortgages" (Bhide 2009, 34).

There were further, even more baroque, financial innovations. Components of CDOs were used as the raw material to build new securities, so-called CDOs squared. Here, traders securitized the mezzanine tranches of an existing CDO to create a new set of AAA-rated securities that were entitled to the first set of repayments from the mezzanine tranche once the senior tranche holders had been paid. "Synthetic" CDOs were an even more esoteric innovation. One limit on the creation of mortgage-backed or other debt-based securities was the constraint on the supply of fresh mortgages or other forms of debt. This is one reason mortgage originators and the banks were so keen to enter the subprime market: they needed fresh mortgages to turn into structured credit products. To overcome this problem, the banks created synthetic CDOs: derivatives whose value was derived not from an underlying physical asset, such as a set of mortgages or credit card repayments, but from potential payments from CDS contracts based on the possibility of default of a given set of reference securities (we discuss the development and role of CDSs in more detail presently). Paul Krugman (2010) called synthetic CDOs "cocktails of credit default swaps that let investors take big bets on assets without actually owning them." Synthetic CDOs increased the supply of securities that had previously been fixed by the supply of real underlying assets. Because synthetic CDOs could be built without the need for fresh mortgages or other forms of debt, the market ballooned. This was especially so at a time when demand for new mortgage loans in the housing market began falling from 2006. The first synthetic security was launched by Goldman Sachs in 2004, and by 2007 the bank had packaged and sold $73 billion of such securities. By the end of 2006 half of all the new securities being issued were synthetic (Lowenstein 2010, 56). The rapid diffusion of synthetic products underlines a particular feature of financial markets—the impossibility of claiming patents over the development of new financial instruments. In a global ranking of firms' assigned patents in 2011, the first financial company in the list was American Express—in joint 259th place (Economist 2012b). The absence of patents meant that in an increasingly competitive market, banks had to either sell more of their existing products or continually discover and launch new ones to boost their profits.

Originate and Distribute?

Securitization in general and the proliferation of CDOs in particular have been identified as key causes of the 2007–2008 crisis. The usual argument here is that securitization resulted in a drop in credit standards because lenders who knew that they would be able to sell their loan to a third party had no incentive to assess whether a borrower would be likely to repay a loan. As Duff McDonald (2009, 205) puts it, "As the most successful version of financial alchemy in history, securitization also planted the seeds of the housing market's implosion, by removing any reason for a lender to care about whether the borrower would be able to repay the loan."

Yet at a time in which the securitization market was booming, it is important to realize that the "originate and distribute" logic of securitization was widely seen to have *reduced* financial risks by allowing the banks to calibrate and manage risk and apportion it to investors with corresponding risk appetites. Investors who were risk averse could manage their portfolios by buying the senior AAA-rated tranches of an RMBS CDO. Other investors who were prepared to take more risks in the pursuit of higher profits could buy a lower-rated junior tranche, the repayments from which would be imperiled if a larger-than-expected number of mortgage holders defaulted on their loans. As we will see in Chapters 5 and 6, regulators and central bankers as well as bank executives believed that the dispersal of risk had made the financial system safer.

Securitization was a financial godsend for the banks. If a bank simply lends money to a borrower, then that money cannot be lent to anyone else until it has been repaid. With securitization, banks could borrow money in order to profit from lending money and then sell that loan in order to lend more money to other borrowers. In this way, small banks like Northern Rock could grow their business at an exponential rate. Furthermore, each time a bank packaged and sold a CDO or other structured product it could expect to earn a commission of around 1–2% of the value of the sale. The key to success in such a low-margin market was volume trading. In 2006 US banks earned around $690 billion in fees from constructing and selling CDOs (McGee 2010, 160). In the decade prior to the crisis, Merrill Lynch alone was estimated to have created over $70 billion of CDOs and earned around $875 million in commissions from selling about half of these. In order to make CDOs or other securities more attractive to outside investors in an increasingly crowded market, a number of banks designed "liquidity puts" that gave buyers the right to return to the bank a CDO at its original price if the market deteriorated.

We now know that the risk-minimizing properties of originate-and-distribute securitization had been exaggerated. One problem was that securitization distributed risk but did not necessarily disperse it. When the housing market turned and repayments fell, the actual losses recorded were no different from what they would have been in the absence of securitization. Indeed, insofar as securitization pumped up the mortgage market and led to falling credit standards, it actually increased total risks. Furthermore, mezzanine and junior tranches were being aggressively sold to naive investors who believed that they were actually acquiring robust investment assets. The logic of originate-and-distribute required that there was always a potential buyer of any securitized asset. Once the housing market turned, this was not the case. Banks were liable for losses on the mortgages they had "warehoused" that were awaiting securitization.

The major problem with the originate-and-distribute system of securitization was that, in the years prior to the crisis, it had been rendered increasingly obsolete. From around 2004 many banks realized that, rather than packaging and selling securities for a fee, they could earn higher profits by holding these securities on their own balance sheets or even buy securities being issued by other banks. The prime motive for this shift in strategy was quite straightforward. The interest payments banks could earn from holding a securitized asset were greater than the fee they could expect to earn for selling that asset to an outside investor. In 2007 the Bank of England (2007, 9) observed that, as a result of the tilt toward originate-and-hold, the balance sheet assets of the largest global banks "more than doubled," from $10 trillion in 2000 to $23 trillion in 2006. By 2007 the Swiss bank UBS alone held $50 billion of AAA-rated securitized assets (Acharya and Richardson 2009, 207). In July 2008 the *Financial Times* estimated that banks were buying 48% of all the senior AAA-rated tranches of RMBSs. Acharya, Cooley, et al. (2009, 284–285) estimate that US banks and Fannie Mae and Freddie Mac held 50% of all AAA-rated securities, with an estimated value of almost $8 trillion. These securitized assets—at least the non-synthetic ones—were, in one sense, loans. The securities were backed by assets, which resulted in interest payments. But these were not necessarily loans that the bank itself had made. The loans had often been made by mortgage brokers or other banks, packaged together, sliced into CDOs and other structured products, and then bought and sold. Instead of distributing risk, the growth in the holdings of these assets hugely concentrated risk in the major banks (Duquerroy, Gauthier, and Gex 2009). When the housing market deteriorated and the market value of securities fell, losses were concentrated in just a handful of systemically important banks whose balance sheets were loaded with securitized assets and that were too big and too interconnected to be allowed to fail. As Duff McDonald (2009, 213) writes: "Wall Street firms issued $178 billion in mortgage-backed CDOs in 2005 and almost twice that in 2006. They effectively over-stuffed the pipeline, and in an increasing volume the securities stayed in-house . . . The idea that

Wall Street functioned merely as intermediary was officially out the window."

Financial regulation also gave bankers an incentive to pursue the policy of originate-and-hold. Under the terms of the Basel capital regulations, banks were required to hold less capital on AAA-rated securitized assets held on their own balance sheet than they were on nonsecuritized loans (Acharya and Richardson 2009, 201–202). Bank executives also genuinely believed that the senior RMBS CDO assets held on their balance sheets were exceptionally safe, not only because they had an enduring faith in the stability of the US housing market but because they believed they would be the first to be paid and because they had also insured themselves against the possibility of future losses. CDSs offered banks a way of offsetting or hedging their risk by paying a monthly or annual fee to a third party, who, in return, committed to compensate the bank or investor if a larger-than-expected number of borrowers defaulted and repayments from the security fell below a certain specified level. Most of the CDS trades were backed by one of a small number of large financial organizations. AIG's London-based Financial Products Division, for example, insured around $450 billion of such trades (McGee 2010, 254). Fannie Mae and Freddie Mac insured upwards of $2 trillion of securitized mortgages. Tett (2009, 264) suggests that the actual market risk embodied in CDS contracts rose to around $24 trillion prior to the crisis.

Derivatives and Proprietorial Trading

CDSs were meant to reduce financial risk. They did not do so. One problem was counterparty risk. CDSs only offered an effective form of insurance insofar as the insurer, the counterparty, was in a position to make payments when it was required to do so. The problem facing AIG and other CDS counterparties was that when the housing market deteriorated they lacked the resources to pay out on a large number of simultaneous claims. This created a further problem during the financial crisis. Not only were banks that had insured their securitized assets via CDSs at risk; banks that had lent money to banks that had used CDSs to insure their risks were also at risk. A second problem with CDSs was that as well as offering a means of insuring risk, they offered banks and other investors a means of speculative trading on future market movements. Banks could structure a CDS deal in such a way that another party had to pay out if the market price of some asset or instrument rose above or fell below a specified value during a particular period. McIlroy (2010) estimates that up to 80% of CDS agreements were "naked" in the sense that the buyer had no ownership stake in the underlying asset and was therefore engaged in financial speculation rather than hedging a risk.

Securitization was presented as a means of reducing and dispersing risk, whereas CDSs were meant to insure risk. Both instruments ended up concentrating risk. The same problem arose with other kinds of derivative financial instruments the banks were trading. One particularly active market was in interest rate and currency forward agreements, swaps, and options. Here, the underlying and publicly articulated logic of the market was, once again, that of risk reduction. Interest rate and currency agreements allowed businesses to reduce risk by locking in particular interest rates and currency exchange rates through a contractual agreement with a bank. In theory, derivatives trading could, from the bank's perspective, be profitable and riskless. It could be profitable because the bank could charge a fee for arranging the derivative. It could be risk-neutral if the bank entered into a series of offsetting exchanges with different parties. The practice was again somewhat different. This is because interest rate and currency exchange derivatives also offered the banks a means of speculating about future price movements by negotiating derivative agreements with *other* banks, investors, and financial institutions. By June 2008 the gross market value of foreign exchange derivatives was around $1.2 trillion and that of interest rate derivatives $4.8 trillion (IMF 2009b, 70). Duncan (2009 271) observes that at its precrisis peak, the nominal value of the global derivatives market exceeded the market value of everything produced on earth during the previous twenty years. This was not, in other words, a market in which derivatives were being used simply to hedge trade risk. A survey by the ratings agency Fitch (2006, 9) showed that speculative trading was the dominant or active motivation for 90% of participants in such markets.

Financial trading was most certainly not an invention of the twenty-first century. Trading in derivatives and "short selling" were established features of the fledgling Amsterdam share market of the eighteenth century (N. Ferguson 2008, 138). Short-term trading in financial markets had long provided a sometimes rich source of profits for investment banks (Mallaby 2010). These kinds of activities—along with the provision of advice on mergers and acquisitions, currency exchange, and other services—had always formed an important part of the business model of investment banks like Lehman Brothers and Goldman Sachs in the United States and merchant banks like Schroders and Barings in the United Kingdom. However, what was new prior to the crisis was the way in which previously marginal activities became an increasingly important part of the business strategy of the largest investment banks and many commercial banks. The growth in securitization and the inexorable rise in derivatives trading are thus emblematic of a historic shift toward high-risk/high-return banking strategies in the financial heartlands of the United States and the United Kingdom (Crotty 2009; Gowan 2009). At Merrill Lynch, revenue from trading and principal investments (in which the firm risked its own money rather than the money of clients or external investors) rose from 47% of pretax earnings in 1997 to 55% in 2007. At Goldman Sachs it rose from 39% in 1997 to 68% in 2007. At Lehman Brothers it rose from 32% to over 80% (Crotty 2009, 18; McGee 2010, 128–129; FCIC 2011, 66). Overall, between 1984 and 2006, the proportion of US and UK bank income derived from non-interest sources rose from 24% to 48% (OECD 2011). Derivatives trading became, in the words of one senior bank executive, "the basic business of banking" (quoted in McLean and Nocera 2010, 53). In Chapter 3 we show how the growth in trading in CDOs, CDSs, and other kinds of derivatives transformed the balance sheets of the largest UK and US banks. At the RBS, for example, derivatives accounted for 12% of total assets in 2000 but 41% of assets in 2007. In 2005 and 2006 trading on derivatives accounted for 30% of the bank's overall profits. In total, and across designated large, complex financial institutions, the proportion of assets held in the trading book rose from 21% in 2000 to 45% in 2008 (Haldane, Brennan, and Madouros 2010, 92). Traditional bank lending continued to grow in absolute terms. The outstanding asset value of the RBS's loans rose from £135 billion in 2000 to £835 billion in 2007. Yet at the same time gross loans as a proportion of overall assets fell from 55% in 2000 to 37% in 2007. At Barclays the proportion fell to as low as 22% in 2008.

Leverage and Funding

Increased competition and declining profit margins in traditional business and mortgage lending gave bank executives an incentive to reengineer their balance sheets toward securitization and financial trading. Competition also gave banks an incentive to grow the overall size of their balance sheets. Securitization and derivatives trading were immensely profitable for the banks. These profits were, however, dependent upon low-margin, large-volume trading. In *After the Great Complacence*, Engelen et al. (2011, 108–110) show that within the largest UK banks, return on assets during the financial boom was running between 0.5% and 1.5%. It followed that, in order to significantly increase their profits, the banks needed to increase the total size of their balance sheets—that is, the overall value of their assets and liabilities. Achaya, Cooley, et al. (2009, 286) estimate that there was a doubling in the size of global banking balance sheets between 2004 and 2007 alone. In the United Kingdom the total assets of the five largest banks rose by 1,500%, from £82,000 billion in 1990 to £1.3 trillion in 2007. In the United States the total assets of the ten largest banks by market value more than doubled, rising from $4.305,987 trillion in 2000 to $9.538,814 trillion in 2006. We provide more detail of the growth in the balance sheets of individual banks in Chapter 3.

One way in which the banks could have funded their growth was by raising additional capital. But the banks did not do this. Haldane and Alessandri (2009, 2) show how the major banks in the United Kingdom, for example, were instead allowed to run down their capital levels by a factor of five over the course of the twentieth century. As Figure 2.1 shows, leverage at the largest UK, US, and European banks increased significantly in the decade prior to the crisis. The rapid growth of the banks through leverage and the substantial run-down in capital had implicitly placed the burden of risk not on the banks but on the state. At the same time the banks were privatizing a far higher level of returns.

High leverage was attractive to the banks because, in a period of financial boom and rising asset prices, leverage was a means of extracting higher profits from any given level of investment. Just as mortgage holders gain a larger windfall profit from rising house prices the lower their initial equity stake, high leverage allowed the banks to increase their total profits

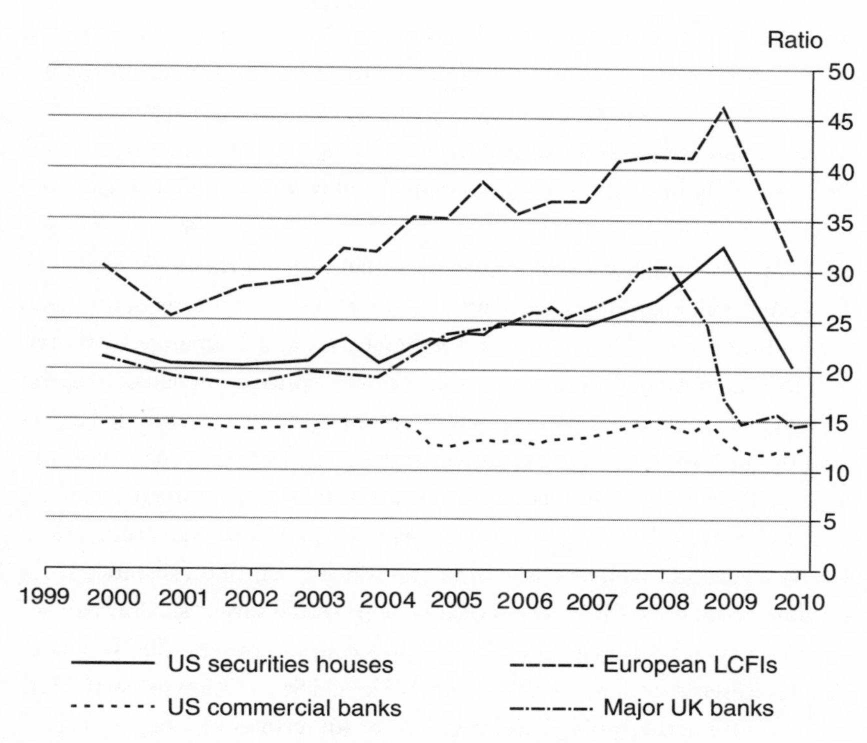

Figure 2.1. Leverage at the large, complex financial institutions (LCFIs). Leverage = assets over total shareholders' equity net of minority interests. Data from Bloomberg, published accounts, and bank calculations. *Source:* Andrew Haldane, Simon Brennan, and Vasileios Madouros, "What Is the Contribution of the Financial Sector: Miracle or Mirage?," in *The Future of Finance: The LSE Report*, ed. Adair Turner et al. (London: London School of Economics and Political Science, 2010), chart 24, p. 15.

and, in particular, their ROE despite recording relatively low returns on assets. This was important because, as we shall see, bonuses were often linked to ROE rather than to overall profitability. There was an intimate connection, in this respect, between higher leverage on the one hand and securitization and financial trading on the other. It is no coincidence that the greatest increases in leverage occurred at the banks that held the largest proportion of trading assets (Haldane and Alessandri 2009, 5; ICB 2011, 10).

Higher leverage was, however, a source of additional risk within the banking system insofar as it amplifies losses as well as profits. High leverage was a key source of risk for individual banks. At a leverage ratio of 30:1, a 3% fall in asset prices is enough to render a bank technically insolvent (Stiglitz 2009, 331). As Alan Greenspan (2013, 42) has come to argue, "In retrospect it is now evident to all that the level of capital that commercial banks and especially investment banks accumulated prior to 2008 as crisis protection was inadequate."

One interesting feature of Figure 2.1 is that it shows that leverage in the US commercial banking system was apparently constant. This is, however, misleading. In the United States, the Securities and Exchange Commission (SEC) continued to enforce stricter capital controls on banks than did British or European regulators. But US accountancy rules excluded assets held by the banks in structured investment vehicles (SIVs) and other off–balance sheet entities such as conduits that the banks maintained (Acharya, Wachtel, and Walter 2009, 366). To expand markets and evade regulation, US bankers and financiers used SIVs and other forms of off–balance sheet conduits to hold securitized assets. Citigroup created seven "shadow banks," or SIVs, which held assets of more than $100 billion. In total the New York Federal Reserve estimates that by 2007 SIVs held $2.2 trillion in assets (Tett 2009, 263). Furthermore, Basel regulations (described in Chapter 1) created a further catalyst for securitization because they allowed banks to reduce their capital reserves for assets held off their balance sheets. Banks were required to hold capital where they were dependent on funding from deposits or long-term loans. The same rules did not, however, apply to bank-sponsored SIVs that funded the purchase of CDOs and other assets using short-term, often overnight funding. Here, the banks' stake in these SIVs was not counted, as it ought to have been, as a liability but as an asset (Acharya and Richardson 2009; Acharya and Schnabl 2009, 89). These shadow banks were nominally independent of their parent entities. They borrowed money on wholesale markets and used it to purchase and then hold CDOs and other assets. In reality, in order to be able to fund their purchase of securitized assets, often from the bank of which they were an offshoot, these shadow banks needed a AAA rating from a credit rating agency, and in order to get this, parent banks needed to guarantee the debts of their offspring. This meant that when the value of the assets that the shadow banks held started to fall and they were unable to meet their own debt repayments, the parent banks were forced to transfer the assets of their conduits back onto their own balance sheets. Banks also felt obliged to cover the losses of their SIVs in order to avoid reputational damage (Barwell 2013, 14).

The total assets of the global shadow banking sector—which includes nondepository banks, hedge funds, special purpose vehicles, structured investment vehicles, and asset-backed commercial paper conduits—rose from $26 trillion in 2002 to $62 trillion in 2007 (FSB 2012a). In order to minimize tax liabilities and regulation, most shadow banks were incorporated within offshore financial centers such as the Cayman Islands, Jersey, and Luxembourg. Citigroup alone had 472 tax haven subsidiaries (Shaxon 2011). The IMF (2010) demonstrates that, rather than providing safe havens for storing assets, these offshore centers constitute the connection points between large banks in different onshore financial centers. More than half of the world's cross-border assets and liabilities were being held in offshore financial centers (Palan, Murphy, and Chavagneux 2010, 25–27). The Cayman Islands was the largest foreign holder of US MBSs (Lane and Milesi-Ferretti 2010a, 3). Rixen (2013), who cites these figures, argues that the existence of these offshore financial centers increased risk and contributed to the origins of the 2008 crisis in a number of ways. First, they made it easier for banks to securitize assets via SIVs. Second, they allowed financial institutions to hide risks from regulators. Third, their low or zero tax rates increased profit margins and encouraged risk taking. Fourth, by locating SIVs in tax havens, certain quality requirements on credit to be securitized could be avoided. Finally, the tax advantages offered by offshore financial centers encouraged banks to fund their trading through debt rather than capital.

One way in which the banks could have purchased additional assets and extended their leverage during the financial boom was by attracting additional deposits on the liability side of their balance sheet. Yet at a time when debt was rising and average savings were falling and the banks were facing increasing competition for consumer and business deposits from pension mutual and money market funds, many banks struggled to secure additional deposits. This was most obviously true of the largest US investment banks, which typically operated without a deposit base, but it was also true of many of the largest commercial banks in the United States and the United Kingdom. The Financial Services Authority (FSA) estimates that the "customer funding gap" at the major UK banks, for example, rose from just £1 billion in 2000 to nearly £600 billion in 2006 (FSA 2011, 46). Banks instead increasingly funded their asset base through short-term borrowings on wholesale financial markets. By 2007, 50% of bank lending was being funded by short-term wholesale sources in the United Kingdom (Milne 2009, 30). It has been estimated that by the summer of 2008 the short-term debt of the ten largest US commercial banks and investment banks exceeded $2.6 trillion. This money was sometimes borrowed directly from pension funds or money market funds, sourced domestically and internationally, and rolled over on a monthly, weekly, or even daily basis. The banks also borrowed through the repurchase (repo) agreement market where they borrowed to purchase securities that constituted the collateral for that loan—a form of lending that only made sense in a market in which asset prices were continuously rising. By the summer of 2008, 50% of leverage growth in the US market was being funded in this extremely risky way.

Slaves of Structures: Systemic Risk

In the years prior to the crisis the traded value of credit securities in general and CDSs in particular rose sharply. But when the market turned and prices fell, this meant that banks had to suddenly revise downward the value of the assets they held on their balance sheets. Whereas in even the most severe recession, the value of assets in the real economy is unlikely to decline by more than 20% a year, it became clear that securitized assets could lose large amounts of their nominal market value in a matter of days. This was particularly so in the case of the senior AAA-rated tranches of CDOs held on bank balance sheets, which had previously been treated as effectively riskless. Moreover, because of the burgeoning international trade in such securities, many banks and financial institutions and a wide range of other international investors were exposed.

The crisis began almost imperceptibly during 2006 and early 2007 when the housing market started to crack in the United States and as mortgage default rates in Arizona, California, Florida, and Nevada started to rise at the same time that house prices started to fall (FCIC 2011, 87). Subprime loans were encouraged in a low interest rate context and in a context of rising house prices, the latter implying that mortgagees could refinance or sell their house at a higher price if they could not service their existing loan.

International macroeconomic imbalances and credit flows were also an important market context (Wolf 2009). Credit flowed from high-saving, surplus countries into deficit countries like the United States and the United Kingdom, reflecting huge international trade and savings imbalances (Bernanke 2005). A key source of funds was China. The Chinese government calculated that it could not invest more of its savings domestically without risking uncontrollable inflation. So it effectively decided to park its trade and savings surplus abroad by purchasing US government, corporate, and bank debt, effectively paying for US investment in the absence of sufficient US savings (Wade 2009a, 2009b). The result was a huge current account surplus in China. Instead of money flowing from the developed economies to the developing world, it ran in the opposite direction. Savings from China and other surplus countries contributed to a credit boom in which ever-larger volumes of cheap money were chasing limited investment opportunities in the West. Much of the savings were used to purchase US government bonds, thus displacing investors into other assets. As Barwell (2013, 17) notes, this "wall of money helped to fuel the rapid and intertwined expansion of both the global banking system and the securitisation markets." Plentiful credit and cheap imports from countries like China also helped suppress inflation and thus interest rates in the lead economies. A further important factor was the cheap money policy run by Alan Greenspan's Federal Reserve during the early 2000s. This reduced the costs of credit and helped fuel booming mortgage and credit markets. Through the so-called carry trade, cheap US funds were also recycled into overseas investments in the United Kingdom and Europe. The US subprime mortgage market that first emerged in the 1980s took off in 2001 when, in the aftermath of the dot-com crash and the 9/11 attacks, interest rates were cut to 1%. In this environment, bank traders could invest in higher-return securities, hedge risk using credit derivatives such as CDSs, and sit back and reap the profits.

In 2005, however, in the face of rising inflation, interest rates suddenly jumped to over 3% and in 2006 to almost 5%. This was the sharpest series of rate rises since the Federal Reserve's big inflation-busting effort in the early 1980s. These interest rate increases hit hundreds of thousands of mortgagees, many of them subprime mortgage holders who had been sold "teaser" loans featuring low initial interest rates, many of which were timed to reset to a higher rate in 2006. This resetting and the rise in official interest rates saw many mortgagees struggling to meet repayments on houses now often worth less than the value of their loans. Taking advantage of "without recourse" rules, which effectively insulated them from bankruptcy, many homeowners simply abandoned their houses and walked away from their mortgages. When these houses were then repossessed and resold, the supply of housing on the market began to massively outstrip available demand, and prices tumbled further. Between 2005 and 2007 there was an 84% drop in residential investment (M. Lewis 2010, 85). The first commercial casualties of the housing crash were, unsurprisingly, real estate agents and mortgage lenders. At the end of December 2006, the California-based real estate investment trust company New Century employed 7,000 people and had a stock market value of $1.7 billion. Yet almost 17% of its loans defaulted within the first three months of origination (FCIC 2011, 157). In March 2007 the company disclosed that it was running short of cash to pay creditors. In April it declared bankruptcy. Hundreds of other similar companies followed.

At this point, in the first few months of 2007, economists and policy makers generally assumed that a temporary correction in the housing market would have little impact on the rest of the economy. During this period the US Federal Reserve (2007a, 4) continued to assume that inflation was the key economic challenge facing the economy. The Federal Reserve's new chairman, Ben Bernanke, reassuringly told Congress in early 2007 that "the impact on the broader economy and financial markets of the problems in the sub-prime market seems likely to be contained" (FCIC 2011, 234). Similarly, former Treasury secretary Hank Paulson thought the subprime meltdown did not pose "any threat to the overall economy" (quoted in Roubini and Mihm 2010, 15). There was a widespread recognition that the banks were exposed to losses in the housing sector, but there was, at this stage, no panic.

One reason politicians, the banks, and regulators remained confident was that the underlying economic indicators remained positive. In the United States annual growth in 2007 was 2%. This was lower than the 3.2% growth figure in 2005 and 2006 but was still regarded as favorable. The same was true in the United Kingdom, where the economy grew by 3.1% in 2007. Insofar as the housing market was thought to be problematic, this was thought to relate exclusively to subprime loans. The subprime mortgage market was worth about $1.4 trillion by 2007, with a substantial proportion of these assets being securitized. There were, however, deep flaws in this market. The securitization chain meant that mortgage originators quickly offloaded mortgages to commercial and investment banks. This meant that neither borrowers (who benefited from without recourse rules), mortgage originators, nor the banks had an obvious interest in ensuring that repayment schedules were plausible. Predatory—if not criminal—lending practices were widespread (FCIC 2011, 10–11). As we shall see in Chapters 5 and 6, the assumption made at executive level within many banks operating in the major UK and US markets was that subprime securities were a small part of the market, that securitized assets and associated risk had been distributed to many parts of the financial system, and that the remaining risks had been hedged either through offsetting trades or insurance measures. The only correct assessment here was that the subprime market was a relatively small part of the overall securities market. As noted above, Milne (2009, 64) estimates that the subprime sector of the overall securitization market was about $800 billion. The overall structured credit market, however, was far bigger, amounting to over $11 trillion in 2006. This far larger market included various forms of ABSs well removed from the subprime market as well as almost $6 trillion of MBSs generated by the mortgage giants Fannie Mae and Freddie Mac. Most of these latter securities were relatively safe, or in the case of Fannie Mae and Freddie Mac, implicitly guaranteed by the government.

The first sign that the housing downturn might morph into a full-scale financial crisis came in the summer of 2007 when various hedge funds belonging to the US investment bank Bear Stearns and the French bank BNP Paribas announced that they had sustained significant losses on securities investments made in the US housing market. Significantly, some of these losses were incurred on assets the credit agencies had rated AAA—that is, supposedly as safe as US Treasury bonds. In October 2008, the IMF estimated the declared losses in the subprime securities markets to be around $500 billion (Admati and Hellwig 2013, 60). Milne (2009, 65) estimates that there could have been a further $4.8 trillion in relatively safe securities sitting on bank balance sheets that became illiquid because of a loss of market confidence. The $500 billion of actual losses sounds like a large number, but it needs to be put into perspective: $500 billion is far smaller than losses associated with the dot-com crash in the early 2000s, where US equity markets lost around $5 trillion (Bernanke 2012). The $500 billion in losses should also be compared with the $2 trillion–plus balance sheets of single banks such as JP Morgan Chase or Citigroup. Onaran and Pierson (2008) suggest that the total losses from the subprime market were equivalent to the average daily gain or loss on the US stock market. Bernanke told the FCIC (2011, 27) that "prospective subprime losses were clearly not large enough on their own to account for the magnitude of the crisis" (on the relative significance of the subprime failure, also see Dodd and Mills 2008).

A key question is why such losses generated a full-blown financial crisis. The answer is that bankers and financiers were operating in a structural context of systemic risk. As British business secretary Vince Cable (2009, 33) puts it, the subprime securities crisis was the "fuse that lit the bomb," and the bomb was in fact systemic risk: a situation in which relatively small perturbations can set off major chain reactions or cascading failures that can bring down the entire financial system (Haldane and May 2011). This is a structural characteristic of the system, but the basic mechanism underpinning it is behavioral dynamics and panics within complex and highly interlinked financial markets in which fully two-thirds of the of the massive growth of banking balance sheets previously described reflects increasing claims from *within* the financial system itself (Haldane and May, 2011, 351).

Systemic risk and its effects were manifested primarily in two ways. First, asymmetric information and the opacity and "almost indecipherable complexity" (Greenspan 2013, 46) of many of the exotic securities rendered financial markets extremely fragile. Within the largest investment and commercial banks, so-called quants with PhDs in physics or mathematics were hired to help develop and construct complex new securities. These allowed for multiple bets on the same underlying assets, thus rapidly multiplying risk and uncertainty. Increasingly, a lack of transparency generated by the complexity of new structured products started to affect the market. The prospectuses of such securities would often run to hundreds of pages, "encased in a nearly incomprehensive language that only a securities lawyer could truly love" (W. Cohan 2011, 480). The complexity meant that rating agencies and risk managers would find them difficult to accurately assess in terms of risk (Crotty 2009, 567). Not surprisingly, the biggest asset losses occurred in the market for these products (Milne 2009, 165).

As soon as the market downturn became obvious, investors began to worry about market reaction and counterparty risk, reflecting interaction effects as a key structural characteristic of the system. Rising fear and uncertainty meant that, increasingly, investors did not discriminate between safer and less safe securities (Milne 2009, 64–65), a situation in which mounting panic and the dumping of assets would soon destroy the securitization markets. Wild swings in financial markets and investor sentiment, from euphoria to panic, combined with myopia and herding behavior, are now well understood features of behavior within financial markets, as outlined in Chapter 1. Despite the fact that the total mortgage and ABS markets were huge compared to the subprime securities market, and despite the fact that a large number of mortgage and asset-backed securitizations were relatively safe, the market panicked. Investors sold securities they held and, as a result, market prices began to fall. It was the losses generated by market panic and not "toxic assets" per se that undermined and nearly destroyed the financial system (Milne 2009, 25). Losses stemming initially from subprime securities were rapidly magnified into a loss of confidence and panic across the entire structured credit market. The market's limited understanding of these instruments was a factor that drove the panic. This was exacerbated by uncertainty about *which* banks had lost the most money amid the crisis. Around 80% of the world's almost $700 trillion derivatives trades had been negotiated over the counter (OTC), that is, bilaterally and confidentially between banks or other entities—trades that had not been registered on a central exchange (Crotty 2009, 566). As a consequence the market was opaque. As Tett (2010, 126) notes: "By 2005 complex credit was evolving so rapidly, and the banks were in such fierce competition with each other, that they kept much of their activity in the CDO or credit default swap world relatively secret from each other. That made it hard for outsiders to track how the market was developing." There were even more complex market interrelationships and potential default correlations between different securities and market segments that were almost impossible to understand or model. Uncertainty about the location of the largest losses therefore had an immediate and incendiary effect, resulting in a massive loss of investor confidence and finally a freezing of the market in all forms of structured securities.

At this point the market value of a wide range of securitized assets of different credit ratings began to fall and fall suddenly. The global financial system became caught in a vicious downward spiral. An ever-growing list of banks, hedge funds, insurers, and mutual funds started to announce losses in the value of the RMBSs and other assets held on their books. As these losses started to accumulate, investors concluded, not unreasonably, that other securities derived from corporate debt, credit card loans, or other assets that had been split into different tranches might also have been overvalued. When the credit rating agencies responded by substantially downgrading these securities, major institutional investors who were legally required to hold AAA-rated assets simultaneously sold their holdings, forcing the market price down further.

Financial markets are particularly prone to chain reaction and contagion effects. This stems from uncertainty and herding effects and from the extraordinary interconnectedness of global financial markets. While the US and UK banks had increasingly switched to a policy of "originate and hold," it was still the case that thousands of CDOs and other securities had been sold to banks, companies, universities, and local government authorities in other countries. Indeed, the US banks routinely sold the higher-risk securities, the first to lose significant value, to overseas investors. It is estimated that between 40 and 50% of the securities generated by US financial institutions ended up in the portfolios of overseas investors (Roubini and Mihm 2010, 81). As the market value of these securities began to fall, the credit agencies downgraded the ratings they attached to those securities. In 2007, 20% of US MBSs were downgraded. In 2008, 91% of securities were downgraded (FCIC 2011, 148–149). The banks increasingly found they were unable to sell securities to other investors and, at a time when their own balance sheets were so fragile, were reluctant to retain them. Increasingly it became impossible to price securitized assets, as the market for them was evaporating.

The loss of value in securitized assets immediately posed major problems for banks and asset holders. Bankers and investors had assumed that the sanguine market assessments offered by the credit rating agencies were correct and that risk had been offset by hedging or insurance measures. Instead, the ratings were incorrect, especially for the more esoteric products, and the CDS market, along with insurance giants like AIG, collapsed under the weight of claims amid the crisis. The banks' internal risk management assessments had also overlooked the havoc that could be wreaked by a synchronized downturn in asset prices. Banks desperately needed to cover losses and fund their activities. But banks had run down their capital levels, leaving little capacity to meet unexpected balance sheet losses. Indeed, most of the shadow banking system was running on virtually no equity. Alan Greenspan (2013, 50) argues that this represents the key difference between the dot-com crash and the 2008 crisis. In the dot-com crash large losses were incurred but not within financial firms run on borrowed money: "If mortgage-backed securities in 2008 had been held in unleveraged institutions—defined contribution pension funds and mutual funds, for example—as had been the case for [dot-com] stocks in 2000, those institutions would still have suffered large losses, but bankruptcies, triggered by debt defaults, would have been far fewer." A number of banks raised additional capital to shore up their balance sheets. The Singapore Investment Corporation purchased $6.8 billion of Citigroup shares and a 9% stake in the Swiss bank UBS. Another Singaporean fund, Temaske, bought a 10% stake in Merrill Lynch. The China Investment Group extended $5.5 billion of credit to Morgan Stanley. The Abu Dhabi Investment Group invested $7.5 billion in Citigroup, the Kuwait Investment Company invested $6.6 billion in Merrill Lynch, and the Qatar Investment Group invested £1.7 billion in Barclays. But this was not enough, and with share prices continuing to fall, a number of banks held asset fire sales, causing further falls in market prices.

In such a context, funding pressures increasingly put the spotlight on bank leverage and dependence on wholesale funding markets. The banks had been operating with a large maturity mismatch: borrowing short in order to hold longer-term assets. Such exposure to short-term funding markets rapidly became a second major structural challenge or source of systemic risk. As the crisis gathered, fear and eventually panic spread through short-term funding markets. The interconnections among the largest banks and, in particular, the ways in which the banks had borrowed money from each other and from other entities meant that the vulnerability of any one bank created a systemic risk for the entire banking sector. Panic in these markets rapidly led to a general liquidity crisis that then started to bring down banks. It was "nothing less than a run on the entire global banking system" (Milne 2009, 52). The banks had assumed that leveraged risk could be dealt with if needed by selling securities in markets that would remain liquid. Charles Goodhart, formerly of the Bank of England, argues that the prevailing view was that "you can always obtain funding to hold assets . . . and that the short-term wholesale market, the inter-bank markets, the asset-backed commercial paper market and so on, would always be open and that you would always have access to them" (quoted in Crotty 2009, 567). This view turned out to be totally incorrect. The funding markets froze amid the panic. As Mark Blyth (2013, 31) describes it: "The crisis spread globally as investors sought the protection of liquidity, but failed to find it. Just as one country's exports [depend] upon another country's imports, so one bank's liquidity depends upon another bank's willingness to be illiquid. And at that moment, no one wanted to be illiquid." When the market for mortgage-backed and other securities collapsed and the securities became illiquid, the banks then got caught by the squeeze on short-term funding. The inability of banks to raise short-term funding was the proximate cause of bank failures such as Northern Rock in the United Kingdom and Bear Sterns and Lehman Brothers in the United States. Hence, the asset and liquidity crises were linked. The scale of the initial asset crisis was greatly exaggerated by market panic, and then the banks were hit again by the subsequent panic in credit markets and the eventual credit freeze. As Ben Bernanke has commented: "The subprime crisis triggered a much broader retreat from credit and risk taking. It became much bigger than I had anticipated. And on top of that we didn't—nobody really did—understand the inter-connections to off-balance sheet vehicles and complex credit derivatives and all of those other things that followed" (quoted in Wessel 2010, 129). This exposure of banks and financial institutions to wider market dynamics and "all of those other things that followed" was greater in this crisis than in previous ones, reflecting greater systemic risk. Milne (2009, 37, 39) argues that this latter condition is the "distinguishing" feature of the crisis, one in which investor panic and the withdrawal of "hot money" greatly amplified the downswing, more so than in any previous financial crisis.

Leverage magnified the scale of the banks' losses during the crisis and meant that many banks were rendered effectively insolvent by their trading losses at a time when the rest of their business remained profitable. As the value of the assets on their balance sheets fell, bank share prices began to fall. The structural cycle was further exacerbated by banks simultaneously being forced to sell assets in a falling market to try to raise funds. A strategy of asset sales to restructure a balance sheet is common practice, but the strategy does not work well when everyone is trying to do the same thing at the same time. The situation was made worse by institutional arrangements like mark-to-market accounting rules that forced banks to value the assets on their trading books based on current market values. These rules made sense insofar as they prevented banks from hiding their losses from shareholders by pretending that assets were worth more than they were (S. Ryan 2009). In an economic boom, mark-to-market rules allowed the banks to constantly revise upward their asset values (Gowan 2009), but in a downturn banks were forced to sell assets in a falling market, a key example of the procyclical effects of regulation (J. Friedman 2009, 168). Another procyclical dynamic was that the banks also risked running afoul of regulatory rules that required them to maintain minimal capital ratios. To meet such requirements banks had to try to obtain more capital (which was not easy amid the crisis) or restructure their holdings, which usually meant forced asset sales. The spiral was further exacerbated when lenders such as money market funds started to experience their own runs.

In early 2008 rumors began to circulate in the United States that two investment banks, Bear Stearns and Lehman Brothers, were sitting on collapsing assets and might be running out of cash and close to insolvency. The rumors were well founded. A number of large investment and commercial banks were at this time sitting on huge losses. The rumors did, however, have a self-fulfilling quality. Money market funds and other wholesale lenders started to withdraw their money from the banks and started to increase the interest they charged the banks to borrow the money they needed to fund their debts. At this point a "liquidity black hole" (Persaud 2003) opened up in the banks' balance sheets. Exploiting this weakness, hedge fund traders began to short the banks, leading to a further fall in their share prices.

In March 2008 Bear Stearns failed and was bought at a knockdown price by JP Morgan Chase. The US Treasury subsidized the deal because, in the words of the then president of the New York Federal Reserve, Timothy Geithner, it feared that "an abrupt and disorderly unwinding of Bear Stearns would have posed systemic risks to the financial system and magnified the downside risk to economic growth" (W. Cohan 2009, 99). The markets were not, however, reassured by the startling news that the government was prepared not only to support commercial banks that held customer deposits but also to support investment banks. Bank share prices continued to fall as short-term credit markets froze. This was an important and distinctive feature of the 2007–2008 crisis. With the notable exceptions of Northern Rock in the United Kingdom and Wachovia in the United States, the banking crisis did not feature customer-led bank runs of the sort that had destroyed banks in the 1930s. This was in part because most bank customers initially remained largely unaware of the scale of the crisis. It was also because government deposit schemes had reduced the incentive for customers to be the first to withdraw their money. The crisis was instead driven by the failure of the wholesale funding market (Brunnermeier 2009; Diamond and Rajan 2009; Gorton 2009). Huang and Ratnovski (2011) demonstrate that a bank's dependence upon wholesale funding was the variable that would best predict its total losses during the crisis.

The crisis reached a defining moment on 15 September when Lehman Brothers, an investment bank with $600 billion in assets and 25,000 employees, was forced to declare bankruptcy after the failure of takeover talks with Barclays (Mishkin 2009, 4). Stung by intense political criticism of their earlier bailout of Bear Stearns, the US authorities resolved not to bail out Lehman. However, the largest corporate losses in US history were recorded at a commercial bank, Citigroup, which hemorrhaged $28 billion in 2008 and only survived through repeated infusions of taxpayer money. The markets reacted violently as investors scrambled to withdraw their investments from banks—almost any bank. In short order, the giant insurance group AIG, the two government-sponsored mortgage providers in the United States, Fannie Mae and Freddie Mac, as well as Washington Mutual and Merrill Lynch, were either taken over or effectively nationalized. In the

United Kingdom and Europe, RBS, HBOS, Bradford and Bingley, Fortis, Dexia, Bayern Landesbank, and ING either failed or were saved from failure by government-brokered takeover deals.

Some semblance of order within the financial markets was established only when, in a series of coordinated moves in September and October 2008, governments across the world responded by cutting interest rates; guaranteeing bank deposits and bank borrowing on short-term markets while also purchasing "toxic" assets from the banks; injecting additional capital into the banks; and swapping increasingly precarious bank assets for cash (see Claessens et al. 2009, 20 for an overview). The costs of these rescue packages were astronomically high. In June 2009 the IMF (2009a, 7) estimated that the liabilities assumed by governments during the final few months of 2008 and the first few months of 2009, when the US Treasury had to announce a second rescue package for Citigroup, and the UK government unveiled its Asset Protection Scheme, were equivalent to an average of 32% of GDP in the G20 countries and more than 80% of GDP in the United States and the United Kingdom.

The immediate effect of the banking crisis on the "real" economy was to reduce bank lending and real investment. Despite low interest rates and extensive government support since the crisis, banks have been economizing on lending to rebuild their balance sheets. Lending has still not recovered to precrisis levels. In order to protect their balance sheets and reduce their leverage, banks either increased the interest they charged on loans, withdrew credit, or demanded more collateral for their loans. Total bank lending to nonfinancial corporations in the United Kingdom fell from £80 billion in new loans in 2007 to £50 billion in 2008. In 2009 net lending was negative £50 billion as banks called in existing and impaired loans and cut new lending (HM Treasury 2010, 17). As consumers scrambled to reduce their debts, the result was a slump in trade and investment. The longer-term effect of the banking crisis on the real economy has been a fiscal crisis and deep recession. In order to fund the bank bailouts and fiscal stimulus packages, governments borrowed money. In the United States central government debt rose from an equivalent of 35% of GDP in 2007 to 61% of GDP in 2010. British government debt rose from 42% of GDP to 85% over the same period. At the start of 2009 governments experienced few problems in funding this debt. Investors were running scared of financial markets and were willing to accept relatively low interest rates on government bonds, which were deemed to be safer. Market sentiment changed in early 2010 as investors began to contemplate the possibility that some governments might be unable to honor their repayments and default. Attention initially focused on Greece, whose already astronomically high public debt prior to the crisis climbed to the equivalent of 150% of GDP in 2010. Fears about default risked being a self-fulfilling prophecy. As confidence in first the Greek and then the Portuguese, Spanish, and Italian governments faltered, interest rates on their debt soared. With an ever-larger proportion of their day-to-day expenditure being consumed by interest repayments, the chances of one of these governments defaulting increased. In order to appease financial markets, governments started to cut their budgets. As consumer spending and investment then started to fall, economies were tipped back into recession.

Systemic Risk and Ecosystem Power

Bankers and financiers had created a fragile asset and debt structure whose ultimate ramifications they did not understand and could not control. The crisis, fueled by systemic risk, was really about the volitions of market actors (panic and herding) in a structural context of high interbank debt dependence and complex financial interconnections: a classic pattern of agent-structure interaction. How should we theorize this interaction?

McAnulla (2005, 32) argues that "causal mechanisms can exist independently of our knowledge of them." As we have shown here, systemic risk was a structural parameter whose presence and ultimate effects were not immediately observable or understood by affected actors. Archer (2000, 465) nevertheless argues that structures are always mediated and actualized by agents: "Structures only exert an effect when mediated through the activities of people. Structures are only ever relational emergents and never reified entities existing without social interaction." The question thus arises as to how agents can mediate or actualize structural effects they do not fully comprehend.

What is the connection between agents and structure here? It is true that our agents did not fully understand the properties and, in particular, fragilities of the system they had created. Nevertheless, they did know that their balance sheets and solvency were threatened once asset prices began to fall. Subsequent market interaction between agents who were simultaneously seeking to secure additional funding while selling assets produced further falls in asset values. Agents then became concerned about debt exposures and counterparty risk. This saw the credit markets freeze. Ultimately, their panic and herding in a structural context of high debt dependence and complex financial interconnections were what fueled the liquidity crisis and the scale of the overall financial crisis. The structural ramifications of agency stemmed from the structure and dynamics of *interaction* between agents, especially when agents were all trying to behave in the same way at the same time. In the classic sense, then, agents and structures were thus mutually constitutive. Kim and Sharman (2014) suggest that their empirical data demonstrates the "primacy of contextual, structural factors over agency." The account here of structure and agency is somewhat different. We argue that agents themselves actualized the structural impacts of the context they inhabited through their behavior and especially their patterns of interaction. In other words, it was not a matter of structure *over* agency, but a process whereby agents and their behavior actualized structural effects: a process demonstrating the mutual constitution of structures and agents.

Haldane and May (2011) have argued that banking and finance are usefully seen as a complex ecosystem, dense with agent-environment and agent-agent interactions that produce systemic risk. These effects, however, can also be seen as a form of structural power. Bankers did not want to have to sell their assets in a falling market; they were forced to. They had little alternative in an institutional and structural environment characterized by asymmetric information, low capital buffers, mark-to-market valuation, and market panic. Similar pressures also existed in the wholesale funding markets. Agents collectively wanted markets to remain open in order to facilitate the rollover of short-term debt, but individually in the context they confronted they had no incentive to lend money and every incentive to withhold it. Bankers and financiers were thus caught in a series of severe collective action problems stemming from an institutional and structural environment they had helped create.

Our agents were therefore confronted by a power dynamic that forced their hand. We thus invoke the language of power because agents were being forced by the actions of other agents to do things they did not wish to do. This is not the simple form of power where an agent A intentionally forces B to do something. Nor is it a form of power strategically wielded by agents in a structurally privileged position, the usual focus of structural power arguments (Lindblom 1977). Nor is this about the forms of disciplinary or discursive power theorized by Foucault (1991). Our agents were not being directly coerced by other agents, nor were they in a privileged structural position, nor were they discursively constrained or self-disciplined. Power is often thought of as a resource that is deployed or used by agents, usually in a strategic manner. But there is another category of power, one where agents mutually exert power over one another through the way they interact in a structured context. In the case we are examining, bankers were subject to a form of power that they themselves created and exerted *collectively*, essentially a form of "ecosystem power" born of agent-agent and agent-environment interactions. It was a form of power that was not exerted strategically but was instead being exerted unwittingly and unwillingly. Our agents were acting in a myopic and self-interested manner, producing large structural effects they could not fully comprehend or control. As noted earlier, agents can sometimes use ideas to mediate structural power relations, but this option was not available. Instead, the power in question was a form of ecosystemic power born of myriad unplanned, uncontrolled interactions between agents in a structured context, with devastating effects.

Ultimately, financial crises highlight the limits of human understanding and control in complex systems and the perverse effects of incentive systems that encourage risk taking. The concept of "bounded rationality" and the findings of behavioral finance theory were never more applicable, excepting the few bankers that did perceive unacceptable risks and refused to join the herd. We have told a story about the limits of human control in complex systems, as contagion and chain reaction effects wreaked havoc in a fragile structure that participants thought was built on rational contracting and sound risk management. This is a striking example of agency-structure interaction. The ideas held by agents about the safety of the system blinded them to mounting systemic risk prior to the crisis. Prevailing ideas and assumptions concealed the true nature of the structural dynamics confronting agents. In this sense, ideas and structures proved to be dangerously congruent. Only as the crisis was breaking did bankers come to realize what they had created. They ceased being true believers at precisely the moment that it became too late to escape.

Conclusion

The 2007–2008 crisis was sparked when the burgeoning industry in the more esoteric forms of RMBSs collapsed in the wake of a downturn in the US housing market. This led to a wave of house repossessions, the bankruptcy of real estate agents and mortgage lenders, and eventually dramatic falls in the market value of MBSs, which had often been awarded the highest possible credit ratings. In 2010 the IMF estimated total losses in the banking sector to be in the order of $2.3 trillion. This includes losses on mortgage lending (especially in the subprime markets) as well as trading losses on MBSs. Such losses were sufficient to render many banks insolvent because they were holding only slivers of capital as a buffer and because they were also exposed to a liquidity crisis in wholesale funding markets on which they had become heavily dependent for funding their trading activities and operations. The transformation of bank balance sheets in the years prior to the crisis is essential to understanding the extent of the losses incurred in 2008 and since. Because banks had invested their resources not simply in physical assets but on bets about the future direction of asset prices, and because the banks were highly leveraged and thus exposed to short-term wholesale funding markets, the losses they suffered were out of all apparent proportion to the scale of the losses in the mortgage securities sector.

In order to explain the banking crisis we need to examine how bankers interacted not only with proximate institutions, such as banks in which they worked, but also with wider institutional contexts and patterns of change, such as liberalization, and with wider structural forces such as systemic risk and other structural changes embedded in major contemporary transformations in capitalism, especially financialization. We have argued that bankers and financiers were authoritative and displayed substantial agency in recasting the institutions of banking and finance. They also were (and remain) highly influential in relation to the state. However, as key markets and institutions changed and developed, they subsequently began to exert strong pressures and constraints on bankers. Here market incentives such as remuneration incentives, intense market competition, and the nature of profit opportunities strongly incentivized certain forms of trading and leverage in the core financial markets. When the real estate and securitization markets collapsed, so too did the boom. In this context the structural effects of systemic risk would eventually overwhelm bankers.

We have two central arguments. First, institutional change shaped markets and thereby incentives that strongly influenced and helped produce different types of banking across our four countries. In the United States and the United Kingdom, liberalized markets and sanguine views held by the majority of bankers drove the securitization boom, whereas in Australia and Canada markets and more cautious banking cultures encouraged more traditional banking, as we show in Chapter 8. Second, wider structural forces also mattered, especially in the crisis-hit economies. The downturn in the US real estate market was a structural shift that impacted on MBSs. The collapse of value in these markets then triggered the crisis, whose scale is explained through the structural impact of systemic risk and market interconnectedness. These structural ramifications saw severe knock-on effects as balance sheet losses rapidly escalated into a full-blown liquidity crisis that then brought down or severely damaged a wide range of banks. The findings of behavioral finance point to the myopia and irrationality of agents in making decisions. But such an account is too narrow because it does not tell us enough about how different institutional and structural contexts also shape behavior and outcomes.

Institutional pressures as well as structural forces are thus key explanatory factors in our account. It is important, however, not to lose sight of agency. In Chapters 5 and 6 we show in detail how bankers in the United States and the United Kingdom perceived and operated in the institutional and structural contexts they confronted. These agents "actualized" the institutional and structural effects in question. Bankers in the crisis-hit markets faced strong incentives to behave in certain ways, but it was only those bankers who also *believed* in the markets and the securitization boom who joined the herd and eventually brought the system down. Other agents were more circumspect. In Chapter 7 we show how some banks and bank leaders in the United States and the United Kingdom questioned and managed to stand against the prevailing pressures. In the United States, for example, Wells Fargo (Veverka 2008) and JP Morgan (D. McDonald 2009; Tett 2009) adopted relatively conservative strategies in relation to MBSs, while Goldman Sachs essentially outwitted the market. In the United Kingdom, relatively conservative banking strategies were also followed by HSBC, Lloyds, and Standard Chartered. Clearly, some bankers and bank cultures were able to go against the market and withstand pressures to join the herd, although the pressures were intense. The influence of market pressures was thus strong but not deterministic. This highlights the importance of at least a degree of agent-centered discretion at the micro level. Despite the findings of behavioral finance, not all bankers became overoptimistic or rushed to follow the herd. Milne (2009, 197) also notes that on the whole, pension funds, insurance companies, and sovereign wealth funds also largely avoided investing in CDO RMBSs. The particular and variable patterns of discretion forged by agents, in different but also even in similar contexts, are an important part of our story.

The transformation of banks' balance sheets also tells us something about how the banking crisis was different from those that had preceded it, especially the banking crisis during the Great Depression. Unlike the 1930s financial crisis, the crisis that peaked in 2008 was bank-led: it was the implosion of the financial system that led to a collapse in the "real" economy, and not vice versa. It is true that the 2008 crisis was preceded by what we now know to have been a credit-fueled asset bubble and that the crisis can, in one respect, simply be described as the bursting of that bubble in the housing market. To this extent, Reinhart and Rogoff (2009) are right to argue in *This Time Is Different* that all of the classic signs of a bubble were present and known to be present prior to the crash. But what was different was the way in which the bubble burst. Bank balance sheets were not, in the first instance, destroyed by rising rates of loan defaults in the real economy. Instead, balance sheet losses were caused by losses on the trading book, which then triggered a crisis of systemic risk and eventual illiquidity. This is the essence of the "banking crisis" that is the focus of this book.

3

Bank Performance in the United States and the United Kingdom

Banking markets in the United States and the United Kingdom were at the heart of the 2007–2008 crisis. These conjoined markets hosted the largest banks and the largest trading operations and sustained the greatest losses. British, American, and European banks were all involved. Yet not all the banks in these countries were equally affected by the banking crisis. In this chapter we describe the postwar evolution of the UK and US banking markets and the growth, balance sheet composition, and varying fortunes of the ten largest investment and commercial banks in the United States and the six largest British banks. In the final part of the chapter we also describe the fortunes of AIG Financial Products and of the London-based investment banking arms of the major European banks Deutsche Bank and UBS. This chapter and Chapter 4, which deals with the major Australian and Canadian banks, are therefore about how the banks in question acted and what they did. We offer a forensic analysis of bank balance sheets and of key assets and liabilities. In particular we detail the extent to which banks reengineered their balance sheets amid the boom and the extent to which they engaged in securities trading and exposed themselves to short-term funding markets by ramping up leverage. These proved to be the key risk factors that accounted for the fate of particular banks.

The chapter is necessarily detailed. Our basic argument is, however, quite simple. Some banks—for example, Lehman Brothers, Merrill Lynch, Bear Stearns, and Citigroup in the United States and the Royal Bank of Scotland (RBS) were heavily engaged in what turned out to be risky securities trading. Some banks, such as HBOS in the United Kingdom, suffered big losses in mortgage lending, and all of these banks were highly leveraged and were exposed to bank runs in short-term funding markets. These banks sustained crippling losses during the crisis and either had to be taken over by another bank or nationalized.

Other banks—Wells Fargo, JP Morgan Chase, and Goldman Sachs in the United States and Standard Chartered and, with some important caveats, HSBC in the United Kingdom—escaped relatively unscathed. Some of these banks did engage in risky trading, but managed to largely exit the market prior to the crisis, while some banks, such as Wells Fargo, largely eschewed risky trading. We link this intracountry variation in performance to differences in balance sheet composition, that is, to the degree to which banks had invested in securitized trading assets and other derivatives, as well as their leverage and dependence upon wholesale funding. We demonstrate that survival or failure during the financial crisis was not a matter of luck. The banks that failed had the weakest balance sheets, and those that survived had the strongest. In Chapter 4 we extend our analysis to the largest Australian and Canadian banks.

The United States

Background

In the aftermath of the Great Depression, US politicians restructured the banking industry and introduced far-reaching reforms to reduce the likelihood of a future banking catastrophe. Key measures included the creation of a securities regulator, the Securities Exchange Commission (SEC); the introduction of deposit insurance for commercial banks through the creation of the Federal Deposit Insurance Corporation (FDIC); a strict prohibition on commercial banks engaging in investment bank trading activity (the Glass-Steagall Act); restrictions on interstate banking to limit the size of banks and to limit and structure competition; interest rate caps to limit price competition and risky mortgage lending; and government-sponsored and insured mortgage origination through what would become the giant government-sponsored enterprise Fannie Mae (later to be followed by Freddie Mac in 1970). The result was a highly regulated banking market and a period of relative stability in banking, with only 243 banks failing between 1934 and 1980 (FCIC 2011, 36). Moreover, at this time, the US banking system was a national one. The most internationalized of all the US banks at this time, National City, still only earned around 15% of its profits from outside of the United States (Christophers 2013, 161).

In the 1970s this regulatory regime came under increasing pressure as a result of the remorseless growth of the largely unregulated nonbank financial sector and the growth of the Eurodollar market, which we describe in the final part of this chapter. Amid concerns that the US banking sector was in decline, the largest commercial banks pressed for financial deregulation (Suárez and Kolodny 2011). In 1980 the Depository and Monetary Control Act eliminated interest rate caps on mortgages. In 1982 the Garn–St. Germain Act allowed thrifts (building societies) to compete with banks to offer mortgages to new customers. In 1984 the Secondary Mortgage Enhancement Act allowed banks to hold and trade in mortgage securities. In 1994 the Riegle-Neal Act finally and fully authorized interstate banking. In 1996 the Economic Growth and Regulatory Paperwork Reduction Act required federal regulators to review their rules every decade and solicit comments on "outdated, unnecessary or unduly burdensome rules." Finally, and most significantly, the 1999 Gramm-Leach-Bailey Act undid the Depression era Glass-Steagall Act by allowing large financial institutions to operate, simultaneously, as commercial banks, investment banks, and insurance firms.

By 2007, on the eve of the banking crisis, the banking and finance industry had been transformed. At the apex of the system were five large commercial banks whose deposits were insured through the FDIC and five "bulge bracket" investment banks. In order of the size of their assets, the five largest commercial banks were Citigroup (total assets in 2007 of $2.187 trillion), Bank of America ($1.715 trillion), JP Morgan Chase ($1.562 trillion), Wachovia ($782 billion), and Wells Fargo ($575 billion). The five investment banks were Goldman Sachs ($1.119 trillion in assets in 2007), Merrill Lynch ($1.020 trillion), Morgan Stanley ($901 billion), Lehman Brothers

($691 billion), and Bear Stearns ($395 billion). These banks had grown rapidly. Citi, Wells Fargo, JP Morgan, Morgan Stanley, and Merrill Lynch had more than doubled the value of their total assets between 2000 and 2007. Bank of America, Goldman Sachs, and Lehman Brothers more than tripled the value of their assets over the same period. In 2007 the total assets of the US banking sector were the equivalent of around 110% of GDP. The largest banks were also extremely profitable. In 1980 financial profits constituted around 15% of total corporate profits. By 2004 financial profits amounted to more than 30% of total profits (FCIC 2011, 64). Average return on equity (ROE) among the 500 largest banks in the United States was 14.9% in 2004, 15.7% in 2005, and 16.4% in 2006. In 2006 the *average* pretax profit at the five largest commercial and investment banks was $33 billion.

Beyond these behemoths, the US banking system was composed of a mixture of over 5,000 local community banks; around 30 regional banks with assets of between $20 billion and $300 billion (Landy 2013), some of whose fortunes we describe presently; a horde of smaller state-based banks; and around 400 overseas banks operating out of the United States. In March 2007 Australian banks held $17 billion in assets in US offices; Canadian banks $302 billion; French banks $377 billion; German banks $383 billion; and UK banks $513 billion (US Federal Reserve 2007b).

The largest American commercial and investment banks operated a business model increasingly predicated upon leveraged trading. Exploiting the opportunities provided by the emergence of regulatory loopholes within the Glass-Steagall Act in the late 1980s and early 1990s and, subsequently, its eventual repeal, the commercial banks began to reengineer themselves as investment banks. At the five largest commercial banks, interest-bearing loans constituted only 50% of assets in 2007, while securities constituted 26% of assets. At the large investment banks, which in the 1980s and 1990s had pioneered the trading model, there was, in the 2000s, a slight shift toward lending as banks developed large commercial property portfolios. Facing growing competition from the commercial banks, the investment banks began to buy mortgage originators in order to assure an adequate supply of mortgage-backed assets to securitize. In 2000 Lehman Brothers led the way by purchasing a stake in a California-based subprime lender, BNC Mortgages. Others soon followed, and in 2006–2007 Bear Stearns purchased EMC Mortgages and Encore Credit Corporation; Morgan Stanley purchased Saxon Capital; and Merrill Lynch bought First Franklin. By 2006 trading securities constituted 32% of assets at the five largest investment banks.

The growth in total assets and the shift toward trading created new sources of systemic risk. Leverage within the financial system appeared to be stable. Kalemli-Ozcan, Sorensen, and Yesiltas (2011, 33) have calculated leverage for US banks, including the largest banks, with assets of over $1 billion in 2000, as well as investment banks and large commercial banks. Average leverage at the investment banks rose from 30:1 in 2003 to 36:1 in 2005 before rising again to 44:1 in 2007. Within other parts of the banking system that were regulated by the SEC, leverage was, however, stable. As we first noted in Chapter 2, these figures underestimate the risks that had accumulated within the banking system. Assets held off the banks' balance sheets were not included in the SEC's calculations. Banks also learned to evade regulatory controls by the simple expedient of temporarily selling assets immediately prior to announcing their leverage figures (Quinn and Farrell 2010). Leverage based on wholesale borrowing was a major source of systemic risk. The largest investment banks, which lacked a deposit base, were almost wholly dependent upon short-term wholesale funding and hedge fund deposits in order to finance their trading activities. The largest commercial banks also borrowed heavily. In 2007 customer deposits at the five largest commercial banks were the equivalent of just 37% of the value of liabilities. This shortfall had to be met through borrowing.

The banking crisis in the United States began with the downturn in the housing market and culminated in the near-collapse of the financial system in September and October 2008. In July 2008 Congress passed the Housing and Economic Recovery Act, which authorized the government to invest money directly in Fannie Mae and Freddie Mac in order to stimulate the housing market. Over the next few months the Federal Reserve extended its liquidity programs whereby banks could, at a time when markets were already freezing, swap assets for liquidity by staking other assets as collateral. The Treasury sought to corral other banks into constructing a rescue package to save Lehman Brothers. When this failed, the Treasury showed itself willing to invest $85 billion in AIG to keep it afloat. In October 2008 the Federal Reserve coordinated international interest rate cuts and announced that it would create a facility to buy commercial paper—effectively guaranteeing the short-term lending needs of all American companies that relied on short-term debt to fund their day-to-day operations. As 2008 unfolded and the crisis deepened, the FDIC, with the Federal Reserve's support, intervened to guarantee the senior unsecured debt of banks, thrift companies, and bank holding companies. The Federal Reserve lent a total of $1.1 trillion to financial firms. Bank of America borrowed $67 billion. Citigroup borrowed $58 billion, as did RBS. Barclays borrowed $50 billion and UBS $35 billion (Gorton 2012, 187). On 3 October, Congress passed the $700 billion Troubled Asset Relief Program, which authorized the Treasury to run an emergency recapitalization program through which the largest banks were required to accept government loans and, in return, control executive compensation and clawback compensation obtained on the basis of inaccurate earnings statements, prohibit golden parachutes to senior executives, and limit tax deductions on executive compensation to $500,000. Over $145 billion in government capital was injected directly into the banks in the final months of 2008 and, in total, over 650 banks received government support.

During the crisis average ROE among the 500 largest banks fell from 16.4% in 2006 to 10.3% in 2007 and –1.2% in 2008 before recovering to 2.4% in 2009. Among the five largest commercial banks, average ROE fell from 16.4% in 2006 to 10.3% in 2007 and –1.2% in 2008 before recovering to 2.4% in 2009. Among the largest investment banks, average ROE fell from 20% in 2006 to 5% in 2007, –43% in 2008, and –11% in 2009. These aggregate figures do, however, mask considerable intracountry variation.

The greatest losses in the US banking system were sustained by Citigroup, Bear Stearns, Lehman Brothers, and Merrill Lynch. With government support, Citigroup survived despite recording a pretax loss of $53 billion in 2008, the largest in US history. Bear Stearns failed in 2008 and was taken over by JP Morgan Chase. Lehman Brothers declared bankruptcy in September 2008, and Merrill Lynch, which had "cornered the market on radioactive waste" (Farrell 2010, 19), was taken over by Bank of America. Underlining the extent of intracountry variation in performance, Figure 3.1 shows the end-of-year share price of each of the largest American banks from 2003 to 2011. Care should be taken in reading these figures because the starting share price of each bank is very different—ranging from a

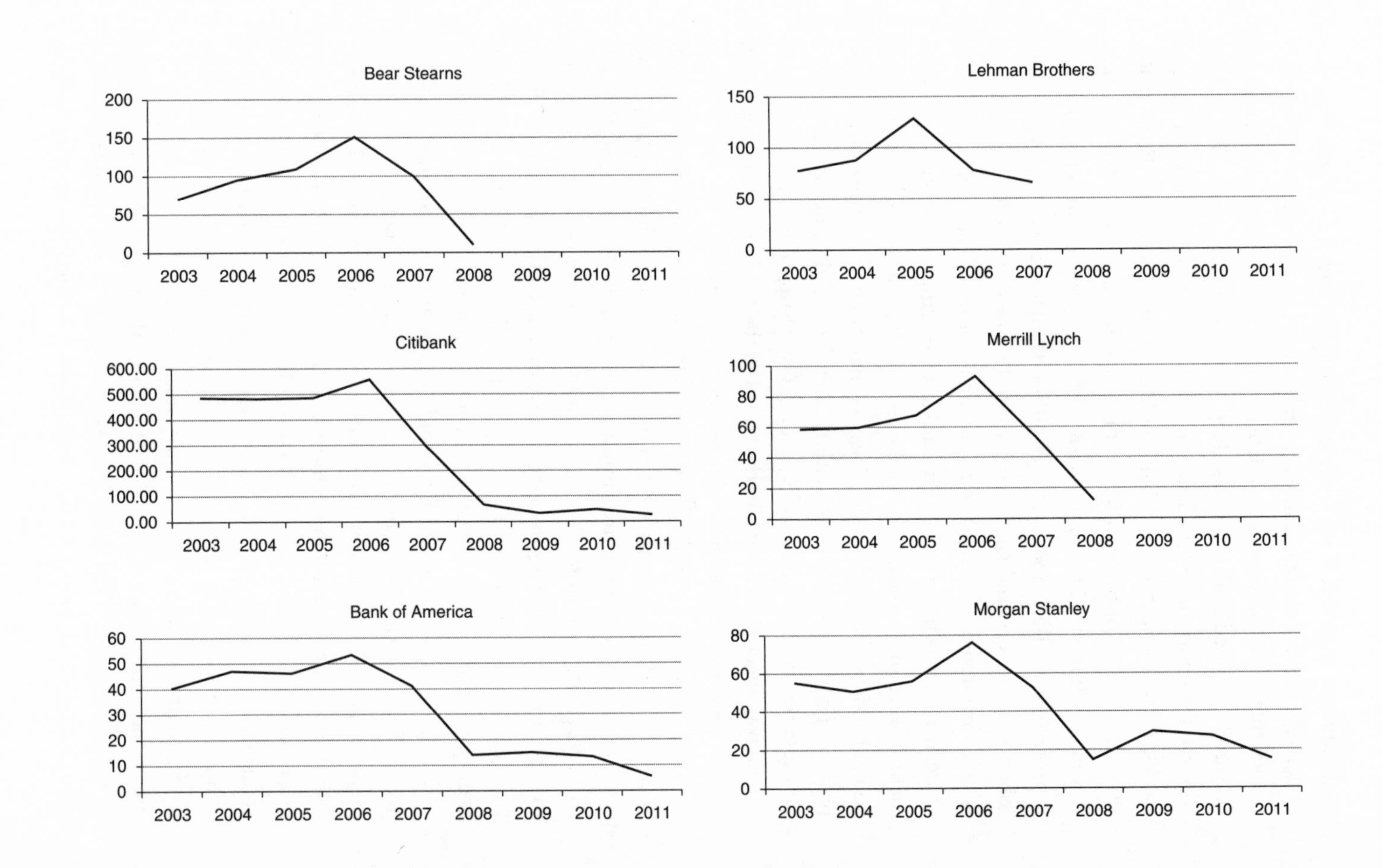
Bear Stearns
200
150
100
50
0
2003 2004 2005 2006 2007 2008 2009 2010 2011
Lehman Brothers
150
100
50
0
2003 2004 2005 2006 2007 2008 2009 2010 2011
Citibank
600.00
500.00
400.00
300.00
200.00
100.00
0.00
2003 2004 2005 2006 2007 2008 2009 2010 2011
Merrill Lynch
100
80
60
40
20
0
2003 2004 2005 2006 2007 2008 2009 2010 2011
Bank of America
60
50
40
30
20
10
0
2003 2004 2005 2006 2007 2008 2009 2010 2011
Morgan Stanley
80
60
40
20
0
2003 2004 2005 2006 2007 2008 2009 2010 2011

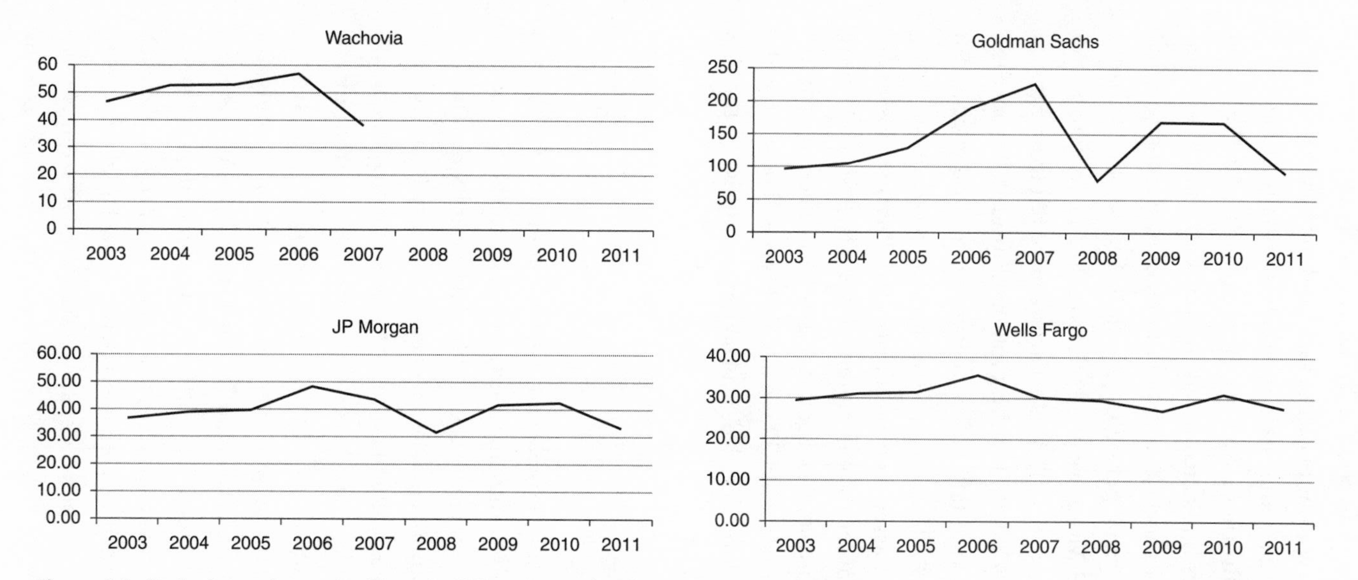

Figure 3.1. End-of-year share price ($), major US commercial and investment banks, 2003–2011.

staggering $481 for Citibank to $30 for Wells Fargo. These differences reflect both investors' perceptions of future value and the volume of shares issued by the bank. The diagrams are nevertheless visually compelling. The series for Lehman Brothers, Merrill, Bear Stearns, and Wachovia simply end as each bank is liquidated or taken over. Citi's share price fell from $557 in 2006 to $33 in 2009 (a 94% fall). Bank of America's price fell from $53 to $15 over the same period (a 72% fall). Yet not all the banks were so badly affected. JP Morgan's price fell from $48 in 2006 to $31 in 2008 and $41.6 in 2009 (a 35% fall). Wells Fargo's price fell from $35.5 in 2006 to $29.4 in 2008 (a 17% fall). Finally, Goldman's price fell from $189 in 2006 to $78 in 2008 (a 58% fall) before recovering to $168 in 2009 (an 11% fall on its 2006 level). These banks still had to record major write-downs on the value of their assets as market prices fell. But these losses did not imperil solvency. In order to understand why the largest banks were treated so differently by investors in 2008–2009, we now need to turn to a more detailed analysis of each bank. These descriptions will be used as the starting point for the more detailed explanatory analysis of the US banking system in Chapter 5.

Lehman Brothers

Lehman Brothers was initially established as a trading firm in Alabama in 1850. Having converted itself into an investment bank in the first decade of the twentieth century, Lehman was bought by American Express in 1984 before being spun off as an independent company a decade later. By 2007 Lehman derived 3% of its $45 billion revenues from asset management; 5% from commissions on trades (largely for hedge funds); 7% from investment banking (primarily mergers and acquisition advice); 20% from own-account principal transactions; and 65% from interest on holdings or profits from trading securities (Lehman Brothers 2007, 41). At this time, the bank held 25% of its assets in Europe (where it operated out of an office in London opened by the then chancellor, Gordon Brown, in 2004), 10% of its assets in Asia, and 65% of its assets in the United States (Lehman Brothers 2007, 52). Lehman operated with a leverage of 26:1 in 2006, although Lawrence McDonald (2009, 279) estimates its true leverage as being closer to 40:1. In 2010 a bankruptcy court examiner found that Lehman had been able to evade capital regulations prior to the crisis through "Repo 105" transactions in which it had temporarily "sold" loans on its balance sheet for short periods of time with the intention of buying the loans back once it had reported an artificially deflated leverage ratio. In the first two quarters of 2008 Lehman undertook $50 billion of such transactions (Merced and Sorkin 2010). Furthermore, the bank was heavily dependent upon short-term funding. Blinder (2013, 120) estimates that in the first quarter of 2008 Lehman required over $200 billion of short-term repurchase agreement (repo) funding. The bank held 40% of its assets in the form of trading securities and a further 5% of its assets in short-term derivative positions. Lehman was heavily exposed to the US housing market. By November 2007 it held on its balance sheet $89.1 billion in mortgage-backed securities (MBSs), of which $3 billion was subprime (Lehman Brothers 2007, 95). Of this sum, only $0.2 billion had been valued on the basis of *actual* market prices. The value of no less than $25 billion of these assets was derived from a management estimate "of what market participants" might pay if the assets were sold (Lehman Brothers 2007, 96–97).

In 2007 and 2008 Lehman's business model collapsed when it was left holding mortgage assets it could not sell or securitize. In 2006 Lehman held $4.1 billion in bonds and loans awaiting securitization (Lehman Brothers 2007, 58). Total securitization revenue dropped by 35% between December 2006 and December 2007 (Lehman Brothers 2007, 101). At this point, and as a part of its self-styled "countercyclical growth strategy," the bank *chose* to retain more of its assets on its own books rather than try to sell them to outside investors at a lower market price (FCIC 2011, 177). Between November 2006 and November 2007 the value of the asset-backed securities (ABSs) held on the bank's balance sheet increased from $55 billion to $89 billion at a time when market prices were falling (Lehman Brothers 2007, 95). At the same time, the bank *also* decided to increase its investment in commercial real estate. Between November 2006 and November 2007 the value of the real estate investment held for sale on the bank's balance sheet more than doubled (Lehman Brothers 2007, 94). As late as March 2007 Lehman led a $22 billion consortium to buy the Archstone-Smith property company. In this one deal, Lehman risked a sum equivalent to 20% of its total equity (Williams 2010, 133).

In June 2008, with little, if any, warning to investors, Lehman announced a second-quarter loss of $3 billion. Investors and irate senior managers forced Lehman's CEO, Dick Fuld, to sack the bank's long-standing president, Jo Gregory. Lehman then tried to reverse its market exposures. It was too late. Lehman was forced to post $8 billion in collateral to JP Morgan to maintain access to its trading positions. Amid rumors that other banks were refusing to lend it money, Lehman's share price tumbled. In September 2008 Lehman unveiled a $4 billion third-quarter loss and, with it, a disastrous and immediately aborted plan to spin off its remaining and now toxic commercial and residential real estate holdings into a separate company. A court auditor's report has since shown that around this time Lehman moved over $50 billion of assets off its balance sheet in order to conceal the extent of its losses and its dependence on short-term borrowing (Valukas 2010). Barclays, which was presumably unaware of these maneuvers, came close to buying Lehman. When the British government refused to waive the usual requirement that shareholders approve any takeover, the deal fell apart, and the firm filed for bankruptcy on 15 September.

Merrill Lynch

Merrill Lynch was established in 1914 and listed as a public company in 1971. Traditionally, Merrill's great strength was its network of over 14,000 brokers and asset managers located in towns and cities across America who provided a steady and relatively riskless stream of revenue. In 2003, with its profits lagging behind those of the other investment banks, Merrill appointed a new and aggressive CEO, Stan O'Neal, with a remit to reengineer the bank's balance sheet (Farrell 2010). By 2006 Merrill derived 34% of its revenue from principal transactions, 24% from commissions, 18% from investment banking, and 25% from commissions and fees on managed accounts (via its brokerage network) (Merrill Lynch 2007, 32). Sixty-four percent of its revenue was derived from operations in the United States, 20% from operations in Europe, and 10% from Asia (Merrill Lynch 2007, 48). At this time Merrill was operating with a reported leverage of 31:1, held 30% of its assets in the form of trading securities, and was recording an annual pretax profit of $10 billion. Like the other investment banks, Merrill relied heavily upon wholesale markets to fund its operations.

In 2006 Merrill was holding $181 billion in long-term debt and $284 billion in repurchase agreements and other forms of short-term borrowing (Merrill Lynch 2006, 20).

Merrill profited from buying a 50% stake in the BlackRock asset management company in September 2006. The bank was, however, massively exposed to the US housing market. In September 2006, after the US housing bubble had peaked, Merrill bought First Franklin, a subprime lender, for $1.4 billion (FCIC 2011, 204). In addition, Merrill also ran another subprime lender, Ownit Mortgage Solutions. By December 2007 Merrill had direct exposure to $2.7 billion of subprime, $2.6 billion of Alt-A nonconforming, and $28 billion of prime loans (Merrill Lynch 2007, 35).* In that year Merrill recorded a $3.1 billion net loss on these holdings (Merrill Lynch 2007, 35). These were not, however, the investments that sunk Merrill. In 2003 Merrill appointed a new vice president, Dow Kim, with a specific remit to develop the bank's languishing collateralized debt obligation (CDO) business. By 2005 Merrill was second only to Goldman Sachs in the value of CDOs sold that year. These CDOs were mostly being sold to outside investors and were being insured through credit default swap (CDS) arrangements with AIG. In 2006—and despite AIG having withdrawn from this market—Merrill's management reportedly issued an instruction to "do whatever it takes" to gain the number one spot in that market (FCIC 2011, 202). In the first six months of 2007 Merrill manufactured $34 billion in CDOs, of which only $3 billion was sold to outside investors (Farrell 2010, 18). By that stage Merrill was holding a total of $48 billion in CDOs.

In July 2007 Merrill's board of directors was told for the first time of the scale of the bank's holdings. In October the bank announced that its third-quarter earnings would reflect the impact of a $6.9 billion write-down on the value of its CDO holdings and a $1 billion loss on its subprime mortgage holdings as market prices fell. In January 2008 Merrill announced that it had lost $10.3 billion in the final quarter of 2007. In July of that year and with a new CEO in place, the bank sold its CDO holdings to a Texas-based private equity firm, Lone Star, for $6.7 billion at a loss of around ninety-five

*An Alt-A loan falls between the prime and subprime categories. Alt-A borrowers will usually have clean credit histories but will be seeking higher loan-to-value or debt-to-income loans or will have incomplete documentation.

cents on the dollar (Farrell 2010, 239). In 2006 Merrill recorded a ROE of 19.2%. In 2007 this fell to −29% and in 2009 to −50%. With the firm's share price collapsing, Merrill's management negotiated a merger with Bank of America in October 2008.

Bear Stearns

Bear Stearns was the smallest of the US investment banks and presented itself to the world as a scrappy outsider. In 1998 Bear refused to join the government-backed bailout of the Long-Term Capital Management hedge fund, which had lost over $5 billion in derivatives trading following the Russian financial crisis. Bear nevertheless thrived. Its annual pretax profits grew from $1.7 billion in 2000 to $3.1 billion in 2006. These profits were derived from four principal sources. First, it charged fees to originate mortgages via the Bear Stearns Residential Mortgage Corporation. Second, it earned fees by securitizing and selling residential mortgage-backed securities (RMBSs) to investors—in 2006 Bear securitized $121 billion in RMBSs (Bear Stearns 2007, 101). Third, it received interest payments on the $39 billion of RMBSs it continued to hold on its *own* balance sheet in 2006 (Bear Stearns 2007, 95). These holdings were often of poor quality. Of the $121 billion in mortgage assets Bear securitized in 2006, it retained $3 billion of AAA-rated assets, $1.3 billion of AA- or B-rated assets, and $1.3 billion of noninvestment grade or "junk" assets. In total, by February 2007 Bear held $36 billion in mortgages, MBSs, and other ABSs on its balance sheet. Two-thirds of its holdings were subprime or Alt-A (FCIC 2011, 286). Fourth, it charged commissions worth 2% of assets and 20% of profits to hedge funds—including hedge funds it had created and invested in—to borrow funds and clear its trades. Bear was the second-largest prime broker in the United States (FCIC 2011, 280).

Bear's business model was a "house of cards" (W. Cohan 2009). The company was being run on debt. In 2006 Bear recorded an official end-of-year leverage ratio of 28:1 but was often running at a day-to-day ratio of at least 38:1 (Lawder and Younglai 2010). The bank was borrowing around $70 billion a day on short-term, often overnight, money markets and was holding $30 billion of assets off its balance sheet in structured investment vehicles (SIVs) (W. Cohan 2009, 32; Williams 2010, 145). As the housing market turned, the repayment income Bear derived from the assets on its books fell. In June 2007 Bear announced an $800 million year-end loss and a $1.9 billion write-down in the value of its mortgage assets. At this time, Bear was also forced to post $1.6 billion in collateral to save its off–balance sheet investment funds, which had lost more than 90% of their value. Bear's solvency ratio—which measures the size of a company's after-tax income relative to its total debt obligations and is a good measure of financial resilience—fell from 3.4 in 2006 to 2.9 by the end of 2007, the lowest of any of the ten largest commercial or investment banks. In order to cover its losses, Bear needed to borrow more money on the short-term money market. Bear's problem was that the value of the assets it was using as collateral on those loans had fallen. Market sentiment turned, and hedge funds (which stood to lose their money if Bear collapsed) withdrew their funds. In March 2008 rumors then circulated that a major bank had denied Bear credit. With the bank's share price falling toward zero, JP Morgan Chase stepped in with an offer to buy Bear in a deal that valued the company at no more than $1.2 billion (L. McDonald 2009, 244). In doing so JP Morgan agreed to meet the first $1 billion in losses on Bear's exposures in return for an assurance that the US Treasury would meet the next $29 billion in losses. Williams (2010, 142) describes the bank's downfall as follows: "Bear has created radioactive funds, took client money, rolled the dice, and lost big."

Citigroup

Citigroup was formed in 1998 following a $140 billion merger between Citicorp and an insurance company, Travelers. By 2006 Citigroup employed 350,000 people and was recording revenues of $131 billion and profits of $24 billion. The company's reputation had, however, already been tarnished. In July 2003 Citi agreed to pay the SEC $120 million to settle allegations that it had helped Enron use structured finance transactions to manipulate its financial statements. In March 2005 the Federal Reserve banned Citigroup from making any more major acquisitions until it had improved its governance and risk management structures (FCIC 2011, 137).

Citi was heavily exposed to a downturn in the US housing market. Through one of its 2,000 operating subsidiaries, CitiFinancial, the bank was responsible for up to $90 billion in annual mortgage lending (FCIC 2011, 19). These loans were then securitized and sold to outside investors. As early as 2003 Citi sold $20 billion in CDOs to outside investors. By 2005 Citi had climbed to third place on the CDO league tables behind Goldman and Merrill Lynch. Three particular problems were to emerge in the bank's business model. First, in order to raise the appeal of its product in an already crowded market, Citi in 2003 started to sell its CDOs with a liquidity put: a promise to buy back a CDO at the original selling price if the market collapsed (FCIC 2011, 137–138). Second, in order to increase the volume of its sales, Citi was "parking" more of its assets in an intricate $100 billion web of off–balance sheet accounts (L. McDonald 2009, 229; Tett 2009, 160). Third, following a 2005 management injunction against the use of liquidity puts, traders started to hold rather than sell their securitized assets. Between January 2006 and August 2007 Citi issued $18 billion in CDOs that it held on its own books (FCIC 2011, 196). By December 2007 the bank held $32 billion of US Treasury securities; $18 billion of municipal and state securities; $52 billion of foreign government securities; $181 billion of corporate and other debt securities; $76 billion of derivatives; and $56 billion of mortgage loans and collateralized mortgage securities (Citigroup 2008, 157). Many of these assets had a low credit quality. In 2007 the bank recorded $37 billion of "sub-prime related direct exposures," $43 billion of "highly leveraged loans and financing commitments," and $22 billion of Alt-A mortgage securities (Citigroup 2008, 10).

Leverage at Citi was 13.6:1 in 2000 and remained stable until 2005, when it rose to 15.7:1. By 2007, with markets already deteriorating, reported leverage rose further, to 19:1. By this time Citi had, however, also accumulated $114 billion in off–balance sheet guarantees. The FCIC estimates that had Citi's assets been properly accounted for, its actual leverage would have been close to 48:1 (Farlow 2013, 140). To fund its day-to-day activities Citi borrowed on wholesale markets. In 2000 total customer deposits (a balance sheet liability) at Citi were the equivalent of 33% of total balance sheet assets. This had actually risen to 37% by 2006. Nevertheless, in 2007 Citi borrowed $304 billion through the purchase of Federal Funds or repurchase agreements and recorded $574 billion in other short- and long-term borrowings (Citigroup 2007, 66).

In September 2007, five months after Bear's collapse, Citi revealed a $13 billion subprime exposure. One month later the bank revised this figure upward to $55 billion and announced an $11 billion loss in the value of its assets (Tett 2009, 205). Citi's CEO, Chuck Prince, resigned, and over the next year the bank, weighed down by losses in the value of assets it was suddenly unable to sell in the market, imploded. ROE fell from 17.9% in 2006 to 3.4% in 2007, −19% in 2008, and −1% in 2009. Total losses on subprime and Alt-A mortgages and CDOs exceeded $55 billion (FCIC 2011, 261). In November 2008 the US Treasury was forced to inject $20 billion of funds into Citi. In February 2009 it announced that it had taken a 36% ownership stake in the bank and guaranteed a further $300 billion of assets against future losses. In February 2009, as the recession worsened, Citi received a further injection of government capital. The academic economist and one-time member of the Bank of England's Monetary Policy Committee, Wilem Buiter, who in 2009 became Citigroup's chief economist, memorably described the bank as "a conglomeration of worst practice from across the financial spectrum" (Buiter 2009).

Bank of America

Bank of America was established in California in the 1920s and expanded aggressively through the acquisitions of Seafirst Bank in Washington in 1983, Security Pacific National in 1992, the failed Continental Illinois in 1994, Nations Bank in 1998, and Fleet Boston Financial in 2004. In 2006 Bank of America held $1.615 trillion in assets, recorded an income of $32 billion, and made a pretax profit of $31 billion. Leverage in 2006 was 27:1 (up from 18:1 in 2000). Taking into account off–balance sheet exposures, the bank's actual leverage may have been closer to 36:1 (FCIC 2011, 65). Total customer deposits were the equivalent of 47% of total balance sheet liabilities in 2006 (down from 57% in 2000). In 2006, Bank of America (2006, 38) recorded $217 billion in purchased Federal Funds and repurchase agreements, $141 billion in commercial paper and other short-term borrowings, and $146 billion in long-term debt. Trading securities constituted 10.4% of total assets (up from 7% in 2000). Gross loans were equivalent to 48% of assets (down from 61% in 2000). Thirty percent of these gross loans were to the corporate and commercial sector. At the end of 2006 Bank of America held $55 billion in US government and government agency bonds; $55 billion in corporate securities; $22 billion in equity securities; and $18 billion in mortgage trading loans and other ABSs. The bank also carried a total $20 billion exposure to CDOs, of which fully $16 billion was composed of subprime assets (Bank of America 2007, 54).

In September 2008 the bank revealed a 31% decline in annual revenues, $3.7 billion in write-downs on the value of its assets, and a $4 billion loss on its off–balance sheet holdings (Farrell 2010, 65). Yet, overall, losses were contained. Pretax profits slumped from $20.9 billion in 2006 to $4.2 billion in 2008 and $4.3 billion in 2009. The bank's solvency ratio fell from 9.2 in 2006 to 8.5 in 2007 before recovering to 9.7 in 2008. Bank of America nevertheless displayed an ability to snatch defeat from the jaws, if not of victory, then at least of a scrambled stalemate. A significant proportion of the bank's 2008 losses were incurred through its New York investment banking unit. Asked at the time whether he planned to expand its operations, the bank's CEO, Ken Lewis, replied, "I never say never . . . but I've had all the fun I can stand in investment banking at the moment" (Cimilluca 2007). A few weeks later, Lewis authorized the purchase of the failing Merrill Lynch investment bank. This was to prove disastrous. In 2008 Bank of America recorded $13 billion in unrealized losses on Merrill's trading assets and was forced to seek a further $20 billion in government support. In 2010 the bank recorded a loss of $1.3 billion and saw its end-of-year share price slump from $13.3 in 2010 to $5.5 in 2011.

Wachovia Corporation

Wachovia was established in 1879 in North Carolina. The bank expanded rapidly through a series of mergers and acquisitions with First Union Corporation (2001), Prudential Securities (2003), Metropolitan West Securities (2003), Sought Trust (2005), Westcorp (2005), and Golden West Financial (2006). Wachovia's total assets grew from $254 billion in 2000 to $782 billion in 2007.

In a number of respects, Wachovia operated a relatively conservative balance sheet. In 2006 the bank operated with a leverage ratio of 9.7:1 (down from 16:1 in 2000). Gross loans constituted 61% of total assets (up from

48% in 2000). Trading securities constituted just 1% of total assets. The bank's loan book was strong. In 2006 impaired loans constituted just 0.29% of total loans. Finally, the bank held customer deposits equivalent to 61% of total liabilities (up from 55% in 2000).

Yet Wachovia nevertheless failed. In 2007 the bank recorded a pretax profit of $8.7 billion. In the first quarter of 2008 it recorded a $0.3 billion loss. In the second quarter this loss rose to $8.9 billion. In order to protect itself Wachovia successfully raised $6 billion in additional capital in January 2008 and a further $8 billion in April 2008. This was not, however, sufficient. In September 2008 investors raced to either withdraw their deposits from Wachovia or to reduce those deposits below the $100,000 threshold covered by insurance payments. In one day in late September 2008, Wachovia lost over $5 billion in deposits. On 29 September the FDIC declared Wachovia to be "systematically important" and simultaneously guaranteed the bank's funding needs while passing its assets and liabilities to Citigroup. The expectation was that Citigroup would buy Wachovia at a fire sale price. On 3 October, however, Wells Fargo announced plans to merge with Wachovia. This deal was eventually completed on 31 December 2008.

Was Wachovia the innocent victim of a generalized loss of confidence in the US banking system? As we have seen, the bank operated with a relatively low leverage ratio and largely eschewed securities trading. Nevertheless, in 2007 the bank did hold $2.2 billion in MBSs and $11.4 billion in "other" ABSs on its balance sheet (Wachovia 2008, 87). Only one-half of these holdings were rated AAA (Wachovia 2008, 15). Wachovia was also exposed to significant losses through one of its subsidiaries, Golden West Financial, which offered homeowners "pick-and-pay" mortgages, which included the option to repay a monthly sum lower than the interest on the loan. In 2007 Wachovia reported $111 million in losses on these mortgages (Wachovia 2008, 16). Wells Fargo (2009, 48) subsequently reported that, as of December 2008, "purchased credit-impaired" loan losses following the merger with Wachovia amounted to $4.8 billion in commercial real estate and foreign loans, $10.2 billion in pick-and-pay loans, and $2 billion in "other" consumer losses. All of this suggests that while Wachovia may not have converted itself into a trader bank in the same way as Lehman Brothers or Citigroup, it did seek to profit from the housing boom by significantly lowering its own credit standards and by acquiring ABSs. It was therefore not an innocent bystander but was directly caught up in the crisis.

Morgan Stanley

Morgan Stanley was formed in 1935 when the Glass-Steagall Act required JP Morgan to separate its commercial and investment banking activities. In 1997 Morgan Stanley merged with the securities and stock brokerage firm Dean Witter Reynolds. In 2004 Morgan Stanley recorded a pretax profit of $6.2 billion and a ROE of 15.8%—only slightly short of Goldman's 16.9%. In June 2005 a group of eight major shareholders and former senior managers nevertheless publicly attacked the firm's chief executive, Philip Purcell, for "the failure to continue to earn a premium return on equity; the failure to maintain earnings growth relative to its peers; and the weak performance of the firm's retail and investment management business over the past five years" (Group of Eight 2005a). The activists were successful in their attempts to secure a management change, and in June 2005 Purcell was replaced by John Mack, who had left Morgan Stanley in 2001 following a power struggle with Purcell. Mack had previously run Credit Suisse's trading operations in New York and been chairman of Pequot Capital, a hedge fund. According to Morgan Stanley's head of global mergers and acquisitions, Paul Taubman, Mack "didn't recognize the place, how lumbering we had become" (Raghanvan 2007). Mack made it clear that he wanted to boost profits and that the key strategies would be "investing in the financial derivatives business, getting more involved in residential mortgage finance, and taking more risk by trading with the firm's own capital" (Raghavan 2007). In the short term the strategy was a successful one. In a letter to shareholders reviewing Morgan's performance in 2006, Mack was able to boast of a 36% increase in share price; a 47% growth in diluted earnings per share; a 44% growth in net income; and a 26% growth in net revenues. This had, in Mack's own words, been achieved by "leveraging our global franchise" to "close the gap" with rivals in areas such as "leveraged finance, residential mortgages and equity derivatives" (Morgan Stanley 2007, 1). Pretax profits jumped from $6.2 billion in 2004 to $11.2 billion in 2006, while ROE rose from 15.8% to 22% over the same period.

By December 2007 Morgan's leverage was 40:1 (up from 22:1 in 2000) (FCIC 2011, 65). At this time Morgan held $23 billion of US government and agency securities; $140 billion in corporate securities; and $77 billion in derivatives on its balance sheet. Morgan also carried significant exposures to the housing market through $8.7 billion of mezzanine-tranche subprime CDOs, $7.8 billion of subprime CDSs, $4 billion of loans, and $8.7 billion of RMBSs for non-subprime assets (Morgan Stanley 2008, 65–66). In 2006 only Merrill Lynch issued more mortgage-related CDOs than Morgan Stanley (FCIC 2011, 202). Once the subprime asset bubble burst, Morgan (2010, 45) recorded $1.7 billion of "mortgage-related losses" and a $7.8 billion write-down on the value of its subprime assets in 2008. The bank's one precarious source of comparative advantage at this time was its funding base. When compared with many of its immediate competitors, Morgan Stanley held more deposits ($31 billion in 2007) and was less dependent upon short-term wholesale borrowing (of its $124 billion in debt only $34 billion was short-term, and only $12 billion of this was secured on a day-to-day basis) (Morgan Stanley 2010, 81; FCIC 2011, 297). This was not, however, enough. Once Lehman Brothers declared bankruptcy on 15 September, wholesale borrowing markets froze and Morgan was forced to borrow up to $35 billion a day from the Federal Reserve in order to remain in business (FCIC 2011, 361). On 21 September Morgan joined with Goldman in applying to change its status from an investment bank to a bank holding company regulated by the Federal Reserve. A few days later Mitsubishi Financial Group, Japan's largest bank, announced that it was investing $9 billion in Morgan. In total Morgan Stanley borrowed $107 billion from the Federal Reserve in 2008. Pretax profits fell from $11.2 billion in 2006 to $2.7 billion in 2007 and $1.2 billion in 2008, and the company lost $1.1 billion in 2009. Morgan Stanley survived the 2007–2008 crisis and returned to profitability in 2010. It is not, however, a success story.

Fannie Mae and Freddie Mac

Our primary focus within this study is on the largest US and UK commercial and investment banks. It is, however, impossible to understand the failings of the US financial system without analyzing the role played by the two giant government-sponsored housing corporations, Fannie Mae and Freddie Mac, and the insurance group AIG. We discuss AIG—whose key trading operations took place in London—presently. Fannie Mae (the Federal National Mortgage Association) was established in 1936 to buy mortgages insured by the Federal Housing Administration. In 1968 Fannie was restructured as a nominally independent trading corporation. In 1970 Congress established a second company, Freddie Mac (the Federal Home Loan Mortgage Corporation), with a specific remit to buy mortgages from nonbank savings and loan "thrifts."* Because Fannie and Freddie were regarded as a surrogate arm of the government and so seen as entirely creditworthy, they were able to borrow money on wholesale markets at lower interest rates than commercial banks. They used this money to buy mortgages originated by banks or local mortgage companies, which they then either guaranteed and sold to outside investors or held on their own balance sheets. Between 2000 and 2006 Fannie's and Freddie's assets grew by an average of 10% a year. In 2004 Fannie and Freddie bought 57% of all mortgages issued in the United States (their market share fell to 36% in 2006 as a result of competition from banks). By the end of 2007 Fannie and Freddie had insured and sold $3.5 trillion in MBSs to outside investors and held $1.4 trillion of mortgages on their own books (M. Lewis 2010, 81). The US banks had bought $817 billion of the assets guaranteed by Fannie and Freddie (Acharya, Richardson, et al. 2011, 25). By June 2008 Fannie's and Freddie's combined debt and obligations totaled $6.6 trillion—larger than the total public debt of the US federal government (Woll 2014, 84).

In the 2000s Fannie and Freddie came under pressure from Congress to extend home ownership and lowered their previously rigorous credit standards and entered the subprime market. In 2004 Fannie and Freddie purchased $160 billion of subprime mortgages (FCIC 2011, 124). In 2006, with their overall market share declining, Fannie and Freddie redoubled their subprime efforts at a time when the market was already showing signs of slowing down (Acharya, Richardson, et al. 2011, 58–60). In that year they purchased $120 billion of subprime mortgages. Fannie and Freddie funded their asset growth through debt rather than equity. Commercial and in-

*A third and smaller company, the Government National Mortgage Association (Ginnie Mae), was also established in 1968 to expand affordable housing.

vestment banks were required to hold capital reserves equivalent to 4% of the mortgage assets held on their balance sheets. This was not sufficient to cover their losses in 2007–2008 but did constitute a buffer for the taxpayer. Fannie and Freddie were, however, required to hold only 0.45% capital against MBSs they had guaranteed and sold to other investors and 2.5% capital against their own holdings. In 2007 Fannie and Freddie were operating with a staggering leverage ratio of 75:1 (FCIC 2011, xx). As soon as repossessions rose and house prices started to fall, this meant that Fannie and Freddie risked insolvency. Acharya, Richardson, et al. (2011, 3) describe Fannie and Freddie as "the largest hedge funds on the planet." In November 2007 Fannie and Freddie reported combined losses of $3.5 billion. In order to maintain liquidity within an otherwise moribund housing market, the government allowed Fannie and Freddie to continue borrowing and purchasing mortgages. But in September 2008 Fannie and Freddie were taken into conservatorship, and by 2010 the Treasury had invested $151 billion of taxpayer money to keep them afloat (FCIC 2011, xxvi).

Bucking the Trend: Survivors and Thrivers in the US Banking System

In contrast to the banks discussed earlier, a number of high-profile investment and commercial banks managed to avoid the worst of the crisis and emerged from it in a relatively strong position. These banks included Goldman Sachs, JP Morgan Chase, and Wells Fargo.

Goldman Sachs

Goldman was established in New York in 1869 and emerged as a significant investment banking firm in the 1930s. In 1999 Goldman converted from a private partnership to a public company, selling a 48% ownership stake to outside investors. By 2005 Goldman was, first and foremost, a trading bank, deriving 15% of its $37 billion revenue from investment banking; 68% from trading and principal transactions (FCIC 2011, 66); and 15% from asset management (Goldman Sachs 2007, 9). Fifty-one percent of net revenues were derived from activities in the Americas; 29% from the United Kingdom, Europe, and the Middle East; and 20% from Asia

(Goldman Sachs 2007, 136). Goldman was the first bank to launch a synthetic CDO, Abacus, in 2004 (FCIC 2011, 143). Between 2004 and May 2007 Goldman sold forty-seven synthetic CDOs with an aggregate market value of $66 billion. By November 2007 the bank held $54 billion in MBSs and other ABSs on its own balance sheet; $39 billion in corporate debt securities; and $50 billion in credit derivatives (Goldman Sachs 2007, 99). It held a further $18 billion in MBSs, $10 billion in corporate CDOs and collateralized loan obligations (CLOs), and $17 billion in real estate in off–balance sheet conduits (Goldman Sachs 2007, 107). Goldman was incredibly profitable. Pretax profits had risen from $2.5 billion in 1998 to $4.4 billion in 2003, $8.2 billion in 2005, and $14 billion in 2006. Goldman was operating with a recorded leverage of 35:1 (up from 22:1 in 2000).

In the months prior to the onset of the crisis Goldman was, however, able to largely reverse its trading positions. Throughout 2006, a small unit of Goldman traders made sizable profits by betting that mortgage prices would fall. In December of that year analysts prepared a management report regarding the "major risk in the mortgage business" for Goldman's chief financial officer, David Vinar, and its chief risk officer, Craig Broderick (FCIC 2011, 235). The following day Goldman's executive directors decided to significantly reduce their mortgage exposures by selling their CDOs and ABSs at whatever price the market would tolerate. Within three days, Goldman had offloaded $1.5 billion in mortgage securities. In 2007 Goldman then started to bet heavily that MBS market prices would fall. Goldman's competitors accused the bank of unfairly forcing market prices down by marking down its own prices in the sure knowledge that other banks could not ignore its marks. The argument is implausible. In 2007 mortgage securities *were* overpriced, which is why, with Goldman in the lead, market prices began to fall rapidly. William Cohan (2011, 591) suggests that the mortgage trading desk that was shorting the market in this way recorded a $3.7 billion profit in 2007, $373 million of which was booked in a single day. In total, the bank recorded pretax profits of $2.3 billion in 2008, $18 billion in 2009, and $12 billion in 2010. ROE fell from 23% in 2006 and 2007 to 3.5% in 2008 before recovering to 17.4% in 2009. Goldman also benefited from its debt structure. In 2006 it held $47 billion in short-term debt but $120 billion in long-term debt with maturities extending to 2036 (Goldman 2006, 95).

Goldman did not emerge from the financial crisis unscathed. A few weeks after the collapse of Lehman Brothers, Goldman, along with Morgan Stanley, changed its status to a bank holding company and accepted tighter government regulation. In its own words, Goldman (2008, 1) became a bank holding company to "address market perceptions that placed a premium on the value of oversight by the Federal Reserve Board and to be able to access a broader set of funding alternatives." Goldman entered the crisis with strong liquidity. Yet following the failure of Lehman Brothers it nevertheless struggled to raise short-term finance to meet its obligations in a market in which investors were panicking and refusing to hold money in anything other than US treasuries.

> Although Goldman was in better shape than its rivals . . . it was no secret that Goldman could be the next target. Its liquidity was draining more slowly but was draining nonetheless; some firms had stopped dealing with it . . . With swap premiums on Goldman's debt reaching $500,000, the market was treating Goldman as only borderline financeable. In such a weakened state, the firm could survive for a matter of weeks but probably not more. (Lowenstein 2010, 227)

Goldman also accepted $10 billion in government support in October 2008 and did not finally repay this money until April 2009. In addition, Goldman suffered significant reputational damage in the aftermath of the crisis. Critics accused Goldman of trading on and benefiting from its close links with Washington: links epitomized by the appointment of two former chief executives, Robert Rubin and Hank Paulson, as Treasury secretaries. Goldman's $18 billion profit in 2009—a profit inflated by government interest rate cuts and quantitative easing—also attracted criticism, especially when Goldman's serving CEO, Lloyd Blankfein, said his bank was doing "God's work" (Gapper 2009). In 2009 the journalist Matt Taibbi (2009) famously denounced Goldman as a "great vampire squid wrapped around the face of humanity, relentlessly jamming its blood funnel into anything that smells like money." A Senate subcommittee subsequently accused Goldman of providing misleading evidence in relation to a claim that it had deceived investors who it had encouraged to buy mortgage-backed CDOs that it was simultaneously shorting. A few months later, Goldman paid $550 million to settle a court case on this issue prior to judgment. Compared with its immediate rivals Bear, Lehman, and Merrill, however, Goldman emerged from the crisis in a strong position.

JP Morgan Chase

JP Morgan Chase was formed from the merger of Chase Manhattan Bank and JP Morgan in 2000. The bank has regularly been presented as one of the "winners of the [banking] crisis" and the new "King of Wall Street" (Lowenstein 2010, 292). The bank's chief executive, Jamie Dimon, has been the subject of flattering biographies (D. McDonald 2009; Tett 2009). The bank's performance during the crisis largely (but not entirely) justifies its reputation. In 2006 JP Morgan recorded a pretax profit of $20.6 billion. This climbed to $22.8 billion in 2007 before falling to $4.6 billion in 2008 and $16.1 billion in 2009. ROE fell from 12.4% in 2006 to 12% in 2007 and 3.3% in 2008 before recovering to 7% in 2009. Throughout this time, the bank's solvency ratio fell only slightly, from 8.5 in 2006 to 7.8 in 2007 and 7.6 in 2008. Compared with the other major commercial and investment banks, these were impressive returns. Furthermore, during the crisis, JP Morgan was able to acquire Bear Stearns and Washington Mutual at fire sale prices. The bank did accept over $10 billion in Treasury funding in 2008, although executives argue that they only did so at the behest of the government and that they repaid the money as soon as they were allowed. Dimon repeated on several occasions that "we didn't ask for it, didn't want it, and we don't need it" (D. McDonald 2009, 310).

Why was JP Morgan able to survive in 2007–2008? During the financial boom that preceded the crisis, JP Morgan maintained a conservative balance sheet. In 2006 the bank's leverage ratio was a relatively modest 11:1 (down from 16:1 in 2000) and its ratio of total customer deposits to assets a healthy 47% (up from 39% in 2000). Furthermore, and unlike Citigroup in particular, the bank did not hold undisclosed assets off its balance sheet. In 2004 the bank sold its only SIV to Standard Chartered for $8 billion and reduced its $12 billion exposure to the SIVs of other banks to just $500 million. The bank also eschewed trading and investment in risky assets. In the late 1990s traders at JP Morgan pioneered both CDO and CDS trading (Tett 2009). JP Morgan was also the first bank to use AIG to insure its holdings of CDO assets. Yet in 2001 the bank decided that the relatively small profit spread between CDO yields and US treasuries did not warrant the risk of holding CDOs on its balance sheet, and decided to exit this market. By 2006 the global league tables of asset-backed CDO issuance ranked JP Morgan in a lowly nineteenth place (L. McDonald 2009, 214). The bank also decided to wind back its proprietary trading exposures in 2005.

JP Morgan did not, however, escape from the financial crisis unscathed. In its 2006 annual report (JP Morgan Chase 2006, 10) the bank admits making the mistake not only of continuing to lend money directly to home buyers but of relaxing its credit standards. By December 2008 the bank had a total (loans and securities) exposure of $0.9 billion to subprime assets, $3.9 billion in Alt-A assets, and $4.6 billion in prime assets (JP Morgan Chase 2009, 169). In this year the bank recorded losses of $369 million on its subprime investments and $4 billion on its prime and Alt-A holdings. In total, JP Morgan recorded $69 billion in write-downs and credit losses between June 2007 and March 2010 (compared with $130 billion for Citigroup, $97 billion for Bank of America, and $55 billion for Merrill Lynch over the same period) (Acharya, Kulkarni, and Richardson 2011, 147). Most of this loss reflects general falls in asset value prices during a period in which the real economy was also contracting. It does, however, also suggest that JP Morgan's postcrisis reputation for prudent banking might not always have fully matched the reality. JP Morgan's reputation was also tarnished in 2012 when a trader, Boaz Weinstein (the so-called London Whale), lost over $6 billion trading in synthetic credit products (Fitzpatrick, Zuckerman, and Rappaport 2012). In its own report into this incident, JP Morgan (2013, 1) blamed these losses on "flawed trading strategies, lapses in oversight, deficiencies in risk management, and other shortcomings." The sheer scale of the losses incurred is, however, difficult to reconcile with JP Morgan's own presentation of itself as a risk-averse bank that eschewed proprietary trading. In November 2013 JP Morgan then agreed to a record $13 billion settlement with the Justice Department in relation to a series of investigations into the way potential investors had been misled about the creditworthiness of RMBSs. The primary (although not exclusive) focus of these investigations was actually on Bear Stearns and Washington Mutual, banks that JP Morgan acquired in the aftermath of the crisis. The settlement nevertheless further tarnished the bank's reputation.

Wells Fargo

Wells Fargo was formed as an express stagecoach company in California in the early 1850s. In its modern form, Wells was created through the merger of the Minneapolis-based Norwest Corporation with San Francisco–based Wells Fargo in 1998. Wells Fargo (2008, 6) operated, in its own words, "a conservative financial structure." By 2006 it was operating with a leverage ratio of just 10.5:1 (the same as in 2000). Its balance sheet was heavily skewed toward mortgage lending rather than securitization or financial trading. It held 73% of its assets in the form of gross loans (up from 62% in 2000). This was more than double the proportion of Citi, for example. Thirty-four percent of gross loans were to the corporate and commercial sector. In 2007 trading securities constituted just 1.1% of its assets. In December 2007 the bank held just $7.4 billion in MBSs. All of these were AAA-rated by "an independent third party pricing service" (Wells Fargo 2008, 113). Wells Fargo was also less dependent upon wholesale borrowing. In 2006 the bank held $223 billion in deposits equivalent to 59% of assets (down from 62% in 2000). In 2007 the bank borrowed just $21 billion on short-term markets (Wells Fargo 2007, 44). This balance sheet placed Wells in a strong position when entering the financial crisis. In a widely cited report published in *Barron's*, Mark Veverka (2008) asked and answered the following question:

> What big bank is likely to find the safest, fastest route through the US's dangerous credit mess? Wells Fargo is an excellent bet. Partially, it's about what Wells isn't. Unlike most of its peers that have been badly singed, the San Francisco–based bank doesn't have a big capital-markets operation exposed to credit derivatives, structured investment vehicles, or mortgage-backed securities. It isn't slowed down by a huge book of subprime residential-mortgage loans, and its balance sheet can withstand more bullets than most.

This confident prognosis was largely vindicated. Wells was "probably less hurt by the mortgage crisis that unfolded in 2008 than any other major bank" (Dash and De la Merced 2009). The bank's proportion of impaired loans rose from 0.38% in the boom year of 2005 to just 0.76% in 2008. In that year Wells recorded a pretax profit of $3.2 billion. Wells was, however, compromised by its takeover of Wachovia. This purchase allowed Wells to more than double the size of its asset base, from $575 billion to $1.309 trillion. As we have seen, however, Wells was then left carrying significant losses from Wachovia's loan book. Wells Fargo's problems were compounded in August 2012 when the SEC charged Well Fargo's brokerage firm and a former vice president with selling investments linked to MBSs to outside investors without fully understanding their complexity or disclosing the risk to investors (Protess 2012).

Within the US banking system a number of small, regionally based banks also escaped largely unscathed from the crisis. The PNC Corporation (formerly the Pittsburgh National Bank) held $138 billion in assets in 2007 and operated banks in fifteen states. It recorded pretax profits of $3.9 billion in 2006, $2 billion in 2007, $1.2 billion in 2008, and $3.2 billion in 2009. Its solvency ratio fell only slightly, from 10.4 in 2006 to 6.8 in 2007, before rising to 9.7 in 2008. Although it was required to accept taxpayer support, PNC was in a strong enough postcrisis position to purchase the Cleveland-based National City Bank for $5.2 billion in October 2008, nearly doubling the size of its asset base. BB&T (Branch Banking & Trust) also maintained a very conservative balance sheet in the years prior to the crisis. In 2006 gross loans were 68% of total assets and trading securities just 1.8% of assets. It recorded a pretax profit of $2.4 billion in 2006 and 2007 before increasing its profits to $2.5 billion in 2008. Finally, the Minneapolis-based US Bancorp, with assets in 2006 of $219 billion, also performed well. It did not hold any recorded trading security assets on its balance sheet and held gross loans equivalent to 68% of total assets. In 2006 it recorded a pretax profit of $6.8 billion. This fell to $6 billion in 2007 and $4 billion in 2008. The bank's solvency ratio fell from 9.6 in 2006 to 8.8 in 2007 before climbing again to 9.8 in 2008. In October 2008 Bancorp bought a part of First Citizens Bank, and in 2009 it purchased nine regional banking networks belonging to the failed FBOP Corporation.

The United Kingdom

Background

In the nineteenth century, London's status as a global trading center was underpinned by Britain's economic hegemony (Gieve 2007, 3). In the twentieth century, London had to reinvent itself as a global financial trading center—one usually referred to as "the City." This process began in the 1960s when British banks were instrumental in the development of the "Euromarkets" that were processing transactions denominated in US dollars held outside of the United States and beyond the purview of US regulators. By 1975, fifty-eight US banks had established branches in London in order to trade in the Euromarkets, and the City had, according to the economist Tim Congdon, become "the hub of a new and vast international capital market without rival anywhere" (quoted in Kynaston 2011, 568). London's resurgence during this period was helped by its location in a time zone that straddled the Asian and American markets. It was also assisted by the Bank of England, which left the Euromarkets almost entirely unregulated. In a move toward what would become the City's famed "light-touch" regulatory approach, the government lifted interest rate caps and credit restrictions on the banks in the 1970s. In the 1990s and 2000s successive Conservative and Labour governments recommitted themselves to further enhancing the City's global appeal through skilled immigration and taxation policies and further regulatory reforms (Augar 2010, 38–44). The 2001 Financial Services Act, for example, gave the Financial Services Authority a statutory responsibility to "consider the international mobility of capital" and "avoid damaging the UK's competitiveness." As a result of this light-touch approach, Gowan (2009, 16) argues that London became to New York something akin to what Guantanamo Bay would become to Washington: the place where you could do abroad what you would not be allowed to do at home. By 2006 the lobby group the CityUK (2008) estimated that financial and banking services together contributed £103 billion to the British economy, accounted for 8.3% of GDP, employed 303,000 people in London, generated a £44 billion trade surplus, attracted £40 billion in foreign direct investment, and accounted for 25% of corporation tax revenue.

Nearly all the world's major banks operated offices in London. By 2006 London held a 49% share of the market in foreign exchange derivatives and a 34% share in interest rate derivatives and was the base for 20% of the world's hedge funds. In 2007 New York's City's mayor, Michael Bloomberg, and Senator Charles Schumer launched a report documenting London's ascendancy and New York's relative decline, with a warning that New York was in danger of being relegated to "regional market status" (Bloomberg and Schumer 2007). Transatlantic banking traffic was not all in one direction, however. RBS boosted its trading in the US markets through a subsidiary, Greenwich Capital Markets, which was a primary dealer in US Treasury securities. In 2007, 15% of RBS's revenue was recorded as having originated in the United States (RBS 2007a, 210). Furthermore, as we shall soon see, HSBC acquired considerable direct exposure to the US housing market through its ownership of Household International and Decision One. In 2007, Barclays (2007b, 2) conducted banking operations in fifty countries and employed staff in twenty countries. Ben Broadbent (2012), an external member of the Bank of England's Monetary Policy Committee, estimates that *three-quarters* of UK bank losses were incurred on their overseas assets. But in the 2000s London was the winner in the race to develop a comparative advantage in financial trading.

We do not know what proportion of the losses sustained during the 2007–2008 crisis was incurred directly through transactions in London or New York. Banks simply do not publish this information. Indeed, it may not always make sense to talk about losses being incurred in one particular place where deals were often constructed by teams working in very different places. Yet in extending our focus beyond the largest American and British banks, we can see how London came to be used as a trading center by a variety of different financial corporations from a range of countries, as we show in what follows.

Despite the City booming, the largest British banks nevertheless fared badly in the 1980s and early 1990s (Augar 2010, 16–27). The manipulation of share prices during the takeover of a large brewer, Guinness, exposed a number of banks to charges of insider dealing and mendacity. The spectacular collapse of the Bank of Commerce and Credit International in 1991 and of Barings in 1995 led to charges of regulatory and management incompetence. In the early 1990s nearly all of the most venerable and ancient

British merchant (investment) banks, including Barings, S. G. Warburg, Smith New Court, and Kleinwort Benson, were taken over by or merged with larger American, Japanese, or European firms. The eventual winners from this shakeout were the largest commercial banks. By 2007 the six largest banks—the giant HSBC Holdings (with total assets of £2.3 trillion), RBS (assets of £1.9 trillion), Barclays (assets of £1.1 trillion), HBOS (assets of £667 billion), Lloyds Banking Group (assets of £353 billion), and Standard Chartered (assets of £329 billion)—accounted for 87% of the assets of the total UK banking sector. The total assets of the UK banking sector rose from the equivalent of 27% of GDP in the 1950s to over 500% of GDP by 2006 (Haldane and Allesandri 2009).

The largest commercial banks were extremely profitable. Between 2004 and 2006 the average ROE of the ninety-four banks for which aggregated data is available was 16.6%. In 2007 HSBC, RBS, HBOS, Lloyds, Barclays, and Standard Chartered announced pretax operating profits of, respectively, £20 billion, £9 billion, £7 billion, £3 billion, £6 billion, and £4.5 billion. These profits were partly driven by an expansion in commercial and domestic lending fueled by low interest rates and consumer debt. In the United Kingdom the annual rate of growth of real household debt was 10% between 1997 and 2007. The total stock of UK debt went from £570 billion (just over 100% of net disposable income) in 1997 to over £1.5 trillion (just over 175% of net disposable income) in 2007 (Farlow 2013, 19). Profits were also driven by an expansion in trading activity. At the six largest banks interest-bearing gross loans as a proportion of total assets fell from 59% in 2000 to just 49% in 2006. Conversely, the value of the securities listed on these banks' balance sheets as being held for trading purposes rose from 3% of total assets in 1990 to 10% of total assets in 2000 and 16% of assets in 2004. The proportion of pretax profits accounted for by trading in derivatives rose steeply, from 9% in 1994 to 12% in 2001, 27% in 2004, and 56% in 2006. The largest banks also extended their mortgage lending to exploit apparently insatiable consumer demand for housing. In the decade prior to 2007 bank lending trebled. Yet it is worth noting that, over this period, most commercial lending was for real estate and that lending to manufacturing companies actually fell. By 2008, of the £6 trillion of banking system assets, only about £200 billion represented lending to businesses, about 3% of the total (Farlow 2013, 57).

In order to fund asset growth, the banks also extended their leverage. Among the six largest UK banks, average leverage rose from 20:1 in 1994 to 26:1 in 2007. In *After the Great Complacence* Engelen et al. (2011, 108–110) persuasively argue that this rise in leverage accounts for much of the rise in bank profits. The banks did not, by and large, learn how to extract more profits from the assets on their balance sheets. ROE throughout the 2000s may have been high, but the return on assets at the banks fluctuated between 0.5% and 1.5%. The banks' profits—and their ROE—grew spectacularly because they used debt to acquire more assets relative to their equity. Total customer deposits at the six largest banks were £2.098 trillion in 2007 (up from £990 billion in 2000). These deposits were, however, the equivalent of just 35% of liabilities (down from 57% in 2000). The Financial Services Authority (FSA 2011, 46) estimates that the "customer funding gap" at the major UK banks rose from just £1 billion in 2000 to nearly £600 billion in 2006. The Bank of England (2007) estimates that in 2006 a median of 44% of UK banks' wholesale debts were scheduled to mature within three months (Hardie and Maxfield 2013, 73). Furthermore, and because executives believed that they would always be able to sell assets in the event of financial problems, banks ran down their liquidity. In 1970 the London clearing banks held about 30% of their assets in the form of cash or short-term liquid instruments. By 2008 this had fallen to just 1% (Farlow 2013, 72). Increased leverage and reduced liquidity meant that the banks had become far more vulnerable in a downturn.

In 2007 the chancellor, Gordon Brown (2007), lauded a "new golden age for the City of London." At this time, nine banks occupied places in the FTSE-100 index of the largest UK companies. Within eighteen months five of these nine banks had either been taken over or effectively nationalized (Treasury Committee 2009c, 7). As we shall see in Chapter 6, the Bank of England and the Treasury saw few signs of an impending financial meltdown. The former permanent secretary at the Home Office, Sir John Gieve, entertainingly describes his arrival as the director of financial stability at the Bank of England.

> I only arrived in 2006 . . . I'd come from four years at the Home Office, which had been the most stressful and frantic four years of my life. I got to the Bank, which anyway looks a bit like a mausoleum

really . . . I remember one of my predecessors saying it's the only place that he's ever been where he could hear the clocks ticking, and discovered this very elaborate long, quarterly timetable with masses of discussion and very academic manner. It seemed like heaven on earth to me and a year later the whole thing blew apart. (Interview, 19 April 2013)

The banking crisis began in September 2007 when the Bank of England was forced to extend liquidity support to and then, following a mass withdrawal of customer funds, to guarantee deposits at the Northern Rock. At this stage, the Bank of England did not foresee the onset of a major crisis. Indeed, Governor King described the turmoil in European markets in August 2007 as "a welcome development" that would lead to a more "realistic appraisal of risks" (Irwin 2013, 6). Yet amid tightening markets, the bank struggled to find a buyer for Northern Rock, which was nationalized in February 2008 and eventually sold to Virgin Money for a mere £0.7 billion in January 2010. In late 2007 and early 2008 an ever-growing list of UK banks announced losses in the value of the RMBSs they held on their books or had bought from other banks. Within a short time the banks found themselves caught in a vicious circle of lower asset prices, higher borrowing costs, and scarce capital from which they could not escape. In April 2008 the Bank of England launched a Special Liquidity Scheme allowing banks to temporarily swap MBSs for UK Treasury bills. In the same month RBS and HBOS announced, respectively, a £12 billion and a £4 billion rights issue to raise new capital. On 18 September—three days after the collapse of Lehman Brothers—Lloyds merged with HBOS and the FSA prohibited short selling of shares in financial institutions. On 29 September the Bradford and Bingley Building Society failed. Bradford and Bingley, like Northern Rock, was a former building society that had demutualized in the 1990s. In May 2008, amid market concerns about the bank's funding model in the aftermath of the collapse of Northern Rock, Bradford and Bingley announced a £300 million rights issue. This was a spectacular failure. Private investors, including a large private equity firm, TPG Capital, which had pledged to buy 23% of the shares being offered, walked away. With the bank struggling to securitize its existing loans and so service its operations, it was split into two parts. The bank's £42 billion mortgage book was effectively nationalized. The branch network and deposits were sold to the Spanish banking group Santander. By early October the Bank of England was estimating that capital losses for the six largest UK banks exceeded £100 billion, threatening the solvency of individual institutions and the stability of the entire financial system (Quaglia 2009, 1068). On 8 October and at a moment when a number of the United Kingdom's largest banks were only days from collapse as a result of the complete failure of wholesale lending markets, the government announced £37 billion in funding to recapitalize UK banks; guarantees for up to £250 billion in short- and medium-term lending and bank borrowing; and a guarantee of wholesale lending requirements. Called upon to explain and justify the bailout, Prime Minister Gordon Brown argued that he had no alternative: that he had not wanted to "reward failure" but that the failure of a number of the banks would have meant economic ruin: "I knew that doing nothing was not an option. We were days away from a complete banking collapse: companies not being able to pay their creditors, workers not being able to draw their wages, and families finding that the ATM had no cash to give them" (Brown 2010, xvii)." On 3 November the Treasury announced that its shareholdings in the banks were to be managed on a commercial basis by a new company, UK Financial Investments. A few days later the Bank of England cut interest rates by a further 1.5% to just 3%. In January 2009, with bank share prices still moribund and lending collapsing as the banks sought to reduce their leverage, the government unveiled a new Asset Protection Scheme that gave the banks the option to insure themselves, at the taxpayers' potential expense, against further losses on their most risky assets. In total the UK government invested £1.2 trillion in bailing out the banks. As of March 2012—and at a time when all the US banks had repaid their debts to the federal government—the UK banks still owed £228 billion (Aldrick 2012). The largest economic and social costs, however, arose from the double recession that the banking crisis caused. In 2012, UK GDP was 3% below its precrisis peak.

Across the largest ninety-four banks, average ROE fell from 17.5% in 2006 to 15.5% in 2007, −12.5% in 2008, and 0.03% in 2009. Across the six largest banks, average ROE fell from 18.2% in 2006 to 16.8% in 2007, −14.2% in 2008, and 2% in 2009. The average share price of the six largest banks fell by 30% between December 2006 and December 2007 and fell

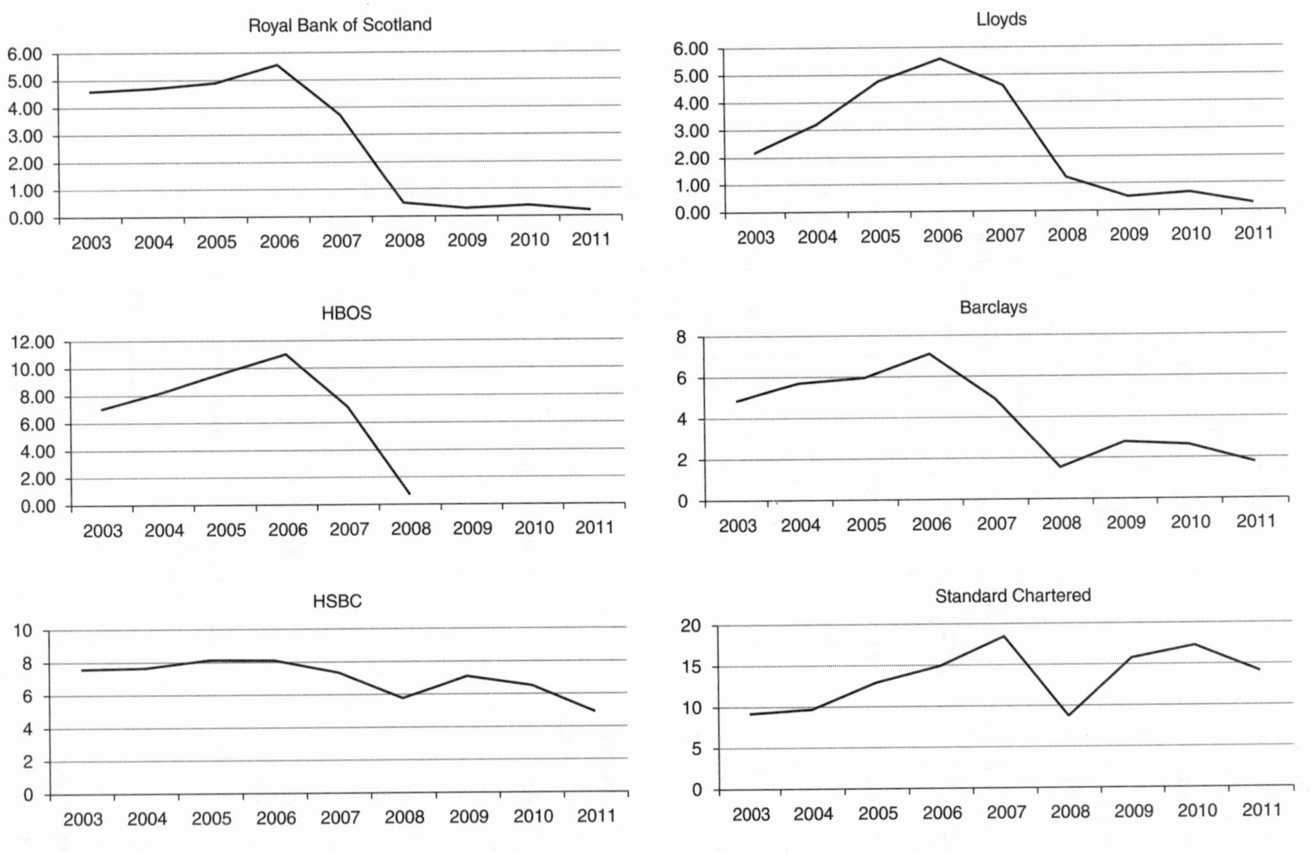

Figure 3.2. End-of-year share price (£), major UK banks, 2003–2011.

by a further 70% between December 2007 and December 2008. Once again, however, these figures mask considerable variation. The banks that sustained the heaviest losses in 2008 were RBS and HBOS. At RBS, ROE fell from 14.2% in 2006 to 8.4% in 2007 and −42% in 2008. At HBOS, ROE fell from 18.6% in 2006 and 18.4% in 2007 to −54.9% in 2008. As we shall see, Lloyds and Barclays also sustained heavy losses during this period, although in the case of Lloyds these losses stemmed largely if not entirely from its ill-fated takeover of HBOS. The two banks that emerged from the crisis in the strongest position were HSBC and Standard Chartered. HSBC's ROE fell from 13.4% in 2006 and 15.1% in 2007 to 6.4% in 2008 and 4.9% in 2009. Standard Chartered's ROE fell from 15.1% in 2006 to 13.7% in 2007, 13.2% in 2008, and 12.3% in 2009. In order to further underline the extent of these differences, Figure 3.2 shows the end-of-year share prices of the six largest banks. Once again, care should be taken in reading these figures because the starting share prices of the banks are very different. The intracountry variation in performance is nevertheless striking. RBS's price fell from £5.5 in 2006 to just £0.49 by the end of 2008 (a 91% fall). HBOS ceased trading as a separate entity in 2008. Lloyds' price fell from £5.58 in 2006 to £0.51 in 2009 after the full impact of the takeover of HBOS had become clear (also a 91% fall). Barclays' price fell from £7.1 in 2006 to £1.53 in 2008 (a 79% fall) before recovering somewhat in 2009. On the other hand, HSBC's price fell from £8.1 in 2006 to £5.77 in 2008 (a 29% fall). Finally, Standard Chartered's price fell from £14.9 in 2006 to £8.7 in 2008 (a 42% fall) before recovering to £15.7 in 2009.

The Royal Bank of Scotland

RBS was established in the early eighteenth century. Its profits and assets grew rapidly in the decade prior to the crisis through a series of takeovers and acquisitions, including those of the Citizens Financial Group in the United States for £0.5 billion in 1998; the hostile takeover of the giant NatWest Bank for £21 billion in 2000; of Mellon Financial in the United States for £1.2 billion in 2001; of Churchill Insurance for £1.1 billion in 2003; of Community Bancorp in the United States for £1 billion in 2003; of Charter One Financial for £7 billion in 2004; and of the Dutch ABN Amro for £16 billion in 2007. RBS's total group assets rose from £77 billion in 1998 and

£309 billion in 2000 (following the takeover of NatWest) to £871 billion in 2006 and £1,900 billion in 2007 (following the takeover of ABN). Profits were correspondingly impressive, rising from £1 billion in 1998 to £4.2 billion in 2001, £7.2 billion in 2004, and £9.9 billion in 2007. RBS's chief executive, Fred Goodwin, was knighted for services to banking in 2004, and the following year the queen opened the bank's new £350 million headquarters building on the edge of Edinburgh. The bank's fall from financial grace was even more spectacular. On 1 October 2008 the Bank of England extended a £36 billion bridging loan to RBS to keep it in business. On 13 October the bank accepted a £20 billion capital injection from the Treasury, making the UK taxpayer the majority shareholder. By November 2009—after a series of additional government interventions—RBS had received a total of £45 billion in government subsidies and was 84% owned by the taxpayer. In October 2008 Sir Fred Goodwin took early retirement from RBS and became a public hate figure for accepting a £700,000 annual pension. In 2010 his home was vandalized, and in February 2012 he was stripped of his knighthood. As for RBS itself, after considerable speculation that the bank would be privatized prior to an expected general election in 2015, executives announced in November 2013 that they would "ring-fence" £38 billion of troublesome loans within the bank.

The FSA (2011, 7) suggests that the 2007 purchase of ABN Amro played a "significant" role in RBS's collapse. RBS led a Europe-wide consortium buying ABN Amro and committed €16 billion to the deal. The takeover required the bank to borrow more money, exposed it to new sources of trading risk, and undermined shareholder confidence. Prior to the takeover of ABN Amro, RBS had, however, already reengineered its balance sheet. First, in order to fund its acquisition of assets, the bank had extended its leverage. In 2006—prior to the ABN deal—the bank was operating with a leverage ratio of 19:1. This was lower than the leverage employed by Lloyds, HBOS, or Barclays. But in 2006 RBS also held £48 billion of assets in off–balance sheet conduits to which it was forced to extend £15 billion in credit in 2007. In total, the bank's "tier 1" (or core) capital ratio was lower than that of any other UK Bank (FSA 2011, 64). Second, RBS increasingly relied upon trading through its global investment banking division rather than lending as a source of revenue and profit. By 2006 only 54% of the group's assets were held in the form of loans—this figure falling to just 43% with the takeover of ABN Amro (down from 55% in 2000). RBS was a late entrant to the trading market. The FSA (2011, 140) suggests that in "mid-2006, RBS took a strategic decision to expand aggressively its structured credit and leveraged finance business" and that this resulted in the "accumulation of significant credit risk exposures in its trading portfolio." In 2005 RBS held £5 billion of trading securities on its balance sheet. This was equivalent to 0.7% of total assets. By the end of 2006 its holdings had risen dramatically, to £112 billion (12% of total assets). Derivatives accounted for a further 14% of assets, and trading in derivatives accounted for fully 29% of the bank's profits in 2006 and 2007. The bank having failed to either reduce or effectively hedge its exposures, these trading assets proved a financial liability. The bank lost £1.4 billion on credit trading—primarily on CDS purchases and sales—in 2008 and a further £12 billion in 2009 and £4 billion in 2010.

Through its US subsidiaries—by 2005 RBS was the sixth largest bank in the United States—RBS was also exposed to losses in the US housing market. In 2008 it had held £33.5 billion in US RMBSs guaranteed by the US government; £5 billion in "prime" RBMSs; £1.1 billion in "non-conforming" RMBSs; and £1.8 billion in subprime RMBSs (RBS 2009, 185). The bank held a further exposure to £50 billion in collateralized mortgage-backed securities (CMBSs) (45% of which originated in the United States); £8 billion in CDOs (95% originating in the United States); £7 billion in CLOs (90% originating in the United States); and a further £97 billion in "other" ABSs (60% originating in the United States). RBS lost huge amounts of money because the securitized assets it bought sustained huge market value losses in 2007 and 2008. By December 2008 its high-grade (AAA- and AA-rated) ABSs were worth just 30% of their 2006 value. Compounding the problems posed by its poor investment and trading decisions, RBS was overreliant upon wholesale funding. Total customer deposits were equivalent to just 35% of total balance sheet assets in 2007 (down from 57% in 2000). By September 2007 RBS was borrowing £70 billion from short-term wholesale funding markets. Fully 70% of this sum was being borrowed on an overnight basis (FSA 2011, 46). When the value of the bank's assets started to fall in 2006, this dependence upon short-term funding proved fatal. The former chairman of RBS's investment bank, Johnny Cameron, told us that "the credit crunch was a credit crunch. The one thing that mattered in late 2008 was your wholesale deposits. That was what the survival was all about. Just when we needed it most we were running a downhill escalator. That was absolutely crucial to the disaster" (interview, 18 April 2013). When the UK government was forced to lend RBS £36 billion on 1 October the bank was, in Mervyn King's judgment, only a "matter of hours" from collapse, having been refused credit by wholesale lenders (Martin 2013, 17).

HBOS

HBOS's business model was focused upon domestic mortgage and commercial property lending in the United Kingdom. In 2007 the bank's retail division accounted for 25% of income; the corporate division 21% of income; insurance and investment 41%; and its international division—through holdings in Australia (Bank West), Ireland (BOS Ireland), Europe (Clerical Medical Europe), and North America (HBOS Canada) only 8% (HBOS 2007a, 172). In 2007 £532 billion of the bank's £667 billion in assets were held in the United Kingdom (HBOS 2007a, 174). Unlike RBS, HBOS ran a relatively small trading book. In 2006, 64% of total assets were in the form of gross loans, a higher proportion than in any of the other large UK banks. In 2006 HBOS held £49 billion in trading securities and £8 billion in derivative exposures, but these amounted to, respectively, only 8% and 1% of total assets. HBOS ceased interest rate proprietary trading activities in 2005 (Parliamentary Commission on Banking Standards 2013a, 70).

HBOS failed in 2008 because it grew too rapidly, lent too much, and was too dependent upon wholesale borrowing and so became caught in the systemic crisis. HBOS's total loan book rose from £201 billion in 2001 to £435 billion in 2008. As the Parliamentary Commission report (Parliamentary Commission on Banking Standards 2013a, 53) into the failure of HBOS concludes:

> HBOS had no culture of investment banking; if anything, its dominant culture was that of retail banking and retail financial services more widely, areas from which its senior management were largely drawn. Whatever may explain the problems of other banks, the down-

> fall of HBOS was not the result of cultural contamination by investment banking. This was a traditional bank failure pure and simple. It was a case of a bank pursuing traditional banking activities and pursuing them badly.

HBOS's corporate lending increased by an average of 15% a year between 2000 and 2008 (Treasury Committee 2008, 7). Total leverage rose from 21.5:1 in 2000 to 24.2:1 in 2005 and 29.9: 1 in 2007. Total customer deposits were £243 billion in 2007 (up from £127 billion in 2000). But total deposits were only 36% of liabilities in 2007 (down from 54% in 2000). Indeed, one of the immediate triggers for HBOS's collapse on 17 September was the publication of a Citigroup report that HBOS had a £197 billion "funding gap," a large part of which was being met through overnight borrowings (Wearden 2008). HBOS management were aware of their dependence upon wholesale borrowing. Indeed, Bank of Scotland executives had wanted to merge with the Halifax Building Society (to create HBOS) precisely in order to secure a larger deposit base (Perman 2013, 53–54). In 2004 and 2005 HBOS management sought to reduce its dependence upon wholesale borrowing by trying to raise new deposits while also holding a larger pool of liquid assets. HBOS also sought to alter the profile of its wholesale funding. The proportion of wholesale funding with a maturity of less than one year was reduced from 86% in 2001 to 50% by 2008. However, the bank used additional long-term funding to support asset growth rather than to reduce short-term debt. By the end of 2008 HBOS had debts with a maturity of less than one year of £119 billion (Parliamentary Commission on Banking Standards 2013a, 76).

HBOS was not fatally compromised by domestic mortgage lending. HBOS's market share had fallen from around 20% of all new mortgages between 2001 and 2005 to less than 10% of all new mortgages in 2006 (Scotsman 2007). This was, however, to prove an unexpected blessing, as HBOS had less exposure to new loans taken out at the peak of the market. The problem for HBOS was that executives sought to compensate for lower profits on mortgage lending by ramping up corporate lending. It was the corporate side of the bank that generated the largest losses. In late 2007 and 2008 commercial property values and the value of HBOS's assets relative to its deposits and other liabilities began to fall. By the summer of

2008 HBOS had recorded £6.6 billion in impairment losses within its corporate division, of which over £4 billion was in the form of commercial property loans. Impaired loans as a proportion of gross loans grew from 2.3% in 2006 to 5.5% in 2008 (significantly higher than for any other UK bank). HBOS did not seek to minimize its exposures by selling down its loan book. As late as February 2008, the head of corporate banking, Peter Cummings, berated the other banks who were winding down their commercial property lending for a "failure of nerve" and promised to continue lending (Teather 2009). In many respects, HBOS was simply reaffirming the Bank of Scotland's traditional culture of "staying at the table" to support customers through the economic cycle (Perman 2013). HBOS's decision to stay in the corporate lending market was, however, an immensely costly one. The bank's losses were compounded by its exposure to the US housing market through investments acquired by an off–balance sheet investment vehicle, Grampian, whose £37 billion in assets HBOS was forced to take back onto its balance sheet in April 2007. By 2008 HBOS held a total exposure to £42 billion in ABSs, including £9 billion in US RMBSs, £3 billion of CMBSs, £3.3 billion of CDOs, and £3.2 billion of CLOs (HBOS 2008a 129). In December 2007 HBOS announced a £736 million write-down in the value of these assets. By April 2008 it was forced to announce a further £2.8 billion write-down.

After a failed attempt to raise £4 billion in new capital in July 2008, the bank's share price plunged following the collapse of Lehman Brothers. Lloyds, with assets of £300 billion, agreed to absorb HBOS's balance sheet in return for an agreement from the government to waive the usual competition rule requirements. In 2008 HBOS recorded a £110 billion pretax loss. In 2009 HBOS lost a further £80.7 billion.

Lloyds Banking Group

Lloyds Banking Group (LBG) was formed following the merger between Lloyds TSB and HBOS in 2008. The merger proved disastrous for Lloyds. Overwhelmed by the unanticipated scale of the losses on HBOS's balance sheet, LBG struggled to raise additional equity through capital markets, and by February 2009 the government owned 43% of the bank's shares and a further £4 billion stake of preference (nonvoting) shares. In total, it has been estimated that LBG wrote off between £45 and £49 billion in bad debts as a result of its takeover of HBOS (Perman 2013, 175). LBG's market position was further undermined by a European Commission ruling requiring it to sell 632 branches, its TSB and Intelligence Finance brands, £64 billion of loans, and £32 billion of deposits as a condition of receiving state aid during the financial crisis. Yet LBG's position was not quite as precarious as that of RBS or HBOS. LBG recorded a pretax profit of £1 billion in 2009 and £0.2 billion in 2010.

How would Lloyds TSB have performed during the crisis if it had avoided merging with HBOS? Lloyds TSB recorded a £4 billion pretax profit in 2007 and a reduced but still healthy £2.2 billion profit in 2008. In his memoirs, the former chancellor, Alistair Darling (2011, 73), describes Lloyds as a "conservative well-run" bank. In his evidence to the Treasury Select Committee, Lloyds' CEO, Eric Daniels, maintained that Lloyds "had entered the financial crisis in a strong position"; that 80% of LBG's losses were incurred by HBOS; and that, left on its own, Lloyds TSB would not have needed any taxpayer support (Treasury Committee 2009b, Ev432). In 2010 LBG's finance director, Tim Tookey, told investors at a New York meeting that of the £225 billion lent by HBOS's retail division, £65 billion would not have been lent by Lloyds under its own rules and that of the £116 billion lent by the corporate banking division, £80 billion would not have been authorized (Perman 2013, 184). Indeed, Sir John Gieve suggests that, paradoxically, it was the very conservatism of Lloyds' operations prior to the crisis that encouraged the chairman and chief executive to buy HBOS.

> I think that [the senior management] probably felt that this was their moment when the tortoise was going to overtake the hare and at the end of this terrible crisis, which hadn't really—I mean it affected them through the economy but it hadn't really had a massive impact on their own operations and profitability—that the rewards for virtue were going to come out and they were going to swallow up this upstart bank and put themselves as the major bank in the UK and show that they'd had a long-term strategy. (Interview, 19 April 2013)

Yet Lloyds' position prior to the merger with HBOS was not unproblematic. In 2006 Lloyds maintained a 29:1 leverage ratio, the highest of any of the major UK banks (and up from 15:1 in 2000). In 2007 Lloyds required £12 billion in short-term wholesale funding and raised an additional £12 billion through securitization (Lloyds TSB 2007, 50). In 2007 customer deposits were the equivalent of 44% of liabilities (down from 60% in 2000). Lloyds had also acquired significant trading exposures. The *Financial Times* (2008) argued that "at a time when other banks were cantering off into new products and new corners of the globe," Lloyds TSB had stuck with the "tedious business" of retail banking, stating that the bank now had the "form to emerge in the winners' enclosure." This was a reasonable but incomplete assessment. Lloyds had indeed decided to focus upon the UK market rather than expand abroad. But in 2006 only 55% of its assets were in the form of loans (down from 69% in 2000). The bank held 20% of its assets in the form of trading securities (up from 4% in 2000). In 2007, Lloyds TSB (2007, 12) reported that it carried no direct exposure to the US subprime market. Yet at this time the bank held £6 billion in available-for-sale RMBSs and £4 billion in "other" ABSs on its own balance sheet (Lloyds TSB 2007, 105). The bank was ultimately responsible for a further £8 billion in ABSs held by an off–balance sheet investment vehicle, Cancara (Lloyds TSB 2007, 12). LBG eventually recorded £2 billion in write-downs on these assets.

Barclays

In 1997 Barclays abandoned its equities and mergers and acquisitions advisory business and renamed its fixed-income and trading business Barclays Capital (BarCap). In 1998 BarCap incurred significant losses in trading on Russian government bonds and through a significant exposure to the hedge fund Long-Term Capital Management. Having reaffirmed its commitment to securities trading, BarCap's chief executive, Bob Diamond, launched the "Alpha plan" in 2003, which set the goal of doubling revenues in four years (Salz 2013, 30). In 2003 BarCap became the first UK bank to enter the synthetic CDO market. By 2007 Barclays was generating £23 billion in revenue, of which £7.2 billion derived from BarCap (Salz 2013, 33). BarCap's status within the bank was confirmed in September 2010 when Bob Diamond was appointed CEO of the Barclays Group.

By 2006 Barclays was operating with a leverage of 36:1 (up from 20:1 in 2000) and a balance sheet in which gross loans constituted just 28% of total assets (down from 53% in 2000). Fifty-three percent of these loans were in the corporate and commercial sector. Trading securities constituted 21% of total assets and derivatives a further 13%. In 2006 Barclays recorded a £3 billion profit on its trading book (59% of total bank profits). The bank also carried significant exposures to the US market. In February 2007 it bought Equifirst, a nonprime US mortgage originator, for $225 million. By the end of 2007 it held £4.6 billion in US residential mortgage loans; £9.9 billion in US subprime and Alt-A RMBSs; £2.8 billion in US commercial property loans; and £1.2 billion in CMBSs (Barclays 2008, 106). It also held a £700 million exposure to two Bear Stearns hedge funds that had invested heavily in subprime securities (K. Kelly and Mollenkamp 2007). Furthermore, while it might have been Barclays' "policy to fund the balance sheet of the retail and commercial bank . . . with customer deposits," the group (including BarCap) was hugely dependent upon wholesale funding. Total deposits were the equivalent of only 23% of total assets in 2007 (down from 46% in 2000).

In August 2008 Barclays revealed that it had sold £6.3 billion of its loans at an undisclosed loss and written down the value of its RMBSs and CBMSs by £2.8 billion (Thal Larsen 2008b). This sum included £0.5 billion in impairment charges and £0.5 billion in market value losses on its subprime and Alt-A lending and securities and £0.7 billion in losses on its "super-senior" AAA-rated CDOs. Yet Barclays was not destroyed by the financial crisis. In 2007 the bank reported a £7 billion pretax profit. In 2008 it reported a £6 billion profit and in 2009 an £11 billion profit. Within the wider group, BarCap reported a £2.3 billion profit in 2007, a £1.3 billion profit in 2008, and a £2.4 billion profit in 2009. Barclays did not have to accept a capital injection from the UK government. Instead, it raised a total of £7 billion in additional private capital, a large part of it from Qatar, in return for a generous 30% stake in the bank (Farlow 2013, 133). Why was Barclays able to record a profit in 2008 and 2009? In 2008 BarCap recorded a £2.3 billion write-*up* in the value of the £72 billion in trading and £1.5 billion in property assets it had bought from the collapsing Lehman Brothers for just $250 million in September (Hughes and Hughes 2008). Without this windfall BarCap would have lost money in 2008. Even so, we now know that Barclays also borrowed money on forty-nine occasions from the US Federal Reserve via the Primary Dealer Credit Facility, which was established in March 2008—these loans ranging from $300 million to $15 billion (Farlow 2013, 125). Barclays also sold one of its business divisions, Barclays Global Investors, to BlackRock for £8.2 billion—generating a net profit gain for Barclays of around £4 billion (Salz 2013, 31). Barclays would no doubt argue that its decision to buy assets from the bankrupted Lehman Brothers is evidence of its good market judgment. Yet it should be noted that in August and September 2008 Barclays had tried to buy Lehman Brothers before it was bankrupted, only to be thwarted by a risk-averse British government (FCIC 2011, 335–336). Barclays had also tried to buy ABN Ambro in September 2007, only to be gazumped by RBS. In these respects, Barclays was lucky in 2008. Its good luck was, however, to run out.

In 2011 Bob Diamond incurred the wrath of senior politicians when he called for an end to the "time of remorse and apology" within the UK banking sector (Kirkup 2011). The following year, traders within Barclays were exposed for their efforts to manipulate the LIBOR interbank lending rate. Barclays' chairman, CEO, chief operating officer, and chief remuneration officer were forced to resign. Barclays' reputation was further tarnished when the Serious Fraud Office announced that it was investigating payments made to advisers in relation to the injection of funds from Qatar in 2008 (Goodley 2012). Barclays has also been widely criticized for the aggressive manner in which it has used an off–balance sheet conduit, Protium, to hide its assets from European regulators conducting stress tests. It was also criticized for the inappropriate sale of payment protection insurance to customers; for charging excessive interest on credit cards; and for aggressive tax avoidance (Salz 2013, 40–52). In July 2013 Barclays announced that, in order to rectify a £12 billion capital shortfall, it would seek to raise an additional £6 billion in shareholder investment (Treanor 2013a).

HSBC

HSBC Holdings was established as a London-based corporation in 1990 following the purchase of the Midland Bank amid concerns about Hong Kong's return to Chinese sovereignty in 1997. By 2011 HSBC was, by some measures, the world's second largest public company (deCarlo 2011). HSBC performed relatively well during the 2007–2008 crisis. In 2007 the bank recorded a pretax profit of £24.2 billion and a ROE of 15.1%. Profits fell in subsequent years, but the bank remained in the black. In 2008 the bank recorded a pretax profit of £9.3 billion and a ROE of 6.4%. In 2009 profits were £7 billion and ROE 4.7%. HSBC raised an additional £12.5 billion in capital via a market offering in March 2009 and did not require direct government capital support. HSBC's solvency ratio remained higher than that of any other UK-registered bank throughout the crisis.

HSBC's record was not, however, an unblemished one, especially in relation to the operations of its US subsidiaries. The bank suffered from a significant exposure to the US housing market both as a mortgage originator via HSBC Finance and through two wholly owned US subsidiaries, Household International (purchased for $14 billion in 2002) and Decision One (purchased for $10 billion in 2003). By December 2007 HSBC had accumulated £5.8 billion in direct subprime loans; a further £12.9 billion in subprime RMBSs; £1.7 billion in Alt-A RMBSs; and £14 billion in CMBSs (HSBC 2008, 152). The value of these assets fell dramatically amid the crisis and led to a $15 billion loss in its North American operations in 2008 and a further $7.7 billion loss in 2009. In addition, HSBC lost a further $984 million it had invested with the convicted fraudster Bernie Madoff. HSBC's former chief economist, Dennis Turner, describes HSBC as traditionally being "boring . . . dull and conservative" (interview, 18 April 2013). However, the investment in Household International and Decision One was not boring. Indeed, one senior risk manager at HSBC suggests that the problems in their loan books were well known.

> I think that—because I was a risk guy at the time—I actually did say, look, I'm nervous about Household International. It's a very low quality book and frankly I think at this point the risk functions views were largely ignored, to be honest, which was fatal, because there were guys like myself who said, look, although the numbers of Household International look good, this is in the backdrop of a ten-year fall [in interest rates] in the States, so even the low-quality portfolios can perform quite well in those situations. Although they've managed to convince you that they have great models, great controls, great procedures for managing for these sorts of portfolios, it's not been tested in a downturn. (Interview, 19 April 2013)

HSBC was able to survive despite the losses it incurred in the US housing market for four principal reasons. First, the American part of HSBC's business was a significant but still relatively small part of the bank's overall balance sheet. As of December 2008, the bank held 50% of its assets in Europe, 25% in Asia, 5% in South America, and 15% in North America (including Canada) (HSBC 2009, 417). In 2008 the £15 billion loss in its North American operations was mostly offset by an £11 billion profit in Europe and Asia and a £2 billion profit in Latin America. Second, and unlike RBS in particular, HSBC did not compound its losses in mortgage lending and securitization with additional trading losses. HSBC did run an investment bank, but this was largely focused upon mergers and acquisitions. In HSBC's own words, its relatively strong performance in the primary markets in which it was focused was "due to our relationship banking strategy, our strong business model, our prudent risk approach and our philosophy of taking a through the cycle approach . . . We had anticipated that the benign economic environment was unlikely to last and had as a result positioned our business to avoid riskier parts of the lending market" (Treasury Committee 2008, 26). In 2006 gross loans constituted 46% of HSBC's assets, trading securities 8% of assets, and derivatives held for trading purposes a further 5% of assets. In 2008 the bank made an overall profit on its trading activities of £6.5 billion. Third, and again unlike RBS, HSBC escaped further damage in the US market by winding down its exposures relatively early. In its 2008 annual report the bank's chairman states that HSBC "saw" and reacted to the problems in the US housing market as early as 2006 (HSBC 2008, 9). The bank publicly announced its intention to reduce its subprime holdings in March 2007. It closed the subprime mortgage originator Decision One in September 2007 and ceased trading in RMBSs in November of that year. Finally, the bank had also managed its overall leverage conservatively. In 2006 the bank had a leverage ratio of 14:1—significantly lower than that of any other British-based bank. It was thus less dependent upon wholesale funding. In 2007 total customer deposits were equivalent to 46% of total balance sheet liabilities (down from 64% in 2000). In its submission to the United Kingdom's Independent Commission on Banking, HSBC (2010, 31–32) argued that it had deliberately eschewed the wholesale funding market in favor of a large deposit base and had, starting in late 2005, sought to improve its capital reserves.

Standard Chartered

Standard Chartered is essentially a UK-based offshore banking operation. It opened its first branches in Shanghai and Mumbai in 1858. Standard's assets rose from £102 billion in 2000 to £329 billion in 2007 as a result of organic growth and the acquisition of Korea First Bank in 2004 and Hsinchu Bank in Taiwan and Union Bank in Pakistan in 2006. Standard was the British bank that sustained the least damage during the 2007–2008 crisis. Its pretax profits rose from £8.6 billion in 2006 to £11 billion in 2007, £13 billion in 2008, and £14.4 billion in 2009. Its ROE fell only slightly, from 15.1% in 2006 to 13.7% in 2007 and 13.2% in 2008. In December 2010 Standard was designated the "Global Bank of the Year" in the Banker's Bank of the Year Awards.

What was different about Standard Chartered? First and foremost, the bank operated largely in Asia and so benefited from sustained economic growth in that region. In 2007, 17% of the bank's operating income was earned in Hong Kong, 18% in India, 8% in Singapore, 8% in Korea, 3% in Malaysia, 18% in the rest of the Asia Pacific, 13% in the Middle East, and only 7% in the Americas, the United Kingdom, and Europe (Standard Chartered 2007, 5). Second, Standard maintained a relatively conservative balance sheet. Leverage in 2007 was 15.3:1 (compared to 16.7 in 2000). Gross loans constituted 47% of total assets in 2007 (down from 53% in 2000). Customer deposits were the equivalent of 62% of liabilities (down from 78% in 2000). Derivative holdings constituted only 7% of assets in 2007. Standard had been an active participant in securitization markets. In 2007 Standard sold $5.742 billion in loans to outside investors (Standard Chartered 2007, 112). Standard did, however, largely avoid buying the securitized assets of other banks. In 2007 Standard held $607 million in RMBSs, $219 million in CDOs, $830 million in CMBSs, and $970 million in "other" ABSs (Standard Chartered 2007, 54). The bank was forced to write down the value of these assets by $274 million (around 10% of their 2007 value). Furthermore, Standard was also forced to bring back onto its balance sheet $1.316 billion in RMBSs, $491 million in CDOs, $308 million in CMBSs, and $1.115 billion in other ABSs it had previously held in an off–balance sheet SIV, Whistlejacket, it had bought from JP Morgan. It recorded a $300 million write-down loss on these assets.

A range of other financial institutions and banks that traded in the City also did badly. The American Insurance Group (AIG) was established in China in 1919 and, by the 1990s, was one of only a handful of US corporations to have been given an AAA credit rating. In 1998, in an effort to exploit this rating, which meant that it could borrow money more cheaply on wholesale markets, executives established AIG Financial Products (FP) initially as a partnership with two former senior traders at the brokers Drexel Burhman Lambert, which at the time was being sued by the SEC for insider trading, stock manipulation, and defrauding its clients. In the 2000s, operating by this time out of an office in London employing around 300 people, AIG FP began to insure securitized assets, particularly CDOs, through CDSs. By 2006 AIG FP had insured a staggering $450 billion of securitized assets. For the banks involved, insuring their assets meant that they could reduce their regulatory capital. In this manner, the largest European banks, for example, were able to reduce their capital requirement from 8% to 1.6% (FCIC 2011, 140). In return, the banks paid AIG FP each year around 0.12% of the value of the assets insured. In a buoyant market in which the market value of these assets was rising, this stipend could be recorded as a pure profit. Indeed, as late as August 2007, AIG FP's chief executive, Joseph Cassano, publicly stated that "it is hard for us, without being flippant, to even see a scenario within any kind of realm or reason that would see us losing $1 in any of these transactions" (FCIC 2011, 268).

AIG began to unravel when auditors discovered that it had, as a part of the deals it had made, promised to post collateral to their counterparties in the event that the value of the assets they had insured began to fall below certain agreed levels. Because, for regulatory purposes, CDSs were not considered a form of insurance, AIG had not been required to hold *any* reserves against those possible payments. When, as a result, AIG lost its AAA rating and when the value of securitized assets *did* begin to fall, it became clear that the company would not be able to meet its obligations. As the chairman of the Federal Reserve, Ben Bernanke, commented: "AIG exploited a huge gap in the regulatory system. There was no oversight of the financial products division. This was a hedge fund, basically, that was attached to a large and stable insurance company, and it made huge numbers of irresponsible bets."

By May 2008 AIG FP had recorded $20 billion in write-downs on its assets. By September 2008, with the company facing bankruptcy, the US government—fearing that the banks that were owed money by AIG would collapse if AIG was unable to pay to those debts—extended the company a $85 billion loan in return for an 80% ownership stake in AIG itself.

Deutsche Bank also incurred huge losses through its London-based investment bank. In 2005 the chairman of the Group Executive Committee, Josef Ackermann, told investors that while the London investment bank had grown, "there is still a distance between us and the world's premier league." It therefore saw potential for "further growth in high margin processes, for example in trading in loans and sales of complex derivatives" (Ackermann 2005a). Later that year, after ramping up its trading operations, profits at Deutsche's investment bank grew by 130%. By December 2007 Deutsche was operating with a leverage ratio of 49:1 (up from 18.5:1 in 2000) and was carrying on its balance sheet a €2.864 billion gross exposure to subprime CDOs. In 2006, 46% of Deutsche's assets were for the purposes of trading (Hardie and Howarth 2013b, 111).

Once the market began to turn, the investment bank could not manage to sell these and other securitized assets and had to write down their value, thus compromising the bank's balance sheet. By April 2008 annual investment bank revenues had fallen from €5.2 billion to €1.5 billion. In August 2008 investment bank write-downs in structured credit products already exceeded €5 billion (Treanor 2008). In February 2009 Deutsche announced a €3.9 billion annual loss—its first loss in fifty years. This was the direct result of a €8.5 billion loss in the London investment bank. The rest of the bank remained profitable. Deutsche did not need a bailout and in 2009 reaffirmed its commitment to investment banking in London.

The Swiss bank UBS was also severely damaged by the 2007–2008 crisis. The headquarters of UBS's investment bank were in London, but it also ran significant trading operations in New York through a subsidiary firm, Dillon Read Capital Management. UBS, like Merrill Lynch, was a late entrant to the trading market. In 2005 UBS management hired an external consultancy firm, Mercer Oliver Wyman, to review its business strategy. The consultants argued that UBS had fallen behind its key rivals in the structured credit, securities, and commodities business. Management accepted this conclusion and adopted a strategy described by the OECD's chief economist, Adrian Blundell-Wignall, as one of "growth at any cost" (Blundell-Wignall and Atkinson 2008, 90). Initially, UBS sought to construct and then sell CDOs. In February 2006 UBS held only $5 billion of CDOs on its balance sheet—and these were all being warehoused awaiting future sales. Traders then noticed that although AAA-rated CDOs earned an income premium above the internal interest UBS charged for capital, UBS's risk management systems regarded these assets as being effectively riskless. Traders therefore switched from a strategy of originate-and-distribute to one of originate-and-hold. By September 2007 UBS was operating with a quite staggering leverage of 61:1 (up from 24:1 in 2000) and was holding $50 billion of the senior tranches of CDO assets (Acharya, Cooley, et al. 2009, 266). Once the market began to turn, UBS was unable to sell these now "toxic" assets, and as early as October 2007 was required to announce over $40 billion in write-downs on its investment bank assets (Straumann 2010, 6). Two-thirds of these losses were attributed to the CDO desk within the investment bank (UBS 2008b, 13). By October 2008 UBS had raised $34 billion in additional private capital but was effectively insolvent. The Swiss government saved the bank by agreeing to buy $60 billion in toxic assets from it, including $5.6 billion in US-originated subprime mortgages; $2.4 billion in Alt-A mortgages; $5.7 billion in commercial real estate; and $17 billion in "other" positions (presumably CDOs and other MBSs) (SFBC 2008). As the board of directors admitted to shareholders:

> Our balance sheet was too large and the systems of risk control and risk management that should have limited our exposure failed. We placed too much emphasis on growth and not enough on controlling risks and costs, particularly in regards to our compensation systems, performance targets and indicators and executive governance structures. Imponderable levels of cross-subsidy and confusion about accountability resulted from complex relationships between our business divisions. (UBS 2008a, 2)

Chastened by its losses, UBS management announced that it planned to scale back its investment banking operations and exit "high-risk and unpromising businesses" (Gow 2009). This did not occur. Indeed, UBS's return to profit in 2009 was fueled by a significant increase in trading income, with the London investment bank setting an annual $3.6 billion profit target (Moya 2009). UBS's reputation was further tarnished in 2011 when one of its London traders, Kweku Adoboli, lost £1.4 billion in global synthetic equities and was arrested and subsequently convicted on charges of fraud through abuse of position and false accounting.

Conclusion

No bank in the world was unaffected by the 2007–2008 crisis. As interbank interest rates increased, the size of the liabilities on bank balance sheets increased. As market prices fell, the assets banks held on their balance sheets had to be marked down. But not all banks were equally affected. The most obvious measure of the difference between the major banks operating in the United States and the United Kingdom is the difference between failure and survival. Lehman Brothers, Merrill Lynch, Bear Stearns, Citigroup, Wachovia, Fannie Mae, Freddie Mac, RBS, and LBG (following its merger with HBOS) were either bankrupted, taken over, or nationalized during the crisis. Contrast this with Goldman Sachs, JP Morgan, Wells Fargo, Standard Chartered, Barclays, and HSBC, which all recorded pretax profits in 2007 and 2008. The difference between failure and survival was not simply a matter of good and bad luck. Barclays *was* extremely fortunate to be gazumped by RBS in its bid to buy ABN Amro and to find its attempts to buy Lehman Brothers vetoed by the British government. In other cases, differences in performance during the crisis are reflective of and can be explained with reference to prior differences in business strategy and balance sheet composition or, in the case of Goldman Sachs, speed of response to changing market conditions.

Bear Stearns, Merrill Lynch, Lehman Brothers, Citigroup, and RBS failed during the crisis because they accumulated securitized assets and trading liabilities on their balance sheets prior to the crisis and compounded this error by sharply extending their leverage and wholesale funding requirements. HBOS and Wachovia failed because they were hugely exposed to downturns in, respectively, the domestic and commercial property markets. All this is, however, to beg a further question. Why did some US and UK banks adopt different strategies and eschew the risks that destroyed others? This is the question we address in Chapters 5 and 6. First, however, we need to extend our analysis through an examination of the fortunes and business strategies of the largest Australian and Canadian banks.

4

Bank Performance in Australia and Canada

In this chapter we describe the balance sheet composition and fortunes of the largest Australian and Canadian banks. In the 1980s and 1990s Australia and Canada, like the United States and the United Kingdom, embarked upon a program of financial liberalization. The banking systems in each country grew rapidly. In Australia the total assets of banks rose from A$319 billion in 1990 to A$690 billion in 2000 and to A$1.747 trillion in 2007 (RBA 2013). In Canada total bank assets rose from C$910 billion in 1997 (the first date for which aggregated data is available) to C$1.403 trillion in 2000 and to C$2.397 trillion in 2007 (OSFI 2013). The financial position of the Australian and Canadian banks was weakened by dislocation within global wholesale funding markets in 2007–2008. Yet of the four largest Australian and five largest Canadian banks, only one Canadian bank recorded a pretax loss over this entire period. In neither country did the government have to directly intervene to bail out individual banks.

In this chapter we argue that the performance of the Australian and Canadian banks during the crisis can be accounted for in terms of the composition of their balance sheets prior to the crisis. In particular, we show that the Australian and Canadian banks had significantly lower leverage and only minimal exposures to high-risk trading securities. There are, however, important differences between these countries. The Australian banks were dependent upon wholesale funding to sustain their balance sheets.

The Canadian banks held significantly higher proportions of their assets in the form of trading securities. There are also differences between the banks in each country. Two of the largest Australian banks, Australia and New Zealand Banking Group (ANZ) and National Australia Bank (NAB), did sustain losses during the crisis as a result of their exposure to the US housing market. The Canadian Imperial Bank of Commerce (CIBC) also sustained heavy losses during the crisis and recorded a C$4.2 billion pretax loss in 2008.

This chapter thus describes the fortunes of the Australian and Canadian banks, while Chapter 7 explains such outcomes. Drawing upon interviews with bankers and regulators, we show in Chapter 7 that key agents within the Australian and Canadian systems held very different views about risk management, leverage, financial trading, and wholesale funding than their counterparts in the United Kingdom and the United States. Regulation explains some but not all of these differences. More centrally, market structure provided strong incentives for bank executives to run relatively traditional balance sheets and not to reengineer them, as was the case for many banks in the United States and the United Kingdom.

Australia

In the wake of the traumas of the Depression in the 1930s, the postwar Australian banking system was tightly regulated. The interest rates banks could charge on loans and pay on deposits were controlled. Banks were subject to directives on the overall quantity of loans they could make, and it was very difficult for a foreign bank to enter the market (Battellino 2007). Financial deregulation began in the 1970s and accelerated in the 1980s as a key part of a more general program of economic liberalization (Bell 1997, 144–146). In 1973 interest rate controls on the banks were progressively removed. In 1983 the exchange rate was floated and capital controls on the flow of money into and out of the country were largely removed. Finally, and again in the 1980s, the government sought to stimulate competition within the banking system by allowing foreign banks to enter the Australian market. As in the United States, the result of this deregulation was a credit boom as the Australian banks sought to defend their market share against foreign competitors through aggressive lending, especially in the commercial property market. Furthermore, as was also the case in the United States, a boom and then bust in property prices led to a major banking crisis in the early 1990s. This crisis destroyed the State Bank of Victoria, the State Bank of South Australia, and the Pyramid Building Society, and, as we shall see, came close to destroying one of Australia's largest banks, Westpac (Carew 1997).

In the aftermath of the banking crisis, successive governments continued to reaffirm the virtues of deregulation and especially competition. In the name of sustaining competition, the government, in 1990, introduced the "six pillars" policy, which prevented any of the four largest banks and the two largest insurance firms from merging. The six pillars policy was the subject of intense criticism from the banks, who argued that it prevented them from achieving the economies of scale needed to compete globally (Bakir 2005). A government-sponsored inquiry into Australia's financial system, the Wallis Inquiry, recommended in 1997 that the policy be ended (Bakir 2003). The government balked at this advice. It agreed to remove the two insurance companies from the reach of the policy but the revised "four pillars" policy has remained in place since.

On the eve of the international banking crisis, the Australian banking system was dominated by the four pillar banks: the formerly publicly owned Commonwealth Bank of Australia (CBA) (total assets in 2007 of A$440 billion), Westpac (A$377 billion), ANZ (A$392 billion), and NAB (A$574 billion). Having grown through a series of mergers with smaller, regionally based banks, these four accounted for 73% of the total assets of the Australian banking system, 75% of total deposits, and 86% of the home loan market (Economics Reference Committee [Senate] 2011, 43). The first source of competition confronting these banks came from a number of regional banks, such as Suncorp Metway in Queensland (total assets of A$84 billion in 2007) and the Bendigo and Adelaide Bank in Victoria (assets of $17 billion). A second source of competition came from a number of building societies and upwards of fifty credit unions located across Australia. A third source of competition came from ten foreign-owned bank subsidiaries with upwards of thirty foreign bank branches. A final source of competition came from a number of nonbank mortgage lenders such as Aussie, Rams, and Wizard, which did not take deposits and funded their loans through wholesale funding markets. In total, the "shadow" banking system composed of nonbank mortgage lenders, monoline insurers, investment banks, and hedge funds accounted for around 20% of the Australian financial system in 2007 (RBA 2010a, 36–37). Firms in the shadow banking system originated wholesale funded mortgages, bundled these as residential mortgage-backed securities (RMBSs), and sold them to local and offshore investors. The traditional banks provided fee-based warehousing services for mortgages waiting to be pooled and securitized. The Australian RMBS market had grown from A$5.4 billion in 1995 to A$204 billion by mid-2007 (Garnaut and Llewellyn-Smith 2009, 59).

Throughout the 2000s strong economic growth and rising house prices fueled asset growth and returns on bank equity that were among the highest in the world (Hawtrey 2009, 108). Among the twenty-three largest Australian banks, average return on equity (ROE) was 15.6% in 2004, 18% in 2005, and 19.8% in 2006. These figures are slightly above those in the United Kingdom, where, between 2004 and 2006, the average ROE for the largest ninety-four banks was 16.6%. Average annual pretax profits at the four largest Australian banks rose from A$3.3 billion in 2000 to $6.3 billion in 2007, while average ROE rose from 17.2% in 2000 to 18.9% in 2007. Importantly, the Australian banks maintained these levels of profitability without reengineering their balance sheets. There are, in this respect, four key differences between the largest Australian banks prior to the crisis and the largest US and UK banks. The first of these is leverage. As we saw in Chapter 3, average leverage at the largest UK banks rose from 20:1 in 2000 to 26:1 in 2007. In Australia the average leverage of the four largest banks was 15.2:1 in 1990. Leverage subsequently fell to 13.8:1 in 1995 before returning to its 1990 levels by 2000. By 2007, average leverage had risen to 19.1:1. The second difference is that the largest Australian banks remained heavily dependent upon traditional banking, with residential mortgages as a key source of income. Between 2005 and 2009 the value of residential loans as a proportion of total assets at the four largest banks remained unchanged at 40%. Gross loans (mortgages and commercial loans) constituted, on average, 72% of assets in 2009 (down slightly from 73% in 2000). In the United Kingdom, by contrast, gross loans at the six largest banks constituted an average of just 49% of assets in 2006. The third difference is that Australian banks largely eschewed the subprime mortgage market. Australia's nonbank mortgage lenders began introducing "no-doc" loans in 1999, and by 2006 these constituted 7% of new loans. But the Reserve Bank of Australia (RBA) (2009, 18) estimates that the nonconforming mortgage market in Australia (the closest equivalent to the subprime market in the United States) accounted for only around 1% of the total mortgage market in mid-2007, compared to around 13% in the United States. One measure of the resulting difference in the quality of loans can be seen in comparative impairment rates. In 2005 an average of 1.7% of loans among the six largest UK banks were impaired. In Australia only 0.24% of loans were impaired.

A fourth difference was that the largest Australian banks had largely eschewed trading in securities and derivatives. The recorded value of trading securities held on the balance sheets of the four largest banks rose from A$33.7 billion in 2000 to A$86.1 billion in 2007. More dramatically, the value of derivative holdings rose from A$41 billion in 2006 (the first year for which aggregate data is available) to A$118 billion in 2008. Yet such increases should be seen in the context of the more general effects of rising asset prices and expanding balance sheets. The key figure here is not the total dollar value of derivative and security holdings but their value as a share of total assets. In 2007 derivatives constituted just 4.9% of the assets of the largest four banks. Trading securities constituted a further 4.5% of assets (up fractionally from 4.4% in 2000). As we saw in Chapter 3, trading securities constituted an average 16% of the assets of the six largest UK banks in 2004. Furthermore, the banks largely avoided holding RMBSs and other asset-backed securities (ABSs) originated in the United States. An assessment of Australia's "bank and corporate sector vulnerabilities" by the IMF (Takáts and Tumbarello 2009, 3) estimates that holdings of RMBSs and asset-backed commercial paper peaked at around A$240 billion during the second quarter of 2007, accounting for about 12% of Australia's financial sector; by June 2009, this figure had dropped to A$160 billion, with a third belonging to the big four banks, almost half to midtier and regional banks, and the remainder to nonbanking financial institutions. Significantly, only 2.1% of this amount rested in subprime RMBSs. The IMF also found that the majority of Australian-originated RMBS trades were made with external parties, rather than internally dispersed through a complex web of group-owned special purpose entities, a common practice among many of the largest US and UK banks. As the RBA argued in its

March 2010 *Financial Stability Report:* "One of the reasons why the Australian banks' earnings have remained comparatively stable is that their business models were focused on domestic lending. As a result, they had relatively little exposure to the kinds of securities that were a significant source of losses in the North Atlantic countries worst affected by the crisis" (RBA 2010a, 18). The RBA board member John Edwards (2008) similarly argues that "Australian banks do not engage in trading activities to the same extent as the major global banks. They are closer to the model of the traditional balance sheet." Jain and Jordan (2009, 6) suggest that "Australian banks focused on a traditional business model, old fashioned banking, rather than diversifying into trading activities or portfolio investment." Similarly, the CEO of Deutsche Bank, Australia, maintained that "the Australian banks largely saw some of the securitized mania—especially where the black boxes contained subprime assets—for what it was and that they were not assets to be involved in" (ASIC 2009, 22).

For all of its other virtues, the Australian banking system remains heavily dependent upon wholesale funding. The gross savings rate in Australia fell from 8% of household disposable income in 1990 to –4% in 2005 (RBA 2011, 43). Furthermore, in the 1990s available savings were increasingly funneled away from bank deposits and toward tax-subsidized superannuation funds. Although total deposits in the four largest banks rose from A$172 billion in 1990 to A$378 billion in 2000 and A$730 billion in 2007, deposits as a proportion of total assets nevertheless fell from 54% in 2000 to just 40% in 2007. In order to fund their asset growth, Australian banks had to borrow on wholesale markets, often from overseas. In 1990 the Australian banks collectively relied upon overseas markets for 10% of their total funding. By 2006 this had risen to 38% (RBA 2006, 31). It was the consequent exposure to currency and offshore interest rate changes that prompted many banks to enter the derivatives market in an attempt to hedge their risks. Wholesale borrowing was thus a key source of vulnerability in an otherwise resilient financial system. In order to remain in business, the Australian banks had to be able to borrow money on global markets. In 2008 they were increasingly unable to do so.

The senior Australian economist Ross Garnaut argues that the Australian banking system was in the process of reinventing itself in the years prior to the crisis. "Although Australian banks were slower to adopt the risks of shadow banking they were on the same track. By this reckoning Australia was saved by the timing of the Great Crash" (Garnaut and Llewellyn-Smith 2009, 142). Garnaut and Llewellyn-Smith are right to point to the growth of the shadow banking system in Australia and, in particular, to the role played within it by nonbank mortgage lenders. They are also right to emphasize—as we have—the dependence of the Australian banks upon wholesale funding (Garnaut and Llewellyn-Smith 2008, 61–62). Finally, they are also right to point to the growing value of the trading securities and derivatives held by the largest Australian banks (Garnaut and Llewellyn-Smith 2008, 59–60). Yet, as we have already argued, this growth must be understood in the context of the overall growth in the balance sheets of the Australian banks. In our view there is little evidence that the largest Australian banks were reinventing themselves in the years prior to the 2007–2008 crisis to anything like the same extent as many of the largest US and UK banks.

On 4 September 2008, with global credit markets in a state of turmoil, the Australian treasurer, Wayne Swan, argued that "if you were any country in the world in these circumstances, the country you would want to be is Australia" (Munro 2008). The RBA (2009, 17) subsequently offered an equally positive assessment of the resilience of the Australian financial system: "The Australian financial system has weathered the current challenges better than many other financial systems. Unlike in a number of other countries, the Australian banking sector continues to report solid profits, has little exposure to high-risk securities, and the largest banks have maintained their high credit ratings." Australia was not unaffected by the crisis. In September 2008 the federal government banned short trading in bank shares. In October 2008 the RBA injected additional liquidity into the market by accepting a broader range of assets from the banks as collateral in return for the provision of short-term cash. In November the government announced that it would guarantee all borrowing by Australia's banks on wholesale funding markets and guarantee all customer deposits up to A$1 million. The government also became a buyer of last resort for *locally* issued RBMSs, allocating A$4 billion for this purpose.

Within the Australian banking industry, the first and most significant casualties of the financial crisis were the nonbank mortgage lenders who were not authorized to take deposits and were completely dependent upon wholesale funding. Although the proportion of impaired loans held by these institutions remained low, they were unable to access funding. CBA eventually bought up to A$4 billion of Wizard-originated loans. Rams sold a part of its business to Westpac and stopped issuing new mortgages. Some of the regional banks also experienced difficulties. In February 2009 the CEO of the Queensland-based Suncorp-Metway Bank resigned shortly after revealing a A$350 million exposure in potential bad loans to property developers. In February 2009 the bank successfully raised A$1.3 billion in additional capital but only by heavily discounting its share price. The proportion of impaired loans at Suncorp rose from 0.3% in 2007 to 2.6% in 2009. Over the same period pretax profits fell from A$1.5 billion to A$0.4 billion.

Australia's largest investment bank, Macquarie, also suffered significant losses during the crisis. Macquarie grew rapidly in the 2000s by acquiring ownership shares in a range of businesses, in particular, finance firms and infrastructure firms specializing in public-private finance schemes. Notable acquisitions included Sydney Airport in 2002, ING Asian Cash Equities in 2004, Thames Water in 2006, and Giuliani Capital Advisors in 2008. Macquarie's total assets rose from $A21 billion in 2001 to $136 billion in 2007. In September 2008 a Credit Suisse report argued that Macquarie was heavily exposed to the US housing sector, and that year's annual report (Macquarie 2008, 86) went on to announce a A$290 million write-down in the value of its holdings. Worse was to come. In 2009 the real estate division recorded an A$360 million loss. Overall pretax profit fell from A$1.9 billion in 2007 to A$0.3 billion in 2008, A$0.6 billion in 2009, and A$0.5 billion in 2010. Macquarie's end-of-year share price fell from $52 in 2008 to just $27 in 2009.

Among the twenty-three largest Australian banks, average ROE rose from 19.8% in 2006 to 33% in 2007 before falling to 14.1% in 2008 and 10.2% in 2009. At the *four* largest banks, average pretax profits fell from A$6.3 billion in 2007 to A$5.1 billion in 2008 before recovering to A$5.4 billion in 2009 and A$7.1 billion in 2010. Average ROE in these banks fell from 18.9% in 2007 to 16.2% in 2008 and 10.1% in 2009 before recovering to 14% in 2010. Significantly, no major Australian bank came close to collapsing during the crisis. Indeed, not one bank had its credit rating downgraded. By late 2009 four of the eleven global banks with an AA credit rating

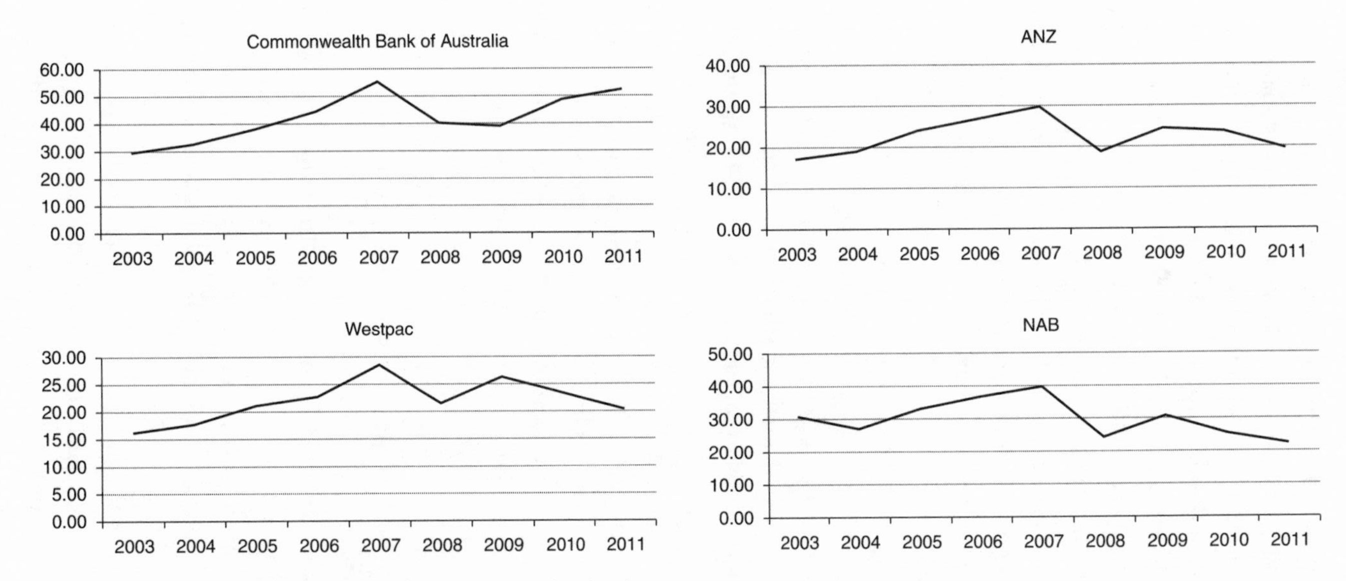

Figure 4.1. End-of-year share price (A$), major Australian banks, 2003–2011.

from Standard and Poor's were Australian (RBA 2009, 25). Yet, just as in the United States and the United Kingdom, these aggregate figures mask some variation in performance. The two strongest Australian banks before, during, and after the crisis were CBA and Westpac. As we shall see, neither bank carried any direct exposure to the US housing market. The same was not true of the other two major banks, ANZ and NAB, which did acquire some exposure to the US market and were forced to write down the value of these assets. Once again, the simplest measure of this difference is market share price. CBA's end-of-year price dropped from A$55.2 in 2007 to A$40.1 in 2008 (a 28% fall). Westpac's price dropped from A$28.52 in 2007 to A$21.4 in 2008 (a 25% fall). ANZ's price dropped from A$29.7 in 2007 to A$18.7 in 2008 (a 38% fall). Finally, NAB's price dropped from A$39.7 in 2007 to A$24.6 in 2008 (a 39% fall) (see Figure 4.1).

Commonwealth Bank

CBA was created as a government-owned bank in 1911 with a dual remit to act both as a commercial and a reserve bank. In 1960 the RBA was established, at which time CBA became a commercial bank; in 1991 it was successfully privatized. The value of the bank's assets rose from A$207 billion in 2000 to A$440 billion in 2007. Over this time it retained a conservative balance sheet. In 2007 the bank operated with a leverage of 18:1 (up from 11:1 in 2000). Seventy-six percent of its assets were in the form of gross loans (up from 64% in 2000). Trading securities accounted for just 4.8% of assets (up from 3.5% in 2000), while derivatives accounted for just 2.8% of assets. One way of understanding CBA's business model is in terms of the sources of its income. In the year up to June 2008 the bank earned A$546 million from trading in securities, most of these domestically issued, A$546 million from "other" (unspecified) trading activities, and A$756 million from interest on available-for-sale securities (CBA 2008, 100). These numbers were, however, dwarfed by the A$25.598 billion CBA earned from interest on loans. Eighty-three percent of the bank's loans had been made to Australian homeowners and companies (CBA 2008, 106). The bank had no direct exposure to the US subprime market (CBA 2008, 12). The bank's only significant vulnerability was its dependence upon wholesale funding. In 2007 deposits constituted just 44% of liabilities (down slightly from 45%

in 2000). In 2009 around 60% of the bank's wholesale borrowing was sourced overseas (CBA 2008, 203).

In August 2008 CBA surprised many analysts with an increase in annual impairment charges from A$434 million to A$930 million. In November 2008 the bank revealed further exposures to a number of failed or failing companies, including Centro, a large retail property developer ($900 million), ABC Learning (A$40 million), Lehman Brothers (A$150 million), and Allco, an Australian finance company ($170 million). In December 2008 CBA's management responded by raising an additional A$2 billion in capital. Its success in doing so was, however, tarnished by an Australian Securities and Investment Commission inquiry into whether the bank had deliberately delayed announcing an increase in the proportion of the bank's bad loans until after this capital had been raised (Gluyas 2008). In June 2009 CBA then admitted to "shortcomings" in its dealings with customers exposed to the failed financial company Storm Financial (CBA 2009, 7). Yet the bank's bottom line was largely unaffected by such difficulties. Pretax profits fell only slightly, from A$6.5 billion in 2007 to A$6.2 billion in 2008, before rising to $6.4 billion in 2009. In August 2008 CBA bought a 33% stake of the mortgage company Aussie Home Loans. In October 2008 it bought the West Australian BankWest from HBOS for A$2 billion. As one analyst remarked of the bank's 2009 profit results, "The Commonwealth's peers around the world would give their right arms to report a result like this" (Gluyas 2009a).

Westpac

In 1817 the Bank of New South Wales was the first bank to be founded in Australia. In 1982 it changed its name to Westpac Banking Corporation following a merger with the Commercial Bank of Australia. In the late 1980s Westpac underwent a period of rapid growth and acquired significant new exposures to the Australian commercial property market. By 1991, with the Australian economy slipping into an unexpectedly sharp recession, Westpac's loan book fell apart. By early 1992 the bank's bad loans exceeded its entire capital, and in May of that year the bank announced a A$1.6 billion loss (Carew 1997, 338). With the bank's credit rating falling, rumors spread that the bank was being kept afloat with cash provided by the RBA.

Eventually, following the appointment of a new CEO and chairman, the bank recovered. Indeed, by 2007 Westpac had been ranked by Dow Jones as the most sustainable bank in the world (Westpac 2007, 7).

In 2007 Westpac was operating with a leverage of 21:1 (up from 17:1 in 2000). This was the highest of any of the four major banks. Furthermore, at this time deposits were the equivalent of just 40% of liabilities (down from 47% in 2000). Yet, crucially, the bank remained focused upon domestic lending rather than trading. In 2007, 73% of the bank's assets were held in the form of loans (up from 71% in 2000). Only 0.2% of these loans were impaired. The value of the trading securities held on the bank's balance sheet had risen from A$7 billion to A$22 billion between 2000 and 2007, but this only constituted an increase from 4% of total assets to 5.8% of total assets. The bank carried no recorded exposures to the US housing market either directly in the form of loans or indirectly through holdings of ABSs. In 2007 the bank earned A$1.069 billion from trading activity (A$660 million from trading in securities and A$409 million from foreign exchange trading), but these figures were dwarfed by the A$19.483 billion the bank earned from interest on loans (Westpac 2008, 140–141).

In 2009, the *Australian* newspaper (Stevens 2008a) suggested that "Westpac [is going into] into banking's most dangerous crisis for two decades in more of a robust, risk-averse condition than any of its local or even regional peers." In May 2009 Westpac announced that its impairment charges to meet the costs of bad loans would increase from A$433 million to A$1.56 billion. By November 2009 impairment charges had risen again to A$3.2 billion (Gluyas 2009b). These losses were primarily recorded in the bank's institutional division, which had a $700 million exposure to three failing Australian companies: ABC Learning, Allco, and Babcock & Brown. In 2009 the bank raised A$3.8 billion in additional capital to reinforce its balance sheet. Yet the bank's core business in home lending remained strong. In October 2008 the CEO, Gail Kelly, boasted that of Westpac's 800,000 mortgages only 165 had been repossessed (Stevens 2008b). The bank's chief financial officer also stated that "the bank may have been overly conservative" in estimating its impairment charges (Stevens 2009). Overall performance did not deteriorate during the crisis. Annual pretax profits rose from A$5.1 billion in 2007 to A$5.2 billion in 2008 and A$6 billion in 2009.

Furthermore, each of the bank's five divisions—including Westpac's asset management and investment banking division, BT Financial—remained profitable. In November 2008 Westpac completed the A$18 billion take-over of the regional St. George Bank. In May 2009 the bank launched a new advertising campaign boasting of its aversion to risk. "We are take a jumper just in case." "We are the designated driver." "We're the safety bar, not the roller-coaster." Indeed, in reputational terms the bank actually suffered most during the financial crisis from accusations that it was *too* profitable and that it was promoting the interests of its shareholders over those of its customers.

Australia and New Zealand Banking Group

ANZ was formed when the Bank of Australia merged with the National Bank of New Zealand in 2003. In 2007 ANZ held assets of A$392 billion, recorded an annual operating income of A$14 billion, and employed over 30,000 people across its personal, institutional, New Zealand, and partnerships and private banking divisions. Although in the early 2000s the bank announced a long-term strategic objective of developing its Asian operations, 93% of group assets were held in Australia and New Zealand (ANZ 2008, 151). In July 2008 ANZ shocked the market by announcing A$1.6 billion in provisions for expected bad debts and trading losses in 2008 and forecast up to A$2.4 billion in potential losses in 2009. One month later a consultancy firm, Wilson HTM, published a report that concluded that a period of "unprecedented prosperity" had hidden significant weaknesses in ANZ's operations and that the bank "is in need of a thorough overhaul" (A. Ferguson 2008b). In October 2008 ANZ raised an additional A$1 billion in capital and in the same month announced a 21% fall in annual profits. ANZ's problems were compounded by the collapse in October 2008 of a securities and stockbroking firm, Opes Prime, to which ANZ had considerable exposures (Ryan 2008).

ANZ was also vulnerable to losses in the US market. As early as February 2008 it revealed a A$206 million exposure to a struggling US monoline insurer, ACA Capital (A. Ferguson 2008c). In July 2008 a Citibank report suggested that of all the Australian banks, "ANZ is most at risk of further [losses] . . . because of its long credit default swaps" (Jimenez 2008).

At the time, ANZ's CEO, Mike Smith, told reporters, "We have no exposure to US subprime or mortgage related CDOs . . . Our total [on-book] exposure to CDOs is A$5.5m" (Butler 2008). This was not, however, the full story. At ANZ's annual general meeting in December 2008 the chairman, Charles Goode, confirmed that the bank could lose up to A$530 million on its US mortgage-backed securities (MBS) positions. In a less than reassuring statement he told investors: "I don't know why we did this. The Board did not know this was happening" (Murdoch 2008). Goode subsequently said of these exposures:

> They didn't get reported up because we took insurance on them and apparently the management reporting showed net exposures were minimal . . . At the Board level we didn't know we'd bought any of these products . . . The documentation for these securitised packaged loans might be six or eight inches thick. These were very complex documents; senior executives just wouldn't have the time to have read the detailed documentation, let alone understand it . . . The complexity of it led them, I think, to rely entirely on the ratings agencies. (Interview, 29 February 2012)

In its 2008 annual report, ANZ (2008 187) confirmed that it held A$1.4 billion of credit default swaps (CDSs), A$395 million of collateralized debt obligations (CDOs), A$140 million of CMBSs, and A$800 million of RMBSs on its balance sheet. It also revealed that A$520 million of these securities were backed by US rather than Australian or New Zealand assets and that A$117 million of these were A- rather than AA- or AAA-rated (no assets were classed as B- or BB-rated).

Yet ANZ's travails were contained. The proportion of impaired loans to overall loans increased, but only from 0.3% in 2005 to 0.7% in 2008. The bank retained its AA credit rating and by February 2009 was posting a record A$1.6 billion quarterly profit. In August 2009 ANZ completed the purchase of the RBS's retail and commercial operations in Asia, and in 2010 it launched its own bank in China and took a major stake in an Indonesian bank, Panin. Overall pretax profits fell from A$5.8 billion in 2007 to A$4.5 billion in 2008 and to A$4.3 billion in 2009 before recovering to A$6.6 billion in 2010.

ANZ was damaged but not imperiled by its exposure to the US housing market. In 2007 the bank operated with a modest leverage of 17:1 (up slightly from 16:1 in 2000). Trading securities constituted just 3.8% of total assets (up from 2.6% in 2000). In 2007 profits from trading in derivatives accounted for just 6% of total profits. Gross loans accounted for 75% of assets (down slightly from 77% in 2000). Like CBA and Westpac, ANZ was dependent upon wholesale borrowing. In 2007 deposits were the equivalent of just 42% of assets (down slightly from 44% in 2000). Despite the losses associated with its US exposure, these figures do not suggest that the ANZ was reengineering its balance sheet in the years prior to the crisis.

National Australia Bank

In its modern incarnation, NAB was formed in 1981 when the National Bank merged with the Commercial Bank of Sydney. In the late 1980s the bank grew rapidly as a result of a series of takeovers, including those of the Clydesdale Bank in Scotland and the Northern Bank in Ireland in 1987; the Yorkshire Bank in 1990; the Bank of New Zealand in 1992; Michigan National Bank in 1995; and Homeside Lending in the United States in 1997. The bank's total assets rose from A$83 billion in 1990 to A$320 billion in 2000. The bank's reputation was tarnished in the early 2000s when its management was accused of trying to cover up a A$360 million loss incurred by a foreign currency trader and when Homeside Lending lost A$2 billion through the incorrect structuring of a tranche of mortgage deals. Having rebuilt its business and recorded a A$7.2 billion pretax profit in 2006 (the highest of any of the four pillar banks), NAB struggled to maintain its momentum during the financial crisis.

In March 2008 NAB signaled a A$180 million provision for potential losses on its US CDO holdings. In July 2008 NAB then revealed a further A$1.1 billion exposure and estimated A$380 million in losses through ten CDO portfolios composed of US RMBSs. NAB's share price immediately slumped by 13%. In August the credit rating agencies placed NAB's AA rating on a negative outlook. At the end of the year, NAB revealed that its total securities and credit impairment charges for the year had risen to over A$1 billion. In July 2009 reports surfaced that NAB was in talks with the Australian Prudential Regulation Authority (APRA) about how to correctly value a *further* A$17 billion of corporate bonds, CDOs, and RMBSs held within the bank's investment arm, NabCapital (A. Ferguson 2008a). At issue here was NAB's reluctance to price these securities at existing market value on the grounds that it planned to hold them to maturity. Faced with a barrage of bad publicity, NAB announced plans to raise a further A$2.7 billion in capital. In October 2009 the bank announced a 40% fall in annual profits and a 50% rise in bad and doubtful debts. In its annual report at the end of that year NAB then revealed that it continued to hold a total of A$1.6 billion in ABSs through off–balance sheet conduits: a sum that included A$266 million in US-originated CDOs (NAB 2009, 154–155). The bank subsequently faced a legal challenge from shareholders who maintained that the bank had deliberately sought to mislead investors about the extent of its CDO holdings (Drummond 2011).

NAB's exposures contrast with those of CBA and Westpac. Yet its overall position was strong. NAB experienced no difficulties in raising capital in November 2008. In May 2009 it raised A$1.2 billion in offshore wholesale funding without government assistance. Pretax profits fell from A$7.8 billion in 2007 to A$4.5 billion in 2008 and 2009, but NAB retained its AA rating. Like ANZ, NAB survived because its exposures to the US market constituted only a small part of its overall balance sheet. In 2007 NAB was operating with a leverage ratio of 19:1 (up from 16:1 in 2000). In the same year 67% of NAB's assets were held in the form of gross loans (up from 62% in 2000). Only 3.7% of assets were held in the form of trading securities (down from 4.7% in 2000). These figures vividly contrast with those of the largest US and UK banks that were taken over or nationalized in 2008.

Canada

An independent Canadian banking system emerged following the creation of the Canadian dollar in 1867. One key difference from the US system was that from its inception, the federal government in Canada possessed the legal authority to charter and regulate banks. In the United States the banking system in the nineteenth and early twentieth centuries was composed of thousands of often locally based and inadequately regulated banks. In Canada a handful of nationally regulated banks emerged and soon dominated the market. The resulting financial system was extremely stable. Not one Canadian bank failed during the Depression of the 1930s (Bordo, Redish, and Rockoff 2011).

In the late 1970s and early 1980s the Canadian government encouraged the banks, trust companies, insurance companies, and securities brokers—the so-called four pillars of the Canadian banking system (Bordo, Redish, and Rockoff 2011, 22)—to compete to provide financial services. A number of banks responded by aggressively pursuing market share. The result was an unsustainable property boom. When this boom turned to bust in 1985 the banks were exposed to huge losses, and a number of banks—including the Calgary-based Northland Bank and the Edmonton-based Canada Commercial Bank—failed. In the aftermath of this crisis, the largest banks learned to cope with the competitive pressures imposed upon them in a different way. They simply bought the previously independent insurance firms and securities brokers that were threatening their market share (Bordo, Redish, and Rockoff 2011, 23). As a result, the Canadian banking system was, by the early 2000s, dominated by five commercial banks that in 2007 accounted for 90% of the assets of the entire Canadian banking system. These were the Royal Bank of Canada (RBC) (assets of C$600 billion in 2007), Toronto-Dominion (TD) (C$422 billion), Bank of Nova Scotia (BNS) (C$411 billion), Bank of Montreal (BMO) (C$366 billion), and CIBC (C$342 billion). The National Bank of Canada (assets of C$113 billion) posed the most significant challenge to these banks' market share. Additional competition was provided by a number of regional banks such as Canadian Western Bank (assets of C$9 billion in 2007) and Laurentian Bank of Canada (assets of C$17 billion) as well as credit unions and foreign-bank subsidiaries. The largest banks were extremely profitable. Among the twenty largest Canadian banks, average ROE was 18% in 2004, 15% in 2005, and 21% in 2006. Average pretax profits among the five largest banks were C$2.6 billion in 2004 and C$4.1 billion in 2007. The Canadian banks were also highly internationalized. The Financial Stability Board (FSB 2012b) estimates that international activities constituted close to half of Canadian banks' income.

When the financial crisis began, the Canadian federal government intervened decisively to protect its financial system. First, through a series of purchase and resale agreements with individual banks, the Bank of

Canada provided C$37 billion in liquidity support by temporarily buying securities and other assets from the banks. Second, in October and November 2008 the Canadian government—through the Canada Mortgage and Housing Corporation—purchased C$19 billion in mortgages held by the banks, immediately and dramatically enhancing their liquidity and capital in doing so. Finally, the Canadian government, like its Australian counterpart, guaranteed the wholesale borrowing requirements of regulated deposit-taking banks (Bank of Canada 2008, 13). Such measures must, however, be understood in context. The Canadian government intervened to protect Canada's banks from the effects of the US crisis. The largest Canadian banks were not in and of themselves in financial difficulty. Only one bank, CIBC, recorded a pretax loss during the crisis, and not one bank had to be rescued. Among the twenty largest banks, average ROE rose from 21% in 2006 to 22% in 2007 before falling to 9.9% in 2008 and 11.9% in 2009. In November 2008, *Time* magazine (Heinrich 2008) described Canada as the "new gold standard in banking." In December 2008 the Bank of Canada's Financial System Review (Bank of Canada 2008, 1) suggested that "the Canadian financial system has proven to be relatively resilient throughout the crisis." Writing in the *New York Times*, Paul Krugman (2010) argued that "we [the United States] need to learn from those countries that did it right. And leading that list is our neighbor to the North."

As we go on to demonstrate in the rest of this chapter, the Canadian banks performed strongly during the 2007–2008 crisis because they had maintained conservative balance sheets in the years prior to the crisis and had not reinvented themselves as trader banks. Across the five largest banks, average leverage in 2007 was 23:1 (up from 20:1 in 2000). Gross loans constituted an average of 45% of assets (down from 51% in 2000) (53% across all Canadian banks). Trading securities constituted 19% of assets (up from 14% in 2000). Derivatives constituted a further 8.6% of assets. In 2006 trading activities generated just 5% of income (up from 4% in 2000) (Leblond 2013, 205). Furthermore, the Canadian banks were not as dependent upon wholesale funding relative to their Australian, British, or American counterparts. In 2007 total customer deposits, a liability on the balance sheet, were the equivalent of 59% of balance sheet assets (down slightly from 60% in 2000). These aggregate figures do, however, mask important differences between the exposures acquired by RBC, TD, and BNS on the

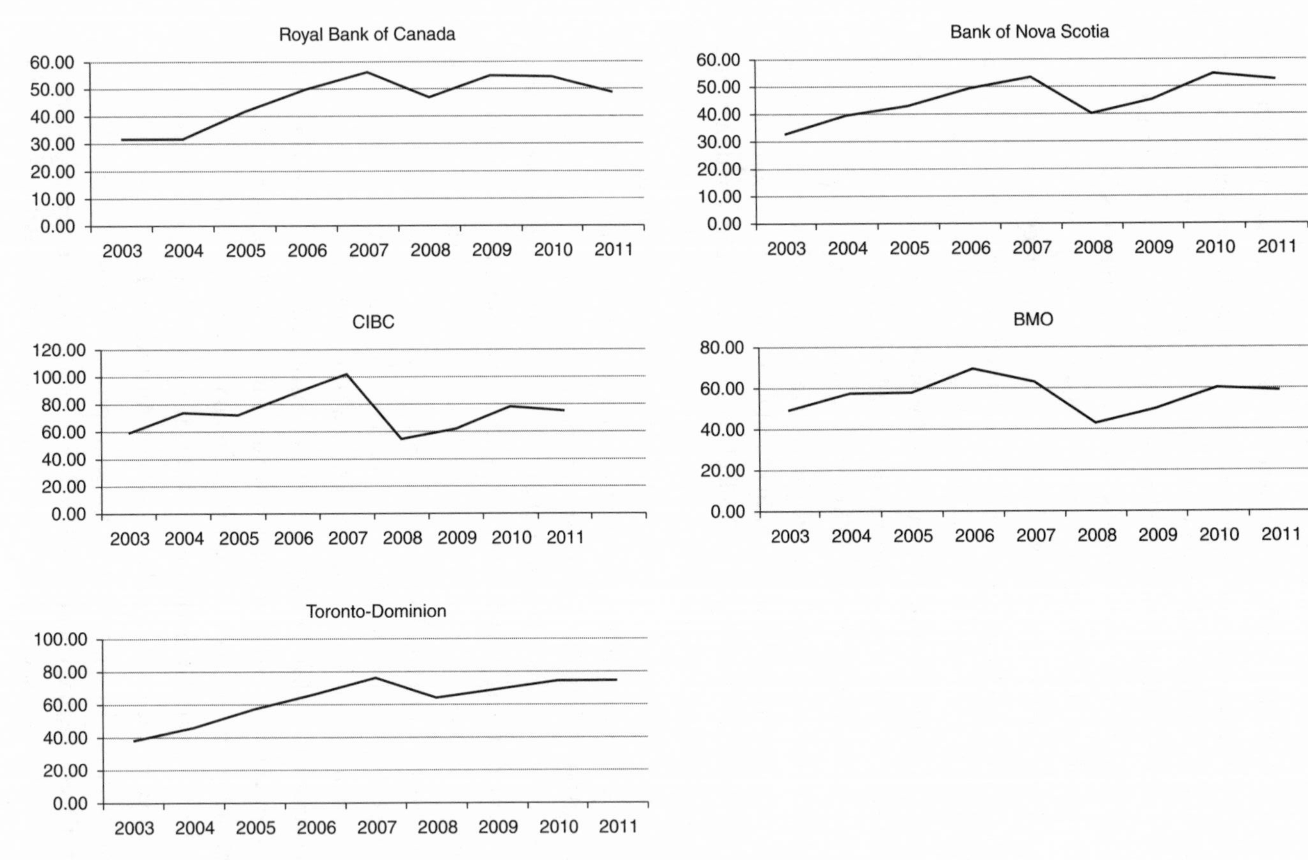

Figure 4.2. End-of-year share price (C$), major Canadian banks, 2003–2011.

one hand and CIBC and, to a lesser extent, BMO on the other. Once again, end-of-year share price provide one measure of this difference. RBC's price fell from C$56 in 2007 to C$46.8 in 2008 (an 18% fall). TD's price fell from C$73.3 in 2007 to C$64 in 2008 (a 16% fall). BNS performed less well. Its price fell from C$53.4 in 2007 to C$40.1 in 2008 (a 25% fall). BMO fell from C$63 in 2007 to C$43 in 2008 (a 32% fall). Finally, and most dramatically, CIBC fell from C$102 in 2007 to C$54 in 2008 (a 54% fall) (see Figure 4.2).

Royal Bank of Canada

The RBC was originally established as the Merchants Bank of Halifax in 1864. The assets of the bank rose from C$173 billion in 1994 to C$289 billion in 2000 and C$600 billion in 2007. Measured by total asset value, RBC was Canada's largest corporation and had been its largest bank since the 1940s. By 2007 RBC derived 48% of income from its Canadian banking operations, 5% from international banking (primarily through RBC in the southeastern United States and its operations in South America), 14% from wealth management, 8% through insurance, and 24% through capital markets and investment banking (RBC 2009, 6).

In his preface to the bank's 2008 annual report, RBC's CEO, Gordon Nixon, argued that "this year, as market and economic conditions were at their most challenging[,] RBC emerged, not unscathed, but strong and stable" (RBC 2008, 4). This was a reasonable assessment. In May 2008 RBC posted a C$855 million write-down in the value of its assets. In April 2009 it announced a further C$800 million write-down (Willis 2009). In 2010 Moody's downgraded RBC's credit rating from AAA to Aa1 because of the size of the bank's capital market operations, which "potentially expose bondholders to increased earnings volatility and [pose] significant risk challenges" (B. Simon 2010). Yet the bank's overall position throughout this period remained strong. Pretax profits fell from C$7 billion in 2007 to C$6 billion in 2008 and C$5.5 billion in 2009 before recovering to C$6.9 billion in 2010. As one market analyst commented: "You're not going to read [Andrew Sorkin's] *Too Big to Fail* and have to look for Royal in the index. They were just bystanders through the crisis really" (Perkins 2009).

Throughout a decade of rapid growth, RBC maintained a prudent balance sheet. In 2007 the bank operated with a leverage of 23.5 (up from 21.3 in 2000). At this time, total deposits were the equivalent of 56% of assets (down from 63% in 2000). Yet, perhaps surprisingly given its overall profile, only 40.1% of the bank's assets were held in the form of gross loans (down from 53.9% in 2000). Trading securities constituted 37.4% of assets (up from 14.7% in 2000). As global asset prices fell in 2007–2008, RBC recorded C$1.5 billion in losses on these securities. Yet upon a closer inspection, the bank's exposures were limited. Most of its loans and securities were tied to the Canadian market. In 2007 RBC held C$24.3 billion in Canadian government and government agency securities, C$3.5 billion in Canadian MBSs, and C$4.7 billion in other Canadian ABSs on its balance sheet (RBC 2008, 44). In 2006, 5.3% of RBC's loans were held in the United States, 2.7% in other countries, and 92% in Canada (RBC 2008, 120). RBC had relatively little exposure to the US market. In 2005 the bank sold its US mortgage origination business, RBC Mortgage Company, to New Century. One anonymous market commentator suggests that "rather than play hot potato with risky mortgages, RBC decided to focus on bread-and-butter lending, the type of business it thrives on" (Perkins 2009). In 2008 the bank had a residual C$262 million exposure to US subprime securities and C$93 million of CDOs that contained subprime assets (RBC 2008, 80). Given the size of the bank's overall balance sheet, these were manageable sums.

Toronto-Dominion

In 2007 TD operated across four divisions: Canadian banking (net income in 2007 of C$2.253 billion), wealth management (C$762 million), US commercial banking (C$320 million), and wholesale banking (C$824 million) (TD 2008, 29). TD's total assets had risen from C$264 billion in 2000 to C$422 billion in 2007. During the financial crisis TD's pretax profits fell from C$5.6 billion in 2006 to C$4.9 billion in 2007, C$4.4 billion in 2008, and C$3.4 billion in 2009. Yet TD retained its AAA credit rating and emerged in a strong enough position in 2010 to buy three regional US banks—Riverside National Bank of Florida, First Federal Bank of North Florida, and American First Bank.

In 2007 TD operated with a leverage ratio of 20.2 (up slightly from 19.7 in 2000) and with total customer deposits that were equivalent to 63% of total balance sheet assets (up from 60% in 2000). TD also managed to reduce its exposures to the US market in the run-up to the crisis. In 2005 TD committed itself to a significant overseas expansion through the US$8.5 billion purchase of the 1,000 branches of the New Jersey–based Commerce BanCorp, which was heavily engaged in subprime lending. At this time, TD was also among the world's ten largest purchasers of securitized assets (Kravis 2009). Yet in the year in which TD completed its purchase of Commerce BanCorp it decided to exit the securitization and subprime market. In an interview published as a part of its 2008 annual report, TD's CEO, Ed Clark, explained this change of strategy:

> A lot of it comes down to strategic decisions we have made, largely around the way we manage risk. One of those decisions involved getting out of the structured products business in 2005. We just didn't like the risk embedded in all those complex, financially engineered investment vehicles. We also didn't think it was wise to put our clients into asset-backed products—so we refused to sell them . . . Another decision was to avoid subprime lending in the US. Our approach is to lend in our local markets to people we know and who we're confident can pay us back. That's meant we have only made loans to creditworthy people in areas of the country that have largely avoided the housing collapse and are relatively stronger economically. As a result of our footprint, conservative lending practices and strong credit culture, our reserves far exceed our credit losses. (TD 2008, 11)

As a result of TD's change in strategy, trading securities as a proportion of total assets fell from 22% in 2000 to 18% in 2007. In 2007 gross loans constituted 41% of assets (down from 46% in 2000). TD continued to securitize assets in the run-up to the 2007–2008 crisis. In 2006 it securitized C$6.349 billion of new residential mortgage loans, C$6.741 billion of personal loans, C$420 million of credit card loans, and C$633 million of commercial mortgage loans (TD 2007, 91). Crucially, it did not, however, hold those securitized loans on its own balance sheet. It sold them to outside investors. In 2006 TD retained C$241 million of securitized assets on its balance sheet, around 2% of the total value of the assets it securitized that year (TD 2007, 91). Furthermore, by 2008 TD had no recorded exposures to the US subprime market or to CDOs derived from US RMBSs.

Bank of Nova Scotia

BNS (colloquially known as Scotiabank) expanded during the 1990s through a series of acquisitions including Inverlat (a Mexican bank) in 1992, Montreal Trust in 1994, and Dundee Wealth in 1998. By 2007 BNS operated through a domestic banking division (C$1.550 billion income in 2007), an investment banking division, Scotia Capital (C$1.114 billion income), and an international banking division (C$1.232 billion income) (BNS 2007, 9). During the financial crisis the bank's pretax profits fell from C$5.2 billion in 2007 to C$3.9 billion in 2008 before recovering to $C4.7 billion in 2009. BNS performed well during the crisis despite carrying a significant exposure to three off–balance sheet conduits it sponsored. One of these was housed in the United States and had acquired US$12.699 billion in assets (including $650 million in MBSs, $372 million in CDOs and collateralized loan obligations (CLOs), and $4.236 billion of securitized auto loans) (BNS 2008, 44). In 2008 BNS was forced to transfer these CDO and CLO holdings back onto its balance sheet and to write down their value by US$298 million (BNS 2008, 25). The other assets remained in the conduit to which BNS continued to provide liquidity guarantees.

BNS's exposures to the US housing market were not insignificant and need to be understood in the context of the bank's overall balance sheet. In 2007 BNS's operating leverage ratio was 21.8 (up from 18:1 in 2000). This was below the Canadian (let alone the UK) average. The bank held 55.7% of its assets in the form of gross loans (down only slightly from 57.7% in 2000). Total customer deposits were the equivalent of 63% of balance sheet assets (up from 57% in 2000). Beyond its US-based conduit, BNS had minimal exposures to the US market. In 2007 it was carrying C$158 billion of outstanding Canadian-based loans, C$53 billion of non-US international loans, and only C$17 billion of US loans (of which $366 million was classified as being impaired) (BNS 2008, 118). BNS had "nominal" exposures to the US subprime market and "insignificant" exposures to the Alt-A mortgage market (BNS 2008, 48; BNS 2009, 49). Furthermore, while BNS was an active participant in securitization markets, it did not retain those assets on its own balance sheet. In 2006 BNS securitized C$2.514 billion of assets, retaining only $67 million of that on its own books (BNS 2007, 109). Finally, BNS operated a relatively small trading portfolio. In 2007 it recorded $517 million of Canadian MBSs and $38 million of commercial MBSs on its balance sheet as being held for trading purposes. By the standards even of other Canadian banks this was quite low.

Bank of Montreal

BMO's performance during the crisis was similar to that of the other banks we have surveyed. Pretax profits fell from C$2.3 billion in 2007 to C$1.9 billion in 2008 before recovering to C$2 billion in 2009. By 2010 BMO was in a strong enough position to extend its US operations through a US$4.1 billion investment in a midwestern bank, Marshall and Isley. Yet BMO's performance masked a number of difficulties on its balance sheet. The first of these derived from the bank's 1984 purchase of the Chicago-based Harris Bank, which in the early 2000s ran a significant mortgage lending business. In 2008 BMO (2008, 62) revealed that it was carrying US$2.5 billion in loans with "subprime characteristics" and a further US$1.6 billion in Alt-A loans through its US subsidiary. In an apparent attempt to reassure investors, BMO announced that it had discontinued its no-documentation loan schemes—but only in early 2008 (BMO 2008, 63). A second difficulty stemmed from the Capital Market division's exposure to US housing securities. In 2008 BMO was carrying C$12 million in CDOs, C$53 million in CLOs, C$69 million of RMBSs, and C$399 million of other ABSs on its balance sheet (BMO 2008, 63). BMO's annual report and accounts do not specify what proportion of these assets derived from US-originated loans. The fact that in 2008 the CDOs lost C$17 million in value and the CLOs $24 million in value is, however, suggestive. A third difficulty arose from funding guarantees BMO had extended to a US firm, Fairway Finance, which had sponsored the off–balance sheet conduits of a number of large US banks (Perkins 2008a). In 2008 BMO recorded a C$247 million provision for future losses as a result of this commitment.

Announcing a "reorganization" of the bank's risk management functions in the aftermath of these losses, BMO's president and CEO, William Downe, admitted that "it's now clear that, in a number of businesses, our positions grew beyond what is in line with our risk tolerance and strategic direction" (Perkins 2008b). BMO was nevertheless able to record pretax profits in 2008 and 2009 because its core business remained profitable. Rather like ANZ and NAB in Australia, BMO made mistakes on the margins of its balance sheet. In 2007 BMO was operating with a leverage of 23:1 (up from 18:1 in 2000). This was the Canadian average. Forty-one percent of BMO's assets were in the form of gross loans (down from 51% in 2000). Nineteen percent of assets were held in the form of trading securities (up from 9% in 2000). Total customer deposits were the equivalent of 53% of total balance sheet assets (down from 57% in 2000). These figures suggest that BMO had gone further than RBC, TD, or BNS to reengineer its balance sheet. They were not, however, of a magnitude that threatened the bank's survival.

Canadian Imperial Bank of Commerce

CIBC was formed in 1961 as a result of a merger between the Canadian Bank of Commerce and the Imperial Bank of Canada. The bank has had a checkered recent history. In 2003 the US Securities and Exchange Commission (SEC) fined CIBC US$80 million for its role in the manipulation of Enron's financial statements in relation to the value of structured credit products. In 2005 CIBC subsequently paid US$2.4 billion to settle a class action lawsuit brought by a group of pension funds that had invested money in Enron (Teather 2005). In 2004 CIBC reached a C$15 million settlement in relation to inadequate disclosure of payment charges on its Visa Card operations. In the same year CIBC announced that it would refund C$24 million to customers who had been overcharged for mortgage payments (Business Monitor International 2010, 41). In 2005 CIBC then confirmed that it would pay US$125 million to settle an out-of-court SEC investigation into irregular trading practices.

CIBC's corporate reputation was further tarnished by the losses it incurred during the 2007–2008 crisis. In December 2007 CIBC disclosed that it had a C$9.8 billion exposure to the US subprime RMBS market via a series of derivative contracts and a further C$1.6 billion exposure to RMBSs and CDOs on its balance sheet that were "related" (CIBC 2007, 40) to the US subprime market. In February 2008 the bank reported that it had written down the value of these assets by C$3.46 billion. In June it announced a further C$2.4 billion write-down on the same assets. In its 2008 annual report, CIBC (2008, 44) recorded a C$811 million exposure to the super-senior tranches of CDOs, a C$365 million exposure on "warehoused" CDOs, and a further C$313 million exposure to "other" nonhedged CDOs. In addition, the bank at this point recorded a $6.6 billion off–balance sheet exposure to a series of conduits for which it had guaranteed liquidity funding. In 2007 CIBC recorded a pretax profit of $3.8 billion. In 2008 CIBC recorded a pretax loss of C$4.2 billion. CIBC's fortunes recovered in 2009 when it recorded a pretax profit of C$1.9 billion. According to the senior equity analyst Peter Routledge, CIBC incurred a large part of these losses because it had bought protection on its CDO holdings with monoline insurers that failed.

> Everyone was looking at this risk on a net basis . . . I remember I looked at this at Moody's because we had details into the transactions. But basically, everyone was looking at it on a net basis including us at Moody's, and it wasn't a net problem, right. They had—and this is public—they had bought CDOs and offset it by buying protection, and their biggest provider of credit protection CDS was ACA [a larger monoline insurer]. No one thought it was an issue, and then when you peel apart the transaction . . . well, it's insolvent . . . If you would have actually split it apart and thought of it, you would have realized, geez, this is just correlation of one and there is actually very little protection in fact. (Interview, 5 June 2013)

CIBC was the only Canadian bank to experience significant financial difficulties during the crisis. Indeed, the *National Post* (Lam 2009) reported that CIBC experienced the fifteenth highest losses of any global bank. Its experiences might have been worse. Barclays was able to record a profit on its trading activities in 2008 in part because it bought Lehman Brothers' assets at a fire sale price. CIBC benefited from Lehman's bankruptcy in a different way. In 2010 the estate of Lehman Brothers sued CIBC in relation to a C$1.3 billion debt on a CDS exposure that CIBC had owed to Lehman but had not had to pay in 2008 when the latter was bankrupted (Robertson 2010).

CIBC did not initially demonstrate a great deal of contrition in relation to its losses. CIBC's CEO, Gerry McCaughey, argued that "the fact of the matter is that this issue [the losses on the US housing market] arose in a small area of the bank and in the least expected of places" (Perkins 2008c). Given that CIBC's losses were of an order of magnitude larger than those of the other Canadian banks, this was hardly reassuring. It is, however, true that the core Canadian part of CIBC's business was relatively healthy. In 2006 CIBC's Canadian banking division recorded a C$1.8 billion pretax profit. In 2007 this rose to C$2.5 billion before falling to C$2.1 billion in 2008. One market analyst argued: "The irony of CIBC's situation is that, without the overhang of its subprime and CDO counterparty exposures, it would likely be the most risk-free bank of the Big Five and should represent the safest harbour in the current uncertainty faced by Canadian banks" (Perkins 2008c).

This assessment must be treated cautiously. In 2007 CIBC was operating with an overall leverage of 25:1 (up from 23:1 in 2000). This was the highest leverage of any of the Canadian banks, and this meant that its losses had an exaggerated impact on profitability. Yet in other respects, CIBC's balance sheet was indeed run conservatively. In 2007, 20% of assets were held in the form of trading securities (up only slightly from 19% in 2009). Forty-seven percent of assets were held in the form of gross loans (the same proportion as in 2000). Furthermore, CIBC was not overly dependent upon wholesale funding. In 2007 total deposits were the equivalent of 63% of balance sheet assets (up from 62% in 2000). Of all the Canadian banks, CIBC found itself in the most difficult position in 2007–2008. The challenges it faced were, however, minimal when compared with those facing some of the largest US and UK banks. It must, however, also be noted that CIBC has, in recent years, worked hard to reform itself. As Peter Routledge emphasized to us, CIBC raised $3 billion in common equity in January 2008 precisely because it wanted to do everything necessary to remove the specter of instability from the bank. Since then, the bank has appointed Nicholas Le Pan, the former head of the Office of the Superintendent of Financial Institutions, to chair its risk management committee.

Conclusion

In this chapter and Chapter 2 we have examined the financial fortunes and balance sheets of twenty-five banks in four countries. We have documented evidence of significant intercountry and intracountry variation in performance. Figure 4.3 shows the ranking given to the American, British, Australian, and Canadian banking systems by the World Economic Forum (higher numbers imply a lower ranking). These country-level variations broadly reflect differences in the composition of bank balance sheets prior to the crisis. In 2007 the UK banks operated with an average leverage of 26:1. Australian banks operated with an average leverage of 19:1 and Canadian banks with a 23:1 leverage ratio. In the United States the commercial banks held an average of 26% of their assets as trading securities. In Australia the equivalent figure was just 4.5%. Conversely, loans constituted 50% of assets among the US commercial banks, 49% of assets among the UK banks, and 72% of assets in Australia. On these measures, the Canadian banking system had more in common with the United States and the United Kingdom than with Australia. In 2007 loans constituted 45% and trading securities 19% of total assets. However, the Canadian banks were less dependent upon wholesale funding. In 2007 total customer deposits were the equivalent of 60% of balance sheet liabilities in Canada, 40% of assets in Australia, 35% of assets in the United Kingdom, and 37% of assets among the five largest US commercial banks. Ratnovski and Huang (2009) argue that this difference was crucial. When wholesale funding markets began to deteriorate in 2007, the Canadian banks retained investor confidence because they could largely rely upon their deposit base for funding. The Canadian banks—like their Australian counterparts—also had far less exposure to the US housing market.

We have also documented considerable intracountry variation in performance. Not all the US and UK banks failed, and not all the Australian and Canadian banks prospered to the same degree. In the United States, JP Morgan and Goldman Sachs accumulated substantial market exposures but then largely reversed their positions (JP Morgan on an ongoing basis in the 2000s and Goldman Sachs in 2006–2007). Wells Fargo maintained a conservative balance sheet throughout the 2000s. In the United Kingdom, Standard Chartered emerged from the 2007–2008 crisis largely unscathed, while

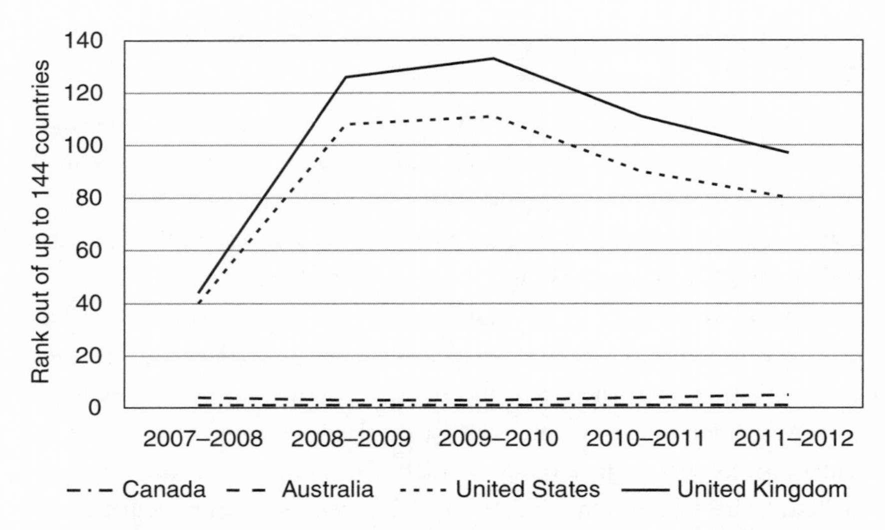

Figure 4.3. World Economic Forum Global Competitiveness Report: Banking system soundness, 2007–2011. (From data in World Economic Forum Global Competitiveness Report.)

Table 4.1. Intercountry and intracountry variation: A summary

	Good intracountry performance	Intermediate	Bad intracountry performance
Good intercountry performance (Australia and Canada)	Commonwealth Bank of Australia WestPac Royal Bank of Canada Toronto-Dominion Bank of Nova Scotia	ANZ NAB Bank of Montreal	CIBC
Bad intercountry performance (United States and United Kingdom)	Wells Fargo Goldman Sachs JP Morgan Chase Standard Chartered HSBC	Bank of America Lloyds (prior to takeover of HBOS) Barclays	Citigroup Merrill Lynch Bear Stearns Lehman Brothers Wachovia Fannie Mae and Freddie Mac Royal Bank of Scotland HBOS

HSBC—despite the huge losses it incurred through its US subprime exposures—recorded pretax profits in 2008 and 2009. The performance of some other banks was more mixed. In 2008 the Bank of America recorded $3.7 billion in write-downs on the value of its assets and a $4 billion loss on its off–balance sheet holdings. Yet the bank remained in the black. In the United Kingdom, Lloyds was in a reasonably strong position prior to its disastrous takeover of HBOS. Barclays recorded a profit in 2008 and 2009 partly as a result of its purchase of a large part of Lehman Brothers' assets. Barclays did not receive any direct support from the UK government but instead raised additional capital through Middle East sovereign wealth funds.

Turning now to Australia and Canada, ANZ and NAB remained profitable but recorded losses on their exposures to the US housing market. The same was also true of the BMO. The only bank in either Australia or Canada to record a pretax loss during or after the 2007–2008 crisis was CIBC. Whatever the rhetorical purchase of the notion of a global financial crisis, there was significant intercountry and intracountry variation in banking performance in 2007–2008. We summarize our overall findings in Table 4.1, which provides a reference point for future discussion.

How do we explain these differences in bank performance? We have argued that the differences are explicable in terms of the composition of bank balance sheets. The banks that emerged from the crisis in the strongest position had either lower leverage, a lower dependence upon wholesale funding, fewer trading exposures to securitized assets, or some combination of all three. Why did the banks operate with such different business models? This is the question we address in the following chapters.

5

US Banking

Exciting but Not Very Safe

The think tank Better Markets estimates the total costs of the financial crisis in the United States at nearly $13 trillion, once balance sheet losses and GDP losses are fully incorporated (Blyth 2013, 45). In assigning the blame for this, the US government's Financial Crisis Inquiry Commission (FCIC) (2011, xvii) declared that the 2007–2008 crisis was the result of "the captains of finance and the public stewards of our financial system [who] ignored warnings and failed to question, and manage evolving risks."

In Chapter 2 we showed how the collapse of the housing bubble in the United States triggered a financial collapse whose scale was propelled by the accumulation of systemic risk within the financial system. In Chapter 3 we showed how Bear Stearns, Lehman Brothers, Merrill Lynch, Morgan Stanley, Citigroup, and Bank of America secured higher profits through highly leveraged trading in securitized assets and how their balance sheets were destroyed or gravely damaged amid the crisis. In this chapter we explain the behavior of these imprudent banks, largely by examining the views, strategies, and behavior of the authoritative CEOs and other senior executives who had a vise-like grip on the leadership of these banks. We saw in Chapters 1 and 2 how a revised version of historical institutionalist theory offered a way of explaining such institutional behavior. We showed how bank leaders faced strong institutional incentives and market pressures to grow their balance sheets and profits, becoming almost slaves of the market. Yet, as we show here, these agents were on the whole also "true believers" who thought that markets were efficient; that securitization had dispersed risk; that risk management systems were effective; and that a national downturn in housing prices was unimaginably unlikely. There is no contradiction between arguing that bank executives appeared as both slaves of the market and true believers. Material incentives and ideas were in accord. Bankers believed in what they were doing and hence did not fundamentally question the pressures and incentives thrown up by the markets in which they operated. Even those bankers who did have some doubts nevertheless had strong remuneration incentives not to question the boom.

The particular combination of incentives and ideas is the key difference between the banks that crashed and the more prudent banks, such as JP Morgan, Goldman Sachs, and Wells Fargo, which survived the crisis and which we examine in Chapter 7. In these latter banks, executives were aware of market pressures to increase profits but also recognized the risks. Our account thus emphasizes institutional pressures on agents, but also shows how agents assess and operate within such contexts. Ultimately, as we argued in Chapter 1, contexts and agents shape one another. The agents who were sanguine about their context surged forward. Those who harbored doubts either resisted pressures to reengineer their balance sheets or reversed their positions prior to the onset of the crisis. This comparative difference in bank behavior underlines the significance of ideas and of individual agency in such contexts. All of the banks in the United States operated in essentially the same market and regulatory system. All were exposed to the broader structures of systemic risk, so the differences in question clearly stem from the banks themselves—from their internal assessments of the markets and their corporate strategies and cultures. Although we have argued that market incentives and institutional pressures seemingly "enslaved" bankers, it was only those bankers who were true believers in the markets who allowed themselves to become enslaved. Those who were more skeptical were more prudent and did not follow the herd.

As the famous sociologist Max Weber argued long ago, "Ideas, have, like switchmen, determined the tracks along which action has been pushed by the dynamic of interests" (Weber 1946, 280). For US bankers, it was ideas about the nature of financial markets and the perceived riskiness or otherwise of leveraged trading that were the focal points of financial innovation and the key drivers of the markets up until the crash. In this regard, as we show, there were strong similarities among the imprudent banks. They were run by authoritative and imperious CEOs. Once relatively sanguine views about the markets and the profit potential of leveraged trading were formed, there was nothing in the operating or institutional environments of these banks to check what would turn out to be disastrous behavior. The basic authority structures and operating procedures within these banks, as well as the main market and regulatory contexts, all supported and even incentivized the headlong rush to financial collapse. The authority of senior managers was sufficient to sideline or crush concerns or dissent regarding bank strategy emanating from less senior managers and especially risk managers. Boards and shareholders were also largely sanguine and sanctioned the forward rush. Ultimately, there were no effective checks on the overweening authority of senior managers bent on turning substandard mortgages into huge profits through what seemed to be a new kind of financial alchemy.

In this chapter, then, our aim is to zero in on the microdynamics of the US banks that got into trouble, showing exactly how bankers understood their situation and reacted to the wider incentives and pressures they confronted. How did the leaders of these banks understand the contexts in which they operated and the risks they were taking? How did they respond to market pressures, and how were their risk perceptions and appetites shaped by greed and ego-driven strategies, by risk-oriented remuneration packages, and by the apparent assurances offered by various risk management strategies? Moreover, to what extent did they understand the complexities of financial instruments and corporate entities they thought they controlled?

Market Pressures

National market conditions were central in shaping bank strategy. There were strong market pressures to grow balance sheets and dramatically elevate profits through leveraged trading. Failure to perform meant negative market reaction, plunging equity values, and perhaps takeover. Competition was also strongly endorsed by the authorities. By threatening traditional sources of profits, competition had the effect of encouraging many banks to reinvent themselves. For example, US investment banks were originally collectively governed on a partnership model. This encouraged a cautious approach to banking because each partner's money was on the line. "We lost the checks and balances, a system that provided a kind of curb on excessive risk taking, when we moved away from the partnership model," says one former senior banker (McGee 2010, 186). Increasingly, the partnership model was abandoned during the 1980s and 1990s as the investment banks became publicly listed, drawing in more capital and debt and increasingly moving into more aggressive trading strategies. Another way in which banks responded to competitive pressures was through mergers and takeovers. In the United States between 1990 and 2005 there were seventy "megamergers" involving banks with assets of more than $10 billion (FCIC 2011, 52). By growing their balance sheets, banks hoped to compensate for lower margins and acquire greater market power. However, the key response, as we saw in Chapter 2, was to engage in leveraged trading and securitization. As one bank insider puts it, the banks "chased yield. And they chased it big time . . . In a virtual feeding frenzy investors placed huge sums in increasingly riskier securities" (Tibman 2009, 100).

Executives and managers operated in a fishbowl, under intense scrutiny from an army of analysts and investors all clamoring for quick, high returns, especially during the frenzy of a boom. In *Businessweek*, Thornton, Henry, and Carter (2006) asked just prior to the crisis, "Why, then, are banks racing ahead to build bigger, more complicated trading operations, risking huge long-term losses? . . . For one, banks think they can handle the risks. For another, their shareholders and clients are demanding it." In such an institutional context, investors punish underperforming capital and see it as a takeover opportunity. Competition became warfare. Dick Fuld, the CEO at Lehman Brothers, thought "every day is a battle . . . You've got to kill the enemy" (Fishman 2008). As one banker put it, "Every quarter we'd get some kind of note about how this was going to be the biggest or most important quarter in the firm's history, asking us to keep focussed and deliver results" (McGee 2010, 85–66). Another banker stated, "From 1999 through to the middle of 2007, anytime you stopped participating, by *not* adding more risk or by *not* aggressively pursuing more transactions, you were wrong" (McGee 2010, 10). Morgan Stanley's CEO, John Mack

(2010), told the FCIC that things had become "so competitive and everyone is looking out for revenues and how to build the business . . . I can pass on this deal . . . but if I pass on the fourth or fifth one you are going to have people possibly leaving, and you are going to have business go away from you." Lloyd Blankfein, CEO at Goldman Sachs, recalls that the bank for a time accepted loose credit standards: "We rationalised [it] because a firm's interest in preserving and growing its market share, as a competitor, is sometime[s] blinding—especially when exuberance is at its peak" (Braithwaite and Guerrera 2010). As Citigroup's CEO, Chuck Prince, famously said amid the euphoria of the boom: "As long as the music is playing, you've got to get up and dance. We're still dancing" (FCIC 2011, 175). Chuck Prince later explained to the FCIC that the banks were under intense takeover pressure from private equity firms and that in such a context it was "not credible for one institution to unilaterally back away" (FCIC 2011, 175). Not dancing, it seemed, was not an option. As a senior banker argued, "What was happening at the bank that did that? The investment analysts downgrading it, the shareholders are unhappy, the employees are unhappy because their bonuses aren't as fat . . . The press are all over it, saying it's not well run" (McGee 2010, 10). Within the banks and investment houses the performance of individual traders and fund managers was also closely monitored. As one insider put it, "Once investing in lower rated, higher risk securities gained a foothold, it became impossible for individual managers to stick to their usual knitting. For any individual fund manager, abstinence would mean lagging performance versus peers . . . Not a recipe for job retention. Investors in funds, often blind to risk, would flee the underperforming ones" (Tibman 2009, 100–101).

Intense competition also explains falling credit standards at Fannie Mae and Freddie Mac. In the mid-2000s Fannie Mae found that its share of the US mortgage market was falling rapidly as "private label" investment banks aggressively started buying and securitizing mortgages. According to Fannie Mae's former chief business officer, Robert Levin (2010), "Our volume of business relative to the market continued to decrease to a level where we were concerned about losing relevance in the marketplace." According to a team of consultants, Fannie faced two "stark choices." It could continue with its existing business model and lose more market share or it could "meet the market where the market is" (Lowenstein 2010, 14). Executives decided to expand their Alt-A and subprime origination and securitization business. According to Kenneth J. Bacon (2010), Fannie's executive vice president:

> There was a consensus that we had to take more risk because we were falling behind the market, and with investors and customers . . . We had plenty of product [in 2008] that we didn't have in 2005 . . . It's not as much that Fannie Mae changed radically, it's that the market changed and we joined the parade later on . . . We couldn't control the pace. There was stuff out there, and we had to adjust to the market.

Bacon was asked by the FCIC whether mortgage originators had threatened to take their business to the investment banks if they refused to underwrite Alt-A loans. He replied that the threat remained "implicit."

> [The] Wall Street thing was not a threat; it was just a viable alternative. That was just real—when you gave a bid to somebody, you knew that they were getting a bid from someone else too. It was just a fact. I don't view it as a threat; it was that customers had new alternatives, which created a pressure on Fannie.

When asked what had gone wrong in the US housing market, he replied, "The market went wrong." Similarly, Daniel Mudd (2010), the former CEO of Fannie, told the FCIC: "Your relative market share with your customers or with the market informs you as to whether you are relevant or not. And obviously, if your market share goes to zero, you don't have a business. And so during this period of time, market share had gone from, as best I recall, the mid 50s down to mid-to-high 20s."

Another key incentive encouraging CEOs to aggressively pursue profits and market share was short-term corporate rivalry. The top ranked or so-called bulge bracket investment banks on Wall Street were clearly led by Goldman Sachs, widely acknowledged as the most innovative and profitable of the big investment banks. In the decade leading up to the crisis, Goldman had generated an annual average return on equity (ROE) of over 25%, while the four other large investment banks earned only around 15% annually. "It was clear to every other Wall Street CEO that chasing

Goldman Sachs was the only way to boost their personal wealth and simultaneously to keep their cantankerous shareholders pacified" (McGee 2010, 9). This competitive dynamic involved not only profits and remuneration but also the egos of rival bank leaders who became fixated on "beating Goldman." In the face of Goldman's surging performance "we all got Goldman envy," recalls one leading banker (Tett 2009, 134). According to a former Lehman Brothers insider, "Lehman Brothers had a Chairman and President who were determined to join the biggest financial operations on the planet" (L. McDonald 2009, 231). At Morgan Stanley in 2005, Phil Purcell was replaced by John Mack, a more aggressive CEO bent on beating Goldman by taking on more risk and leverage. As one banker observed, "It was very, very apparent to every CEO on Wall Street that Phil Purcell had been run out of Morgan Stanley because he couldn't keep up with the ROE that Goldman had, because he wasn't using enough leverage and taking on enough risks" (McGee 2010, 150).

Similarly, at Merrill Lynch, with its profits lagging behind those of the other bulge bracket investment banks, a new, aggressive CEO, Stanley O'Neal, was appointed in late 2002. "O'Neal turbocharged Merrill's profits, transforming a company that was held back by the modest profits of its financial advisory network into an aggressive, risk-taking operation that placed billion-dollar bets in the capital markets. O'Neal's vision had been to make Merrill more like Goldman Sachs, the perennial profit machine of Wall Street" (Farrell 2010, 231). In 2003, Merrill's co-president of global markets and investment banking, Dow Kim, instructed his underlings to do "whatever it takes" to take over the number one ranking in the collateralized debt obligation (CDO) business (FCIC 2011, 202). By 2006 Merrill had beaten the competition by originating almost $35 billion in mortgage-related CDOs, while second-ranked Morgan Stanley originated $21.3 billion (FCIC 2011, 202). A key and fateful decision at Merrill was to hire Osman Semerci to head the fixed-income division, which traded CDOs and other exotic instruments, in July 2006. Semerci's experience was mainly in sales, with little experience in fixed income. He was appointed to drive growth, and on his own reckoning had "six months to make this work or I'm out of here" (Farrell 2011, 29). Semerci drastically expanded trading in mortgage-backed securities (MBSs) during the latter part of 2006 and early 2007. In Farrell's (2011, 27) account this was like "taking a salesmen with the instincts of a riverboat gambler and making him the general manager of the casino." At the time, CEO Stanley O'Neal was challenged by a senior manager, Greg Fleming, over the move, and the following dialogue ensued: "But, Stan, you know what Semerci is like. This would be completely dysfunctional." O'Neal responded, "What you don't seem to understand, Greg, is that sometimes dysfunction is a good thing. Some of the most successful people on Wall Street operate that way" (Farrell 2011, 27). O'Neal was constantly pushing various divisions within the bank to take on more risk. "You didn't want to be in Stan's office on the day Goldman reported earnings," one senior manager recalls (Farrell 2011, 162).

The situation was similar at Bear Stearns. Williams (2010, 139) writes: "Bear's inferiority complex cannot be underestimated when trying to understand its surge in risk taking. Year after year, the corporate ethos at Bear remained the same: one day Bear would eclipse the Big Three—Goldman Sachs, Morgan Stanley and Merrill Lynch . . . Deep down, both Bear and Lehman remained envious of their much larger rivals." This type of competitive envy propelled Bear Stearns forward to take on bigger risks and aggressively expand its MBS trading, even as the market was turning down. None of these Goldman pretenders ended up besting its performance, and a number collapsed in the process.

The forward rush was also fueled because swashbuckling market traders and risk takers, who had largely displaced more traditional investment bankers, had risen to the top of corporate hierarchies during the boom (L. McDonald 2009, 92–93). By 2004 at Lehman Brothers, for example, capital markets activity, including trading and sales, accounted for 66% of the firm's revenue, compared to only 20% of revenue from more traditional investment banking activities (Williams 2010, 107). At Lehman Brothers, Dick Fuld made it clear to senior staff that he wanted the bank to take on bigger deals. Fuld "wanted risk, more risk, and if necessary bigger risks," according to a former insider (L. McDonald 2009, 233). He also supported major new investments in commercial real estate and gave aggressive traders like Mark Walsh, the head of the global real estate group, almost free rein within the bank. Lehman was one the largest MBS underwriters on Wall Street, with its balance sheet of global real estate bets ballooning to $89 billion in 2006, two-thirds of which was in commercial property (Williams 2010, 133). Within the mortgage division, as one insider puts it, "the risks they took were nothing short of awesome . . . It seemed everyone was admiring them and helping them . . . Whatever they needed—extra budget, permission for more risk—they got" (L. McDonald 2009, 111).

True Believers

Executives within the largest banks were responding to strong incentive structures. But what were they thinking? Perrow (2010, 309) derides the key agents responsible for the crisis, arguing that they "were aware of the great risks" they took and were "fully aware that [they] could harm their firms, clients and the public." We dispute this view. Instead, most bankers seem to have been true believers. Ideas that we now regard as not only flawed but quite bizarre survived because bankers were not rational but "boundedly rational" and were susceptible to myopia, overoptimism, and bandwagon effects, as outlined in general terms in Chapter 1. In 1996 the Federal Reserve chairman, Alan Greenspan, had expressed concern about "irrational exuberance" and the dangers of an asset price bubble in equity markets. Greenspan did not, however, seek to raise interest rates in order to calm markets because he also believed that the enlightened self-interest of shareholders whose capital was at stake would constrain bankers and reduce risk taking. In the wake of the 2008 crisis, however, Greenspan (2009) shifted to a view that recognized financial manias and how "an inbred propensity of human nature fosters speculative fever that builds on itself . . . [creating a crisis] much broader than anything I could have imagined." At the height of the euphoria in the run-up to the crisis many bankers were willing to take huge bets based on hunches and seemed only too willing to blindly follow the business leads set by their immediate competitors. They discounted what now seem like obvious warning signs, believing in overoptimistic assumptions about asset prices and risk management. Clearly, we need to understand how bankers understood the financial world and how they perceived and assessed risks.

The prevailing view among bankers was that the real estate market was sound; that securitized assets and associated risk had been distributed to other parts of the financial system; that asset and funding markets would remain liquid; and that the remaining risks had been either hedged through offsetting trades or covered through insurance mechanisms such as credit default swaps (CDSs). As late as 12 September 2008—three days before the failure of Lehman Brothers—JP Morgan predicted that the US growth rate would accelerate in the first half of 2009 (Greenspan 2013, 8). Bankers thought that the huge leverage they were carrying was safe because they assumed they could sell assets in highly liquid markets if needed to service debt. They simply did not envisage asset markets freezing. Nor did they assume that wholesale funding markets would freeze, so causing an immediate and, in many cases, a fatal funding crisis. The majority of bankers and commentators believed that the financial system was one in which risk had been calibrated, managed, and distributed through the financial system and that the profits being made by the largest banks were entirely sustainable. This is why so many senior bank executives lost so much of their own money when the crash came. In 2008 Dick Fuld, the CEO of Lehman Brothers, personally lost $260 million he had invested in the firm. The CEO of Bear Stearns lost closer to $700 million (see Haldane 2011 for a more general analysis of the personal losses incurred by senior bankers).

A core assumption made by these true believers was that markets were both efficient and self-correcting. In this cognitive world, past financial crashes were not interpreted as evidence of fragility but as indicating a capacity for self-correction. The economy and the banking system *had* recovered rapidly from the collapse of Long-Term Capital Management in 1998 and from the dot-com crash of 2000. In the years immediately prior to the crisis, bank share prices remained high and CDS premiums to insure bank debt remained exceptionally low (Eichengreen et al. 2009, 28). Bankers simply assumed markets worked—that those making poor decisions or taking excessive risks would be exposed and forced out of the market and that this could be done efficiently without causing *systemic* damage. Bankers also believed "senior" securitized assets on their own balance sheets rated AAA by the credit ratings agencies were extremely unlikely to default. This faith in the enduring value of securitized assets reflected the view that tranching had made these assets safe (especially the senior assets), but it also reflected a further and underlying faith in the stability of the US housing market. One senior banker had raised concerns about the housing market with the Federal Reserve but was told that house prices always tracked income and jobs growth and that both were rising (FCIC 2011, 19). Bankers did not discount the possibility of a housing downturn occurring in some parts of the country. But they believed that a major and synchronized downturn was exceptionally unlikely. The former chairman and CEO of Freddie Mac, Richard Syron (2010), told the FCIC: "You had all these dollars looking for deals, people chasing yield. And they said what product seems pretty safe? And housing seemed pretty safe. There hadn't been any national decline in housing prices since the great depression."

Bankers also believed they had sound risk management systems. The largest commercial and investment banks had invested heavily in risk management processes in the 1990s and 2000s and believed that, as a result, they could not only measure but minimize risk. There had been prior banking crises to sensitize senior management, such as the savings and loans crisis of the 1980s, the large CMO-related trading losses at Merrill Lynch in 1987, and the Long-Term Capital Management derivatives collapse in 1998. By the 2000s many bankers thought securitization as a system of risk dispersal as well as quantitative risk management strategies would help deal with risk vulnerabilities. But as trading in complex new securities boomed, risk management was found wanting. As one senior insider put it: "I was foolish enough to swallow the widely distributed, popular Lehman doctrine . . . I completely believed that over the years we had learned important lessons about risk from several brushes with death, and was absolutely certain we had become extremely risk averse" (Tibman 2009, 51).

In particular, senior bankers thought their corporate risk management systems using quantitative risk analysis systems such as value at risk (VaR) were first-rate. At Lehman's, according to Lawrence McDonald (2009, 176), "no one wanted to be the renegade who stepped over the sacred VaR guidelines. Should there be a disaster, there could only be one scapegoat, the man who . . . failed to obey the tried and true rules of VaR. Therefore, right or wrong, VaR was obeyed." Methodologies such as VaR estimated potential losses for a specific time period from a portfolio of securities or across a bank's entire operations and had been developed by the banks in the 1990s as a part of their efforts to persuade regulators that they could be trusted to manage their own balance sheets and reduce capital. Handing over risk analysis to the banks in this manner effectively handed a key element of regulatory authority to the private sector. Despite offering the apparent assurance of advanced quantitative risk assessment, in the wake of the crisis VaR has been widely criticized. The modeling tended to be based on parameters established from sampling commonly occurring events from past financial data, data that was limited in time span and that had typically been collected under relatively benign market conditions. Nor did VaR estimates include risk contained within off–balance sheet vehicles. The approach was weak at picking up tail risks or so-called black swan events (Taleb 2007). As the Long-Term Capital Management crisis of 1998 had shown, VaR modeling had completely failed to capture major tail risks in volatile markets. The backward-looking nature of the analysis was poor at factoring in dynamic or systemic changes as markets evolved, a major limitation in fast-moving markets. The complex securities at the heart of the crisis were novel and lacked an observable track record (Williams 2010, 102). In other words, they had no historical precedent and were thus impossible to model using past data. The new securities were also subject to new forms of nonlinear risk and correlation risks that were poorly understood. High levels of leverage within the system also meant that markets faced greater uncertainty and volatility (Williams 2010, 108). The net effect of VaR was to give firms an erroneous sense of security, to seriously underestimate risk and leave banks with too little capital in the face of the looming crisis. As Andy Haldane, the executive director of financial stability at the Bank of England, suggests, "These models were both very precise and very wrong" (quoted in Blyth 2013, 37). At the height of the crisis, when an alarmed Stan O'Neal at Merrill asked a senior risk analyst about the value of the bank's VaR calculations, "worthless" was the response (McLean and Nocera 2010, 316). As Alan Greenspan was later to admit, one implication of the crisis was that "the whole intellectual edifice [of risk management] had collapsed" (Andrews 2008).

Nor were risk analysis systems focused on broader systemic risks in market liquidity and wholesale funding markets that would be the undoing of many banks. We argued in Chapter 2 that banks had assumed that leverage risk could be dealt with if needed by selling securities in asset markets that would remain liquid. Bankers had also assumed that funding markets would remain liquid. Paul Friedman (W. Cohan 2009, 71), a senior managing director at Bear Stearns, told the FCIC that the bank did have some concerns about funding pressures and had started to reduce its exposure to short-term unsecured funding in the commercial paper market in late 2006 and into 2007. Funding requirements in this market were reduced from around $26 billion to $11.6 billion by the end of 2007. Such funding was seen as "confidence-sensitive" and was exposed to "rollover risk" if lenders refused to renew short-term funding lines. The bank also moved to increase the maturity of its funding. "By increasing the amount of its long-term secured funding, the firm believed that it could better withstand a liquidity event." Subsequently, however, by early 2008, other funding markets started to reduce the maturity of loans and insist on higher-quality collateral. Then, in March 2008, Bear Stearns confronted a full-on run. Despite Bear's efforts to reduce risk, William Cohan offers an objective assessment of the situation: "Bear Stearns had become absolutely addicted to cheap financing. They were totally reliant in the end on overnight repo financing. They essentially gave their creditors a vote about whether they would keep in business, which is absurd" (interview, 12 March 2012).

For those within the bank, the market reaction came as a shock. It was completely unexpected, largely because the bank had (wrongly) assumed that the markets would behave in a basically rational fashion and not fall prey to herding behavior. Bear Stearns and other banks did not comprehend or anticipate the sorts of systemic risks and vulnerabilities that had built up within the credit system. As Paul Friedman (2010) explains:

> Bear Stearns suffered from a run on the bank that resulted, in my view, from an unwarranted loss of confidence in the firm . . . This was prompted by market rumours, which I believe were unsubstantiated and untrue about Bear's liquidity position . . . It resulted in a rapid flight of capital from the firm that could not be survived . . . The firm did not anticipate—and, I believe could not have reasonably anticipated—that lenders would be unwilling to lend on a short-term basis even when the loans were fully collateralised by agency securities and other high quality assets.

The 2007–2008 crisis, then, was not some freak event but an organic outgrowth of prevailing and largely uncontested views about new financial opportunities and the wonders of "financial innovation." Charles Prince (2010b, 3) of Citigroup describes the crisis as "wholly unanticipated." Lloyd Blankfein (2010a) of Goldman Sachs likens it to a "hurricane." The Federal Reserve chairman, Ben Bernanke (2010), suggests that the crisis was a "perfect storm." Yet the FCIC (2011, xvii) concludes that "there were warning signs" and that "the tragedy is that they were ignored or discounted." McGee (2010, 241) argues that bankers became deluded by "magical thinking."

Prior to the crisis, explicit concerns had been raised about securities based on subprime mortgages, about the dangers of complex structured products, about the steep rise in leverage within financial firms, and about assumptions that the real estate market would remain solid. Warren Buffett had raised concerns about "financial instruments of mass destruction" as early as 2002. Dick Fuld had raised early concerns (which he was later to ignore) about the state of the US housing market and about how low interest rates were potentially creating a bubble (Tibman 2009, 85). In 2005 Lew Ranieri, a pioneer of MBSs, thought that the market had entered an "insanity phase." He warned about the risks of CDOs and thought that "too many investors don't understand the dangers" (W. Cohan 2009, 318). In 2005 a large money management firm, PIMCO, began to worry about MBSs and "severely limited" its participation. Paul McCulley, a managing director at PIMCO, told the FCIC that he and his colleagues began to get worried about "serious signs of bubbles" in 2005. They sent out credit analysts to twenty cities to do what he called "old-fashioned shoe-leather research," talking to real estate and mortgage brokers and local investors about the housing and mortgage markets. They witnessed what he called "the outright degradation of underwriting standards . . . And when our group came back, they reported what they saw, and we adjusted our risk accordingly" (FCIC 2011, 4). In the same year, former Federal Reserve chairman Paul Volcker warned of "really disturbing trends: huge imbalances, disequilibria, risks . . . as dangerous and intractable as any I can remember" (W. Cohan 2009, 293). In early 2007, a journalist from the *Financial Times*, Gillian Tett, published the concerns of some market participants in an article in which one senior analyst stated: "I have never seen anything quite like what is currently going on. Market participants have lost all memory of what risk is . . . I'm not sure what's worse, talking to market participants who generally believe 'this time is different,' or to more seasoned players who . . . privately acknowledge that there is a bubble waiting to burst" (quoted in W. Cohan 2011, 513). Steve Eisman, one of the heroes of Michael Lewis's (2010) *The Big Short*, as well as the hedge fund manager

John Paulson and the financial analyst Meredith Whitney (Banks 2011, 135–139), all predicted the crisis. A number of economists, including Wynne Godley, Stephen Keen, Nouriel Roubini, and Robert Shiller, not only predicted a downturn in the US housing market but predicted that the downturn would lead to a significant economic contraction and financial distress (Bezemer 2009). Even within the generally gung-ho ratings agencies there were concerns. As one senior analyst at Standard and Poor's wrote in an internal e-mail in late 2006, the CDO market was a "house of cards" awaiting collapse (W. Cohan 2011, 486). Some actors, then, were aware of the risks that had accumulated within the financial system. Furthermore, as we will see in Chapter 7, some leading bankers in the United States and the United Kingdom were also worried and acted on their concerns.

Most bankers and investors discounted the concerns noted above and were increasingly gripped by what Angelo Mozilo, the CEO of the giant mortgage originator Countrywide Financial, called a "gold rush mentality" (FCIC 2011, 5). As one banker put it, "There's a tendency for things to go crazy, for innovation for innovation's sake to take over" (McGee 2010, 87). Or as Erin Callan, a senior Lehman executive, put it in early 2006, "We're in one of those temporary nirvanas where issuers and investors both seem very happy" (Beales 2006, 26). Large banks often held large warehouse inventories of securities waiting to be assembled into CDOs, and super-senior tranches of CDOs were also piling up on bank balance sheets or in associated shadow banks. Increasingly, as an analyst in Merrill Lynch noted, the banks were "absorbing the risk that their clients were looking to get rid of" (Thornton, Henry, and Carter 2006).

Yet these senior assets were seen as safe; only the lower tranches would get hit if there were problems, or so it was thought. Amid the boom, bankers and investors simply assumed that subprime mortgagees would pay their mortgages and that house prices would not fall (FCIC 2011, 134). Even if problems were encountered, lenders assumed that collateral could be redeemed by liquidating assets. In contrast to assets held on the loan book, the assumption was that securitized assets held on the trading book were highly liquid and could be sold if needed (Barwell 2013, 22). When the securitization market collapsed, however, this assumption was found to be incorrect. No one wanted to buy MBSs at the height of the panic; value and liquidity evaporated.

Citigroup's chief risk officer (CRO), David Bushnell (2010), agreed with a characterization by the FCIC that "management had felt there was very little risk inherent in the super senior CDOs." Chuck Prince was assured by his co-head of investment banking, Tom Maheras, "We are never going to lose a penny on these super seniors" (FCIC 2011, 264). As Prince (2010a, 264) later testified before the FCIC, "Everybody believed . . . that the strength of the structuring process would keep the rising flood waters away from the super seniors." Even as the market started to show signs of turning in late 2006 and early 2007, most bankers continued to believe that concerns about a housing downturn were being exaggerated and that the market still presented good opportunities. Indeed, despite growing signs of a downturn, 2006 saw record sales of mortgage-backed CDOs totaling $470 billion. From late 2006, the banks created and sold over $1.3 trillion in MBSs and more than $350 billion in mortgage-backed CDOs (FCIC 2011, 18). As late as April 2007, "Citigroup's CDO desk increased its purchases of mortgage-backed securities because it saw the distressed market as a buying opportunity" (FCIC 2011, 261). Chuck Prince had been assured by David Bushnell that "house prices would have to go down 30% nationwide for us to have . . . problems, and that hasn't happened since the Depression" (FCIC 2011, 262). Later, Citigroup's Tom Maheras (2010, 212) would testify that "it was not within anyone's frame of reference that housing was going to drop on a national aggregate level by 30% over a year or two." Similarly, at Morgan Stanley, John Mack (2010) explained to the FCIC that he'd started to see cracks in the housing market by the second quarter of 2007, but "made the judgement that the mortgage market would not be as severe as it ended up being. So that was clearly a miscalculation, but we were not alone." Fundamentally, there was the basic view that the new securities were just not going to be a problem. As Chuck Prince (2010a, 190–191) explained to the FCIC:

> The context I bring to the analysis is this: We had a $2 trillion balance sheet for the company as a whole . . . We ended up in a situation where a very, very small relative dollar value of assets caused great harm to the company . . . I have said earlier that simply having the information that was known at the time, I am not sure would have made much difference. If David Bushnell would have come to me in June

> or July or a year earlier, the end of '06, and said I want you to understand that we are increasing our activity in this particular area or had said we are retaining these super seniors and had described to me what that meant and what the quality of the assets were and so forth as believed by the rating agencies, as believed by him as a risk professional, I think he would have pointed to the reported comment of Alan Greenspan that super seniors were as safe as U.S. treasuries. I think he would have pointed to Bernanke's comment that he did not see a large real estate crisis coming. I saw something from our chief economist, Lou Alexander, contemporaneous which said he did not think we were going to have a serious recession.
>
> If I had gone to Tom Mahera'[s] office in the spring of 2007 . . . and I had said Tom, I am nervous about these super seniors . . . and I said I want you to sell these triple A rated securities. And he would have said well, why? And I would say because I am nervous that in the long run, we are going to see a real estate crisis like we have never seen since the Depression. And I think that despite all the smart people who have done all the structuring, that the flood waters will actually get all the way up to that super senior level, *I think I would have sounded like a lunatic. No one thought that would be the case in the industry.* (Emphasis added)

Dick Fuld at Lehman Brothers was similarly sanguine. As late as December 2007 he was opining: "Our global franchise and brand have never been stronger, and our record results for the year reflect the continued diversified growth of our business. As always, our people remain committed to managing risk" (Tibman 2009, 106). Lawrence McDonald (2009, 110), a former Lehman bond trader, writes that "CDOs seemed safe, well recommended, highly rated in the hottest market around—a market with a fantastically low default rate. The real granite-hard backup for these securities was, of course, the house . . . the US housing market had never dropped more than five per cent in any year since the Great Depression." On the other hand, another Lehman insider writes that he was "stunned that so many believed the risk in these securities was close to zero" (Tibman 2009, 50). At Merrill Lynch, as the market was turning in 2007, Jeffrey Edwards, the chief financial officer, attempted to reassure investors by saying that "revenues from sub-prime mortgage-related activities comprised less than 1% of our net revenues," and that the bank's "risk management capabilities are better than ever and crucial to our success in navigating turbulent markets." Edwards, however, avoided mentioning the large increase in the bank's holdings of super-senior CDO tranches, the difficulty in selling these, even at a loss, or that the total holdings of Merrill's retained CDOs had reached over $30 billion (FCIC 2011, 258). As Dow Kim stated in 2007, "Everyone at the firm and most people in the industry felt that super-senior was safe" (FCIC 2011, 258).

At Bear Stearns, when the market began deteriorating in 2007, top executives saw only opportunities. The long-held view was that Bear had traditionally done well during market downturns. As a key Bear executive, Warren Spector, put it, "We are not afraid of a bear market . . . We've gained market share in these cycles" (W. Cohan 2009, 314). Another senior Bear Stearns executive argued that "the market has overreacted" and that predictions of worsening problems in the mortgage market should be taken "with a large grain of salt" (W. Cohan 2009, 317). The view that the market had overreacted was widely shared on Wall Street (W. Cohan 2011, 501). Bear thus expanded its mortgage-related business despite evidence of the market turning down, as did other firms such as Merrill Lynch and Citigroup (FCIC 2011, 281). In early 2007, Bear was even ramping up its mortgage origination business by purchasing Encore Credit, effectively doubling its capacity. Bear's 2006 annual report crowed about the bank's "number one position for the third consecutive year in US mortgage-backed securities underwriting." The report also emphasized the bank's "dedication to risk evaluation and management that has given us the ability to expand carefully and conservatively" (W. Cohan 2009, 321).

Internal Governance

Once CEOs and senior managers formed the view that what they were doing was safe, they were in a position to impose their views on their organizations. The standout feature of corporate governance within both investment and commercial banks in the United States was the sheer imperious authority wielded by CEOs. They had very substantial authority to hire and fire senior staff, define and steer corporate strategies, and if necessary sideline risk management staff. In many respects banks came to resemble prisons or the military, the kind of impersonal and disciplined "total institutions" famously analyzed by Erving Goffman (1961). Bank executives and traders were routinely expected to work between seventy and eighty hours each week, be available to work on weekends and public holidays, and be available for corporate social events. Loyalty was expected. Carney (2011) describes the fate of a new staff cohort at Goldman Sachs, summoned to a late Friday afternoon meeting. Upon arriving and waiting for five hours without any further communication, a number of them drifted off. Those that did were subsequently terminated. Meanwhile, at Lehman's, CEO Dick Fuld and his wife had strong connections with New York's Museum of Modern Art. Such was the hierarchy of the bank that senior Lehman managers were expected to attend museum events and donate to the museum (Ward 2010, 128).

Lehman Brothers was dominated by CEO Dick Fuld and by Joe Gregory, the firm's president. Although the bank had appointed Madelyn Antoncic as its CRO in 2000, she and the rest of the risk management team at Lehman were increasingly sidelined. As a former insider puts it, in her quest to better manage risk and hedge more effectively, "Madelyn eventually came up against an obstacle that also derailed others that stick to their principles: Joe Gregory" (Tibman 2009, 97). Antoncic was quoted at an industry conference in 2007 saying that at Lehman's the hedging of risk in MBSs was frowned upon because it reduced profits. Antoncic was eventually demoted after she had raised concerns about bank strategy (L. McDonald 2009, 268–269). Fuld and Gregory were intolerant of contrary views. At one meeting, Fuld, who was growing increasingly angry with Antoncic, told her to "shut up" (L. McDonald 2009, 268). As one insider puts it, "The CEO's authority was widely regarded as absolute . . . No one wanted to deliver bad news to Dick, fearing he would shoot the messenger" (Tibman 2009, 94). Two detailed insider accounts of the fall of Lehman's provide firsthand details of the suppression of internal debate and dissent within the bank (L. McDonald 2009; Tibman 2009). The most notable instance was when the global head of fixed income, Mike Gelband, and several other senior executives expressed serious reservations about Lehman's strategy and especially about its highly leveraged real estate exposures. Gelband and several other senior managers confronted Fuld and Gregory on a number of occasions in the run-up to the crisis, arguing that the real estate market was about to implode and that Lehman should be winding back its exposures (L. McDonald 2009, 234–235). As Lawrence McDonald (2009, 2) recounts:

> If only they had listened—Dick Fuld and his president, Joe Gregory. Three times they were hit with the irredeemable logic of three of the cleverest financial brains on Wall Street—those of Mike Gelband, our global head of fixed income, Alex Kirk, global head of distressed trading research and sales, and Larry McCarthy, head of distressed-bond trading. Each and every one of them laid it out, from way back in 2005, that the real estate market was living on borrowed time and that Lehman Brothers was headed directly for the biggest subprime iceberg ever seen.

Fuld and Gregory were unmoved; "the two of them steamrolled all dissent" (Tibman 209, 52). On one occasion Fuld said to Gelband, "You're too conservative. You don't want to take risk"—a deep insult to a trader (Tibman 2009, 86). In May 2007, Gelband resigned. He was replaced by Roger Nagioff, who had little experience in the fixed-income business (Ward 2010, 168). Within Lehman Brothers, "there were a lot of people in important positions without deep experience at a crucial time," as one senior manager put it (Fishman 2008).

Risk management was also deficient at Citigroup. The bank's regulator, the Office of the Comptroller of the Currency (OCC), had criticized Citigroup's risk management and had warned the bank as early as 2005 that "earnings and profitability growth have taken precedence over risk management and internal control," but to little avail (FCIC 2011, 199). Jaidev Iyer, a senior risk analyst at Citi, was reportedly barred from risk meetings because his seniors thought his vocal concerns about risk might jeopardize the standing of the risk division with the firm. As McGee (2010, 233) notes, this was not an isolated incident: "Across Wall Street, numerous other risk managers or business-unit heads who detected the risks their institutions were running and who tried to apply the brakes were fired, sidelined or stripped of power." An internal auditor at AIG, Joseph St. Dennis, raised concerns about the way in which the firm was pricing CDSs. The CEO,

Joseph Cassano, responded by saying, "I have deliberately excluded you from the valuation of the Super Seniors because I was concerned you would pollute the process." St. Dennis resigned the following month (Lowenstein 2010, 113). David Bowen, who was responsible for overseeing the quality of loans underwritten and purchased by Citigroup, had become concerned about loan quality, discovering in mid-2006 that 40 to 60% of the loans Citi was buying were defective. Bowen says his highly explicit warnings to senior management were largely ignored, "so we joined the other lemmings headed for the cliff." Later, Bowen's bonus was reduced, he was downgraded in his performance appraisal, and he went from supervising 220 staff to supervising just 2 (FCIC 2011, 19). The board at Citigroup was also kept in the dark. David Bushnell (2010, 40, 201), the CRO, recalls that the first time data on risk analysis stress tests were broken out for the super-senior tranches and presented to the board was as late as October 2007. Murray Barnes, Citigroup's risk officer assigned to the CDO desk, later admitted to "complacency" about the risks the desk confronted. As part of the escalation in risk taking, Citigroup's daily VaR limits increased from $63 million in 2001 to $105 million in 2005 (McGee 2010, 233). The risk management division also increased the CDO desk's limits on retaining super-senior tranches on the bank's books in the first half of 2007 (FCIC 2011, 261). In July 2007, Citigroup's CFO, Gary Crittenden, told investors that the firm had wound back its subprime exposures from $24 billion in late 2006 to $13 billion by June 2007. He reassured investors about the firm's "good risk management," but made no mention of the firm's super-senior exposures or the liquidity puts it had offered buyers since 2003 in which it had promised to buy back a CDO at the original selling price if the market failed (FCIC 2011, 263). Another member of Citi's risk management division admitted to the FCIC that she "was seduced by structuring and failed to look at the underlying collateral" (FCIC 2011, 262). Regulators later wrote, "Acknowledgment of the risk in its super senior AAA CDO exposure was perhaps Citigroup's biggest miss . . . Management felt comfortable with the credit risk of these tranches" (FCIC 2011, 261). For its part, the FCIC (2011, 303) concluded that Citigroup's regulator, OCC, "failed to take forceful steps to require mandatory corrective action, and it relied on management's assurances in 2006 that the executives would strive to meet the OCC's goals for improving risk management."

Similar dynamics were apparent at Bear Stearns under CEO Jimmy Cayne. As William Cohan (2009, 215) writes, "There were legendary stories within the firm about the viciousness with which Cayne could publicly dress down subordinates." As one senior executive noted, "The number of people admitted to the inner circle was very, very small and they had to have a similar mind set" (W. Cohan 2009, 222). Stan O'Neal at Merrill was also imperious. "After becoming CEO in 2002, he systematically eliminated any executive who had enough experience to challenge him" (Farrell 2010, 69). On one occasion, after being challenged by a senior legal officer over an investment, O'Neal ordered security to remove the offender from the building (Sorkin 2009, 144). O'Neal also insisted that senior executives speak only to him about important matters and not to each other. He rarely asked for any input when making decisions (McLean and Nocera 2010, 161). As a *Wall Street Journal* profile of O'Neal concluded: "Some former colleagues say Mr. O'Neal's talent and steely drive came with a tragic flaw: He didn't much engage in debate, kept his own counsel and had little use for the kind of strong-willed subordinates who might have helped him steer clear of the sub-prime troubles that brought him down" (Smith 2007).

Our argument, then, is that CEO imperiousness meant that good advice was often ignored, especially when it urged caution in the run-up to the crisis. As the FCIC (2011, 18) concluded, "At too many financial firms, management brushed aside the growing risks." Risk managers were often seen as wet blankets, as dampeners on profits. Consequently, risk management functions were often poorly resourced, understaffed, and lacked authority. At Washington Mutual the CRO circulated a memo to all his staff advising that the bank's risk management functions were being adapted to a "cultural change" and that, in future, the risk department would play a "customer service" role so as to avoid imposing a "burden" on loan officers (Lowenstein 2010, 33). Using a sample of seventy-four of the largest bank holding companies in the United States, Ellul and Yerramilli (2010) report that only a little over 50% had appointed a CRO as an executive officer, while only 20% had a CRO among the top five executives. In some cases, traders, who were obliged to seek approval for new product innovations from risk departments announced such deals only at the last minute after much of the groundwork had already been put in place in order to put pressure for approval on risk managers (McGee 2010, 219). The Senior

Supervisors Group (2009) found that across many financial institutions, risk management was fragmented, senior management did not routinely specify acceptable risk levels, compensation practices were only weakly linked to risk and were focused instead on staff recruitment and bonuses, and boards were often out of touch on key risk issues. At Bear Stearns, the FCIC (2011, 283) reports a postcrisis SEC review which found that the "risk management of mortgages at Bear Stearns had numerous shortcomings, including lack of experience by risk managers in mortgage-backed securities" and "persistent understaffing; a proximity of risk managers to traders suggesting a lack of independence; turnover of key personnel during times of crisis; and the inability or unwillingness to update models to reflect changing circumstances." A consultant's report prepared for Bear Stearns in early 2008, at a time when the bank still had almost $37 billion of mortgage-related securities on its balance sheet, noted that the bank's risk assessment was "infrequent and ad hoc," "hampered by insufficient and poorly aligned resources," "lacking authority," and "understaffed," and considered a "low priority" (FCIC 2011, 284).

Part of the problem here was internal institutional conflict and power struggles that saw risk-taking traders rise to the top of corporate hierarchies, with risk managers and analysts often shunted aside. As Tett (2009, 135) argues in relation to Merrill: "As with most Wall Street banks, departments competed viciously for resources and power, and the department that was most profitable usually had the most clout. As the CDO team posted more and more profits, it became increasingly difficult for other departments, or even risk controllers[,] to interfere." Similarly, as Williams (2010, 50) writes:

> A firm faces a built-in conflict between the managers and traders who are paid to take risk and the risk managers who are paid to prevent excessive losses from occurring. And while traders earn sizable bonuses when they make money, risk managers do not get paid similar bonuses when they prevent the firm from losing money. Traders have an asymmetric payoff on the upside, which encourages greater risk taking, while the risk managers have an asymmetric bias on the downside to avoid a blow-up that could cost them their jobs. It is not uncommon

for the middle and back office to be viewed as cost centers only standing in the way of the firm making additional profit.

CEOs also promoted the introduction of bonus systems that encouraged risk-taking behavior. The former Treasury secretary, Timothy Geithner, maintains that while "the financial crisis had many significant causes . . . executive compensation practices were a contributing factor . . . Incentives for short-term gains overwhelmed the checks and balances meant to mitigate the risk of excessive leverage" (Geithner 2009). Between 1995 and 2005, inflation-adjusted mean bonuses for senior executives in US commercial banks rose from $390,000 to $1.1 million (Mehran, Morrison, and Shapiro 2011, 38). Stanley O'Neal at Merrill had a package of $91 million in 2006. In 2007 Goldman's CEO, Lloyd Blankfein, had remuneration totaling almost $69 million. In 2006 the Goldman Sachs bonus pool totaled $16 billion (Crotty 2009, 565). As one insider puts it, "At Lehman, where employees owned nearly a third of the firm, share price performance was our religion" (Tibman 2009, 80). As another former Lehman's insider stated, "For all of us, the bonus pool was of paramount importance because the bonus pool represented most of our income" (L. McDonald 2009, 164). Because trades within banks were usually executed by individuals or small teams of traders, bank executives could measure performance and, in an increasingly competitive market, reward traders who had made the most profit for the bank with large bonuses. Poaching staff from other banks with large sign-on bonuses was also widespread. Although the rationale for tying employees' financial compensation to their performance was relatively uncontroversial, the actual operation of the bonus system was profoundly dysfunctional. Bonuses were calculated on the basis of the end-of-year mark-to-market profits or, incredibly, sometimes even on the basis of the volume of trades completed (Clementi et al. 2009). This gave traders a powerful incentive to make short-term trades—colloquially known as "I'll be gone, you'll be gone trades." Traders who decided to hold securitized AAA assets could also "book" as profit the difference between the amount the asset was worth on the market at that moment and the amount it was valued on the bank's balance sheets for bonus purposes. Frequently, the difference between these two was relatively small precisely because AAA assets were viewed by traders as being riskless. That is why in order to sustain large profits and bonuses, bankers had to retain tens of billions of dollars of such assets, exposing their bank to a considerable longer-term tail risk (FSF 2008, 9; BIS 2009, 8–9).

Within the banks, CEOs were not effectively checked by boards. Ideally, a key component of effective corporate governance is the capacity of boards to monitor, challenge, and discipline management. However, in virtually all of the banks in question, boards were instead heavily influenced by senior management. In many cases, the CEO was also the board chairman. Jamie Dimon at JP Morgan, Lloyd Blankfein at Goldman Sachs, John Mack at Morgan Stanley, and Jimmy Cayne at Bear Stearns were both CEO and board chairman. At Lehman's, Lawrence McDonald (2009, 226) writes, Richard Fuld "had turned Lehman's board of directors into a kind of largely irrelevant lower chamber . . . yet another group to rubber stamp his decisions." Nine members of the ten-person board were retirees, with only two board members with any direct experience in the financial sector, albeit from a very different era (Williams 2010, 188–192). Boards had limited authority and a limited purview. For example, boards often failed to clearly define their risk management role. A 2009 survey by Deloitte found that only seven out of the thirty banks it surveyed had boards with clearly defined risk roles (Economist 2010a). Information asymmetries were another problem. Many boards were simply unaware of the fine-grained details of risk exposures, and many board members knew little about complex structured finance. Keeping track of trading details was a major problem. As Goldman's president, Gary Cohn, explains, "Unless bank boards want to sit in the executive office and look at the composition of the balance sheet every day, it's going to be very difficult for them to set the real leverage targets and understand what they're doing" (Deogun 2009). According to Citigroup's Robert Rubin, it is the company's risk management executives, not the board, who are primarily responsible for avoiding problems. "The board can't run the risk book of a company . . . The board as a whole is not going to have a granular knowledge" of operations (Blodget 2008). At Merrill Lynch, the board was not informed about the bank's massive exposures to CDOs until as late as September 2007, at which point the board was apparently "startled" at the news. To better understand the situation, some members asked for tutorials on CDOs (McLean and Nocera

2010, 317). At a shareholders' meeting amid the crisis, one of Merrill's founding CEOs, Win Smith, stated, "I stand here today to say shame to both the current as well as former directors who allowed . . . CEO [Stan O'Neal] to wreak havoc on this great company" (Farrell 2010, 403). Once bank profits started to fall in late 2006 and early 2007, boards did start to exert greater authority by demanding the resignation of suddenly tarnished CEOs. There is, however, little evidence that boards played an active governance oversight role in the years in which the banks were recording record profits prior to the crisis. Boards met infrequently, lacked key information, and often had no experience in banking or finance. They failed to effectively challenge—let alone change—bank strategy (Mehran, Morrison, and Shapiro 2011, 18).

While CEOs were imperious, this did not mean that they were able to effectively control every aspect of their organizations. A key problem with bank governance was that many CEOs and top managers did not have much experience in the rapidly evolving and highly complex world of structured finance. For example, many CEOs were often unaware of the fact that their banks had shifted from a policy of originate-and-distribute to one of originate-and-hold. Dick Fuld maintained that Lehman was "in the business of removal not storage" (Farlow 2013, 66). But this was simply incorrect. At Citigroup, the incoming CEO, Vikram Pandit, who had previously been the CEO at the subsidiary firm Citi Alternative Investments, had to be told that Citigroup had insurance to cover itself on defaults on CDOs but not on declines in their market value (Lowenstein 2010, 121). As the Wall Street veteran Henry Kaufman (2012) writes: "Top executives must navigate through a blizzard of arcane formulas and oversee activities in far-flung operational units in order to assess and manage risk properly. Because they often lack the time and tools to monitor diligently, they must rely on the veracity of others." This is an important insight because, despite the overarching authority of CEOs and senior management, they cannot easily control the organization at a more detailed level. This means that increasingly, as the complexity of the organization grows, detailed operational "power resides in middle managers" (Kaufman 2012). Indeed, as the FCIC (2011, 260) reports, at Citigroup, CEO Chuck Prince and the chairman of the executive committee of the board, Robert Rubin, were not aware that the firm's total subprime exposure by late 2007 was $55 billion, far more than had been previously disclosed to investors. Moreover, Prince and Rubin did not know that the investment banking division had retained large volumes of CDOs on the bank's books, to the tune of almost $20 billion. Nor did they know that the bank had sold large volumes of CDOs covered by liquidity puts totaling more than $25 billion. The bank's financial control group had warned about the liquidity puts in 2006, but to no avail (FCIC 2011, 260). Eventually the bank was forced to buy back all of the paper that had been subject to the puts. It was also the case that the firm's securitization division had become concerned about the deteriorating quality of mortgages in 2006 but had failed to warn other divisions within the bank, including the CDO desk, again highlighting the bank's fragmented corporate structure and the fact that there was "no dialogue across the business" (FCIC 2011, 261).

This siloing effect and lack of communication across business units was in fact typical of many financial institutions. Tett (2009, 241) writes that "by 2007, Citi was operated as a vast empire of business silos, which tended to be so fragmented—and feuding—that they rarely interacted. As a result, few of the bankers outside the CDO silo knew the details of how the securitization machine worked." Robert Rubin told the FCIC, "I don't think anybody focussed on the CDOs. This was one business in a vast enterprise, and until the trouble developed, it wasn't one that had any particular profile" (FCIC 2011, 262). And as Citigroup's co-head of investment banking, Tom Maheras (2010), puts it: "I don't think it would have been possible for me to have a hands-on role in a business as small as that. It would have been an impossible task given the number of businesses we were in . . . It did not rank as an area with significant risk in it, so it didn't get much of our focus or attention." Maheras said he spent "a small fraction of 1 per cent of his time thinking about or dealing with the CDO business" (FCIC 2011, 262). Similarly, Chuck Prince (2010a, 105) told the FCIC:

> I am not sure that I at that point in time even had any specific understanding of our, of the mechanics of our CDO business. This was a very small part of one part of one division of the company. I mean, we had a large business. There would be no reason, unless I happened to have worked in the fixed income business, for me to have any familiarity with that detailed level of product activity.

This compartmentalization and lack of effective understanding and communication also afflicted Bear Stearns. Warren Spector, the head of the fixed-income division, was the only member of the five-person Bear Stearns executive committee who was familiar with the firm's burgeoning reliance on such instruments. "Spector was the architect of the strategy to bulk up the fixed income division . . . Cayne, the former broker, had only a vague understanding of these exotic financial instruments." The committee was thus "exceedingly dependent on the expertise of Spector, who was himself becoming imperious and distant" (W. Cohan 2009, 291). Moreover, a series of personal spats between Spector and Cayne had increasingly left Spector on the outer edge, at a time when "the bull market in credit stampeded to unprecedented levels" (W. Cohan 2009, 291). It was also the case that Bob Steinberg, the CRO, "was unable to get from Spector a full accounting of what was going on" (W. Cohan 2009, 291). Later, following the sacking of Spector, Cayne attempted to better understand the business, but according to one senior manager, "It was clear when Warren left, Jimmy had no idea what we did for a living in fixed income" (W. Cohan 2009, 421). Soon after the collapse of two of the bank's major hedge funds in July 2007, in a boardroom conference call with investors, Cayne was asked a relatively simple question about the CDO business. According to a senior executive, Paul Friedman, "All heads in the room swivelled to Jimmy, who . . . went blank, like a deer in the headlights. Sam Molinaro jumped in to save him and said Jimmy had left the room. Our vaunted CEO was incapable of answering a single question" (W. Cohan 2009, 380–381). Soon after, on 17 July, the firm announced that one of its major hedge funds had lost 90% of its value. Instead of attempting to lead the firm through the crisis, the very next day Cayne and Spector absented themselves to go to Nashville to play in a ten-day national bridge tournament. Cayne resigned as CEO in January 2008 but remained as nonexecutive chairman of the board. He later told the FCIC (2011, 285), "I take responsibility for what happened."

At Lehman Brothers, senior management was also out of touch. Fuld was often out of the office and left the day-to-day running of the bank to Joe Gregory. But neither Fuld nor Gregory was aware of the intricacies of the MBS market. Nor were they much involved in the management of the investment banking arm of the business (Tibman 2009, 52). A senior executive had pointedly warned Fuld that Gregory "was not minding the store . . . He's not watching your back on risk" (Sorkin 2009, 118). But Fuld was increasingly isolated. He "worked within a tight palace guard . . . As the years went by Fuld had tightened his circle, shutting out more and more key people from downstairs floors where the daily action seethed" (L. McDonald 2009, 90–91). At one point, Mike Gelband tried to explain the dangers of CDOs and structured investment vehicles to Fuld, but "Fuld just didn't get it" (L. McDonald 2009, 235). As the firm's head of fixed income, Mike Gelband confided, "neither [Fuld] nor [Gregory] understands the dangers of securitization, the leverage in the system. They cannot understand . . . When I beg of them to listen . . . their eyes glaze over" (L. McDonald 2009, 235). Both Fuld and Gregory were operating on hunches and a manic quest for growth. In a classic illustration of "bounded rationality" and the tenets of behavioral finance theory, Gregory once said he believed in "trusting your instincts, even if analysis told you something completely different" (Fishman 2008). As the FCIC (2011, 177) notes, "Senior management regularly disregarded the firm's risk policies and limits." Even as the market was declining, Lehman was selling some of its subprime assets but was simultaneously plunging into new commercial real estate ventures, such as taking a $5.4 billion stake in Archstone Smith, a publicly traded real estate trust, in late 2007 (FCIC 2011, 176).

Merrill Lynch also suffered from similar dysfunctions. Merrill's chief economist, David Rosenberg, was ignored when he warned of the increasingly parlous state of the mortgage market in early 2006 (L. McDonald 2009, 157). Despite the fact that CDS insurance costs on CDOs were rising because of perceived riskiness, Merrill continued to load CDOs onto its balance sheet. One senior manager, Jeffrey Kronthal, tried to limit Merrill's holdings, but to no avail. Kronthal subsequently resigned, to be replaced by Osman Semerci. Semerci drastically expanded MBS trading during the latter part of 2006 and early 2007. However, few people outside Semerci's tight circle were told about the rapid buildup of super-senior CDO tranches on the bank's balance sheet. Semerci had even assured the board in early 2007 that the firm's exposures to the subprime market were limited and amounted to only 2% of the bank's revenues. In July 2007 O'Neal had sent out a memo saying "Over the last six months we have worked successfully to position ourselves for a more difficult market for CDOs and have been proactively executing market strategies to significantly reduce our risk exposure . . . We are very comfortable to with our current exposure to this asset class" (Farrell 2010, 170). Although the bank had reduced its exposure to lower-rated CDO tranches, O'Neal did not know the full extent of the bank's exposures to the more senior tranches. A week later, on 22 July, at a meeting of the board's finance committee, Semerci finally revealed that Merrill had accumulated over $34 billion in CDOs on its books in the first half of 2007 (Farrell 2010, 18).

> Under normal risk controls, Merrill Lynch traders would not be able to amass a $1 billion position in a liquid, reliable stock like General Electric. When bankers in Merrill's private equity division wanted to invest $475 million in a joint buyout of Hertz in 2005, the approval process had taken months and required the backing of the board of directors. Somehow Merrill's FICC department had amassed the largest single CDO position in the history of Wall Street. (Farrell 2010, 22)

O'Neal himself could have been more proactive, but his understanding of the finer points of super-senior risk was limited. The risk department did not even report directly to the board. O'Neal and the firm's co-president, Ahmass Fakahany, finally became alarmed and asked for a full investigation into the firm's CDO exposures. This took time because Semerci was uncooperative. Farrell (2010, 23) reports one instance where Semerci called up John Breit, head of market risk management, and told him to stop inquiring into the fixed-income division's books—specifically because their contents were "none of your fucking business."

Finally, after further investigations, the firm was confronted with the full scale of its exposures and its insufficient hedges as the market was collapsing. It was found that in his year as head of fixed income, Semerci had created over $70 billion in new CDOs, sold $40 billion of these, and retained $35 billion on the bank's books. In August 2007 the decision was belatedly taken to sell off the firm's CDOs, but by then few buyers were forthcoming other than at fire sale prices. O'Neal himself "had never been the kind of CEO who walked the trading floor. The intricacies of the firm's trading positions held no interest for him, except when they showed profits or losses" (McLean and Nocera 2010, 234). As Farrell (2010, 36) concludes,

"Merrill Lynch had just violated the cardinal rule of every financial institution on Wall Street, which holds that no business unit should ever be given enough leeway to sink the entire firm." Increasingly, O'Neal had become isolated.

> At the same time Goldman executives were cancelling vacations to deal with the burgeoning subprime crisis, O'Neal was often on the golf course, playing round after round by himself. He had little or no direct contact with any of the firm's operations . . . Always a loner, he had become isolated from his own firm. He had no idea that key risk managers had been pushed aside or that people he had put in important positions were out of their depth. (McLean and Nocera 2010, 314)

In October 2007, a senior manager dropped into O'Neal's office to find the lights off and O'Neal slumped in his chair, muttering, "That fucking Semerci . . ." (Farrell 2011, 73). On 24 October, Merrill informed the market of third-quarter losses amounting to almost $8 billion, mainly from its CDO and subprime mortgage holdings. Six days later O'Neal resigned from the bank, taking home a severance package of $161 million.

A key problem was that corporate development and financial innovation had greatly increased the scale and complexity of banking operations as well as the complexity and opaqueness of the securities being traded. "Bank officers faced with this sort of complexity naturally struggle to manage every aspect of their business effectively" (Mehran, Morrison, and Shapiro 2011, 20). As Lloyd Blankfein of Goldman Sachs admitted in a speech in 2009, the banking industry "let the growth and complexity in new [financial] instruments outstrip their economic and social utility as well as their capacity to manage them." As a former senior Lehman's insider puts it, "There are no CEO's on Wall Street who, in today's world, understand the complexities of all aspects of the firm's business" (Tibman 2009, 86). Part of the problem here was the sheer size and sprawling multidivisional nature of the banking operations in question. During the 1990s and 2000s, the banks had grown into huge behemoths through mergers and acquisitions. JP Morgan, for example, had grown from $667 billion in assets in 1999 to $2.2 trillion in 2008, a compound annual growth rate of 16% (FCIC 2011, 65). Such rapid growth had in many cases produced large, complex entities.

Citigroup, for example, was a vast and complex multidivisional organization, with nearly 2,500 subsidiaries and with operations spread across eighty-four countries.

Financial markets themselves had also become highly complex. Alan Greenspan had commented that "the complexities of some of the instruments that were going into CDOs bewilder me" (Sorkin 2009, 89). As a former Lehman executive notes, "What differentiates the financial meltdown . . . from crises that preceded it is the utter complexity, the hopelessly tangled tentacles of today's financial markets" (Tibman 2009, 110). Greenspan (2009) comments that "it is clear that the levels of complexity to which market practitioners, at the height of their euphoria, carried risk-management techniques and risk-product design were too much for even the most sophisticated players to handle prudently." A key issue was the novel and complex nature of the securities that were developed and traded. CDOs often contained thousands if not hundreds of thousands of mortgages packaged into complex, tranched structures that could take six months to construct. In 2006 Bear Stearns constructed a CDO composed of 2,800 Alt-A mortgages divided into thirty-seven tranches (Lowenstein 2010, 51). Most investors and traders and even most risk analysts had not bothered or found it too difficult to assess or look in detail at the quality of the underlying mortgages that were used to build these structures. As Citigroup's Tom Maheras (2010) admits, his own bank was deficient. "I recall coming to the conclusion . . . that there was not a significant enough amount of expertise about subprime mortgage collateral embedded within the structured credit unit." John Mack (2010) at Morgan Stanley similarly admitted that "we should have had much more robust risk systems . . . Risk management [is] clearly something we should have done better . . . I think complexity had something to do with it." Secrecy and lack of transparency were also affecting the market. As Tett (2010 126) notes: "By 2005 complex credit was evolving so rapidly, and the banks were in such fierce competition with each other, that they kept much of their activity in the CDO or credit default swap world relatively secret from each other. That made it hard for outsiders to track how the market was developing." CDOs were complex enough, but CDO squared and synthetic CDOs were even more complex. Ultimately they were all based on bets on the performance of underlying securities. Synthetic CDOs could be built without the need for fresh mortgages, thus allowing the market to balloon. They also allowed for multiple bets on the same underlying securities, thus rapidly multiplying risk and uncertainty and the scale of the ultimate collapse. Goldman alone had packaged and sold $73 billion in synthetic CDOs from 2004 to early 2007. A further problem was the complexities in the CDS markets—those over-the-counter swaps and trades that were supposed to act as insurance on the mortgage-backed assets. As the FCIC (2011, xxiv) notes, the CDS market "fueled the mortgage securitization pipeline" and further inflated the real estate bubble by reassuring investors that they had insured or covered their bets. The problem was that the monoline insurers, such as AIG, would collapse under the spiraling weight of claims amid the crisis. When Stan O'Neal at Merrill finally realized the catastrophic exposures of his firm, he asked a senior risk manager, John Breit, "What about all the protection we bought?" Breit replied that AIG had already collapsed and that the other big monoline insurers would be insolvent long before they could pay Merrill (McLean and Nocera 2010, 316).

External Governance

CEOs may have been able to sideline internal sources of opposition and scrutiny, but outside institutional investors, credit ratings agencies, and regulators had, on paper at least, not only the responsibility but the authority needed to check bank behavior. Yet they failed to do so.

Shareholders tended to be opportunistic, short-term equity holders with a narrow focus on bottom-line returns, with few incentives to reduce risk taking given the high rewards during the boom. Reward structures were thus asymmetrical. On the downside, investors might lose their equity. But on the upside, there were potentially huge gains to be made from riding the boom. Moreover, downside risk was limited by deposit insurance in the commercial banking sector and by the promise of a government bailout if the bank was threatened. US federal regulators had, after all, intervened to rescue the savings and loan industry in the late 1980s and then, in 1984, the seventh largest bank, Continental Illinois. During a subsequent congressional hearing, the comptroller of the currency stated what many observers had previously only suspected, that the government would not allow the eleven largest "money center" banks to fail. One congressman responded by suggesting that "we [now] have a new kind of bank. It is called 'too big to fail'" (FCIC 2011, 37). As a report by the Federal Reserve Bank of New York (Mehran, Morrison, and Shapiro 2011, 18) concludes, "Each of these effects reduced the sensitivity of bank investors to bank risk taking, because investors anticipate a degree of state support even in failure conditions. The consequence is a severe attenuation of market discipline." To use a distinction first employed by Hirschman (1970), investors had little incentive to employ "voice" because they could so easily "exit," often at minimal cost.

The market intelligence provided by credit rating agencies such as Moody's, Standard and Poor's, and Fitch fueled rather than restrained the markets. These firms had traditionally assessed the creditworthiness of companies and governments. In the decade prior to the crisis, the agencies found a lucrative new role rating complex securitized assets. This was important because in a number of countries regulatory rules precluded certain classes of investors, most notably pension funds, from investing in assets that were not rated AAA (Bruner and Abdela 2005). The credit ratings agencies therefore played a major role in legitimating and popularizing securitization and the market for CDOs (Richardson and White 2009). In 2004 both Moody's and Standard and Poor's changed their ratings methodologies to make it easier to give high ratings to CDOs. Up to a point, it is clear that the ratings agencies were true believers: they genuinely thought it would be almost impossible for an AAA-rated security to default. Yet it is also true that the ratings agencies stood to profit substantially from issuing AAA ratings.

From the late 1990s under the Basel accord process, the ratings agencies had been handed a huge outsourced responsibility to play a key role in assessing risk within the banks and financial markets. As the CEO of Goldman Sachs, Lloyd Blankfein (2009), would later write:

> Too many financial institutions and investors simply outsourced their risk management. Rather than undertake their own analysis, they relied on the rating agencies to do the essential work of risk analysis for them. This over-dependence on credit ratings coincided with the dilution of the coveted triple A rating. In January 2008, there were 12 triple A-rated companies in the world. At the same time, there were

> 64,000 structured finance instruments, such as collateralised debt obligations, rated triple A. It is easy and appropriate to blame the rating agencies for lapses in their credit judgments. But the blame for the result is not theirs alone. Every financial institution that participated in the process has to accept its share of the responsibility.

As the FCIC (2011, 146) concludes, "The machine churning out CDOs would not have worked without the stamp of approval given to these deals by the three leading ratings agencies." As Citigroup's Chuck Prince (2010a, 118), puts it, "If the rating agencies hadn't approved the products, hadn't certified them as it were, people wouldn't have bought them. The more complex the instruments are, the more people rely on the ratings." At Lehman's, "it was one heck of a plus for a Lehman salesman to go out with a bond that they could prove was investment grade rated, because investors needed little encouragement to go for AAA-rated CDOs. CDOs were considered the same as government bonds, AAA-rated by the most prestigious ratings agencies in the United States" (L. McDonald 2009, 110, 175). CDO managers like Wing Chau, who managed CDOs mostly underwritten by Merrill Lynch, commented, "Unfortunately, what lulled a lot of investors, and I'm in that camp as well, what lulled us into that sense of comfort was that the ratings stability was so solid and that it was so consistent" (FCIC 2011, 133).

Part of the reason for the failures here is that "at no time did the ratings agencies 'look through' the securities to the underlying subprime mortgages" (FCIC 2011, 146). Moreover, the agency analysts tended to use the same methodologies they had previously applied to less risky mortgages and applied these to the new breed of structured securities based on subprime mortgages (Tibman 2009, 65). Part of the problem was the novelty of the new products. "There isn't any performance information available on any of these products just yet because they are still very new to the market," explained one senior Standard and Poor's analyst (W. Cohan 2011, 485). The agencies were also chronically understaffed and analysts overstretched (FCIC 2011, 149). The agencies were also increasingly earning a high proportion of their profits from such ratings. Indeed, as much as 80% of the growth in their revenue in the run-up to the crisis was coming from rating complex securities (McGee 2010, 293). Offering high ratings implied more repeat business from clients (FSF 2008, 33). More insidiously, the ratings agencies were also being paid by the banks to offer advice on how best to package securities to get a AAA rating. Banks would often threaten to boycott the agencies if they failed to deliver appropriate ratings. Richard Michalek, a former Moody's vice president, when asked by the FCIC whether banks threatened to withdraw business if they didn't get the desired ratings, answered, "Oh God, are you kidding, all the time . . . I mean, that was routine" (FCIC 2011, 210).

We have shown how the postwar system of financial regulation was progressively dismantled or watered down in the 1980s and 1990s. Nonetheless, regulatory bodies retained overall authority for the well-being of the US financial system. In 2005 the SEC (2005, 6) received $913 million in funding, employed 3,800 staff, and initiated 947 investigations, 335 civil proceedings, and 294 administrative proceedings in relation to mutual fund and investment adviser fraud, accounting fraud, and failures at self-regulatory organizations. Yet financial regulation in the 2000s increasingly resembled a Potemkin village. Regulatory bodies, whose leaders were appointed and budgets set by politicians, adopted a largely benign view of markets and the financial system. A key cheerleader was Alan Greenspan. Although real estate prices were rising by more than 10% per annum, ten times the long-term average, Greenspan reassured Congress in 2005 that "a 'bubble' in home prices for the nation as a whole does not appear likely" (FCIC 2011, 158). In the same year, Ben Bernanke, the then chair of the President's Council of Economic Advisers, agreed. Rapidly increasing house prices, he argued, "largely reflected strong economic fundamentals" (Tett 2009, 122). Even if house prices did fall, Greenspan thought this would "not have substantial macroeconomic implications" (FCIC 2011, 16). Greenspan and others also argued that financial innovation had made markets safer and more resilient. In 2004 he argued, "Not only have individual financial institutions become less vulnerable to shocks from underlying risk factors, but also the financial system as a whole has become more resilient" (Williams 2010, 186). In 2005 Greenspan argued that "nationwide banking and widespread securitization of mortgages makes it less likely that financial intermediation would be impaired" in the event of falls in house prices (FCIC 2011, 16). He also thought that "the use of a growing array of derivatives and the related applications of more sophisticated approaches to measuring and managing risk are key factors underpinning the greater resilience of our largest financial institutions." Shortly after he had been appointed chairman of the Federal Reserve, Ben Bernanke (2006) argued that "the management of market risk and credit risk has become increasingly sophisticated" and that "banking organizations of all sizes have made substantial strides over the past two decades in their ability to measure and manage risks." Even when the crisis started to unfold in 2007, Bernanke reassured Congress that the "problems in the sub-prime market were likely to be contained" (FCIC 2011, 17). As late as May 2007, Bernanke boldly declared, "We do not expect significant spill overs from the sub-prime market to the rest of the economy or to the financial system" (Williams 2010, 128). Treasury Secretary Timothy Geithner also claimed that "in the financial system we have today, with less risk concentrated in banks, the probability of systemic financial crises may be lower than in traditional bank-centered financial systems" (Crotty 2009, 572).

Deep liquid markets that could accurately price risk and risk dispersal strategies, as well as advanced risk analysis and hedging devices, were all seen in a highly sanguine light and as key innovations that underpinned the new resilience. In 2003 the vice chairman of the Fed spoke of the "truly impressive improvements in methods of risk measurement" within financial institutions (FCIC 2011, 53). Despite the fact that banks were loading up on CDOs and thus concentrating risk, the IMF (2006, 25) claimed that "the dispersion of credit risk by banks to a broader and more diverse set of investors, rather than warehousing such risk on their balance sheets, has helped make the banking and overall financial system more resilient."

Market participants were also seen as seasoned professionals. Former Treasury secretary Lawrence Summers told Congress that the "parties to these kinds of contracts are largely sophisticated financial institutions" (Williams 2010, 186). As late as spring 2007, Hank Paulson, the former CEO at Goldman Sachs and, at that point, Treasury secretary, told an audience that "an open, competitive, and liberalized financial market can effectively allocate scarce resources in a manner that promotes stability and prosperity" (McGee 2010, 273). Greenspan believed that the "self-interest of market participants generates private market regulation" (FCIC 2011, 53) and that government regulation is not "only unnecessary . . . [but] potentially damaging" (Lowenstein 2010, 62). He thought the "regulation of derivatives transactions that are privately negotiated by professionals is unnecessary" (Greenspan 1998). Therefore, there seemed to be little need for activist regulation by government. Later, in the wake of the crisis, Greenspan would admit to the House Committee on Oversight and Government Reform that "those of us who have looked to the self-interest of lending institutions to protect shareholders' equity, myself included, are in a state of shocked disbelief" (Andrews 2008).

The financial crisis also exposed failings not only in regulatory philosophy but also in regulatory structure. US banks faced an "alphabet soup" of regulators, more than one hundred in total (Joyce 2009, 60). This mattered because financial institutions that fell under multiple regulatory agencies were allowed to select their primary regulator. Kwak and Johnson (2010, 96) argue that because some regulators depended upon regulatory fees paid by firms for a large part of their income, there was a regulatory "race to the bottom." For example, the giant mortgage originator Countrywide changed from the OCC to the Office of Thrift Supervision (OTS) after the latter promised to be more "helpful" (McGee 2010, 259). Alan Greenspan defended this structure of regulation, arguing that it would help *discipline* regulators. "The current structure provides banks with a method . . . of shifting their regulator, an effective test that provides a limit on the arbitrary position or excessively rigid posture of any one regulator. The pressure of a potential loss of institutions has inhibited excessive regulation and acted as a countervailing force to the bias of a regulatory agency to overregulate" (FCIC 2011, 54).

The banks were also very adept at circumventing regulation, especially through over-the-counter (OTC) derivatives trading, through off–balance sheet activities, and through offshore shadow banks. The main regulatory agencies, the Federal Reserve and the SEC, as well as other key agencies such as the OCC and the OTS, also had limited purviews. In 2004 Treasury Secretary John Snow had urged regulators to address the proliferation of poor lending standards, but was struck with the limited remit and purview of individual regulators. "Nobody had a full 360-degree view. The basic reaction from financial regulators was, 'Well there may be a problem. But it's not in my field of view'" (FCIC 2011, 172). Regulatory agencies also lacked assertiveness and were administratively weak and often understaffed. Some regulators also seemed averse to the very principle of regulation. The head of the OTS until 2005, James Gilleran, had posed in a photograph wielding a chain saw cutting regulatory red tape and went on to cut the agency's staff by 25%. Not surprisingly, the OTS became a favored regulator. The financial institutions it regulated ended up being the biggest suppliers of subprime mortgages that helped fuel the meltdown (McGee 2010, 258). The head of the SEC, Christopher Cox, also adopted a benevolent view of the markets and cut back on regulation and enforcement activities. The net effect was that the banking sector lacked effective "adult supervision," as McGee (2010) puts it. The dilution of regulatory standards during the 1990s and early 2000s in the United States liberated banks and investors and enabled them to increase leverage and develop and trade in ever more exotic securities. The prevailing regulatory view also meant that regulators were reluctant to shift the focus of their activities in response to the evolution of financial markets. The rapid growth of subprime lending and the rapid growth of the securitization markets in the 2000s are clear examples the effects of regulators looking the other way. The FCIC (2011, xvii) points to the "Federal Reserve's pivotal failure to stem the flow of toxic mortgages, which it could have done by setting prudent mortgage-lending standards." Political leaders and regulators also generally resisted demands that they regulate the shadow banks or complex OTC derivatives trading. In the late 1990s, the chair of the US Commodity Futures Trading Commission, Brooksley Born, argued for stricter regulation of OTC trading, provoking a fearsome backlash. The deputy Treasury secretary, Lawrence Summers, reportedly phoned the commission to say, "I have thirteen bankers in my office, and they say if you go forward with this you will cause the worst financial crisis since WWII" (Kwak and Johnson 2010, 9). Congress subsequently passed the Commodity Futures Modernization Act, which formally and definitively exempted derivative trades, including CDSs, from any further regulation.

In the case of Fannie Mae and Freddie Mac, government regulation actually encouraged risk taking (Wallison 2009, 2011). In 1994 the Federal Housing Authority ordered Fannie and Freddie to direct 30% of their mortgage financing to low-income borrowers. In 2000 this target was raised to 50% and, eventually, by 2008, to 55%. The aggressive entry of "private label" banks into the securitization market in the 2000s therefore threatened not only Fannie's and Freddie's market share but their capacity to meet their regulatory targets. This was one factor encouraging the banks to expand their Alt-A loan portfolios from around 2005. Freddie Mac's former CEO and chairman, Richard Syron (2010), told the FCIC that by 2004–2005 Freddie had started to run "short of mission-rich product of the sort that would satisfy your mission demands . . . You had orders from HUD [the Department of Housing and Urban Development] which continuously escalated the share of your business which was to low and moderate income." James Lockhart (2010), the director and chairman of the oversight board of the Federal Housing Agency, told the FCIC:

> Both CEOs told me that one of their worst fears was missing their affordable housing goals . . . which they ended up doing in 2008. HUD had the power to require a consent agreement if they did miss their goals. Probably worse from the CEO's standpoint[,] it would have incurred the wrath of their Congressional supporters. I believe that high affordable housing goals and the resulting political pressure compounded by the Enterprises' drive for market share and short-term profitability . . . were major reasons why they lowered their underwriting standards.

Despite these pressures, prior to the onset of the crisis, Fannie and Freddie's affordable housing remit was a source of considerable influence that its CEOs could exploit to fend off potentially hostile regulators and lobby for reduced capital. As Helen Thompson (2009, 20–21) observes, between 1990 and 2008 Fannie and Freddie directed an estimated $19 million in contributions to politicians and invested a further $170 million in lobbying while also "creating a language of political justification for their expansion around affordable housing, especially for minorities, that was tied closely to the political agenda and concerns of many in Congress." Daniel Mudd, when he was Fannie's chief operating officer, told the then CEO, Franklin Maines, that "the old political reality [at Fannie] was that we always won, we took no prisoners . . . We used to . . . be able to write, or have written rules that worked for us" (FCIC 2011, 180). Armando Falcon (2010), a former director of the Office of Federal Housing Oversight (OFHO), told the FCIC that his office was "constantly subjected to malicious political attacks and efforts of intimidation" and that in 2003 Fannie Mae had secured his "enforced resignation" after OFHO had published a critical regulatory report. One critical issue was capital. By statute, Fannie and Freddie were allowed to operate with a minimal capital requirement of 2.5%. OFHO sought permission to raise this minimum but was rebuffed following intense lobbying.

Conclusion

In contrast to the strong themes of institutional constraint in much existing institutional theory, we have shown how authoritative CEOs within US banks could shape and bend their institutions in pursuit of their strategies. In doing so, they faced little in the way of institutional resistance, which the FCIC (2011, 279) now characterizes as a "substantial failure of corporate governance." Boards, stakeholders, risk managers, ratings agencies, and regulators either played no restraining role or, if they did, as occasionally happened with regulators and risk managers, they were ignored or silenced. The US government is founded on a system of checks and balances that provides institutional incentives to different branches of government to monitor and constrain each other's behavior. Few such limitations were imposed upon the authority of chief executives who were able to impose their vaulting ambitions and their often limited competence on the banks they led. As Hall and Soskice (2001, 5) argue, "The effects of an institution follow from the power it confers on particular actors through the formal sanction that hierarchy supplies."

Bank leaders got the leveraged trading revolution they wanted and hence are directly culpable for what happened regarding the crisis. As Paul Friedman of Bear Stearns noted on the day of the JP Morgan shareholder vote to take over Bear: "We did this to ourselves. We put ourselves in a position where this could happen. It is our fault for allowing it to get this far, and for not taking any steps to do anything about it. It's a classic case of mismanagement at the top. There's just no question about it" (W. Cohan 2009, 149). As we have shown, bank executives were on the whole true believers. They really did believe that securitization and risk management tools such as VaR meant that "this time is different." As Thornton, Henry, and Carter (2006) argued in *Businessweek*, "For all the risks they're taking on, banks insist they're safer than ever. They've hired many of the greatest mathematical minds in the world to create impossibly complex risk models. They deal in so many markets that the chances of them all going haywire simultaneously appear miniscule." And as Alan Greenspan (2013, 92) now argues, "The willingness of many financial firms to allow their tangible capital, at the height of the boom, to become razor thin was a folly largely explained by their behavior and an underestimation of the ephemeral nature of market liquidity."

These problems of perception were compounded by the fact that many of the markets in question were quite opaque. It is also true, as we have seen, that many bank leaders were not across the detail of their banks' operations and were in many cases ignorant of the risks being taken. In fact, risk was being dispersed *and* concentrated at the same time. Yet the sanguine views of the majority of bankers and regulators prevailed. This, combined with strong market pressures, saw the markets reach new heights in the 2000s in the run-up to the crisis as banks were pushed to achieve ever higher returns on equity. New profit opportunities and new market openings were forged by bankers and financial innovators displaying a combination of bounded rationality and irrational fervor. Very few bankers, however, had any idea of how the system as a whole was evolving, producing extreme levels of systemic risk that would eventually see key asset and funding markets collapse. Ultimately our bankers were destroyed by structural systemic risk forces they did not see and could not control.

6

The United Kingdom

Banking and Bankruptcy

The UK government committed £117 billion in cash to purchase shares in and lend money to UK banks at the peak of the 2008 crisis (National Audit Office 2009). In addition the government insured around £600 billion of financial assets and guaranteed £250 billion of wholesale bank borrowing. As we saw in Chapter 3, the largest losses within the UK system were incurred by the Royal Bank of Scotland (RBS) and HBOS. Barclays incurred significant trading losses in 2008–2009 but recorded a pretax profit. Lloyds TSB entered the crisis in a relatively strong position but was destroyed by its purchase of HBOS. The London-based investment arms of Deutsche Bank and UBS also incurred significant losses. The Northern Rock and Bradford and Bingley building societies were also fatally undermined.

In Chapters 1 and 2 we explained the broad institutional and structural dynamics that drove the banking crisis. In this chapter we explain the behavior of the largest UK banks from the perspective of the banks' leaders as well as regulators and politicians. Drawing upon interviews with these actors, we demonstrate that the UK banks were operating in a highly competitive market that made it extremely difficult for bank executives to resist pressure to pursue ambitious profit and return on equity (ROE) targets. Most bankers nevertheless believed that their business models were safe and that risk had been effectively distributed and controlled. Market pressures and sanguine ideas thus complemented each other. At RBS and HBOS—the two banks that sustained the worst losses and that have been the subject of extensive public inquiries—senior executives were not so much optimistic as Panglossian in their assessments. Emboldened by their convictions, executives either sidelined or failed to listen to risk managers. They also introduced bonus systems that encouraged risk taking. Nonexecutive directors (NEDs), external auditors, and institutional investors had the authority and opportunity to challenge bank executives. They singularly failed to do so. In addition, the Financial Services Authority (FSA) oversaw a "light-touch" regulatory regime that allowed the banks to overextend themselves, engage in risky securities trading, and extend their leverage and dependence upon wholesale funding.

Market Pressures

In his detailed account of the history of the Bank of Scotland, Ray Perman (2013, 17) describes how, until the 1980s, the three largest Scottish banks, the Bank of Scotland, RBS, and the Clydesdale, met together in the Committee of Scottish Clearing Banks "ostensibly to discuss items of mutual concern, but in effect to collude on interest rates, fees and charges." This was, he writes, a "closed and comfortable world" in which "a gentlemen's agreement" first reached in 1876 prevented English banks from operating branches in Scotland or Scottish banks from expanding beyond their London offices (Perman 2013, 17). In England in the 1950s and 1960s the largest commercial and investment (merchant) banks also operated in a secure market in which regulatory controls on interest rates and credit creation sustained profits but impeded competition. David Kynaston (2011) suggests that bankers working in the City at this time would have been performing much the same kind of work in the same buildings as their nineteenth-century counterparts. This world was disturbed by the rise of the Euromarkets in the 1960s and the secondary banking crisis of the early 1970s, but it survived until the 1980s when, starting with the "big bang" reform of the stock exchange, successive Conservative and Labour governments sought to protect consumer interests through the promotion of competition.

In 1987 legislation was passed to encourage greater competition within the banking sector by allowing locally based building societies to take deposits, provide lines of credit to borrowers, and increase their capital base by "demutualizing" and becoming privately owned companies listed on the stock exchange. A number of building societies—most notably the Alliance and Leicester and the Newcastle-based Northern Rock—went on to develop a national market presence. By June 2007 Northern Rock held assets of £113 billion and a 10% share of the mortgage market. In 2001 the Cruickshank Report addressed issues around the costs of switching accounts and hidden fees that tied consumers to particular banks. Finally, in the years immediately preceding the crisis, the FSA encouraged new firms such as Tesco Finance and Virgin Money to enter the market. At the same time, and through a series of successful mergers and takeovers, a number of smaller banks, including RBS (which took over the giant but ailing NatWest bank in 2000 and the Dutch ABN Amro in 2007) and the Bank of Scotland (which merged with the Halifax Building Society in 2001 to form HBOS), extended their market shares. By this time the other large UK banks, Barclays, HSBC, and Lloyds, also faced competition from demutualized building societies and from overseas banks that had either established offices in the United Kingdom or bought British merchant banks. Morgan Grenfell was acquired by Deutsche Bank in 1990. Barings was sold to the Dutch firm ING in 1995. Kleinwort Benson was sold to Dresdner in the same year. S. G. Warburg was bought by the Swiss Bank Corporation (which became UBS) in 1995. Hambros was bought by Société Générale in 1998. Schroders sold its investment banking division to Citigroup in 2000.

In this new and highly competitive world, banks that offered slightly higher interest rates to savers would, according to the director-general of the Building Societies Association, Adrian Coles (interview, 19 April 2013), be "deluged with money." Banks that were able to lower their interest rates on mortgages or increase the amount of money they were willing to lend could also attract waves of new customers. Banks that were unable to match their rivals' pretax profits and, crucially, ROE found their share price sliding and became the subject of takeover speculation. Bank executives who found themselves in this position had little job security. Of the largest UK banks, Lloyds TSB came under the most intense pressure to increase its profits in the years prior to the crisis. In 2005 analysts described Lloyds as the

"British Leyland" of the banking sector and suggested that the bank's executive leadership had "lost its way" (Independent 2005). Even though Lloyds recorded a £3.8 billion pretax profit in 2005, the financial press carried a number of reports that Citigroup or the Spanish Banco Bilbao would launch a hostile takeover. In this environment, bank executives faced tremendous pressure to set and achieve ambitious growth and profit targets. In his review of corporate governance within the UK banks, Sir David Walker (2009, 27) describes a pervasive and "myopic" focus on "short-term horizons" sustained by "the increased weight placed on full reporting of company performance on a quarterly basis, increasing short-term pressures on market valuations that inevitably feed back to the way in which chief executives, and by inference, their boards seek to run their businesses." The UK Treasury Committee (2009a, Ev73) similarly argues that "if one of those banks in 2005 decided to be more conservative and hold back in their activity, they more than likely would have had their CEO and board replaced in 2006 for failing to take advantage of the opportunities." Andy Haldane at the Bank of England told us that the banks had no alternative but to

> juggle their own internal incentives because times were good and it was very difficult for any firm individually to step back—to step out of the party . . . Was too much business being written? Absolutely. They'd say, well we've got a friend who stopped two years ago and they're not in a job any more. So there was this locomotive that was steaming ahead, it was impossible to step off this profitability merry-go-round. People were conscious that that meant running a bit more risk than they'd like but they couldn't stop themselves because their loss would have been someone else's gain. So I think externally there was, at least towards the end, a pretty strong sense of the risks that were being piled up . . . In a way that led, collectively, to everyone to pile over the cliff. (Interview, 9 May 2013)

The former chairman of RBS's investment bank, Johnny Cameron, concurs.

> I think that's true of every company, every bank, in those days that shareholders expected a lot . . . I'd said . . . in March, April 2007 that

> I'm quite worried, the market seems very febrile to me in London. I used the word "febrile." People laughed at me and said, what do you mean, febrile, Johnny? But if we'd said Johnny thinks the market is febrile, we're going to pull back from underwriting leverage loans and pull back more generally, I think the market would have given us absolutely zero credit. I think any bank that said that would have got punished by the market. It would have been a very brave man that said do you know what, we're going to give up market share because we are concerned about risk. (Interview, 18 April 2013)

Adrian Coles told us that in relation to mortgage lending

> there's a danger sometimes with too much competition and that's what happened in pre-2007. Huge competition to lend 95% of house values to people at six times income . . . Now was that competition beneficial . . . ? The free market led to a competing away of underwriting standards which sowed the seeds of its own problems. So you can add too much competition sometimes that destroys rather than creates. (Interview, 19 April 2013)

The effects of intense competition on decision making are perhaps most clearly revealed at HBOS. Following its merger with Halifax, the new bank's executives planned to "break the mould" and mount "a strong challenge to the four clearing banks" (HBOS 2001, 24). The CEO, James Crosby, set a target of achieving and sustaining a 20% average ROE. This required setting sales targets for individual staff in every branch of the bank and, as Crosby (HBOS 2003, 1) recognized, "taking share from our competitors, ideally in every channel and every product." Ray Perman (2013, 110) records one senior manager at HBOS as saying that, at this time, the "divisional chiefs would draw upon their budgets and send them up to Mike Ellis [the finance director]. When they came back they had been pushed up, but they were then carved in stone and you had to deliver. If you were to compete, you had to lend more."

In 2005 HBOS met its 20% ROE target for the first time and recorded a pretax annual profit of £4.8 billion. By this time, however, the bank's mortgage business was coming under intense pressure from new entrants to the market such as Egg and Direct Line and from Northern Rock, which had launched a "together mortgage" allowing customers to borrow up to 125% of the value of the house they were buying. When HBOS announced in 2007 that its share of the new mortgage market had fallen from 20% to 8%, over £1 billion was wiped from the bank's market value in a matter of days (Rutherford 2007). HBOS executives came "under huge pressure" because they believed that the "market expected them to go on achieving higher growth" (Ray Perman, interview, 16 April 2013). Executives reportedly pressed HBOS's head of retail, Benny Higgins, to introduce new "equity release mortgages." Because these mortgages were premised on the assumption of rising house prices, they could be used to lower short-term repayments and so entice new borrowers. Higgins refused and resigned a few months later. Perman (2013, 138) quotes a member of HBOS's board of directors as follows: "Benny was a hero. He called it right on the mortgage market, but the executive and the rest of the board did not have the courage to back him." Once Higgins had left, executives lowered the bank's credit standards and offered a 125% mortgage to compete with the Northern Rock. HBOS also decided to grow its "nonstandard" mortgage lending business, particularly buy-to-let and self-certified mortgages, where profit margins remained higher. By the end of 2008, £66.5 billion (28%) of the bank's retail mortgage lending was classified as nonstandard and 62% of the division's book had a loan-to-value ratio of over 70% (Parliamentary Commission on Banking Standards 2013a, 74).

In order to compensate for tough and competitive conditions in mortgage lending, bank executives also placed more pressure on HBOS's corporate lending division to increase its market share and profits. Ray Perman (2013, 110) describes how divisional managers initially proposed a target of increasing their lending by 6% and profits by 9%, only to be ordered to double their profits by HBOS executives. Cummings, the head of corporate banking, who was fined £500,000 by the FSA in 2012 for his part in HBOS's downfall, told the Parliamentary Commission that he was under pressure to keep increasing profits because "there was a point where the retail bank was not performing and not delivering on the expectation, and I was asked to step in" (Parliamentary Commission on Banking Standards 2013a, 41). In pursuit of further growth, the corporate division "sought out and found 'sub-investment grade' business" and began to take equity stakes in the firms to which it was lending, further increasing its exposure (Parliamentary Commission on Banking Standards, 2013a, 11). The FSA (2012b, 12) concludes that "the increasing pressure to increase growth . . . meant that less attention would necessarily be paid to risk management." In 2007 Peter Cummings assured investors and market analysts that the bank's property portfolio was "truly diversified in terms of lending approach, asset type, location and tenant concentration" and that he had "no concerns with the quality of our book." In fact, the FSA (2012b, 8) found that at this time HBOS had a "high degree of exposure" to property and single-name borrowers as well as a "substantial exposure" to equity and subordinated tranches of debt and to highly leveraged transactions, and that fully 75% of its portfolio was sub–investment grade.

HBOS was not the only bank whose executives believed that market competition left them with little alternative but to set higher growth and profit targets. Barclays, in particular, was driven throughout the early 2000s by a determination to establish itself as a "T5" (top five) global bank. Shortly after being appointed CEO, John Varley spoke about his "impatience" with Barclays' standing and the need to raise the bank's "metabolic rate" (Thal Larsen 2006a). In July 2012 Barclays appointed a senior solicitor and former BBC governor, Sir Anthony Salz, to review the bank's culture and business practices in the wake of the LIBOR scandal. He observes that "winning and commercial drive are not necessarily wrong as values for a commercial organization" but that within Barclays "the interpretation and implementation of 'winning' went beyond the simply 'competitive' in the sense that it 'was sometimes underpinned by what appeared to have been an 'at all costs' attitude" (Salz 2013, 82).

Similarly at RBS, CEO Fred Goodwin was driven by a desire to outperform Barclays. According to one former colleague: "What Fred wanted was to get bigger. He was determined that RBS would be bigger than Barclays" (Martin 2013, 7). One former board member argues that this sense of competition encouraged RBS to mount an unexpected bid for ABN Amro in 2007. "Fred wanted to be bigger than Barclays and here was a chance to do it" (Martin 2013, 233).

Meanwhile, at Deutsche Bank, the CEO, Josef Ackermann (2005a, 5, 7), admitted to shareholders that

> there is still a distance between us and the world's premier league . . . In the markets that are relevant to us, we want to grow more rapidly than the market, and thus accelerate the bank's profitable growth. We intend to do this primarily through organic growth. We see that there is further growth potential, in particular, in high margin products—for example, trading in loans and the sales of complex derivatives.

Finally, as we noted in Chapter 3, UBS's aggressive entry into the collateralized debt obligation (CDO) market in 2005 was prompted by an external consultancy review that showed how the investment bank division was lagging behind its competitors. This led to "a 'growth at any cost' mentality in which market share, revenue gaps and beating the competition is the topic of every morning meeting at all levels in the bank, and for senior management can be a question of holding your job" (Blundell-Wignall, Atkinson, and Lee 2008, 10).

True Believers

In the face of such market competition and pressure, prevailing market opportunities in banking meant that business activity was increasingly focused on risky lending and in some cases risky trading, all fueled by ever-higher leverage. Yet senior executives at RBS, HBOS, and the other major banks that failed in 2007–2008 did not believe they were taking dangerous risks. As the BBC's business editor, Robert Peston (Peston and Knight 2013, 17), comments, "Banks and bankers behaved [in a] reckless way not because of some terrible conspiracy to bankrupt us all, but because—perhaps wilfully, perhaps innocently—they did not believe they were behaving recklessly." Senior executives believed that internal risk management procedures were robust; that the world economy would continue to grow and that this would generate new business opportunities for their banks; that house prices would continue to rise as income levels increased; and that "originate-and-distribute" securitization had dispersed risk. The former director of financial stability at the Bank of England, Sir John Gieve, told us:

> When I used to go and talk to the chairmen and chief executives of the banks, both in London and New York—it was always, well John,

> you're quite right to be worried. I mean, you know, these markets are so good they can't last for long. But you've got to understand that since the last crisis, which was in the early 1990s . . . risk management has been completely transformed and our hedging strategies—you know, we're confident we can handle it. (Interview, 19 April 2013)

In February 2007 the president of BarCap, Bob Diamond (Barclays 2007a), proclaimed "three or four more years where we're truly looking at the golden age of risk management." Earlier, in 2003, an interesting spat occurred between Diamond and his colleagues at Barclays and the American Warren Buffett. In 2002 Buffett famously described derivatives as "financial weapons of mass destruction" devised by "madmen," with derivatives trading constituting a "mega-catastrophe risk" (Berkshire Hathaway 2002, 13, 15). In a reference to Buffett's stand-alone derivatives business, Gen Re Financial Products, which had run aground a few years previously, Diamond suggested that Buffett was wary of the derivatives business "because he failed in it" and that his views were without merit. Diamond's colleague, Jerry Del Misser, Barclays Capital's global head of rates, assured executives that "the derivatives market has grown every year. Risk management and derivatives as risk transfer tools have grown from strength to strength." Citing Alan Greenspan's favorable views on derivatives, Del Misser concluded that "there are not large pools of risk concentrations" (Jeffery 2003). RBS's chairman, Sir Tom McKillop (Treasury Committee 2009a, Ev240), also believed that securitization had led to the dispersal of risk.

> Can I give you my own view here of what has happened? Securitisation, the originate and distribute model, was seen as a stabilising influence in the financial systems. It has been discussed in many forums that I have participated in. This was distributing risk. This was making the whole system more stable. It has not turned out that way. It has turned out completely the opposite to expectations. Everyone has been surprised about that, the regulators, the companies and the banks involved in it.

AT HBOS the CEO, Sir James Cosby, told the Parliamentary Commission on Banking Standards (2013d, 12), "We always believed and my colleagues in the corporate bank always believed that they had a good and clear understanding of the risks they were taking and we in aggregate as a bank had no evidence to the contrary."

Bank executives in the United Kingdom also shared with their counterparts in the United States an unwarranted faith in internal value at risk (VaR) measures. At Barclays, the use of VaR systems led the then CEO, John Varley, to suggest that "credit risk is mostly a science not an art" (Mackintosh 2002). At RBS, Fred Goodwin (RBS 2006a, 23) accepted that VaR "is not a perfect measure," but nevertheless argued that it had helped bank executives understand the risks to which they were exposed. His precise words are worth quoting:

> The outlook for the Group [RBS] is a positive one. The economic outlook is net positive. Yes, there are risks out there, there are always risks out there. The risks which are out there funnily enough feel like lesser risks because they are recognised and they have been around for some time and they are on pretty much everyone's agenda. That, to my mind, helps diminish them and creates a greater likelihood that they will be managed through in a way which is sensible and constructive.

At UBS executives relied upon VaR assessments using five years of data (UBS 2008b, 38). Managers did not recognize that this data might be flawed because it related exclusively to a period of economic boom and so could not describe the way in which losses might accumulate across different classes of trading assets once an asset price bubble started to deflate. To compound this error, UBS's senior management were given information only about the bank's net holdings of subprime assets. This meant that when positions had apparently been hedged through credit default swaps (CDSs) with firms like AIG products or monoline insurers they were effectively invisible to senior management (SFBC 2008, 12).

Investors, bank executives, and regulators were also reassured by the positive assessments being issued by credit ratings agencies. Moody's awarded RBS a long-term debt credit rating of Aa1 (one notch below its maximum of AAA) in 2006. Moody's placed RBS on a review for a negative downgrade in April 2008 but only announced an actual downgrade in June. Even more startlingly, Moody's only downgraded HBOS from Aa1 to Aa2 in

September 2008. Fitch actually raised HBOS's rating from AA to AA+ in August 2006 and raised RBS's rating from AA to AA+ in March 2007. It did not downgrade RBS's rating until as late as September 2008 (Hindmoor and McConnell 2013, 2014).

In their own risk assessments and presentations to market analysts, bank executives relied heavily upon the credit ratings being awarded to the financial instruments they were creating and trading to assure investors that they were not taking unsustainable risks. Time and again in trading updates and market analysts' conference calls, bank executives responded to critical questions about risks by citing the proportion of assets rated AAA or AA. Robert Peston (Peston and Knight 2013, 169) quotes a "renowned senior [British] banker" as saying that "if you were in charge of risk at an investment institution or bank and you saw that your colleagues were loading up your organization with AAA investments, you didn't check what the investments were, you didn't think twice, because if they were badged as AAA you knew they would be fine." The group finance director at HBOS, Phil Hodgkinson, told market analysts in December 2007 that the securitized assets on the bank's balance sheet were "all super senior, its 96% AAA" (HBOS 2007b). The group finance director at HBOS, Mike Ellis, similarly assured investors in July 2008 that "93% of the ABS book is rated AAA . . . only 1.3% of the book is below investment grade" (HBOS 2008a, 10). The director of retail at Lloyds, Helen Weir, described the assets of the bank's off–balance sheet conduit, Cancara, as "all AAA ABS, primarily vanilla assets . . . I think we've described it before as the Rolls Royce of conduits" (Treanor 2007a).When Peter Kurer, the former chairman of UBS, asked about the CDOs being accumulated on the bank's balance sheet, he was "told by our risk people that these instruments are like triple-A, like Treasury bonds" (quoted in Tett 2009, 139). Johnny Cameron of RBS provides a compelling account of the status accorded to credit ratings:

> The balance sheet of RBS totally was £2 trillion. The balance sheet that I was responsible for was £1 trillion. That's £1,000 billion, it's a huge number. The subprime part of it, even on the most broad definition, was around £5 billion (though this eventually became almost worthless) and yet almost all of it was rated—quote, *better than AAA.*

> So all the people responsible to me, and indeed to the Group, the group risk people, never ever highlighted it or focused on it so as to put it on the dashboard of things to worry about. Until very near the end, we never thought of it as subprime. It was better than AAA, it was on the books yielding LIBOR plus an eighth—one of the lowest yielding assets we had because it was so good. I will go to my grave saying that it is not realistic or fair to expect me to have focused on this tiny apparently very safe part of the overall portfolio. I'd like to say my risk people let me down, they should have told me about it—but I don't think I can even say that. If "it's better than AAA" one shouldn't have to think about it. (Interview, 18 April 2013)

Senior executives at RBS and HBOS were resolutely optimistic about future economic and financial growth right up until the point at which the financial crisis began. Johnny Cameron at RBS suggests: "It was the zeitgeist at the time. It was a bullish time and up until 2007 it was upwards and onwards in anything you care to name" (interview, 18 April). In November 2006 RBS's Fred Goodwin told an investors' conference that "whatever the economy, whatever the world throws at us, I am very confident that we will deliver growth which when compared to our peers is superior and sustainable" (Martin 2013, 204). In August 2007, Goodwin assured investors that "we do operate within an economic environment that is positive and looks set to remain positive whoever's numbers you want to believe or prefer" (RBS 2007b, 11). At this time RBS's Johnny Cameron described the downturn in the US subprime market as a "blip" (Interactive Investor 2007). In an interview with the FSA, Cameron was asked why the bank had not sought to reduce its risk exposure once it had started to incur significant losses in late 2007. Cameron suggested that Fred Goodwin "is and was an optimist and he tended to take an optimistic view of what was likely to happen and had often in his life been proved right" (FSA 2011, 380). Goodwin was not alone. In August 2007 Bob Diamond of Barclays predicted that the downturn in the subprime market could take "more than a year to be resolved" but that "we would expect at some point over the next two to three months to see the market at more normal volume levels" (P. Cohan 2007). Three months later Diamond accepted that "we have a serious situation around subprime as an asset class" but told investors that "the optimist in me . . . wouldn't bet that the originate and distribute model is anything other than enforced by this" (Urry 2007).

At HBOS, the CEO, James Crosby, dismissed out of hand any concerns that the US downturn in subprime lending might be a portent for future problems:

> A decade ago, in the aftermath of the 1980s housing boom, repossessions were running at record levels. It seemed that Britain's unique obsession with home ownership was over. Today, repossessions are running at their lowest level since 1984 and house prices rose last year by almost 30 per cent. Not everyone accepts that this is good news. In the grip of a pervasive bear-market psychology, investors are challenging the fundamentals of the market. Some American investment bankers have even made naive comparisons with the property market in the US. They argue that the housing market emperor is not well clothed—that Britain is heading for a residential property crash . . . Lenders have meanwhile been more cautious than during the 1980s. They are lending on the same multiples of earnings as fourteen years ago, when mortgage interest rates were twice the level of today. Competition has forced them to offer better deals to existing customers, leading to smaller discounts for new borrowers . . . [The] British housing market still has solid fundamentals; this emperor has clothes. (Crosby 2003)

Crosby's replacement at HBOS, Andy Hornby, responded to questions whether the bank's profits could be sustained by predicting "continuing GDP growth in each of the major economies in which we operate" (HBOS 2006, 13). Peter Cummings, the head of corporate banking at HBOS, echoed this analysis: "The economy is certainly benign, but the benign[n] ess of the economy is stimulating a lot of activity . . . The sustainability of our investment book is beginning to show through and grow. I remain confident about the quality of our investments, the diversity of our investments and their sustainability going forward. I am very optimistic" (HBOS 2007c, 17). The same year, Andy Hornby responded to questions about corporate lending by arguing that "discussions of corporate credit quality are beginning to have a *Groundhog Day* theme. There is a certain amount of repetition and, each time we stand up and say it cannot get better, it then does" (HBOS 2007c, 4). In October 2007 Hornby told delegates at a Merrill Lynch banking conference that while there had been a "sea change" in attitudes toward risk, HBOS could increase its profits as its rivals reduced their lending (Croft 2007).

Did bank executives appreciate that high leverage and dependence upon wholesale funding created sources of systemic risk? The simple answer is that they did not. Executives at the Northern Rock and HBOS recognized the desirability of growing their deposit base. They did not, however, do so because they were concerned about the possibility of wholesale markets freezing in the event of a downturn but because they wanted to secure a means of further increasing their balance sheet assets while hedging against the possibility of subsequent interest rate rises in wholesale markets. Executives did not imagine the possibility that wholesale funding markets could freeze in a crisis, leaving them unable to roll over debt. Indeed, looking back at speeches given by bank executives and transcripts of their conference calls with market analysts, what is remarkable is that bank executives simply did not feel the need to discuss and justify their leverage or dependence upon wholesale funding. The managing director of Nestor Advisors, Stilpon Nestor, suggests that the use of risk models obscured the existence of sources of systemic risk and that boards of directors "ended up missing more than one elephant in the risk room, such as rapidly increasing gross leverage and decreasing liquidity" (HM Treasury 2013, 120).

It might be objected that we ought not to invest too much significance in the public statements of bank executives who were being paid to put the best possible spin on their banks' performance. There is, however, no evidence that, behind closed doors, bank executives were expressing serious concerns about the state of the economy and their balance sheets. In March 2008 Andy Hornby was so confident about HBOS's future that he invested £413,000 of his own money in buying the company's shares. He was joined by six other executives who invested a further £1 million (P. McMahon 2008). Fred Goodwin lost around £7 million of his own money when RBS failed. The former CEO and later chairman, George Matthewson, lost around £5 million (Martin 2013, 297). Frits Seegers, the head of global retail and commercial banking at Barclays, lost £1.9 million of his own money when the bank's share price tumbled in 2008. Bob Diamond lost around

£300,000. The actions of RBS executives also suggest that they had a genuine faith in the virtues of their banking model. RBS pressed ahead with its takeover of ABN Amro in 2007 and continued to build its trading portfolio during the rest of that year (FSA 2011, 144–146). At UBS, management were so confident of the enduring value of the super-senior CDOs they held on their balance sheet that they insured these assets for only a maximum loss of up to 4% of their value (Martin 2013, 244). The simplest explanation of why so many bank executives proclaimed that their financial prospects were so good is that they genuinely believed that they were good.

We now know that bank executives' beliefs about their risk management practices and the state of the economy were deeply flawed. Yet executives had good reason to believe that their beliefs were correct. The UK economy was growing at above trend, and inflation had remained relatively low. As we shall see presently, politicians and regulators also believed that the boom was sustainable. So, too, did market investors. CDS premiums to insure bank debt remained exceptionally low (Turner 2011, 28). The share prices of the largest banks did not fall significantly prior to the collapse of Northern Rock. Barclays' share price peaked at £6.9 in June 2007 before falling to £6.1 in August. Lloyds' price peaked at £5.67 in April 2007 before falling to £5.4 in June. RBS's share price actually rose from £5.9 in June 2006 to a peak of £6.8 in January 2007 before falling slowly to £6.3 in June 2007 and then more rapidly to £5.7 by August 2007. Clearly, at this point, investors had finally recognized weaknesses in the bank's balance sheet. HBOS's share price fell from a peak of £11 in January 2007 to £9.6 in June 2007 and then to £9 in August. This was a significant fall, but it does not suggest that investors were aware of just how vulnerable the largest banks had become (Hindmoor and McConnell 2013).

Internal Governance

CEOs in the UK banking system exercised a measure of authority similar to that of their US counterparts. They were able to set overall strategic goals, including the bank's "risk appetite"; appoint key executives; set bonus payment systems; and initiate discussions on mergers and acquisitions. In Chapter 5 we saw that US executives often sidelined or even dismissed senior risk officers who expressed doubts about their strategy. Did this happen in the United Kingdom? Yes. The most high-profile incident here concerns the fate of Paul Moore, the head of group regulatory risk at HBOS. In the years prior to the banking crisis he raised a number of concerns relating to inadequate risk controls and the privileging of sales over a risk culture at HBOS to both the CEO and the board of directors, where he requested that his concerns be minuted. Moore (Telegraph 2009)—who had warned about a "cultural indisposition to challenge" within certain parts of the firm—was subsequently reprimanded and told by a KPMG auditor that an unnamed senior HBOS executive had said that he, Moore, must have a "death wish." Moore was subsequently dismissed and replaced by someone with little risk management experience. Reflecting upon his experiences before the Treasury Select Committee, Moore suggested that

> in simple terms this crisis was caused, not because many bright people did not see it coming, but because there has been a completely inadequate "separation" and "balance of powers" between the executive and all those accountable for overseeing their actions and "reining them in" i.e. internal control functions such as finance, risk, compliance and internal audit, non-executive Chairmen and Directors, external auditors, The FSA, shareholders and politicians. As I recently commented on the BBC: "Being an internal risk and compliance manager at the time felt a bit like being a man in a rowing boat trying to slow down an oil tanker." If we could turn that man in the rowing boat into a man with a tug boat or even the Pilot required to navigate big ships into port, I feel confident that things would have turned out quite differently. (Telegraph 2009)

The FSA's report into the failure of HBOS vindicated Moore's analysis. It finds that there was a "culture of optimism" within HBOS, which meant that risk management was regarded as a "constraint on the business rather than integral to it" (FSA 2012b, 4, 13). Moore has subsequently conducted research into the experiences of other risk managers. The *Risk Minds* survey of over 500 risk managers finds that "most risk professionals saw the technical factors which might cause a crisis well in advance . . . The risks were reported but senior executives chose to prioritise sales" (Moore, Carter & Associates 2010, 2). Half of all respondents to the survey said that they had

had major concerns about financial and market risks within their organization prior to the 2007–2008 crisis. One-half of this group—that is, one-quarter of the total sample—said they had felt inhibited in raising concerns (Moore, Carter & Associates 2010, 13). One respondent suggested that the "first time I raised concerns I was denied a promotion and was moved to another department." Another said that "there was limited tolerance for bad news in a sales-driven optimistic organisation" and that "the culture of all organisations prioritised sales and profits, and any attempt to raise matters relating to risk or regulation were considered 'spoil sport.'"

Risk managers were sometimes punished for raising objections to bank strategy. More often, however, the voices of risk managers were simply not heard at a senior level within the bank as a result of decisions taken to exclude them from key decision-making forums. The FSA's report into the failure of RBS finds no clear instances in which risk officers tried to alert managers or board executives about the dangers inherent in the bank's strategy. The report did, however, find that it was not until February 2008 that the chief risk officer (CRO) sat on the group executive management committee or attended the CEO's morning meetings.

When losses started to rise in RBS's US trading operations, Fred Goodwin raised concerns about profit targets but did not ask any questions about the underlying business issues. "The RBS Chief Executive said . . . 'You've got your income projections wrong. Why aren't you getting the growth you promised me?' He didn't then go to Cameron or Crowe and ask what the underlying problem might be with the markets or whether there was a serious issue" (Martin 2013, 240). Later, Cameron reportedly had to draw a picture for Goodwin on a piece of paper showing how CDOs were constructed. Similarly, the Salz Report (Salz 2013, 160) finds that between 2005 and 2009 Barclays' executive committee meetings did not include the CRO and head of compliance. Jo Dawson, Paul Moore's replacement at HBOS, told the Parliamentary Commission investigation into the failure of HBOS that she had influence rather than authority within the bank and that her ability to effect change was dependent upon the quality of her relationships with other senior managers (Parliamentary Commission on Banking Standards 2012). When Dawson did raise concerns about the growth strategy being pursued by the corporate lending division, the CEO and the chairman told her that they were comfortable with the current position and that competitors were "mudslinging" (Parliamentary Commission on Banking Standards 2012). At UBS the senior managers of the investment bank had strong sales backgrounds but no experience in risk management. Indeed, UBS did not appoint a senior risk manager in the fixed-income trading division where the largest part of that bank's losses were incurred until after the crisis had almost destroyed the bank (UBS 2008b, 37). As a result, concerns expressed by more-junior risk officers were either ignored or not relayed to senior executives. A senior risk manager at one of the largest UK banks also told us that while risk managers were given the opportunity to express their views, they had only limited authority.

> Sometimes you've got authority to actually block something and there's often negativity and backlash around those sorts of decisions, which is unfortunate. I certainly experienced some of that myself, particularly people who have come in from other banks who want to do what they did at the previous bank. Sometimes you've got to say well actually I don't think that's the appropriate thing [to do]. So if you want to continue that activity you're very welcome to return from which you came. But of course you've only so many bullets you can fire because the other businesses can tend to gang up on people who are deemed to be just nay-sayers . . . So you have to pick your battle and put it gently. (Interview, 19 April 2013)

On top of weak risk management, executives also oversaw the growth of bonus systems that gave employees an incentive to maximize short-term profit returns even where this resulted in the significant accumulation of risks. Mervyn King argues that the bonus system was fatally flawed:

> The real question about the pension for Fred Goodwin is not a debate now about whether you should undo a contractual entitlement, the real debate is how on earth was it that at the time shareholders, boards, the financial press, all thought it was a great idea to reward people in this way. These bonuses were absolutely astronomic. It was a form of compensation which rewarded gamblers if they won the gamble but there was no loss if you lost it. It is obvious that if you do

> that you will give incentives to people to gamble. (Treasury Committee 2009a, Ev314)

At HBOS, the FSA (2012a, 17) found that "staff were incentivised to focus on revenue rather than risk, which increased the appetite to facilitate customers, increase lending and take on greater risk." Peter Cummings, for example, was awarded a £1.3 million bonus in 2007 for meeting lending and profit targets (FSA 2012a, 21). Appearing before the Treasury Select Committee in February 2009, Andy Hornby made no effort to defend the bonus system.

> There is no doubt that the bonus systems in many banks around the world have been proven to be wrong . . . in that if people are rewarded for purely short-term cash form and are paid very substantial short-term cash bonuses without it being clear whether those decisions over the next three to five years have been proven to be correct, that is not rewarding the right type of behaviour. (Treasury Committee 2009e, 14)

At Barclays bonuses were judged in terms of individual financial performance and were "highly dependent on the judgment of individual line managers" (Salz 2013, 140). This created a culture that encouraged individuals to "follow their manager" and not question decisions. Furthermore, "risk and control themes were rarely mentioned in the actual performance assessments and were typically not explicitly weighted in the overall performance grade" (Salz 2013, 156). Similarly at UBS, bonus schemes encouraged traders to record a short-term profit on the higher-risk mezzanine tranches of CDOs left on the bank's balance sheet because "the compensation structure generally made little recognition of risk issues or adjustment for risk" (UBS 2008b, 42). At UBS bonuses constituted, on average, between 64 and 70% of salaries between 2000 and 2006 (Treasury Committee 2009e, 11). Johnny Cameron told us:

> Looking back with hindsight I can see that what happened to compensation in banks is that compensation went up, just more or less in line with leverage. We all increased the leverage from [the] early '90s

> through to 2007. Hey, we made more and more money. We could pay ourselves more and more and still give the shareholders a decent return. Clearly it's more complicated than that. But it's not a lot more complicated. (Interview, 18 April 2013)

The structure of bonus payments reflected the intensity of market pressures. Executives justified bonuses linked to short-term profits by arguing that there was no other way of retaining key staff. Executives believed that they were effectively managing and distributing risk. But they also believed that they had little alternative but to act as they did, given the market pressures and incentives they faced.

The key responsibility for safeguarding the long-term interests of shareholders and, where appropriate, challenging management and formulating long-term business strategy lay with boards of directors. There is little evidence that boards questioned executive strategies in the years prior to the crisis. In his review of corporate governance within the banks, Sir David Walker (2009, 53) highlights the failure of NEDs on boards to "challenge the executive on substantive issues as distinct from a conventional relatively box-ticking focus on processes."

In 2003 the FSA (2011, 233) warned RBS that the "challenging management culture led by the CEO" had discouraged the board of directors from asking effective questions about strategy. Indeed, around this time the FSA asked to hold individual meetings with board members and hired an outside firm to conduct an investigation into governance standards (Martin 2013, 218).

This culture did not, however, change. In its review of the failure of RBS, the FSA (2011, 226) found that the board "failed adequately to identify and address the aggregation of risks across the businesses . . . and therefore properly to assess the bank's overall exposures and, ultimately, its vulnerability to a major downturn in the markets and collapse in asset prices." As Johnny Cameron suggests, the board actively supported RBS's expansion.

> The stock market was saying, go for it. Everyone was saying, go for it. The board was saying, go for it. The board was very supportive of the executive. All my time at the bank before I was on the board and

> after, the view was, we're with you, we're supporting you, Johnny. That was the sort of feeling. (Interview, 18 April 2013)

Looking back at this period, Goodwin's replacement as CEO, Stephen Hester, suggests that "lots of people thought Fred Goodwin wasn't much constrained by the board or regulators. It's very difficult for anyone, over time, to make the right judgments if they are not much challenged" (Martin 2013, 296).

Unlike the situation in the United States, bank CEOs in the United Kingdom did not also serve as the chairman of their board. This institutional arrangement was not, however, a guarantee of independence. Cameron argues that the RBS board was compromised by a strong bond between the CEO, Fred Goodwin, and the chairman, Tom McKillop. Similarly at Barclays, Salz (2013, 105) concludes that "at times the Board might have given greater challenge to management assurances, for example that issues were 'industry issues' or known to the regulators. Such assurances were no doubt given in good faith—but they did not always turn out to be a reasonable basis for not taking more urgent action."

Ray Perman (interview, 16 April 2013) describes a significant difference between the old Bank of Scotland, where, prior to the merger with the Halifax, directors would regularly undertake a "fairly rigorous process of cross-questioning executives particularly on large lending proposals," and the culture at HBOS. He quotes one former director as saying: "Stevenson [the chairman of HBOS] didn't see the point of close questioning the executives . . . Over time you could see a growing over-confidence: we lent money and we were never wrong. The board lost the habit of challenge" (Perman 2013, 97). The group director of risk at HBOS, Peter Hickman, told the Parliamentary Commission on Banking Standards (2013a, 30) that there was an "expectation that the Board would approve the executive business plans." He also said that he could not recall any significant change to any decision making being made by the board during his time at the bank.

Why did NEDs fail to challenge bank strategy? The most obvious explanation is that they were overshadowed by and were unable or unwilling to challenge the executive directors (EDs) who were responsible for the day-to-day management of banks but who also sat on boards of directors. At RBS seven of the seventeen members of the board were EDs—including the group CEO (Fred Goodwin), the group finance director, the CEO of corporate markets, and the chairman of RBS America. At HBOS seven of the fourteen members of the board were EDs—including the CEO (Andy Hornby), the director of corporate banking (Peter Cummings), the group finance director, and the treasurer of the Bank of Scotland. At Barclays six of the fifteen members of the board were EDs—including the group CEO (John Varley), the president of BarCap (Bob Diamond), the group finance director, and the chief executive of global retail and commercial. The NEDs may have constituted a numerical majority on the boards, but they necessarily lacked the detailed knowledge of the bank's day-to-day operations possessed by their management executive counterparts.

This structural weakness was compounded by a rapid turnover. In 2007 the ten NEDs at RBS had served on the board for an average of four years. At HBOS the eight NEDs had served for an average of just over two years. Ray Perman (2013, 111–112) observes that term limit rules meant that NEDs seldom served for long enough to "experience a whole business cycle, from boom to bust." Lord Myners (2008), the former Labour minister and director of a private equity firm, suggests that the unwillingness of NEDs to challenge EDs reflects the latters' lack of experience of and knowledge about banking and finance: "The typical bank board resembles a retirement home for the great and the good: there are retired titans of industry, ousted politicians and the occasional member of the voluntary sector. If such a selection—more likely to be found in Debrett's Peerage than the City pages—was ever good enough, it is not now."

It is true that only a minority of NEDs had direct experience working within banks or other parts of the finance industry. At RBS in 2007 only four of ten NEDs had direct banking experience (RBS 2007a, 92–93). At HBOS only one of eight NEDs had direct banking experience (HBOS 2007a, 112–113). At Barclays only three of nine NEDs had a background in banking (Barclays 2007b, 128–129). Indeed, in 2010, in what might be taken as an admission of past failures, Barclays resolved that, in future, half of its NEDs should have "banking and/or financial experience" (Salz 2013, 100). Jo Dawson (2012) has said that "with hindsight . . . having a Board with more banking experience and better management information would have been desirable." Yet NEDs did have extensive business experience. At HBOS, NEDs included a CEO of the multinational Compass Group; the

CEO of the Carphone Warehouse Group; the founder and CEO of Café Rouge; the corporate treasurer of Bank of America; and the head of legal and compliance for Standard Chartered. The issue of whether NEDs had sufficient banking and financial experience may not, in the end, be a significant one. The simple point to make here is that NEDs who *did* have backgrounds in banking and finance were no more likely to raise concerns about bank strategy than those who did not.

NEDs were inhibited not only by the presence of EDs but by the combination of relatively infrequent meetings and crowded agendas that required them to approve large numbers of individual decisions, providing few opportunities for considered reflection. Ray Perman describes the pressures on boards that were, on average, meeting around ten times a year in full session.

> They were served by quite a large corporate department which produced for the boards numerous big thick papers describing what was going on, reporting back statistics on the month for borrowing in all the different sectors that they lent money in. Deposit and wholesale and so on . . . Well, you can imagine the HBOS papers were probably two inches thick and there was no opportunity to go and cross question people about individual banking transactions. You just had to get through this wad of paper, make the decisions that were needed on the day, and move on. (Interview, 16 April 2013)

In evidence to the Parliamentary Commission on Banking Standards (2013c, 333), Professor Julian Franks argued that

> banks are complex and if you think that you can fix boards to fix these problems, that is a great mistake. You need structural changes. We can improve boards, but do not lay too much emphasis on that as a way of stopping the problem . . . [Large] banks are very complex organizations and increasingly I am coming to the view that bank boards do not have the information to pinpoint problems early enough. Problems of fraud, misselling as well as excessive leverage should tell us that with the best of directors some banks are simply too complex for boards to manage with confidence.

The size and complexity of the largest UK banks were also major constraints on effective management. The total assets of the largest UK banks had risen dramatically in the 2000s. At RBS total assets rose from £309 billion in 2000 to £1.9 trillion in 2007—a figure that exceeded total British GDP. At Barclays assets rose from £307 billion to £1.2 trillion over the same period, while at HBOS they rose from £235 billion to £666 billion. In 2007 RBS operated in fifty-three countries and Barclays in fifty-one countries. The RBS group operated through 8 principal subsidiary operations (RBS 2007a, 69) but a total of over 1,300 registered subsidiary companies. The Parliamentary Commission report into the failure of HBOS concludes that senior management was "incapable of even understanding the risks that some elements of the business were running, let alone managing them" (Parliamentary Commission on Banking Standards, 2013a, 31). RBS executives often seemed completely unaware of the level of their market exposures. In August 2005 Larry Fish, the chairman of RBS's US operations, assured investors, "We don't do any capital market trading activities . . . We don't do subprime lending" (RBS 2005, 28). In February 2006 Fred Goodwin maintained that "we've always had a history of being quite conservative on the assets side of the balance sheet and I expect that to continue" (RBS 2006b, 30). Read with the obvious benefit of hindsight, such statements seem quite disingenuous. By 2008 RBS actually held £33.5 billion in US mortgage-backed residential securities (RBMSs) guaranteed by the US government; £5 billion in "prime" RBMSs; £1.1 billion in "nonconforming" RBMSs; and £1.8 billion in subprime RBMSs (RBS 2009, 185). Yet, as Johnny Cameron has said, this constituted only a small fraction of RBS's overall business and was not "on the dashboard of things to worry about" (interview, 18 April 2013).

Andy Haldane suggests that the largest banks in the United Kingdom and beyond were simply too big to manage:

> Nothing I've seen during the crisis has led me to change my view that firms of the size and scope and complexity of the world's biggest banks can be effectively risk managed on a consolidated basis . . . So the fact is, there literally isn't a big bank that's escaped over the course of the last four or five years. In one way or another, everyone's risk management has been found wanting; sometimes in life-threatening ways,

> other times just in career-threatening ways. The more time that passes, the more confident I am in my assertion . . . that at their existing scale and complexity, the world's largest banks are too big to manage, certainly too big to risk manage. (Interview, 9 May 2013)

Sir John Vickers told the Parliamentary Commission on Banking Standards (2013c, 114) that "the complexities of management and the lack of awareness at the top of these banks" were "a major issue." Mervyn King shared this assessment.

> If we had had a discussion around this table before the crisis, and you had said, "We are getting a bit worried that it is too complex and too big. Let's choose four people whom we really trust to put into Citibank, and they will surely know what is going on." Well, we might have said, "Let's start with Bob Rubin, Treasury Secretary in the US, who used to run Goldman Sachs; Sandy Weill, streetwise trader who built up Citibank; Stan Fischer, one of the world's most respected economists, former No. 2 at the IMF, now central bank governor at the Bank of Israel; and Bill Rhodes who has seen every emerging market debt crisis there has been." I think we would all genuinely have thought that you couldn't get four better people to sit there and say, "Well, let's see what's going on." But they didn't see what was going on. I think that is evidence that these institutions were simply too big and complex for anyone to genuinely know exactly what was going on . . . These institutions have become absolutely enormous. (Parliamentary Commission on Banking Standards 2013c, 115)

External Governance

We have argued that bank CEOs operated within extremely hierarchical governance arrangements within their banks where there were few, if any, effective checks on their authority. Outside of the immediate confines of the banks, institutional investors, external auditors, and, crucially, regulatory authorities provided a supportive institutional environment and did little to challenge bank decision making. The Walker Review (Walker 2009, 71) notes that "before the recent crisis phase there appears to have been a widespread acquiescence by institutional investors and the market in the gearing up of the balance sheets of banks . . . as a means of boosting returns on equity." Ninety-four percent of shareholders voted to approve RBS's ambitious takeover of ABN Amro (Martin 2013, 249). Large investors tended to be short-termist and did not develop any long-term relationship with banks. Haldane (2011, 12) shows that for a sample of UK banks the average length of time investors held their shares fell from around three years in 1998 to less than three months in 2008. As a result there was almost no contact between NEDs and the largest shareholders (Lord Myners, interview, 7 April 2013). The prime interest of shareholders in a market in which ownership was frequently changing was to maximize short-term profits. Far from acting as a check on bank executives, institutional investors encouraged bank executives to pursue high-growth strategies. The chairman of the RBS, Sir Tom McKillop, told the Treasury select committee in 2009:

> There is no doubt—and my experience of my institutional shareholders goes back beyond the bank—it would be a very unusual institution that was not seeking a company to grow and to deliver more earnings or better dividends or whatever. That is a kind of given, that they would always be pushing the organisation to perform better and I do not blame them for that. I would say the drift from the most institutional shareholders was increase the dividend, share buybacks, return capital, do not sit on capital and run a very efficient balance sheet. (Treasury Committee 2009a)

Auditors—who had to inspect and approve the banks' accounts—also failed to raise significant concerns. Ray Perman notes that auditors were in an invidious position in that they were expected to challenge managers who approved their contracts:

> I think one of the things that is a problem and has been a problem in the crash is that auditors essentially work for the management. Technically they are auditing the accounts on behalf of the shareholders, and the shareholders have to vote on the reappointment of the auditors

> and the remuneration of the auditors. So it's usual that the shareholders vote on a resolution which says it will leave the management to set the remuneration of the auditors. But in reality auditors work for the management, and it's the management which recommends to the shareholders a change of auditor or carry on. (Perman interview, 16 April 2013)

In 2000 RBS appointed Deloitte as its new auditor. By 2008 this contract was worth £30 million a year to Deloitte. In addition, Deloitte earned a further £20 million in contracts from RBS in 2008 for other work on tax advice and corporate finance (Martin 2013, 223). Lord Myners offers a particularly damning assessment of the work of auditors:

> I met the chairman of the audit committees on four major banks. Quite frankly—within a few minutes it was clear that the only expertise they brought to their role was: "I don't understand all the detail, but I've been around long enough to tell whether a man is being straightforward with me; I can tell from his eyes whether I'm getting honest answers." It was lamentable. (Interview, 7 April 2013)

Auditors are legally authorized to privately raise any concerns with regulators. In 2011 the House of Lords Economics Affairs Committee reported that the FSA did not hold a single private meeting with the external auditors of either Northern Rock or HBOS and that only one meeting was held with RBS's auditors (Martin 2013, 224).

Regulators did little to discourage rapid growth and the pursuit of higher profit returns. Primary responsibility for the regulatory supervision of individual banks belonged to the FSA, which was established by the Labour government in 1997. Overall responsibility for financial stability remained with the Bank of England, with the Treasury playing a coordinative role. The establishment of the FSA constituted a significant extension of state authority relative to the discredited system of self-regulation within the City it superseded (Moran 2003). Yet while the FSA was given the legal authority to demand disclosure of market-sensitive information, fine banks, and even suspend or revoke their licenses, its day-to-day operations were animated by a conviction that markets and market competition were the most effective regulatory tools and that bank executives could be trusted to manage risk and protect the long-term interests not only of their shareholders but of the City as a whole. Employing a beautiful turn of phrase, Engelen et al. (2011, 10) note that "the FSA was an imposing Potemkin village: behind its impressive façade, all informed observers agree, it deferred . . . to elites in the market." When combined with a desire to attract footloose banks and investment from abroad—the Financial Services and Markets Act of 2000 explicitly required the FSA to have regard to "the international character of financial services and the desirability of maintaining the competitive position of the UK"—this light-touch or, as it was often described, "principles-based" approach risked degenerating into an "anything goes" philosophy which, in the words of the former UK chancellor, Alistair Darling (2011, 318), encouraged a "culture of lackadaisical supervision [and a] climate where too often regulators and boardrooms alike were happy to look the other way."

This regulatory regime was, to quote Lord Turner (2009b, 88), "underpinned by the then dominant philosophy of confidence in self-correcting markets." Subsequently, Turner (2011, 4) returned to this theme. "It is striking in the pre-crisis years how dominant and how overconfident, at least in the arena of financial economics, was a simplified version of equilibrium theory which saw market completion as the cure to all problems, and mathematical sophistication decoupled from philosophical understanding as the key to effective risk management." Sir David Walker also suggests that the FSA was just one of many "victims of the intellectual environment. They thought that markets were inherently stabilizing and efficient. Many of us certainly were part of that belief, which proved to be wholly erroneous" (Treasury Committee 2012b, 24). In its report into the failure of the RBS, the FSA admitted that, prior to the crisis, it had operated with "an overt supervisory philosophy that it should, wherever possible, rely on a firm's senior management to ensure that risks were well-controlled." Speaking after the crash, Hector Sancts, the FSA's former chief executive, said that a "prevailing climate at the time and indeed, right until the crisis commenced was that the market does know best" (Farlow 2013, 314).

FSA supervisors did engage with individual banks to collect data on their market exposures, to ensure that they had credible internal risk control systems, and to ensure that they had disclosed appropriate information to investors. Indeed, McPhilemy (2013) points to the apparent paradox that the light-touch FSA nevertheless produced a handbook of intricate secondary legislation running to 8,000 pages. The result was, however, a superficial "box ticking" exercise (Treasury Committee 2012a, 87). FSA supervisors failed to step back and consider whether the banks were operating a sustainable business model. Describing his own experiences as a former director of a large private equity firm, Lord Myners recalls:

> We were based in Bermuda, where we had a UK FSA-regulated subsidiary. We submitted about a billion data points to the FSA each year. I used to think, What are they doing with this information? We're providing them with a massive amount of data. How can they make sense of it? Not once during the time that I chaired this business—which was three years or so—did anybody from the FSA come and say to me "Chairman, how do you see the markets in which you operate? What are your thoughts on the current pricing of risk? What do you make of the behaviors of your competitors? Where is your anxiety level highest?" That's the sort of engagement that you expect an effective regulator to have with the senior people at banks and other regulated institutions. The FSA just didn't see things in this way. They were obsessed with data and the small things—they appeared institutionally incapable of seeing the big things. (Interview, 7 April 2013)

Reflecting upon a similar experience at RBS, Johnny Cameron told us:

> It's not a problem of how far down they [the FSA] went. They went to some extraordinary levels of detail. It's how far up they went that would be the issue. But standing back from the whole thing, the fact is our leverage was too high, both in terms of capital and more particularly in terms of the key loan to deposit ratio which was about our funding. That is where at the end it all went wrong, the funding side . . . in a sense, more importantly than the capital. I don't recall anybody ever saying to us, are you sure you're comfortable with all this wholesale funding? (Interview, 18 April 2013)

Bank executives and market analysts failed to recognize that organizational complexity, leverage, and a growing dependence upon wholesale funding had generated systemic risk. Regulators did not compensate for this failure. The FSA now recognizes that prudential supervisors did not sufficiently assess and challenge key strategic decisions and business model risks. Speaking with the benefit of hindsight, Mervyn King (Parliamentary Commission on Banking Standards 2013c, 416) has argued: "It did not take complex reporting to see that the balance sheet of the banking system nearly trebled in five years, or that leverage ratios had reached levels of 50 or more. The obsession with detail was in fact a hindrance to seeing the big picture." RBS's takeover of ABN Amro, which, as we saw in Chapter 3, was an important staging point in the bank's eventual implosion, occurred in the absence of any executive-level discussion at the FSA (2011, 180–181). Indeed, far from seeking to restrain the banks in 2006–2007, the FSA actually allowed RBS, Northern Rock, and HBOS to reduce their capital buffers (Martin 2013, 248).

The FSA was thus focused upon the quality of the banks' individual balance sheets rather than the overall level of risk within the financial system. Turner (2009b, 84) argues that the failure to recognize the need for a broader regulatory approach, or what is now called a "macroprudential" regulatory approach, prior to the 2007–2008 crisis was a key flaw:

> It is not unfair to characterise what occurred as follows. The Bank of England tended to focus on monetary policy analysis as required by the inflation target . . . The FSA focused too much on the supervision of individual institutions, and insufficiently on wider sectoral and system-wide risks. The vital activity of macroprudential analysis, and the definition and use of macroprudential tools, fell between two stools. In the words of Paul Tucker, former Deputy Governor of the Bank of England for financial stability, the problem was not overlap but "underlap."

In the years prior to the onset of the 2007–2008 crisis the FSA expressed few concerns about financial stability. In a press release accompanying the publication of its 2005 *Financial Risk Outlook*, the FSA's chairman, Sir Callum

McCarthy, argued that economic growth would continue to underpin financial stability. In January 2006 the FSA did express a concern that low interest rates might have led financial institutions to underprice risk and urged companies to conduct rigorous stress tests on their portfolios. Yet this must be seen in the context of the FSA's overall judgment that "our central macroeconomic case is one of continued economic and financial stability" (FSA 2006, 1). By January 2007 the FSA (2007, 1) had recognized "an increasing risk that the business operating environment we will face over the next 18 months, both in the UK and abroad, could be more challenging than in recent years" and warned of the possibility of a "disorderly" unwinding. Yet, even then, such concerns were qualified by an assessment that "our central economic scenario is one of relatively benign economic conditions and financial stability, a view which is in line with consensus forecasts." In June 2007 the director of wholesale firms at the FSA, Thomas Huertas, told Robert Peston (Peston and Knight 2013, 18–19) that "the major institutions are very well capitalized. They show very very strong earnings. Anywhere short of a major depression, the firms are much better placed than they have been to withstand economic shocks."

The FSA, widely pilloried for its failings, was abolished in 2013. It was replaced by the Prudential Regulatory Authority, a new body within the Bank of England. Looking back, it is clear that the FSA operated under significant constraints. It had only a relatively modest number of staff. The team responsible for the supervision of HBOS, for example, consisted of a manager and five staff members who were also expected to oversee the activities of two other smaller retail banks (Parliamentary Commission on Banking Standards 2013a, 27). The FSA team charged with supervising RBS consisted of just one manager and six officials (Martin 2013, 219). In 2006 the FSA then decided to separate the regulation of RBS's investment bank operations from that of the rest of the bank. Iain Martin (2013, 219) quotes one board member as saying, "What I really think they don't understand at the FSA is that the Royal Bank was a retail bank that now had a mini, or not so mini, Goldman Sachs lodged inside it." The chairman of the FSA, Hector Sants, told the Treasury Select Committee (Treasury Committee 2012b, 26) that "the quality and quantity of the supervisory staff that I inherited in the summer of 2007, as well as the procedures and philosophy they were operating to, was inadequate . . . We had almost no investment banking expertise in the FSA. We had very limited risk analysis expertise in the FSA." Furthermore, the FSA was under considerable political pressure to reduce the regulatory burden on UK banks. In May 2005 the then chancellor, Gordon Brown (Farlow 2013, 313), celebrated the fact that the FSA operated "not just with a light touch but a limited touch" in which there was "no form filling without justification, and no information requirements without justification." As he went on to argue:

> A risk-based approach helps us move a million miles away from the old assumption—the assumption since the first legislation of Victorian times—that business, unregulated, will invariably act irresponsibly. The better view is that business wants to act responsibly. Reputation with customers and investors is more important to behavior than regulation, and transparency—backed up by the light touch—can be more effective than the heavy hand. (Farlow 2013, 313)

Later that year, in response to a query from Tony Blair about regulatory standards, the FSA's chairman, Sir Callum McCarthy, reassured the prime minister that the FSA applied to the largest UK banks only a fraction of the supervision applied by US regulators to banks of an equivalent size. In June 2006 the then economic secretary to the Treasury, Ed Balls, told an audience of bankers, "We must keep the UK's regulatory system at the cutting-edge—the best in the world . . . At all times we will apply a principled system of risk-regulation, without unnecessary administrative burden" (Treasury Committee 2012b, 13). The FSA's (2011, 29) report into the failure of RBS suggests that "it is likely that, if the FSA had proposed before the first signs of the crisis (i.e. before the summer of 2007) the measures that in retrospect appear appropriate, such proposals would have been met by extensive complaints that the FSA was pursuing a heavy-handed, gold-plating and unnecessary approach." Similarly, Mervyn King (Kirkup 2009) has suggested that any regulator who had sought to persuade politicians that the banks were underregulated would have confronted a "massively difficult task." Ray Perman (interview, 16 April 2013) told us that "the banks like to always talk to the prime minister, the chancellor of the Exchequer, anybody else's ear they can get," and that if the FSA had raised concerns about a bank's behavior they would have been told "We don't want these people leaving and going to Frankfurt or New York or Hong Kong."

The relationship between the banks and the Labour government was sustained by financial contributions to political campaigns and by the appointment of senior bankers to the FSA and to government commissions. By 2010 nearly 50% of cash donations to the Conservative Party were from the financial services sector (Syal, Treanor, and Mathiason 2011; see also Engelen et al. 2011, 145). We now know that policy makers ought to have done more to question whether the growth of the financial sector was potentially counterproductive, let alone sustainable. But it is not hard to see how, in particular, incumbent politicians had become addicted not only to the tax revenues generated by the banks but also to the mystique of a booming "new" economy in which the United Kingdom appeared to have retained its comparative advantage. "The government benefited from high tax revenues enabling them to increase public spending on schools and hospitals. This was bound to create a psychology of denial. It was a cycle fuelled, in significant measure, not by virtue but by delusion" (Besley and Hennessy 2009, 2).

The FSA's regulatory record prior to the collapse of Northern Rock in 2007 is consistently poor. The Bank of England offered a more nuanced set of reflections about financial stability in the years prior to 2007 but, ultimately, it too failed to anticipate the banking crisis. The bank's 2006 *Financial Stability Report* identifies six "vulnerabilities" within the UK system: unusually low premia for bearing risk; large financial imbalances among the major economies; rapid releveraging and underpriced corporate risk; high UK household sector indebtedness; rising systemic importance of large, complex financial institutions with expanding balance sheets and risk appetites; and the dependence of UK financial institutions on market infrastructures and utilities for clearing and settling payments and financial transactions that might be disrupted in a crisis. The bank reports that it conducted stress tests on these vulnerabilities and that the "scale of the losses associated with them" could be "significant" (Bank of England 2006, 10). These concerns were echoed in speeches given by senior bank officials. As early as January 2004, the deputy governor of the Bank of England, Andrew Large (2004, 4), pointed to the financial stability problems posed by the "dynamics of collective, and sometimes irrational behaviour."

The following year Large (2005) expressed concerns about the absence of any clear targets for or measures of financial stability. Large's successor, John Gieve (2006b), argued that a bonus culture within the City of London had underpinned the growth in leverage. Later that year, the ED of financial stability, Nigel Jenkinson (2006), warned that commercial property price rises were unsustainable and that any sudden crash could imperil financial stability. Jenkinson (2007) also persuasively argued that the downturn in the US housing market had exposed limitations in the UK banks' risk assessment procedures (Hindmoor and McConnell 2014).

The Bank of England did not, however, sound any clear warnings about financial stability prior to the implosion of Northern Rock in 2007. Indeed, in a public mea culpa delivered in 2012, Mervyn King acknowledged that while the Bank of England "had warned that financial markets were underestimating risks," it had not "imagined the scale of the disaster that would occur"(King 2012, 5). According to a member of the Bank of England's Monetary Policy Committee, Kate Barker, "financial stability became a downplayed part of the institution," something Mervyn King was not "initially very interested in" (Irwin 2013, 7). Bank of England officials failed to recognize the fragility of the financial system they were responsible for because they shared the conviction of many bank executives and market analysts that bank risk management systems were effective and that securitization had allowed the banks to manage their own balance sheet risk. Andrew Large (2003) argued that the way markets had absorbed crises such as the failure of Long-Term Capital Management and the 9/11 attacks had shown how financial innovation had actually "contributed to flexibility and resilience in the system." John Gieve (2006a, 4), argued that "the probability of a contagious crisis may have fallen" because risks had been dispersed across a larger number of firms. Similarly, Mervyn King (2007) thought that

> securitisation is transforming banking from the traditional model in which banks originate and retain credit risk on their balance sheets into a new model in which credit risk is distributed around a much wider range of investors. As a result, risks are no longer concentrated in a small number of regulated institutions but are spread across the financial system. This is a positive development because it has reduced

> the market failure associated with traditional banking—the mismatch between illiquid assets and liquid liabilities.

Officials also failed to see the way in which the apparently separate parts of an incredibly complex banking system might interact with each other during a crisis. Andy Haldane describes how risk factors were multiplicative rather than additive:

> I think the part that we perhaps got most wrong was in not joining the dots between the individual vulnerabilities that we pointed towards. I suppose, for no especially good reason, we'd thought of them in a fairly idiosyncratic way, this could go wrong or that could go wrong, or the other could go wrong, but we hadn't yet told ourselves a story about how they could all go wrong at around the same time. What's more, once you add—this is more than a question of simple addition, so if you add risk 1 going wrong, risk 2 going wrong, risk 3 going wrong, what you get is more than one plus two plus three, because they compound and they amplify and they add to the sense of not knowing. What were virtuous circles became vicious circles, the feedbacks stopped being stabilising and began becoming destabilising. It was that aggregation problem, that aggregation mistake that I think caught most of us out. (Interview, 9 May 2013)

Conclusion

In the years prior to the onset of the financial crisis, the largest banks in the United States and the United Kingdom recorded dizzying profits. In 2007 Barclays announced a pretax profit of £7 billion, RBS a profit of £9.9 billion, and HBOS one of £5.4 billion. Gordon Brown (2007) lauded the City as a "great example of a highly skilled, high value added, talent driven industry that shows how we can excel in a world of global competition" and added that "Britain needs more of the vigour, ingenuity and aspiration" demonstrated by its bankers. In the United States, financial sector profits constituted 27% of all corporate profits in 2006—up from just 15% in 1980 (FCIC 2011, xvii). During this period of unrelenting financial optimism, the senior US economist Robert Lucas (2003) argued that the "central problem of depression prevention has been solved." Bank executives, market analysts, institutional investors, regulators, and politicians really did believe that "this time is different" (Reinhart and Rogoff 2009): that house prices would continue to rise; that risk management tools had allowed the banks to quantify and control risk; and that securitization had reduced balance sheet risk. In his memoirs Gordon Brown (2010, 19) suggests that he had been growing increasingly concerned about financial stability and had pressed for coordinated international action to address the issue prior to 2008. Yet, as his successor, Alistair Darling (2011, 3), acidly observes: "Many people have claimed to have predicted what was going to happen . Most of them failed to mention it at the time."

The financialization of the UK and US economies during the decade preceding the financial crash resulted in the creation of new kinds of systemic risk. Once the US housing bubble burst in 2006–2007, an ever-growing list of banks, hedge funds, insurers, and mutual funds in the United Kingdom, the United States, and Europe started to announce losses in the value of the MBSs they held on their books or had bought from other banks. In themselves, these losses were manageable. But the same market investors, analysts, and credit ratings agencies who had previously displayed absolutely no qualms about the high leverage and the enduring value of AAA-rated financial products now started to assume the worst about the future direction of market sentiment and the long-term value of the financial assets on bank balance sheets. Bank executives who, in a supreme exercise in individual agency, had re-created the financial environment within which they operated suddenly found themselves trapped within a vicious circle of lower asset prices, higher borrowing costs, and scare capital from which they could not escape.

Yet, as we demonstrated in Chapter 3, while all the major US and UK banks were adversely affected by the financial crisis, they were not all affected to the same degree. In the United States, Wells Fargo consistently operated with a conservative balance sheet, while JP Morgan and Goldman Sachs managed to exit the market or successfully hedge against major losses on the eve of the financial meltdown. In the United Kingdom, HSBC, Standard Chartered, and, to a degree, Lloyds TSB prior to its takeover of HBOS entered the crisis in a relatively strong position. These banks operated in the same institutional environment as Lehman Brothers, Citigroup, RBS, and HBOS. Yet, as we go on to show in Chapter 7, key agents within these banks interpreted this environment very differently and, for this reason, carved out distinctive banking strategies. Hence an important part of the explanation of intracountry variation in the United States and the United Kingdom lies in the significance of authoritative individual agency and the ideas that animated such agents.

7

The Survivors

Why Some Banks in the United States and the United Kingdom Avoided the Carnage

In the United States and the United Kingdom, intensely competitive markets gave banks a powerful incentive to adopt aggressive growth strategies in order to increase their market share, return on equity (ROE), and share price, and to avoid hostile market reaction or takeover. However, not all bank executives succumbed to these market pressures. For example, PIMCO, one of the larger investment funds in the United States, announced in 2005 that it would be winding down its exposures to mortgage-backed securities (MBSs). Scott Simon, PIMCO's managing director, told an industry conference in 2005, "There is an awful lot of moral hazard in the sector . . . You either take the high road or you don't" (FCIC 2011, 190). Similarly, as we saw in Chapter 3, among America's many regional banks, BB&T, PNC, and US Bancorp all adopted deliberately low-risk banking strategies and so escaped serious losses during the crisis, while other financial firms such as Lazard, Brown Brothers Harriman, Evercore Partners, and Greenhill did not participate in the securitization of mortgages at all.

Our focus in this book is, however, upon the largest banks. The author William Cohan, formerly a banker in the United States, told us that "people think that these banks are monolithic and they all behave the same way.

But in fact that is not even remotely true" (interview, 12 March 2012). Some banks succumbed to the crisis while others sidestepped or escaped it. Wells Fargo maintained a conservative balance sheet and JP Morgan and Goldman Sachs reversed many of their exposures to risky securities. Of the largest UK banks, HSBC adopted relatively prudent strategies in its core European and Asian markets, though it did lose substantial sums as a result of its ill-fated purchase of Household International in the United States. Lloyds entered the crisis in a relatively strong position but was later undone by its ill-considered purchase of HBOS in 2008. Standard Chartered was not much exposed to Western financial markets. In 2007 only 7% of its operating income derived from the Americas, the United Kingdom, and Europe (Standard Chartered 2007, 5). It emerged from the crisis largely unscathed, deriving most of its profits from personal and business lending in Asia and Africa. There is no evidence that its executives contemplated or came under pressure to change their business strategy during the boom years and enter risky securitization markets. Standard Chartered therefore remained very much on the periphery of the calamity that brought down so many other banks.

The more prudent banks that are the focus of this chapter confronted the same market pressures and regulatory systems as the banks that succumbed to the crisis. Yet they responded in a very different way. Therefore the differences in question clearly stem from the banks themselves: from their internal assessments of the markets and their corporate strategies and cultures. Although we have argued that market incentives and institutional pressures seemingly "enslaved" bankers, ideas were a crucial mediator. As we have argued, it was only those bankers who were "true believers" in the markets who became "enslaved" by them.

What was different about the banks that survived the crisis? First, the banks that bucked the market and survived were led by CEOs and management teams that thought differently than their counterparts in the banks that crashed. The leaders of the banks that survived were well aware of market pressures to increase profits but, crucially, they also recognized the risks. They held different ideas about the financial world and how to operate within it. Whether as a result of their personal experiences or their natural caution, the banks that survived were led by CEOs and management teams with a strong commitment to careful risk management who believed that the financial boom would end, that securitization had not resulted in the emergence of a new financial paradigm, and that high leverage and high dependence upon wholesale funding were major sources of risk.

Second, the agents that held more cautious ideas about banking needed to have the authority and support to be able to act on their views. As we have seen, risk managers on many occasions voiced concerns, but they lacked the authority to steer banks and were typically sidelined or sacked if they ran counter to the views of more aggressive senior managers. Even senior managers who were questioning or not performing were jettisoned. As we have seen, this was the fate of Morgan Stanley's CEO, Phil Purcell. In 2005 major shareholders and senior managers removed Purcell for his "failure to continue to earn a premium return on equity [and] the failure to maintain earnings growth relative to [Morgan Stanley's] peers" (Group of Eight 2005a). As we have also seen, Chuck Prince at Citigroup thought he would have lacked support and been regarded as a "lunatic" if he had seriously questioned the value of the bank's collateralized debt obligation (CDO) assets. The bottom line is that leaders who questioned the market needed authority; at the very least they needed the supported of senior colleagues and a broader bank culture that was also risk averse. As we show in this chapter, the CEOs and other senior managers in the banks that survived typically invested in the promotion of a culture in which risk was carefully managed and where growth, sales, and quarterly profits were not exalted above all other goals. These banks were also characterized by "flatter" organizational structures in which there were more open and fluid lines of communication and a greater willingness to share ideas and challenge prevailing assumptions and models.

The challenge for the banks that did not follow the herd was how to buck the wider market and institutional pressures they confronted. In the years prior to the financial crash, market analysts and activist shareholders often criticized executives at the banks that survived for their excessive caution and reluctance to emulate their rivals' more bellicose strategies. Once the crisis had passed, JP Morgan's CEO, Jamie Dimon, was eulogized by politicians and journalists as the "last man standing" (D. McDonald 2009). Yet JP Morgan was criticized prior to the crisis for being too cautious. It is even possible that Dimon would have been forced aside if the crisis had not occurred when it did. Nevertheless, most of the senior bankers who survived could afford to behave more cautiously without being removed because their banks did record satisfactory profits without having to reengineer their balance sheets. Although JP Morgan was under pressure prior to the crisis, HSBC and Wells Fargo, for example, were able to attract deposits and highly profitable prime mortgage business, putting them in a strong market position. The fact that they were able to do so is a reflection of niche institutional capacities that reflect the successful efforts of earlier generations of bank leaders to acquire a reputation for good financial stewardship, reflecting again the impact of corporate cultures.

JP Morgan Chase

JP Morgan recorded significant write-down losses on the value of the assets on its balance sheet once market prices fell in 2007–2008. The bank was nevertheless in a strong position because it had only limited exposures to risky MBSs by the time the financial crisis began, having decided to largely steer clear of such investments in 2006. Like most other CEOs of the leading banks, JP Morgan's Jamie Dimon was authoritative, if not imperious. However, unlike many other CEOs, he was not imprudent. As the *Economist* (2010a) observed, "Imperial bosses and sound risk cultures sometimes go together." Dimon—who was named CEO at JP Morgan in December 2005 and chairman in December 2006—operated on the principle that "no one has the right not to assume that the business cycle will turn. Every five years or so, you have got to assume that something bad will happen" (quoted in Tett 2009, 113). On this basis Dimon justified his pursuit of a "fortress balance sheet" and a cautious risk management strategy that eschewed off–balance sheet activities and risk concentrations. Dimon was aware of the structural pressures facing the banks. He told the FCIC: "We support proper regulation . . . I think the regulation of mortgages was unfortunate because it was basically unregulated . . . It caught us in a race to the bottom and so you are going to lose business if you don't cut your fees and get more aggressive on underwriting" (Dimon 2010). He was also aware that traders and managers had been lulled into a false sense of confidence by the boom. "For twenty years they weren't taking losses . . . They got sucked into this whole sense of security because there were no losses . . . We have to write a letter to the next generation to tell them" (Dimon 2010).

Dimon also warned that "there's so much pressure on companies to expand their business that they end up pushing their own people to grow, grow, grow . . . Such pressure can lead to dangerous outcomes for all businesses—and especially for volatile business[es] like investment banks that take risks" (JP Morgan Chase 2007, 12–13).

Dimon was a stickler for detail and had a sound grasp of the business. Shortly after becoming CEO, he started spending hours every morning examining detailed accounts prepared for him by every division head, with key data from the prior month. Dimon believed that "every single risk you're taking can be broken down to its smallest components and therefore be better understood. All it takes is time and effort" (D. McDonald 2009, 197). In the first half of 2006, Dimon told analysts in a conference call, "Run your business knowing it might be more sunny, it might be stormy, or in fact it might be a hurricane . . . and be honest about how bad a hurricane might be" (D. McDonald 2009, 207).

Dimon also adopted a holistic approach to corporate management. He worked hard to overcome the siloed nature of the various divisions and departments within the bank and brought senior managers together to improve communications and the exchange of views (Tett 2009, 114). JP Morgan's chief risk officer (CRO), Barry Zubrow (2010), argues that, within the bank, there is a "fluid" communication of information and a "lack of hierarchical shielding of information." He tells the story of how, shortly after arriving at JP Morgan, he received a phone call from the chairman of the board of directors' risk committee, Jim Crown, asking for some information. After answering the question he went to tell Dimon what had happened and what he had said to Crown. "Jamie sort of looked at me and said 'why are you telling me this'? I cite this as an example that is emblematic of the culture here, which is that the Board can and should have whatever information it wants and that people in the organization should feel comfortable sharing with them." The story is interesting not just for what it tells us about JP Morgan's culture but for what it says about the culture of other banks. Zubrow (2010) clearly believed the incident to be a memorable one and went on to say that, in his experience, the culture at JP Morgan was "unique."

Dimon also acted to improve the pay, status, and independence of risk managers within JP Morgan (Tett 2009, 115). CROs within each of the bank's divisions sat on the executive committees of those divisions but also had a direct line of reporting to the group's CRO and, through him, to the board to ensure that risk management was "wholly independent of the trading or origination side." Zubrow argues that the culture at JP Morgan was one in which risk managers were given an effective veto over decisions. "If it comes down to a conflict between what risk thinks should happen and what the [rest of] the organization thinks should happen . . . risk gets fifty one per cent of the vote and the revenue side gets forty nine per cent of the vote . . . and in my own experience it has always been that way."

Dimon also sought to ensure that risk management was not regarded as a separate decision-making silo. Traders and managers were sent on training courses organized by the risk department, and senior managers were told to attend risk meetings. Dimon insisted that the staff should think about risk in a truly holistic manner. It was not enough, he declared, to "subcontract risk management to one department" (D. McDonald 2009, 189).

Dimon was also careful not to place too much emphasis on single risk management instruments, such as value at risk (VaR). Warren Buffett has reflected on Dimon in the following way: "Too many people overemphasize the power of these statistical models . . . but not Jamie. The CEO of any of these firms has to be the chief risk officer . . . You have to have somebody that's got a real fear in them of what can happen in markets" (D. McDonald 2009, 232). Zubrow (2010) describes how risk models were employed by analysts at JP Morgan but how "model validation" was undertaken by an entirely separate group to ensure a "clear check and balance" and how risk models were never substituted for "management judgment."

The bank was also cautious about using off–balance sheet vehicles such as structured investment vehicles (SIVs), which relied upon short-term funding. Senior managers had debated the idea of creating a network of SIVs in the 1990s but decided against it. When Bill Winters became deputy CEO of the JP Morgan investment bank in 2004, he drastically cut the $12 billion of credit JP Morgan had already extended to other banks' SIVs to a mere $500 million. "I could never work out why anyone thought that SIVs were a good idea," he said (Tett 2009, 128).

JP Morgan's record was not, however, perfect. In the early 2000s the bank started to increase its mortgage origination business through a subsidiary company, Chase Home Finance. In 2005 it also began to build an infrastructure to more fully engage with mortgage securitization and trading.

However, in 2006 Dimon started to get "cold feet" (Tett 2009, 121). He had become involved in a debate within the bank's mortgage group that had been examining the falloff in house price increases and the rise in mortgage default rates during 2006. In October 2006, Dimon told the head of mortgage trading, Bill King: "I really want you to watch out for subprime . . . We need to sell a lot of our positions. I've seen it before. This stuff could go up in smoke" (Tett 2009, 143). Within weeks, the bank had sold more than $12 billion in subprime mortgages it had originated (D. McDonald 2009, 215). At the same time, Dimon resolved to raise the bank's underwriting standards on new corporate loans. The bank also purchased credit default swaps (CDSs) to try to insure its exposures. Here, however, there was concern about how much protection CDS insurance would offer if there were a major crisis and an avalanche of claims on the big monoline insurers (Tett 2009, 127). In the late 1990s, Terry Duhon, a member of JP Morgan's CDS team, had become concerned about the emerging CDS market in mortgage protection. This market had started in the commercial debt arena, where data on the credit risk of firms was widely available. But the lack of data about the credit histories of the referenced borrowers in the mortgage market made JP Morgan's analysts nervous. Duhon's supervisor, Blythe Masters, argued that "mortgage risk was just too uncharted" (Tett 2009, 68).

In the years prior to the crisis, Dimon and other senior managers, such as Bill Winters, had also become increasingly convinced that the profit margins and the potential risks of securitization business didn't make sense. Given the relatively small margins, we "just could not work out how to make the business profitable enough for the risks," recalls Dimon (Tett 2009, 140). By late 2006 Winters "had concluded that it was no longer worth the risk to underwrite or hold any such product on the company's books. At the time, CDOs were yielding just 2 percentage points more than Treasuries. [Plus] to hedge the CDO risk, JP Morgan Chase needed to buy credit default swaps, but the cost of those was rising" (D. McDonald 2009, 210). Winters had no problem convincing Dimon of his concerns, and the bank began exiting the business of underwriting CDOs while also selling the majority of subprime mortgages originated by the bank during the year. "I'd love to say we saw what was coming," Winters later said, referring to the housing collapse, "but that would be a lie. We just couldn't see the return in them" (D. McDonald 2009, 213).

Dimon communicated well with his senior managers and trusted their judgment. But the question in their minds was why so many other banks had reached different judgments about the sustainability of the boom. Was the leadership of JP Morgan missing something? As winter approached in late 2006, Dimon was becoming increasingly worried. The bank redoubled efforts to increase underwriting standards and hedge its bets. But there were also mistakes. As senior managers were debating the firm's strategy, a unit of the bank went ahead and purchased a $2 billion CDO that wiped $1 billion off the firm's fourth-quarter earnings for 2007 when the instrument lost half its value. Bill Winters called the episode an "outright control lapse" and "the biggest single mistake we've made in a long time" (D. McDonald 2009, 236–237).

Notwithstanding such errors, JP Morgan's reluctance to jump headlong into the booming MBS and CDO markets had taken its toll on the bank's bottom line, especially from 2005 to early 2007. Its profit and share price performance were clearly lagging behind those of its more aggressive rivals. Increasingly, JP Morgan's business strategy was being criticized. From the beginning of 2005 through mid-2006, the bank's share price rose just 7.7% while Goldman's climbed by over 44%. In 2005, JP Morgan's ROE was just 7%, compared with 21% at Citigroup and 14% at Merrill Lynch. In 2006 JP Morgan was ranked nineteenth in asset-backed CDO issuances. Analysts responded by giving the bank what one manager called "a world of shit for our fixed income revenues," arguing that the bank was being too cautious (D. McDonald 2009, 214).

> The Bank's CFO, Mike Kavanagh, recalls being harangued by investors demanding a reason why they should bother with JPMorgan Chase stock when they could own "best-in-class" competitors like Goldman Sachs in investment banking or American Express in credit cards . . . Analysts were losing interest in merely watching costs go down. They craved big news like an acquisition, or significant gains in market share. (D. McDonald 2009, 208)

Yet in the immediate wake of the banking meltdown, JP Morgan's cautious approach was entirely vindicated. "During the previous seven years, JP Morgan staff had become accustomed to feeling like laggards," but by 2009, "now suddenly they were stars" (D. McDonald 2009, 215). Nevertheless, to underline the fact that no bank was immune to the problems of risk management and internal control, the "London Whale" episode at JP Morgan lost over $6 billion trading in synthetic credit markets in 2012, an incident to which we return in Chapter 9.

Wells Fargo

Wells Fargo had the lowest exposures to MBSs and recorded the fewest losses of any of the major American banks during the crisis. Its pretax profits fell from $16.9 billion in 2007 to $2.59 billion in 2008 but recovered sharply to $11 billion in 2009 and $9.9 billion in 2010. Wells Fargo's share price fell by just 17% between 2006 and 2008. Wells had a large mortgage origination business but focused largely upon prime lending and subprime lending, but only where borrowers were in a position to verify their income and job status. In 2004 Wells published a Responsible Lending Code that committed the bank to making loans only where it was convinced that the loan was not only affordable but in the customer's best interests. Wells retained a small proportion of mortgages on its own books but sold most to Freddie Mae, Fannie Mac, and the other large banks. It made its profits from retaining, servicing, and refinancing rights over these mortgages, which allowed it to build an ongoing relationship with clients to whom it could then sell other financial products. According to Mark Oman (2010), the senior executive vice president of home and consumer finance, Wells operated a "vanilla" business model. "We were taking a long view. We were serving customers for a long view and we wanted to have customers for life. So we didn't view this as just a transaction, let's make as much money as we can, we don't care what happens in the future . . . We want that long-term relationship." In late 2006 and early 2007 senior executives identified weaknesses in the housing market and closed Wells Fargo's subprime mortgage origination business (W. Cohan 2011, 523). According to John Stumpf (2010), the president and CEO, "We knew that dog probably wouldn't hunt for ever . . . It did not make sense . . . It was a disaster waiting to happen."

When asked to explain their conservatism, Wells executives often pointed to the company's long history and its reputation for eschewing financial excess, an approach it had developed over a number of decades. According to Stumpf:

> When you think about Wells, we celebrated our 158th birthday on July 15th . . . We have a culture around here that is very much about long term kinds of activities. We're here for the long term. Our investors, Warren Buffett being our largest, only talk about long term. So when fads come and go . . . we're aware of them but we don't get seduced by them. We stick to our vision and values, stick to what we know. I like to say that we're meat and potatoes, if you want tuna tartar[e] and fennel you gotta go someplace else.

Wells employed a "flotilla" of around 6,000 risk officers and insisted that individual loans be approved by named regional executives who could be held accountable for their decisions rather than by loan committees (Stumpf 2010). Risk management was consistently prioritized over market share and growth.

> Control is the ticket to play. In Wells Fargo if you were to go back and say what's the mantra: its control, profitability, growth. You don't get to grow the business unless that's last. You've got to have it under control and you have to have a business model that shows you can make money and then you can grow. (Oman 2010)

Wells also adopted a holistic approach to managing risk and saw the diversity of the firm's businesses in this light. As Richard Kovacevich (2010), Wells Fargo's CEO between 1998 and 2007, told the FCIC:

> I think that comes back to the business model that Wells Fargo has where we are purposefully diversified in many many businesses across many geographies where we can not only diversify our risk but also diversify risk over cycles. We have over 80 businesses . . . pulling the stage coach. And we know in any environment some businesses are going to be doing well and some are going to be doing less well. One of the tenets of our company is that you don't push too hard . . . You trust the business model as there'll be other businesses picking up the

> slack here. I think now the diversified companies are the ones that are still standing.

Did Wells pay a price for its conservatism during the boom years? Wells Fargo's executives, including Oman (2010), certainly believe that they did.

> Did we pay a price? Absolutely . . . We lost market share and the market share that we did have was at a fairly low margin because . . . We stuck to our knitting . . . We were plodders . . . We were not as aggressive as others . . . There were temptations . . . but we were successful in resisting those temptations. In hindsight we look very smart. It didn't feel like that at the time. We had investors saying "why aren't you doing those things?" We had analysts saying "why aren't you doing those things?" We were criticized a lot . . . there's not some magic potion here which says you are always going to do the right thing but we tried to stay true to our vision and values and it worked out.

Richard Kovacevich (2010) agreed that, during the boom years, "we were maybe not as competitive in the non-prime spaces as other people . . . but we were concerned however that we'd seen this movie before." At Wells, unlike at JP Morgan, there is, however, little indication that executives came under sustained pressure to change their overall strategy. When asked to explain why, John Stumpf (2010) suggested that Wells attracted relatively conservative institutional investors like Warren Buffett who shared its commitment to long-term growth. This might well be true, but the underlying figures suggest that Wells did *not* actually pay a significant price for its conservatism. Wells did pay significantly lower dividends to shareholders than its rivals during the boom period between 2004 and 2006 (around a third of the amount paid at Citigroup and Bank of America). But its average ROE of 18% during this period was *higher* than that recorded by Citigroup, JP Morgan, Bank of America, or Wachovia. Furthermore, its end-of-year share price, far from falling, rose from $31 in 2004 to $35 in 2005. It may well be true that Wells could have recorded still-higher profits and ROE if it had more aggressively entered the subprime securitization market and extended its leverage. Wells Fargo's performance during the boom years was, however, impressive, reflecting its deep presence in traditional lending markets.

Wells Fargo's reputation for prudent management helped the company attract prime mortgage business. Its strategy also meant that the company was in a good position to acquire additional assets once the boom had ended.

> We've always had this view that we [have] to have a fortified balance sheet and strong capital. And the difference is made during the go-go times, don't do stupid things, stick to your guns in the go-go times because when times turn tough then you're gonna have the resources at your disposal to make some very good financial decisions for the company . . . The time when Wachovia came up, we're probably the only company in the country that could have bought them without any special support from the government. We used our own money. (Stumpf 2010)

Goldman Sachs

In contrast to JP Morgan and Wells Fargo, Goldman Sachs was a substantial originator and trader in MBSs. In 2006 it was ranked tenth globally in a league table of mortgage underwriters. Goldman was, however, content with being in the middle of the pack and decided not to invest further in this business by purchasing a mortgage originator (W. Cohan 2011, 482). Furthermore, in late 2006 the bank started to actively wind down its exposures. Josh Birnbaum, one of Goldman's key mortgage analysts, increasingly thought "the housing market was starting to lose steam" (W. Cohan 2011, 493). In this context, the bank's mortgage analysts calculated that relatively small increases in default rates could have a substantial impact on the value of tranches within MBSs. At this stage, the bank's VaR numbers were not showing much cause for concern. As CEO Lloyd Blankfein (2009) would later write about the banking meltdown and the pathologies of the sector:

> Risk models failed to capture the risk . . . It seems clear now that managers . . . did not appreciate the full magnitude of the economic risks they were exposed to . . . Complexity got the better of us. The

> industry let the growth in new instruments outstrip the operational capacity to manage them. As a result, operational risk increased dramatically.

At Goldman, however, executives were able to identify weaknesses in the bank's risk systems *before* it was engulfed by the crisis. Trading prices in MBSs started to decline in late November 2006. Traders at Merrill Lynch, Bear Stearns, and UBS did not appreciate that prices were collapsing until early 2007. They recognized that markets were increasingly illiquid and that there were few buyers for their products. Yet they did not connect this lack of demand to a change in price. Indeed, they were misled by relying on hypothetical price quotations in the markets. As a result, senior risk managers and executives at these banks did not realize that the market had turned and that the assets on their balance sheets were significantly overvalued. In contrast, Goldman was able to escape this trap because its risk management systems were predicated on the strict use of mark-to-market pricing on the basis of *actual* exchange prices. In its written evidence to the FCIC, CEO Lloyd Blankfein (2010b, 3) suggested that

> our approach to risk management is rooted in accountability, escalation and communication. A large part of this discipline is reflected in the marking process, which assigns current values to financial assets and liabilities. We believe that rigorous fair value accounting for financial instruments is fundamental to prudent management because it facilitates a clear view of risk. It allows us to manage market risk limits, monitor exposure to credit risk and manage our liquidity requirements. For Goldman Sachs, the daily marking of positions to their fair value was a key contributor to our decision to reduce risk relatively early in markets and in positions that were deteriorating. This process can be difficult, and sometimes painful, but we believe it is a discipline that should define financial institutions. We fair value our positions, not only because we are required to, but because we wouldn't know how to assess or manage risk if market prices were not reflected on our books.

This was not simply rhetorical glossing. Drawing on a variety of sources, Hardie and Howarth (2013a, 33) show that in 2007 Goldman valued 86%

of its assets using mark-to-market accountancy conventions compared with only 27% at Bank of America and 39% at Citigroup. In mid-December 2006 Goldman's chief financial officer, David Viniar, noticed that the daily profit and loss returns from the mortgage desk indicated that there had been ten straight days of trading losses. Daniel Sparks, the head of the mortgage trading department, was also becoming concerned about the bank's mortgage positions and about the bank's inventory of warehoused loans waiting to be packaged and sold. On 14 December, Viniar called a meeting of key traders and risk managers. They reviewed the data and agreed to rapidly reduce the bank's risk exposure. This strategy entailed selling Goldman's long mortgage positions, even if this meant incurring losses. As Blankfein (2010a) told the FCIC:

> It was very very hard to sell them except at distressed prices, which we were willing to do. So as part of our protocols, we actually sold things down faster than others and took losses that in hindsight look like very good transactions but at the time we were doing it we assumed we were going to feel stupid after the fact but we just have these protocols that require us to get our risk down when we're losing money and as it happened, they kept going down further so we didn't feel as stupid as we thought we would when we figured that the market would rally.

In November 2006, the bank had over $7 billion in mortgages on its balance sheet and another $7.2 billion in subprime residential mortgage-backed securities (RMBSs) (McLean and Nocera 2010, 274). In March 2007, despite these sales, the bank still had over $4 billion in CDOs on its books as well as very substantial amounts of RMBSs that it was attempting to offload into an increasingly difficult market. In order to further reduce its exposures, Goldman employed two strategies. First, in late December 2006, Stacy Bash-Polley, a partner and co-head of fixed income, realized that while Goldman was struggling to sell the intermediate mezzanine tranches of its securitized assets, it could still sell its higher-grade senior equity tranches. On her instructions traders therefore "structured like mad" to repackage the mezzanine assets and, according to Daniel Sparks, "make some lemonade from some big old lemons" (FCIC 2011, 236). Second, Goldman also started to actively short the market by taking out CDS insurance, betting against subprime MBSs, and shorting the ABX indexes of some of the firms with which it did business (FCIC 2011, 237).

At the same time as the bank was seeking to reverse its own exposures, traders were continuing to sell MBSs to outside investors. Between December 2006 and August 2007 the bank created and sold approximately $25.4 billion of CDOs, including $17.6 billion of synthetic CDOs (FCIC 2011, 236). Clearly, the bank's "whatever it takes" approach to the bottom line had taken precedence over its more traditional focus on client service and relations. Goldman would later be heavily criticized and sued for its actions. In a subsequent US Senate inquiry, Senator Carl Levin accused Goldman of "repeatedly putting its own interests and profits ahead of the interests of its clients and our communities . . . Goldman's actions demonstrate that it often saw its clients not as valuable customers, but as objects for its own profit" (W. Cohan 2011, 19). In testimony before the FCIC, Blankfein admitted that the practice was "improper and we regret the result." Next day, in a press release, the bank essentially retracted this statement (FCIC 2011, 236). In August 2013 a jury found the former Goldman Sachs trader Fabrice Tourre guilty on six charges of civil securities fraud. The SEC had accused Tourre of deliberately misleading investors about the contents and creditworthiness of a CDO containing subprime asset and of failing to inform them that it had advised a Goldman Sachs client, Paulson & Company, to bet that the security being sold was overpriced.

Other than its adherence to mark-to-market pricing, what was distinctive about Goldman's management strategy and structure? Communications flows, collegiality, and activist risk management were important. As one of Goldman's risk managers comments: "Having been at Deutsche Bank and Morgan Stanley, I can just say here that information flows to people that need that information and the collegial atmosphere in terms of sharing that information—you know, the businesses aren't siloed, risk isn't siloed here—and that's the big difference from what I've seen at other places" (W. Cohan 2011, 498). William Cohan told us that "at Goldman they have this culture of sharing information . . . the information flow, the communication from the bottom of the firm to top of the firm is much, much better tha[n] it is at any other firm . . . in other firms they don't listen to people at the bottom" (interview, 12 March 2012). Cohan also argued that Goldman relied on "very, very selective hiring practices," hiring bright young recruits.

The bank rarely hired from other banks, "so they rarely got infected with the bad behavior at other banks" (interview, 12 March 2012). Trust relationships, a relatively flat hierarchy, and joint decision making within the firm also allowed executives to challenge each other's assumptions and better source information flows (Anderson and Thomas 2007). In contrast to the situation in many other banks, risk managers and traders were also in close contact with each other. Indeed, risk managers and traders were routinely invited to swap jobs for a period of time to learn more about each other's activities and viewpoints. Viniar also took an active role in risk management. He made a daily routine of visiting and talking to traders and the firm's risk managers to check developments in the markets and assess the firm's positions. Lloyd Blankfein and Gary Cohn, Goldman's president, did much the same (W. Cohan 2011, 499). Daniel Sparks from the mortgage trading department sat on the firm's powerful risk management committee. Crucially, according to David Viniar (2010), risk managers were offered "absolute independence and the authority to do things."

HSBC

During the financial boom, HSBC consciously presented itself as a conservative bank. While senior executives at RBS and HBOS were talking up the economy's prospects and their own profitability, senior executives at HSBC consistently articulated a more cautious and skeptical worldview. In 2002 the group chief executive of HSBC Holdings, Keith Whitson, told analysts that "boring is good" and admitted that "we could be criticised for being a little bit cautious when everything is going gung-ho" (Leahy et al. 2002). HSBC's chairman, John Bond, warned investors that the use of a common set of risk management tools like VaR within banks raised the threat of financial booms and busts as banks made the same kind of decisions for the same reasons (Guerrera and Pretzlik 2004). In March 2006, HSBC's CEO and incoming chairman, Stephen Green, warned that continuing financial and trade imbalances could lead to a sharp downturn in economic growth and that any recession in the United States would soon undermine the global economy. In December 2006 the new group CEO, Mike Geoghan, warned that HSBC "won't chase revenues just to make that growth line work in the short-term to take it below the line later on . . .

I've been here for long enough to see some of the covenants that I know are now missing in most loan documents . . . I suppose you can call it deja-vu. We've been there before" (HSBC 2006). In June 2007 Stephen Green told reporters that he was "worried by the degree of leverage in some big ticket transactions" and that the financial boom would "end in tears" (Tucker, Mallet, and Thal Larsen 2007). Green also went on to express doubts about securitization as a risk management tool: "When your risk has been parcelled up hundreds or thousands of times, it's much more difficult to orchestrate a reconstruction of a difficult situation and, therefore, the write-off then risks being worse than it needs to be" (Tucker, Mallet, and Thal Larsen 2007). HSBC's caution about the economic boom was a reflection of the bank's long-standing organizational culture. RBS's Johnny Cameron suggests that HSBC "had a sort of corporate memory," which was strengthened by its exposure to the East Asian financial crisis in the late 1990s (interview, 18 April 2013). This memory was sustained through a habit of filling senior executive positions through internal promotions rather than external recruitment. According to Sir John Gieve, "They've got a pretty cohesive top management team. They've mainly been there for a long time. They've known each other for a long time" (interview, 19 April 2013). An HSBC manager told employees they should

> see themselves as long-term HSBC people. Although Stephen Green came in as a consultant, I think from McKenzie, he'd actually worked there for quite a long time before he ended up being chief executive and then chairman. I think about Stuart Gulliver [current CEO]—he joined HSBC straight out of university and so he didn't see his future as "throw the dice and hopefully it'll come up and I'll make lots of money in a few years." He saw his career as long term—wanted to rise through the ranks . . . Playing that long game I think is very much a trait of HSBC. (Interview with a senior risk manager, 19 April 2013)

A number of people we spoke to about HSBC also pointed to the personal religious convictions of a number of senior executives. HSBC's former chief economist, Dennis Turner, observed that the former CEO, Stephen Green, was also a lay preacher who "never felt there was any compromise between good commercial practice and high moral values" (interview, 19 April 2013).

HSBC's reputation was severely tarnished in 2013 when it was fined almost US$2 billion for failing to stop criminals from using its banking systems to launder money. Prior to the crisis the bank had, however, acquired a reputation for probity and restraint.

The cautious attitudes of senior executives shaped HSBC's business strategy. Leverage and dependence upon wholesale funding were consistently lower than at other UK banks. In 2006 HSBC operated with a leverage ratio of just 14:1 compared to a nominal 19:1 at RBS and 27:1 at HBOS. Furthermore, the bank largely eschewed the wholesale funding market by funding its loans from deposits. In 2006 gross loans were the equivalent of 98% of deposits at HSBC, 122% at RBS, and 179% at HBOS. HSBC also chose not to develop a major investment bank operation. In the late 1990s and early 2000s, HSBC operated an investment banking arm through James Capel, a formerly independent UK securities dealer. Following a series of poor profit results, HSBC cut bonuses to zero and let staff numbers dwindle (Saigol 2002). HSBC subsequently surprised analysts in 2003 by recommitting itself to its investment banking operations, poaching John Studzinski from Morgan Stanley and promising him £220 million a year in resources to fund growth. At the time, HSBC senior executives emphasized that this investment was to be focused upon developing mergers and acquisitions activity and the development of long-term client relationships rather than fixed-income trading (P. Smith and Thal Larsen 2006). In 2005 HSBC advised Mittal Steel on its successful £18 billion bid for Arcelor. One senior executive at a rival firm described HSBC as a "nonfactor in investment banking" (Thal Larsen 2005). In 2006 Studzinski was given a new nonexecutive position, and the investment banking business was allowed to stagnate. Throughout the economic boom HSBC also retained strong risk management controls. According to a senior risk manager at HSBC:

> I think what we did have was a very good process of new product approval. So the business was not simply allowed to just go off and do what it wanted . . . We have a very, very strong process whereby anything that's done outside of existing product bounds had to go through a quite rigorous process of examination and approval by multiple disciplines. That was a source of great complaint sometimes because people would say we've only got a certain amount of time to exploit

> this trade idea and you're too slow. So there was a lot of tension around that. But I do believe that the proper examination from multiple angles—a credit risk view, a market risk view, an operational risk view, a legal sign-off, a tax sign-off—if you looked at this in the round does it make sense from all angles or can we see ways in which this could potentially . . . So I think that was a strength at HSBC to make sure everything was contemplated, was properly examined beforehand. (Interview, 19 April 2013)

Between 2003 and 2006 HSBC's unwillingness to pursue a more aggressive market strategy affected its financial performance. Despite recording a £24 billion pretax profit, in 2006 ROE at HSBC was 13% compared to 25% at Lloyds and 18% at Barclays. In evidence to the Treasury Select Committee (Treasury Committee 2009a), HSBC's managing director, Paul Thurston, told members of Parliament:

> In 2006 I think there were a number of commentators who were suggesting banks like ours were probably over-capitalised, ought to be returning capital, should be leveraging the balance sheet, so most of our discussions with institutional investors were about going through our risk model with them and explaining to them why we believed in strong capital and strong liquidity.

Similarly, the chairman of HSBC, Douglas Flint, told the Treasury Committee (2011, Ev132) that

> there was a great deal of pressure coming from shareholders who were looking for enhanced returns and were pointing to business models that have, with hindsight, been shown to be flawed and in particular very leveraged business models and saying, "you guys are inefficient. You have a lazy balance sheet. There are people out there that are doing much better than you are," and there was tremendous pressure during 2006/2007.

Management discussions with shareholders were not always productive. Stephen Green was accused of being "asleep at the wheel" by one anonymous institutional investor (Treanor 2007b). One of the founders of Knight Vinke Asset Management, Eric Knight, publicly criticized the bank and called for Stephen Green to be replaced as CEO.

HSBC's generally risk-averse culture was tarnished by its exposure to the US subprime market. In 2002 HSBC unexpectedly announced its acquisition of the mortgage lender Household International for £14 billion at the same time that it pledged to expand its other banking operations through the subsidiary HSBC USA. Entering the US market in such a manner was a significant new departure for HSBC. As a result, HSBC became the largest consumer lending bank in the United States, with 53 million customers, 37% of whom were subprime (Rigby and Saigol 2002). At this time HSBC executives spoke about how the Household model of subprime lending, particularly to recently arrived immigrants, could be adopted by other parts of the bank. HSBC's 2002 annual review described Household as possessing a "best in class technology that is exportable to markets where we see potential" (HSBC 2002, 8). In 2003 Stephen Green suggested that "we now have the opportunity to use the Household model in other markets—the French market is an obvious one as it has an immigrant population" (Croft and Pretzlik 2003a).

Why did HSBC move into the US market? Dennis Turner suggests that market pressures account for HSBC's entry into this market.

> There was a corporate raider, Knight, that people had to take seriously. I think there was pressure then to try to up the performance. I think that was probably a feeling there was saturation in the UK market and how much money you could go, it was an oversubscribed market and there was a need to expand elsewhere and the US was always a hole in the portfolio. (Interview, 18 April 2013)

The chronology here is not straightforward, however. HSBC purchased Household in 2002 *before* Knight emerged as a fierce critic of the bank. Indeed, in 2006–2007 Knight was calling upon HSBC management to abandon its US ventures and focus on its Asian operations. It is tempting to view HSBC's US adventures as an organizational aberration. Yet, in one respect, it was an adventure that, paradoxically, also serves as a testimony to HSBC's prudence. This is because, like Goldman Sachs, HSBC showed that it was willing to bear short-term losses and exit markets once economic conditions changed. In March 2007 North American profits at HSBC fell by 87%. Stephen Green announced that HSBC would seek to "significantly" reduce its subprime portfolio (Phang and Wong 2007). In September HSBC announced the closure of its subprime wholesale lending unit, Decision One, which securitized HSBC's loans. In November 2007 HSBC closed its MBS trading operations (Thal Larsen 2007c). This change in strategy was not enough to insulate HSBC from losses; since 2006 it has written off $20 billion in mortgage debt and other bad loans (Thal Larsen 2008b). These losses could, however, have been much worse if HSBC executives had followed their counterparts at HBOS and Merrill Lynch in believing that the downturn was temporary.

Lloyds TSB

In February 2008, Lloyds TSB announced a 6% rise in profits, a significant rise in shareholder dividends, and plans to expand its domestic mortgage lending (Croft and Thal Larsen 2008). At the time, Lloyds' CEO, Eric Daniels, described the increase in profits as being the result of good "old-fashioned banking." Lloyds' chairman, Sir Victor Blank, suggested that his bank would "thrive and grow and not just withstand the downturn but continue to grow through it" (Croft and Thal Larsen 2008). In July 2008 the finance director, Tim Tookey, boasted of the bank's "lower risk, more conservative operating model," and minimal exposure to the US subprime market (Lloyds TSB 2008, 2). Helen Weir, Lloyds' finance director, described Lloyds as a low-risk banking operation: "You don't get the highs, but you don't get the lows either. What's ironic is that what was previously considered to be dull and boring is now considered prudent and the right way to do banking" (Moore 2008). Lloyds' position was perhaps not quite as robust as executives implied. Lloyds was operating with a high leverage ratio and in 2008 was holding £6 billion in available-for-sale RMBSs and £4 billion in "other" asset-backed securities on its balance sheet (Lloyds TSB 2007, 105). The bank was ultimately responsible for a further £8 billion in ABSs held by an off–balance sheet investment vehicle, Cancara (Lloyds TSB 2007, 12). Yet relative to the disaster unfolding at RBS and HBOS, Lloyds was in a strong position. The Lex column in the *Financial Times* (2008) praised

Lloyds for having made "a virtue of boring investors silly" at a time when its "rivals were cantering off into new products and new corners of the globe."

Lloyds' successes in the first part of 2008 represented a considerable turnaround in fortunes. In 2003 Eric Daniels had been appointed CEO and had announced a long-term plan to focus on "organic growth" within the United Kingdom and the "nitty-gritty" of management (Croft and Pretzlik 2003b). Daniels argued that Lloyds' expansions into overseas markets in the 1990s, particularly Latin America, where the bank suffered enormous losses from sovereign write-downs on debt, had been driven by a desire for short-term growth rather than long-term profits (Foley 2003). At the time, Daniels's strategy was questioned by market analysts and investors who argued that there was little opportunity for growth in the UK market and that, unless it expanded, Lloyds would be weighed down by the losses it was then incurring within its Scottish Widows insurance business. In December 2005, the *Independent* (Warner 2005) described Lloyds as being in a "strategic bind" and quoted one analyst describing Eric Daniels as "stumbling around like a blind man in the forest." In 2005 Lloyds' pretax profit of £3.8 billion was the lowest of any of the UK banks. At this time there was considerable speculation that Lloyds would be the subject of a takeover bid by Citigroup or the Spanish Banco Bilbao (Batchelor 2006).

In order to appease shareholders and reduce the threat of a takeover, Daniels decided that he had to maintain a relatively high 6% dividend payment. This was effective. Despite recording lower profits than its main rivals, Lloyds' end-of-year share price rose by 257%, from £2.17 in 2002 to £5.58 in 2006. Over the same period Barclays' price rose by 146%, RBS's by 121%, and HBOS's by 156%. Yet, within Lloyds, the decision to maintain such a high dividend relative to earnings was controversial because by consuming available capital, it effectively locked the bank into an organic and incremental growth strategy. Indeed, in 2004 Lloyds' finance director, Phil Hampton, suddenly resigned following a speech in which he appeared to criticize Lloyds' conservatism and its focus upon shareholder dividends at the expense of growth (Stevenson 2004). One important reason Lloyds could not expand its trading or subprime operations during the financial boom was that its resources were focused on the priority of increasing shareholder dividends. After several years of intense criticism, Daniels's strategy began to pay off as pretax profits rose from £3.8 billion in 2005 to £4.2 billion in 2006. By early 2007 Lloyds suddenly appeared to be one of the strongest of the UK banks. In part its success can be attributed to Daniels's conservative, UK-focused model. Yet Lloyds was also lucky insofar as market pressure to maintain a high dividend meant that the bank did not have the opportunity to rapidly expand its balance sheet. The *Financial Times* (Hughes and Edgecliff-Johnson 2008) offered a clever satire on Lloyds' fortunes:

> Shareholders, I am delighted to say that your bank has come through the credit crisis in excellent shape. How did we do it? The answer is a strategy that some have called "management by inertia," although nowadays we refer to it as our "prudent business model." You will have seen from Tuesday's trading update the fruits of our unambitious strategy. Our write-downs were only £387m in the first quarter. I scarcely need to remind you that certain Scottish rivals, who championed riskier strategies, recently announced losses of £9 billion between them. Our cautious approach started nearly five years ago with the appointment of Eric Daniels as chief executive. To re-cap, Mr Daniels did NOT cut the dividend to free extra capital that we might only have invested recklessly in complex collateralised debt obligations. Nor did he sell Scottish Widows, the life assurance company that we agreed to buy at an inflated price in 1999. Widows still brings a little volatility to our earnings, but we have to spice things up somehow, don't we? Also, your bank did not jump on the securitisation bandwagon to fund new mortgage lending.

Conclusion

This chapter has underlined the significance of agency, bank cultures, and niche institutional capacities. Executives at JP Morgan, Wells Fargo, Goldman Sachs, and HSBC operated in the same markets as their rivals at Lehman Brothers, Merrill Lynch, Bear Stearns, Citibank, and RBS. They also confronted the same regulatory constraints. Yet in the final analysis they adopted very different business strategies. Executives in these banks perceived risks that their counterparts in the banks that collapsed, the true believers, did not. At Wells Fargo and HSBC, for example, caution and skepticism had been institutionalized within the banks' culture, and this created incentives for new employees and aspiring executives to adapt their behavior accordingly. The banks that survived the crisis behaved differently prior to the 2007–2008 crisis because their executives reached different conclusions about the desirability of extending leverage, wholesale funding, and trading in securitized assets. The banks that survived also managed to buck strong market pressures to follow the herd. The cohesiveness of senior management and prudent corporate cultures helped here, but the banks that survived did need to assuage shareholders and other stakeholders. Here, as we have seen, different banks adopted different strategies, with all the banks in question exploiting niche institutional capacities. As we have seen, Goldman Sachs adroitly exited the market in the nick of time and then bet against it in a highly profitable manner. Other banks such as Standard Chartered largely avoided Western banking markets, while banks such as Wells Fargo did well because of their deep presence in traditional lending markets. The bottom line is that those banks that survived had leaders that did not follow the herd, who were supported by other senior executives and prudent corporate cultures, and that had the niche institutional capacities to perform strongly enough in markets to appease shareholders and avoid takeover. All these elements needed to come together. This happened, however, only in a minority of the major banks.

8

Getting It Right

Australia and Canada

In 2008–2009 the World Economic Forum judged Australia and Canada to have, respectively, the third safest and the safest banking systems in the world. The four largest Australian banks, the Commonwealth Bank of Australis (CBA), Westpac, Australia and New Zealand Banking Group (ANZ), and National Australia Bank (NAB), recorded substantial pretax profits in 2007, 2008, and 2009. One of the large Canadian banks, Canadian Imperial Bank of Commerce (CIBC), made a significant loss in 2008 largely as a result of exposures to the US housing market. The other large banks, Royal Bank of Canada (RBC), Toronto-Dominion (TD), Scotia Bank, and Bank of Montreal (BMO), remained profitable. The Australian and Canadian federal governments intervened in their domestic markets in 2008 to provide significant liquidity to the markets. These governments also had to guarantee bank deposits, and the Australian government also had to guarantee wholesale borrowing due to the freezing of global wholesale credit markets. Yet, relative to their counterparts in the United Kingdom and the United States, the Australian and Canadian banking systems emerged from the 2007–2008 crisis largely unscathed.

In Chapter 4 we showed that, relative to their American and British counterparts, the largest Australian and Canadian banks operated with lower leverage and maintained balance sheets mainly focused upon mortgage and business lending rather than financial trading. Why was this conservative banking model pursued in Australia and Canada? To answer this question we apply the explanatory template used in Chapters 5 and 6, starting with a discussion of market structure and then of the role of agents within banks before finally examining differences in regulation. Unlike New York and London, Sydney and Toronto are not global financial centers, nor are they dominated by an investment banking culture. This further explains the stability of the Australian and Canadian systems: they were operating in quite different market contexts and quite different institutional settings compared to those found in New York and London. This also meant that regulators were not compromised by the need to maintain the "international competitiveness" of their banking systems, at least compared to the pressures on regulators in the core financial markets. Australian and Canadian investors and market analysts were judging the performance of their banks against other Australian and Canadian banks rather than against international market-leading investment banks such as Goldman Sachs. This one factor cannot, however, explain all the differences between the United States and the United Kingdom on the one hand and Australia and Canada on the other. In a globalized market there was nothing to prevent Australian and Canadian banks from trading in securitized assets or from opening trading offices in London and New York. Nor is it the case that Australian or Canadian regulators prevented such activity. Indeed, CIBC in Canada and, to a lesser extent, ANZ and NAB in Australia did engage in trading strategies. The question, however, is why these banks nevertheless limited their exposures and why other banks chose not to enter these markets.

In Australia and Canada a number of complementary factors together reduced the incentive and capacity for bank executives to reengineer their balance sheets during the financial boom. The most important of these was the market context in which banks operated. In both countries, this was partly due to regulation. While the largest banks actively competed for market share, regulations on mergers and foreign bank entry protected the position of the largest banks from takeover, thus moderating competitive pressures to a level substantially below that found in the US and UK markets. Market contexts mattered in a second way as well. Because banks in Australia and Canada were able to sustain very high levels of profit from traditional lending in booming domestic markets, there were few incentives for these banks to become heavily involved in leveraged trading. It is also the case that a number of CEOs and risk managers were alert to the potential dangers of entering such markets. Despite the fact that a few major banks in Australia and Canada did enter these markets, exposures were relatively limited, and overall the major banks adopted relatively traditional banking practices. This was in some cases the result of collective lesson learning from earlier bank crises and the emergence of an institutionalized culture of caution. In other cases, most notably that of TD, a CEO imposed a change in strategy. Finally, it is also the case that the key regulatory bodies—the Australian Prudential Regulatory Authority (APRA) and, in Canada, the Office of the Superintendent of Financial Institutions (OSFI)—eschewed a "light-touch" regulatory approach and required the banks to maintain higher capital bases and demonstrate their commitment to effective risk management. Agency and structure cannot, however, be analyzed separately. In the United States and the United Kingdom, bank executives and risk managers were operating in intensely competitive markets in which there was an unrelenting pressure to increase market share and return on equity. Executives and credit managers who raised concerns risked sacrificing their careers. In Australia and Canada it was easier for agents not only to express but to act upon their concerns because the market environment was very different.

Market Contexts: Constrained Competition and Strong Profits

Prior to the onset of the financial crisis, the four largest banks accounted for 73% of total Australian financial assets (Economics References Committee [Senate] 2011, 42). The five largest Canadian banks accounted for over 90% of total assets. These banks competed with each other to attract deposits, mortgage lending, and large-business accounts. A senior manager at NAB told us that "having worked in two of the major banks, competition against each other is furious" (interview, 8 May 2012). A now-retired adviser on regulatory policy at the Bank of Canada, Clyde Goodlet, argues that competition, although often intense, varies. The Canadian banking system is, he says, "competitive in many ways . . . Mortgage rates and nonprice terms are very competitive. The market for loans to large borrowers is quite competitive owing to the range of substitutes available to these borrowers, not so much for small and medium-size borrowers. Parts of the consumer loan market are quite competitive" (interview, 11 June 2013).

Relative to their American and British counterparts, however, the largest Australian and Canadian banks do enjoy several sources of protection. In both countries competition rules prevent the largest banks from merging with or taking each over other. This has reduced the pressure on executives to maximize short-term profits while also giving these banks the opportunity to take over their smaller regional competitors, so consolidating their market position. The Australian and Canadian governments have also continued to place restrictions upon the entry and operation of foreign banks. Cumulatively, these institutional rules protect the *collective* market share and profits of the largest banks, thus reducing the pressure on them to reengineer their balance sheets. In the United Kingdom and the United States, competition policy encouraged regional banks such as RBS, Northern Rock, and Bank of America to aggressively expand their balance sheets through takeovers or organic growth. This threatened the market position and profits of the established commercial banks. In Australia and Canada markets have been more stable and forgiving.

In Australia, as we first noted in Chapter 4, bank competition policy is underpinned by the four pillars policy, which prevents any of the four largest banks from merging with each other. The explicit rationale of the four pillars policy is to increase competition within the Australian banking system. The six pillars policy (as it then was) was introduced in 1990 amid rumors of a merger between ANZ and a large insurance company, National Mutual. In 1998 the Wallis Inquiry report recommended that the six pillars policy be abolished in order to increase competition. The government, fearing that doing so would allow the CBA or Westpac to take over ANZ or NAB, demurred, although it did agree to remove insurance companies from the remit of the policy. The Australian Bankers Association (Bakir 2005; Weihart 2007) has consistently opposed the four pillars policy on the grounds that it handicaps the Australian banks from competing effectively on global markets. The policy has not, however, prevented the largest banks from acquiring greater market share through takeovers of smaller regional banks such as the National Mutual Royal Bank (bought by ANZ in 1990), the Colonial State Bank (bought by the CBA in 2000), BankWest (bought by the Commonwealth in 2008), and St. George (bought by Westpac in 2008). Indeed, during the period in which the four pillars policy has operated, the asset share of the four largest banks rose from 66% in 1990 to 73% in October 2008 (Economics References Committee 2011, 42).

The former governor of the Reserve Bank of Australia (RBA), Ian Macfarlane (2009, 42), argues that by reducing the threat of corporate takeover, the four pillars policy reduced the pressure on the largest banks to protect their share price and short-term profits by engaging in "excessive lending and risk taking." The policy reduced competition "to a sustainable level and thus prevented our banks from moving too far in the risky direction . . . that saved us from the worst excesses that characterized banking systems overseas." The CBA's senior risk officer, David Grafton, agrees: "In a market dominated by the four major banks none of us had compelling incentives to go down the risk curve and grow our books as much more contested markets have" (interview, 29 February 2012). Charles Goode, formerly chairman of the ANZ, similarly argues that "if you look at the countries that came through this crisis well, in a banking sense, you think of Australia, Canada, Singapore, Hong Kong, and Israel. They're all countries where in domestic banking there were three or four major banks—and really stable. So you'll find an oligarchic structure without much international presence in domestic banking in the countries that survived" (interview, 29 February 2012).

The largest Australian banks also received some protection from foreign competition during the 2000s. Restrictions on the entry of foreign banks into the Australian market were formally lifted in the mid-1980s. By the mid-2000s nine foreign-owned bank subsidiaries operated in Australia, while thirty five-banks maintained Australian branches. These banks continued to operate under a number of restrictions, however. First, foreign-bank branches were not allowed to accept retail deposits with an initial balance below A$250,000. Second, foreign banks were subject to a withholding tax on interest paid to a nonresident lender. Third, any proposed takeover of an Australian bank by a foreign company had to be approved at ministerial level. These were not draconian restrictions. The key point here, however, is that restrictions on foreign banks worked with the grain of the four

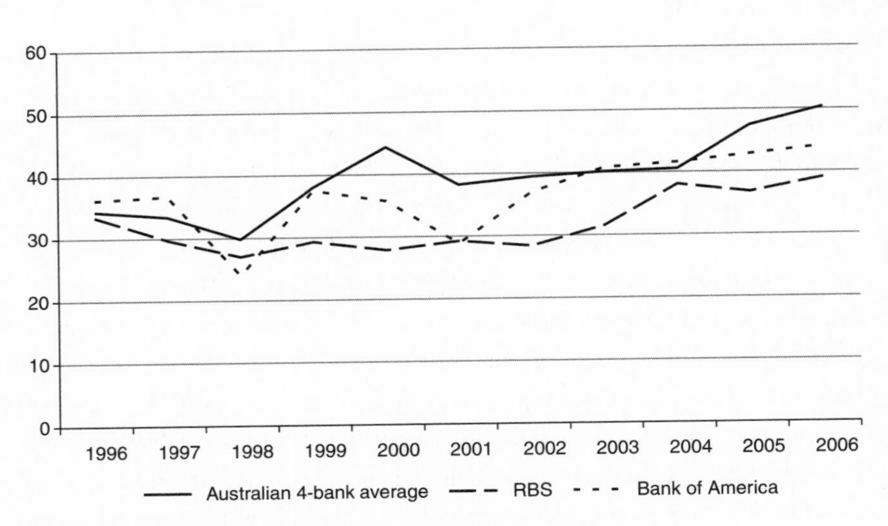

Figure 8.1. Australian bank profit margins, 1996–2006 (%).

pillars policy to protect the market share of the *largest* Australian banks, which were, in turn, protected from takeover.

Throughout the 2000s the largest Australian banks were extremely profitable. Figure 8.1 shows the average profit margins of the four largest Australian banks between 1996 and 2006 compared with Bank of America and RBS. Profit margin is a ratio of profitability calculated as net income divided by revenues expressed as a percentage. The higher the percentage, the more profitable is the bank. Bank of America and RBS were, throughout this period, among the most profitable of American and British banks. While operating with lower leverage and a more conservative balance sheet, the four Australian banks were, however, as profitable, if not more profitable. Indeed, at the height of the boom between 2004 and 2006, the average Australian profit margins of, respectively, 47% and 50% were significantly higher than those of Bank of America or RBS.

In Canada, federal-level banking regulation facilitated the emergence of a handful of large national banks in the nineteenth century (Bordo, Redish, and Rockoff, 2011). The position of the largest banks was further strengthened in the 1980s and 1990s when, in the course of an attempt to increase competition, the four pillars policy, which had prevented mergers between banks, trust companies (broadly the equivalent of savings and loan companies in the United States and building societies in the United Kingdom), insurance companies, and securities brokers, was progressively lifted, allowing the largest banks to simply buy the four largest independent principal securities dealers: Wood Grundy, Dominion Securities, Nesbitt Thomson, and Levesque Beaubien (Allen and Engert 2007, 34). The largest banks are still not allowed to offer insurance services or buy an insurance firm. In other respects the largest Canadian banks now operate as universal banks. The vice president for policy and operations of the Canadian Bankers Association, Marion Wrobel, argues that this constitutes a key source of stability within the Canadian system:

> The existing structure right now . . . is really a product of 100-plus years of mergers and consolidation and the modernization of financial sector policy . . . Just as Canadian banks can diversify their revenues across geographies and across regional economies they can diversify across product lines. I think that's been a source of strength. Some of the banks are more heavily involved in capital markets than others are. But there are limits and I think they recognize the volatility of capital markets, the risks inherent with that. Canadian banks are essentially retail banks with a number of other different product lines that help to diversify income and risk. (Interview, 5 June 2013)

Canada also operates a noncodified but widely recognized prohibition on mergers between the five largest banks. This policy was first articulated in 1998 when the finance minister, Paul Martin, blocked proposed mergers between RBC and BMO and between CIBC and TD on the grounds that they would lead to an "unacceptable concentration of economic power" and a "significant reduction in competition" (Crary 1998). As in Australia, the prohibition on mergers has reduced the pressure on the largest banks to maximize short-term profits in order to deter a takeover bid. This proscription may have prevented one of the Canadian banks from trying to reinvent itself as a major global trading bank. The senior equity analyst Peter Routledge argues that if the 1998 mergers had been allowed,

> there certainly would have been more capacity to go after leverage lending in the US via the structured credit market. More hubris and

> willingness to do so . . . Once you get to the point where you have [smaller] banks that are smaller in overall capital relative to their US bank peers, they can't compete in the same level. They don't have the balance sheet size to do so. There's less hubris and a little more focus on shareholder value. (Interview, 5 June 2013)

The former deputy governor of the Bank of Canada, David Longworth, echoes this argument:

> One of the arguments that was being made by the banks [in 1998 when bank mergers were being discussed] was we're too small to play in some of these markets, in these derivative markets. We can't become a big player in these markets because you need to be bigger in total size so that people see your total capital as being larger. Then you can play in those markets. So I think there would have been an incentive for them to do that if they had received permission for those mergers. (Interview, 10 June 2013)

In the decade prior to the banking crisis, competitive pressures within the Canadian system were also restrained by continuing restrictions on the entry and operation of foreign banks. Under the so-called widely held rule, no person or group is allowed to own more than 10% of a bank without the express approval of the minister of finance. This restriction was first introduced in the late 1960s in response to rumors that the US Chase Manhattan Bank was going to launch a bid for TD. It makes foreign ownership of a Canadian bank "virtually impossible" (Gouvin 2001, 399). Furthermore, while foreign banks have been allowed to open branches in Canada since 1998, they are not allowed to compete for retail deposits, must have total assets of over C$35 billion, and must pledge their total capital as collateral for any losses incurred. Relative to the situation in the 1980s when foreign banks were simply not allowed to operate in Canada, Gouvin (2001, 399) argues that "all of the recent changes in foreign access to Canada's banking market have been essentially cosmetic, appearing to make foreign access more liberal while in reality changing the status quo very little."

The takeover of securities dealers and trusts, the prohibition on mergers, and restrictions on foreign entry have protected the market share and profit margins of the largest banks. This has reduced the pressure on these banks to search for new sources of profit through financial trading. The former governor of the Bank of Canada, David Dodge (quoted in Freeland 2010b), argues: “You had a set of banks that had essentially very profitable domestic commercial banking franchises. They had to be pretty bad in their other businesses to lose money overall.” Peter Routlege (quoted in Goodfellow 2011) agrees: “They [the largest banks] had no incentive to stretch out along the credit curve for loan growth, and were happy to grow loans, perhaps at a slower rate than what they were seeing south of the border, and still make a lot of pretty decent return.” A senior regulator at OSFI told us:

> I do think, though, that one of the criticisms of the Canadian system, the Canadian structure, is that as a result of the difficulty of entry innovation has been slower. I remember sitting talking to a global supervisor in about 2005 when he said, as a result of this you don’t get forty-year mortgages, you don’t get 125% loan to value as you did in the UK. You don’t get all this stuff . . . To me, it was almost a foreign language because—I suppose you could say that there is a little less innovation in the Canadian marketplace. I’m not sure that all innovation’s good when it comes from a risk point of view. (Interview, 11 June 2013)

Simon Johnson (Boone and Johnson 2010, 254) argues that market “concentration can also generate risks for taxpayers as each [bank] is too big to fail.” This may well be true, but the important point here is that market structure reduced the incentive for the largest Canadian banks to reengineer their balance sheets and so made them less likely to fail. Figure 8.2 shows that throughout the 2000s the largest Canadian banks operated with lower profit margins than the RBS and Bank of America. In 2004, for example, Bank of America recorded a profit margin of 41%, RBS a margin of 38%, and the five largest Canadian banks an average of 30%. This difference is not insignificant. What should, however, also be noted is that following a downturn in 2001, the Canadian bank profit margins increased for four consecutive years until 2005 and that, over this time, the gap between them and Bank of America and RBS narrowed.

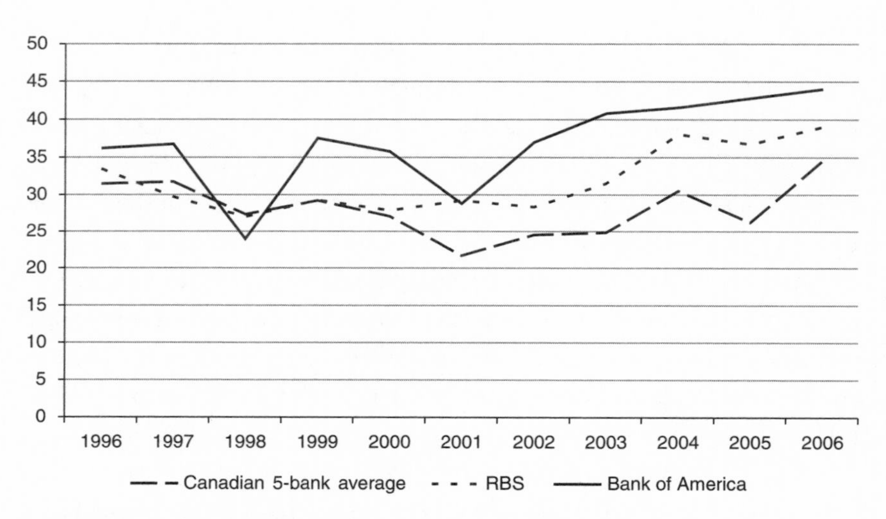

Figure 8.2. Canadian bank profit margins, 1996–2006 (%).

Competition rules thus shaped the domestic market structures within which banks operated. Yet banks were also helped by the underlying health of the Australian and Canadian economies and by lucrative opportunities in banking markets. In both countries mining booms, high levels of skilled immigration, and low inflation and interest rates stimulated economic growth (IMF 2008, 9; Debelle 2009; Jain and Jordan 2009). In Australia, GDP grew by 3% in 2003, 3.5% in 2004, 2.7% in 2005, and 2.7% in 2006. In Canada, GDP growth was 1.9% in 2003, 3.1% in 2004, 3% in 2005, and 2.8% in 2006. In this context, the largest banks had plenty of opportunities to generate business through additional mortgage and business lending. As the RBA's Ric Battellino (ASIC 2009, 48) has argued, "The banks chasing profitable lending opportunities in Australia could grow their balance sheet by 15 per cent a year . . . without having to take on new additional risks." Similarly, the former chief economist at ANZ, Saul Eslake, comments that "the Australian banks didn't feel under any need to enhance their income or profit-generating performance by acquiring risky, and as it turned out toxic securities, in the way that US and European banks did" (interview, 10 November 2011). Simon Johnson (Boone and Johnson 2010, 256) similarly argues that "Canada simply got lucky because the commodity boom [which started around 2004–2005] came so late in the cycle."

The Australian and Canadian banks generally operated within very similar market structures. There is, however one important difference between them. As we first noted in Chapter 4, the largest Australian banks relied upon overseas wholesale markets for around a third of their funding (RBA 2006, 31). The Canadian banks were able to fund their activities almost entirely through domestic deposits. Ratnovski and Huang (2009) argue that this fact largely accounts for the resilience of the Canadian banking system once the crisis started in the United States and wholesale funding markets froze. The Canadian banks did not experience significant liquidity difficulties because they did not have to roll over their funding to sustain their balance sheets. In Australia the banks were exposed to the international crisis and required their wholesale borrowing to be guaranteed by the government. This argument can, however, only take us so far. The Canadian banks did not simply perform well because they had a high deposit base. They performed well because they had relatively low leverage and conservative balance sheets. One interesting question therefore is whether the largest Australian banks behaved more conservatively *because* they needed to attract wholesale funding. Charles Goode argues that the cost of borrowing made trading in securitized assets less attractive. “It would have been pointless borrowing internationally to buy these things [structured credit products] when we were borrowing internationally quite extensively to fund our domestic lending” (interview, 29 February 2012). It is certainly true that the costs of borrowing would have made trading less attractive. But why, in this case, were American and British banks not also deterred from trading? They, after all, were also dependent upon large amounts of wholesale funding. This leads us to a second argument. The former governor of the RBA, Ian MacFarlane (2009, 45), suggests that the fact that banks were raising funds in competitive offshore markets was a discipline on the banks because it meant that they needed to maintain their credit ratings and so had to avoid potentially risky investments. This argument is equally unpersuasive. If credit ratings mattered then, they should also have mattered to the American and British banks that were heavily engaged in leverage and trading. The simple fact of the matter here is that the credit ratings agencies assessed investments in the senior tranches of securitized assets to be exceptionally safe. It is overall market structure, and not the structure of funding arrangements, that generated a distinctive set of incentives for Australian and Canadian banks.

Banker Agency

We have argued that the largest Australian and Canadian banks were not under the same market pressure as their American and British counterparts to reengineer their balance sheets through higher leverage and financial trading. Yet market structure did not *determine* behavior. It is here that the evidence of intracountry variation is, once again, significant. In December 2007 CIBC disclosed that it had a C$9.8 billion exposure to the US subprime residential mortgage-backed security (RMBS) market via a series of derivative contracts and a further C$1.6 billion exposure to RMBSs and collateralized debt obligations (CDOs) on its balance sheet that were "related" (CIBC 2007, 40) to the US subprime market. These assets had been acquired through its investment bank division, CIBC World Markets, which in 2006 generated an income of C$646 million (compared to a net income of C$1.858 billion for the retail bank) (CIBC 2006, 3). According to Peter Routledge, CIBC ran into problems because

> basically, they allowed the investment bank to run free and they did. First they got way too involved with Enron and supported Enron and its transactions. Then they got way too deep into structure[d] credit too late in the game. They didn't get any of the upside to structured credit from 2000 to 2004 right. They got in sort of 2005, 2006 . . . they arrived late, and started drinking heavily. (Interview, 5 June 2013)

In the early 2000s TD was also exposed. It was among the world's ten largest purchasers of securitized assets (Kravis 2009). Yet in 2005 the bank withdrew from these markets, and by 2008 had no recorded exposures to the US subprime market or to CDOs derived from US RMBSs.

In Australia, ANZ and NAB also acquired some significant although not life-threatening exposures to the US subprime market. NAB, for example, acquired assets through its investment bank arm, NabCapital. A senior investment banker at NAB argues that the bank "was in a bit deeper than other Australian banks," partly because the bank wanted to expand its investment banking arm and partly because the new securities trading was seen as relatively safe (interview, 8 May 2012). John Stewart, NAB's CEO, explained the bank's exposure by saying, "It's very hard to say that buying AAA assets with a tiny chance of default is reckless; it's actually not" (Cornell 2009). As that investment banker told us:

> We were under pressure. Basel II was dragging more and more capital into the banks. So we had to get leverage up on the capital and the easiest way to do that was in off–balance sheet and investment banking activity. We were also competing here against global investment banks that were coming out here . . . So we were pushing just as hard back into their markets . . . We were learning offshore and we were competing with them in offshore markets. (Interview, 8 May 2012)

The trading was done in NAB's offshore operations in London and New York in order to, as a senior manager at NAB put it, "satisfy the investment needs of short-term money market investors who wanted high-quality investments with a bit of yield on them." Such offshore trades "didn't need approval from Australia because they weren't going onto our balance sheet." The business was making NAB in the order of $50 million a year according to that manager. "It was not huge in the context of our total revenues." But when the crash came NAB lost $1.2 billion. As that manager puts it, "It was an extremely low-probability but high-consequence event that everyone discounted."

NAB's risk management functions in such markets were not well developed. Attention was paid to the legal and policy aspects of such deals, but as that senior managerputs it, "The risk people would come along after the event . . . Portfolio-level risk analytics were really nowhere in those days compared to where [they are] is now." Importantly, that manager thinks that the timing of the crisis was fortuitous. "One could argue that if this had gone on for another two to three years that the damage that would have been inflicted may well have been far more crippling for NAB. We were really only on the cusp of this business." It is worth pondering whether the escalation of such trading would have attracted the attention of senior managers within NAB or whether other Australian banks might also have started to reinvent themselves as trader banks. Certainly, the strength of traditional banking in Australia and the broad commercial banking focus would have been a damper. As David Stoten, a former risk manager at ANZ, puts it, "There's the hope that a basic commercial banking culture would have kept things in reasonable proportion" (interview, 23 April 2012).

On the whole, the major Australian and Canadian banks, especially the Commonwealth, Westpac, RBC, and Scotia Bank, did maintain consistently conservative balance sheets. This did not happen by chance. Senior executives at these banks identified problems in trading markets and chose not to participate. A senior risk manager at the CBA, David Grafton, conveyed serious concerns about US RMBSs to senior management and to the board. "We really did feel that there [were] serious risk concerns attached to these kinds of portfolios . . . We had a good look at what the true risks were and we just didn't like them . . . There were a whole heap of reputational and other risks that we thought outweighed any financial benefits that might come from a little bit of extra business we might be able to book" (interview, 29 February 2012). At Westpac the head of group risk, Edward Bosworth, argues that the bank applied a "subjective overlay" to risk assessments about the purchase of US RMBSs based on earlier negative experiences with the corporate debt market in the early 2000s following the collapse of Enron and Worldcom.

> There was a debate inside the firm, between those who were inclined to support the model output, which said these investments would actually hold their value, and those who remembered that a model can't tell you everything. It was the subjective call to stay out that held us out . . . We elected, by conscious decision, that it was not an appropriate strategy . . . [Instead we sought] to derive growth from our domestic market, where both subjectively and quantitatively we felt we had a better handle on the risks . . . The judgment call was whether we believed we had learned sufficiently from prior experience to step back into those waters. (Interview, 8 May 2012)

The Australian banking crisis of the early 1990s was an experience that also saw substantial institutional learning and internal governance reform. Financial deregulation during the 1980s and the entry of foreign banks encouraged Australian banks to defend their market share through aggressive credit practices that led to a credit-fueled asset price boom, especially in commercial property (P. Kelly 1992, 487–508). Subsequent monetary policy responses led to a severe recession in the early 1990s that took a heavy toll on exposed banks, including the near-implosion of one of the majors, Westpac, which saw it write off nearly $6 billion in bad debts (Carew 1997), as well as causing severe troubles for ANZ. Saul Eslake, a former chief economist at ANZ, suggests that "there were plenty of people within ANZ who retained a very strong corporate memory of the fact that they almost went out the door" (interview, 10 November 2011). David Morgan, who became Westpac's CEO in the late 1990s and institutionalized the bank's "risk/reward" committee, which brought together all major risk managers and senior managers within the bank, recalls: "Westpac had a near death experience in 1992 . . . We didn't forget it." This conservative culture is reflected in Westpac's attitude to the sorts of structured investment products that were regularly offered to the bank by overseas investment banks. As one insider commented: "On one occasion a note went round. Do we understand this product? Does it make sense to rely on the credit ratings agency? Do we know the underlying exposures? Do we have an appetite for the volatility we have seen in these things before?" (quoted in Cornell 2009).

Similarly, APRA's John Laker (2009, 52) argues that there were "enough reminders that good times come to an end for boards to stay focused." "There was a whole generation of bankers who'd been burnt. That corporate memory was very important." It led, as Laker explains, "to greater visibility and much greater punching power for risk management functions within the banks" (interview, 23 November 2011). John Edwards, a former bank chief economist, argues that "an entire cohort of bankers were emptied out after early 1990s and replaced with more cautious bankers" (personal communication, 15 November 2011). Ian Harper, a member of the 1998 Wallis Inquiry into Australia's financial system, comments that during the 1990s, "inside the banks there was a titanic struggle between the investment bankers and the credit risk managers. It was a culture war. But throughout the period, the chief executives were old-style bankers; the tyre-kicking cautious bankers in the end swept aside those who were hungry for yield" (quoted in Colebatch 2009). As Saul Eslake (interview, 10 November 2011) explains, "The Australian banks are commercial as distinct from investment banks and perhaps more importantly are run by commercial bankers as opposed to investment bankers." This is important because, according to Ian Harper, "there may have been a different outcome had any of the major banks been run at the chief executive level by an investment banker rather than a traditional balance sheet banker" (interview, 2 May 2012). John Laker argues that the Australian banks "weren't building huge trading desks, they weren't setting up large offshore operations . . . and their Treasury functions weren't doing large amounts of proprietary trading." The banks, as Laker explains, "were really focused on growing their retail books in Australia, because that's where the opportunities were . . . We have an inward-looking banking system. Our major banks are focused on growing the domestic markets . . . 2005, 2006, and 2007, these were golden years for the Australian banking system doing domestic business" (interview, 23 November 2013).

The largest Canadian banks also appear to have demonstrated a capacity for lesson learning. In the mid-1980s two Alberta-based banks, Northland and Canadian Commercial, failed amid a sudden collapse in commercial property prices. In the ensuing confusion, two other banks, the Bank of British Columbia and the Continental Bank of Canada, were destabilized and forced into mergers with HSBC and Lloyds. In a system in which bank failures were extremely rare, this was a significant moment. Greg McNab, a partner at Baker and McKenzie and a member of the firm's corporate and securities practice group, argues:

> We tend to think now the world has become very much focused on the short term, but the eighties and the nineties were not that long ago. So there's still people in the banking industry in Canada today, just like every other country, that were involved in the banking sector back then and still remember those risks and those different crises and how they were dealt with. So at the back of their mind is still going to be "We still need a solid foundation and a risk averse foundation on which to grow the business" and so I think it's just going to take a very long time before that gets whittled away. (Interview, 4 June 2013)

RBC and Scotia Bank retained conservative balance sheets throughout the 2000s. TD, on the other hand, entered the subprime securitization market and then exited in 2005, as noted earlier. What prompted this decision? Greg McNab argues that

> TD has always been, I would say, probably the most conservative bank in Canada. They've always been known as being risk averse. They study things, they monitor them, and they tend to prefer to expand into markets and be involved in things where they can be closely integrated and involved in their actual business. So they don't go off into countries and have joint ventures and let somebody else run them and just kind of wait for the results to come back. So they're generally a cautious bank to start with . . . If there was a bank that would have spotted anything—any cracks in the foundations early on—it would have been them because, as I said, they monitor everything in real time as they stay involved with it. (Interview, 4 June 2013)

This argument might help to explain why TD exited the market in 2005, but it does, however, prompt an obvious question about why the bank entered the subprime market in the first place. In this respect, the judgment exercised by TD's CEO, Ed Clark, was critical. Speaking at a conference of Canadian bank executives, Clark (2007) offered a pithy summary of his banking strategy:

> The thing that I think I find when I talk to people is that—I don't mean this [disrespectfully], people really don't get what a retail bank looks like and how different it is from a wholesale bank and how much a Canadian bank differs from a US bank . . . To a certain extent, US banks are restaurants. They have to open for business every day because they sell off their assets. We're not like that . . . We did so much better than everyone else because we just didn't do all the stupid things, which is, as you know . . . my theory of banking. Just stop doing the stupid things, and these are money machines like God has never created before.

In 1998—shortly after its proposed merger with CIBC had been blocked—TD completed an A$8 billion purchase of one of the largest and most successful trust companies, Canada Trust. Ed Clark, who shortly afterward took over as CEO of the combined company, used Canada Trust's management team, information technology systems, and retail culture to overhaul and increase the profitability of TD's existing retail lending business. By 2005 this business generated a high profit base for TD. Clark then decided that the US subprime market was too complex and too peripheral to TD's core business. Speaking of the subprime market in 2007, he argued: "Risk-weighted assets don't capture tail risk, [nor] does Value at Risk capture tail risk . . . If I cannot understand the risk, we should not be taking it. If an average person with average intelligence can't figure this out, why are we doing this? It is way too complicated" (TD 2007).

Were Australian and Canadian executives pressed into adopting conservative strategies by their boards prior to the crisis? It is certainly true that regulators have acted to empower board decision making. In Australia, APRA has encouraged strong, independent boards and an active role for board audit and risk subcommittees. It has also required the entire board rather than simply the CEO or chief risk officer of a bank to sign off on risk statements (Laker 2006). APRA also communicates with the entire board, not just with senior management. It also has the power to vet and recommend against board candidates, which helps reinforce a strong board culture. As a CBA director has argued: "I think Australian directors by and large are prepared to ask questions, not to take things at face value. If they don't understand they speak up. That helps sustain a culture that is disciplined and risk averse" (quoted in Colebatch 2009). In Canada, OSFI presents its supervisory reports to boards of directors and requires them to collectively debate and respond to their findings (J. Dickson 2009b, 6). It is also true that a number of the weaknesses that afflict boards in the United States and the United Kingdom, which we described in Chapters 5 and 6, do not arise in Australia and Canada. In both countries independent directors dominate boards on which CEOs and, at most, one or two other executives sit. In Canada, unlike in the United Kingdom, independent directors also serve, on average, for lengthy terms of office. In Chapter 6 we noted that in 2007 the independent directors at HBOS had served for an average of just four years. At RBC the average was eight years; at Scotia Bank thirteen years; at Bank of Montreal eight years; and at CIBC seven years. Australian banks also tend to have independent directors with more experience of banking and finance. In 2007, five of twelve directors of the CBA had a background in banking. At Westpac five of six directors did. At ANZ three of seven did, and at NAB seven of eleven did. Yet boards in Australia and Canada still operate under significant constraints. Echoing the sentiments we saw expressed by Ray Perman in Chapter 6, Clyde Goodlet argues that boards ultimately lack the resources to effectively challenge executive decision making:

> How can a board be independent without the resources to challenge what's on the table? Everything comes to you in this big binder from management with a lot of analysis and recommendations. If I, as an independent board member, was to challenge management's analysis and recommendations, I'm going to need some independent analytical horsepower myself . . . You can't leave that to the individual board member. You need to provide board members with resources—significant resources—to be able to challenge management. No bank . . . provides board members with resources to challenge management. (Interview, 11 June 2013)

We found no evidence that CEOs in Australian and Canadian banks were pushed into adopting conservative strategies by boards. In the Australian and Canadian banking systems, CEOs and other senior managers have played a key role in shaping bank strategy.

Regulation

Bank CEOs in Australian and Canada were operating in a market in which regulators played a significant role. In Australia, the former federal treasurer, Peter Costello, explains Australia's banking sector resilience in terms of strong "regulatory and prudential arrangements that kept capital requirements strong, subprime lending low and toxic derivatives out of systemically important institutions" (Costello 2009). It is not at all clear, however, that prudential regulation kept "toxic derivatives out of systemically important institutions," given the exposures of ANZ and NAB to such assets. Nevertheless, regulators in both Australia and Canada discharged their regulatory responsibilities in a way that supported prudent mainstream banking and contrasts with the light-touch or permissive regulatory approach in the United Kingdom (Turner 2009b, 86–88) and the United States (FCIC 2011, 52–66).

APRA assumed responsibility for prudential regulation from the RBA after a recommendation from the Wallis Inquiry in 1998. In the words of its former chief executive, Graeme Thompson, APRA was initially encouraged to adopt a "non-intrusive [and] non-prescriptive" regulatory stance (quoted in A. Clark 2009). This approach changed when Australia's second largest insurance company, HIH, was liquidated in 2001 with losses of around A$5 billion. According to John Laker, APRA took a "public lashing" from politicians and commentators in the aftermath of this failure (interview, 23 November 2011). Charles Littrell, an executive general manager at APRA, says that HIH's failure was a "huge jolt" to the organization (interview, 23 November 2011). The HIH Royal Commission (2003) subsequently encouraged APRA to adopt a "more sceptical, questioning and, where necessary, aggressive" regulatory stance. Interestingly, the Royal Commission report drew heavily upon a report that APRA had itself commissioned from the former head of OFSI, the Canadian John Palmer (Palmer et al. 2002). Palmer drew APRA's attention to the virtues of the risk analysis model used by Canadian regulators (Black 2006, 10).

APRA's John Laker argues that the HIH debacle was a "clarion call" (Cornell 2009). It is certainly the case that, since the HIH crisis, APRA has adopted a tougher approach to insurance and bank regulation and an active supervisory role. As one bank insider stated, "People here are scared of APRA . . . You don't want to have them looking over your shoulder" (interview, 10 December 2011). A senior risk officer in one of the major banks says he "used to groan when [he] knew there was to be an APRA visit because, inevitably, they asked a mountain of questions" (quoted in Colebatch 2009). On the whole, APRA has established a close but authoritative relationship with the banks. It relies far less on black letter law enforcement of the kind found in jurisdictions such as the United States, and more on supervision and suasion, trying to inculcate sound risk management principles among the banks. As APRA's Charles Littrell puts it, "The way to do it is not to have a rule that says, 'don't make silly loans'; it's to have supervisors that understand what a silly loans looks like and they go and deal with it. So we look more like a shepherd if you will, not a traffic cop" (interview, 23 November 2011). As APRA's David Lewis (2008, 6) notes, "It is a relationship that recognises that regulation works best when its goals and principles are internalised within the culture of the institutions being regulated."

In the years after the HIH crisis but prior to 2007–2008, APRA intervened to reduce systemic risks in a number of ways. In 2002 the regulator introduced a new risk assessment system, the Probability and Impact Rating System (PAIRS), which requires banks to estimate their risk exposures on the basis of rules set by APRA (2009) and defend these assessments during site visits. Individual audits of banks have been complemented since 2002 by a series of system-wide stress tests that have assessed the banking system's resilience to exogenous shocks. APRA has also sought to minimize risk exposures through capital adequacy controls. First, APRA has, in its chairman's words, "taken a pretty strong approach" to the question of what banks are allowed to count as tier 1 capital" (ASIC 2010, 14). In particular, APRA adopted a stringent approach in the run-up to Basel II implementation in 2008. According to John Laker, "Where we had discretion [with Basel II] . . . we always took the conservative approach" (ASIC 2010, 14). Second, APRA (2004) has required banks making "low-documentation" housing loans to set aside additional capital. Third, APRA (2006) has required banks to hold additional capital against securitized assets or interest rate or currency derivative trades. Finally, APRA has also insisted that banks using third-party loan originators must ensure that the credit assessment standards used by the originators match the standards of the host bank.

APRA deserves considerable credit for its regulatory stance prior to the 2007–2008 crisis. Its record was not, however, a perfect one. APRA's regulatory and supervisory effort was mainly focused on risks associated with mainstream or traditional balance sheet banking in mortgage markets and commercial lending. It was the latter that had gotten some of the banks into trouble in the early 1990s. Yet the fact that NAB and ANZ engaged in what turned out to be risky securities trading prior to the 2007–2008 international financial crisis underlines the fact that APRA did not directly seek to limit nontraditional banking through, for example, limits on proprietary trading or fixed limits on the value of derivatives banks could hold as a proportion of their total assets. What was significant in terms of the timing of the crisis is that the Australian banks were undergoing the Basel II accreditation process in the years prior to the crisis. APRA was insisting on high standards within that process. This lent a degree of caution to the local banks as regards the quality of their assets. As David Grafton puts it, "The last thing that the banks in this market wanted to do was to engage in practices that would put their [accreditation] under threat" (interview, 29 February 2012). On the other hand, APRA was not particularly focused on US mortgage-backed securities as a source of risk. Indeed, as APRA's Charles Littrell, explains, as far as exotic securities were concerned:

> There wasn't a lot of analysis going into it. One of the flaws in our current process is the requirements to monitor credit risk on a trading floor versus market risk is not particularly strong. Certainly, it wasn't in the mid-2000s. The banks themselves seemed to have lost track of the fact that when you're trading credit products you're actually trading credit risk . . . I have talked to a number of people who were trading those products, saying this is great you know, just using the base balance sheet and whacking those things on and getting big bonuses. It was just like Christmas . . . People were looking at the risk of the price changing because of the relative value and demand of different sorts of securities, but no one was looking at, well, what if they are not worth anything? . . . No one was doing that analysis. Because everyone had essentially bought in, and I think to some extent APRA was in that camp. You know, its AAA-rated, it's well secured. All these people were saying there's absolutely no problem with it. (Interview, 23 November 2011)

Banks such as Westpac and the CBA avoided trading in the US securities markets not because of APRA but because of their own risk management judgments. As Alan Oster, chief economist at NAB, explains: "So I actually think it's a combination of a lot of things. APRA sure, but the honest answer to me is that it had a lot more to do with the way banks operated in their environment" (interview, 20 October 2011).

Overall, then, while APRA's role as a regulator and supervisor may have helped discipline and shepherd the banks in the arena of traditional lending risk, APRA did not act as a significant and direct restraint on the kind of securities trading that compromised ANZ and NAB. As a senior manager at NAB explains in relation to APRA's oversight of the bank's US RMBS trading: "We wouldn't have been doing it if APRA had concerns about it, okay? Now whether they understood it any more than the banks . . . I don't think so" (interview, 8 May 2012).

Whatever APRA's specific strengths and limitations, it is true that successive federal governments have supported APRA's robust approach to traditional bank regulation and the monitoring of systemic risk. Ian Harper, an economist at Deloitte Access Economics, argues that in Australia, "we are allowed to get on with regulation. We can distinguish between the role of the executive government and the public service. Regulators are allowed to get on with the job" (quoted in Cornell 2009). APRA's Charles Littrell (2011, 5) underlines the importance of political support for the bank regulator: "Effective intervention over the necessary years and decades is impossible without broad public sector support, most of all from politicians across the political spectrum. If you show me a country where politicians listen to the banks more than they listen to regulators, I will show you a country which is guaranteed to have a banking crisis."

In Canada, regulators also received strong political support. OSFI was established in 1987 following the failure of Northland and Canadian Commercial banks and the publication of a stinging report on the inadequacies of the existing regulatory system (Estey 1986). Following the failure of a large insurance company, Confederation Life, in 1994, OSFI was given new early-intervention powers to order banks to "cease and desist" activities (Black 2006, 7). At this time OSFI was also given a new mandate to

> monitor and evaluate system-wide or sectoral issues that may impact institutions negatively; supervise federally regulated financial institutions and private pension plans to determine whether they are in sound financial condition; and promptly advise institutions and plans in the event there are material deficiencies and take, or require management, boards or plan administrators to take, necessary corrective measures expeditiously. (OSFI 2009, 2)

OSFI's superintendent, Julie Dickson (2011), argues that having such a precise mandate has helped the organization.

> We think it is a pretty good mandate. It seems to work. It does require that we be very focused because it says things like "understand the financial condition of an institution; take action expeditiously." That is the word, "expeditiously." Other countries did not have a mandate like that . . . The mandate in the UK was to promote London as a financial centre. If that is the mandate, you, as a supervisor, would take completely different decisions than you would under our mandate.

OSFI's mandate complements a general organizational skepticism about the capacity of financial markets to self-regulate. The former OSFI superintendent Nicholas Le Pan (2005) argues that "financial systems don't in my view always work according to perfect financial economic models." Similarly, Julie Dickson (2009a) argues that "institutions, unfettered, will take risks that may produce outcomes that are very costly for society."

OSFI, like APRA, has required the banks it regulates to maintain relatively high capital standards, with Canadian banks prior to the 2007–2008 crisis required to reach a 7% tier 1 capital and a 10% total capital ratio (compared to, respectively, a 4% and 8% ratio under Basel II rules) (FSB 2012b, 12). Additionally, OSFI has maintained a total leverage ratio which, regardless of the risk weights being attached to different classes of assets, imposes a limit on the value of debt a bank can carry on or off its balance sheet relative to its capital. This total leverage ratio was initially set at 30:1 in 1982 but was revised downward to 20:1 following the failure of Confederation Life in the mid-1990s. Since 2000 banks have been able to apply to OSFI for permission to extend their leverage to a maximum of 23:1. This would, at face value, appear to constitute a loosening of regulatory standards. The discretion given to OSFI within this framework has, however, given regulators the opportunity to signal early concerns to CEOs and boards about market exposures: "Unbeknownst to the world, financial institutions' leverage ratios here are moved around relatively frequently . . . depending on our assessment of the risk in an institution. So when we see heightened risk, we'll lower the leverage multiple. So, effectively, it controls growth again" (interview, senior OSFI regulator, 11 June 2013). Another regulator agreed with this robust view about regulation:

> Time and time again, I've seen instances where—if the system allowed it, the banks would try to exert influence. But the system just doesn't allow it. I remember a conversation with a group of bankers pre the crisis when they were saying, "We can't compete as long as we've got this asset to capital multiple limit." I looked at them and said, "It isn't happening." That was the end of the discussion. (Interview, 11 June 2013)

By the time the financial crisis began, Booth (2009, 14) suggests that the Canadian banks collectively held 40% more capital than they were required to by OSFI. This suggests that OSFI may, at times, have been preaching to the converted: that OSFI's conservatism complemented rather than competed with the banks' own attitudes toward risk. The counterfactual question about how the banks might have behaved if the leverage ratio had not been in place may, however, be a misleading one. OSFI would argue that the effectiveness of its regulatory effort resides not in the application of any particular rule but in the inculcation of sound risk management practices within the banks and the maintenance of an ongoing dialogue with banks about their approach. Julie Dickson has described OSFI's supervisory approach as being one of

> wanting to be told everything that is going on. We don't want to have a list of boxes that we tick because that's not very effective . . . Having lawyers looking at this line or that clause and debating about whether something is do-able or not is not the right conversation to have. The right conversation is the principle. You have to know what risks you are undertaking. (Freeland 2009)

According to Marion Wrobel of the Canadian Bankers Association, "One of the strengths of the Canadian regulatory system is that there is a continual dialogue with the prudential regulator" (OSFI) (interview, 5 June 2013). According to Greg McNab:

> We'd go to our regulator and say "We have a client that's proposing to do A, B, and C, we're of the view that that's analogous to D, E, and F which the banks are traditionally already doing or the securities dealers are already doing, but we just want to open up a dialogue with

> you and get your views ahead of time." So sometimes we do it on a name basis. Sometimes it's a no-names basis. But that's a frequent role that we play in this process and so that only happens because regulators here will sit down and actually have that discussion with you. Whereas I think in the US they would basically just say, "Look, it's either against the law or it's not, and you decide if it is or it isn't, but if you're wrong we'll come after you afterwards." (Interview, 4 June 2013)

As in Australia, OSFI did not intervene to prevent CIBC and TD from entering the US subprime securitization market. Regulators also collectively failed to appreciate the risks entailed in the exposure of a number of Canadian banks and financial securities dealers to the short-term asset-backed commercial paper market, which, since the early 2000s, was being used to fund the purchase of securitized assets via conduits and other off–balance sheet arrangements (Puri 2012, 180). Overall, levels of securitization were much lower in Canada than in the United States and the United Kingdom. Yet in 2006 this market nevertheless raised C$116 billion in funding. Two-thirds of this amount was guaranteed by the Canadian banks. Around one-third of the market was guaranteed by external investors including US monoline insurers. When the US subprime market began to implode in 2007, this part of the market collapsed and had to be restructured with government support (IMF 2008, 20–23; Standing Senate Committee on Banking, Trade and Commerce 2008). OSFI was responsible for the overall condition of financial institutions, but securities trading was regulated at the state level. However, the failure to effectively regulate this market was indicative of a more general failure to recognize the value of a macroprudential regulatory approach. David Longworth (2013) argues that, prior to the crisis, OSFI focused upon the balance sheets of individual banks and did not recognize procyclical effects and systemic risks. The Bank of Canada, for its part, was focused narrowly on conventional inflation and exchange rate concerns, not on broader questions of financial stability. Such mistakes must, however, be placed in the context of Canada's overall record. As a senior OSFI regulator has argued: "Monday mornings, it's always easy to judge what happened in the football match" (interview, 10 June 2013). Whatever their specific failures, OSFI and APRA had enviable records when compared with the performance of the US and UK regulators.

Finally, effective bank regulation was supported by careful regulation of the housing market, which discouraged the banks from engaging in speculative lending. In Australia, APRA required banks making low-documentation housing loans to set aside additional capital. Subprime lending and housing speculation were also discouraged by the existence of full-recourse mortgages, which meant that banks could pursue the assets of a person defaulting on a loan, and by a Uniform Credit Code that imposed clear legal obligations on lenders to properly assess the creditworthiness of borrowers. In addition, Australian households were not allowed to count mortgage interest payments against their tax liability, thus discouraging borrowers from maintaining a higher mortgage balance for tax reasons. Monetary policy was also important in controlling the growth of the housing market. The RBA ran a higher interest rate policy conservatively, especially when it raised interest rates to deliberately help cool and stabilize the property market in 2003 and 2004, when a degree of overheating was apparent. In preemptively raising interest rates, the RBA was one of the few Western central banks prescient enough (and perhaps bold enough) to tackle this form of asset price inflation (Bell 2004). The result of such actions, together with strong demand, helped stabilize the market, underpin economic growth, expand the balance sheets of the banks, and support strong bank profit performance in a *sustainable* manner.

The Canadian mortgage market was also a relatively conservative one, characterized by full-recourse loans and the use of fixed-rate mortgages that reset every five years rather than variable-rate or interest-only loans (Kiff 2009). What most clearly distinguishes the Canadian market is, however, a rule requiring loans where there is less than a 20% initial deposit to be fully insured with either the Canadian Housing Mortgage Corporation or an approved federal insurer itself backed by a federal government guarantee (FSB 2012a, 13–14). In the United States the presence of government-backed mortgage providers Fannie Mae and Freddie Mac encouraged banks and mortgage brokers to make irresponsible loans that they could then securitize. In Canada the banks were constrained by a further rule that precluded them from making loans where the loan-to-value ratio was greater than 95% or where annual repayments would be greater than 32% of household income. As a result, less than 3% of Canadian mortgage loans had the same characteristics as US subprime mortgages (FSB

2012a, 13). These regulations also help explain why the securitization market was so much smaller in Canada. One consequence of the loan guarantees given to mortgage holders was that, from the bank's perspective, a large part of the mortgages on its book were effectively riskless. As a result, capital risk weights on mortgage loans were lower, and this reduced the incentive Canadian banks had to securitize their loans. In 2007 only 30% of Canadian loans had been securitized—compared to over 60% in the United States (Kiff 2009, 5). Furthermore, around 80% of the loans that had been securitized had been bought by one of the five largest Canadian banks. This meant that when the financial crisis began, the balance sheets of the largest banks were underpinned by an extremely safe asset class.

Conclusion

Market structures and conditions that limited competition and takeover threats and that supported high profits through conventional banking emerge as major factors that explain Australian and Canadian bank conservatism. This was supported by the approach of bank executives and regulators who had learned to act cautiously as a result of the Canadian banking crisis of the mid-1980s, the Australian crisis of the early 1990s, and, in each country, the collapse of a major insurance firm. Market conditions and lesson learning did not prevent some banks from engaging in high-risk leveraged trading, but in general Australian and Canadian banks acted far more cautiously than most of their American and British counterparts. Lesson learning in Australia and Canada, however, raises the question of why UK and US bankers and regulators did not learn from their *own* earlier failures in the run-up to the 2008 crisis—for example, the failure of the Bank of Credit and Commerce International (1991), Barings Bank (1995), or the Equitable Life Assurance Society (2000) in the United Kingdom or, in the United States, the savings and loans debacle of the 1980s or the implosion of Long-Term Capital Management in 1998. The main reason, it seems, is that competitive pressures in the United States and the United Kingdom were more intense, militating against lesson learning and giving bankers strong incentives to pursue high profits through innovative financial channels, especially given prevailing market opportunities. On the other hand, executives at HSBC and Wells Fargo, for example, invoked previous examples of financial downturns to justify their conservatism. Nevertheless, the impediments to policy learning were very substantial in the United States and the United Kingdom, where any executive who failed to generate adequate short-term profits was liable to be removed from his or her position. In Australia and Canada politicians and regulators ostensibly remained committed to market competition. This underpinned the four pillars policy in Australia and Canada, as well as government opposition to bank mergers. Yet in both countries competition rules had the unintended effect of strengthening the market position of the largest banks, so securing their profitability and the opportunity for lesson learning. Agency and structure in this way combined to generate resilient banking systems.

Although domestic market dynamics were central in shaping bank behavior in Australia and Canada, also apparent is the fact that markets and regulation all broadly worked in a complementary fashion, helping to propel the banks mainly in a conservative direction. These complementarities also helped align the interests of bankers and regulators, reducing the likelihood of conflict between the two sets of institutions. This type of institutional conditioning and complementarity is in line with broader institutional theory such as the varieties of capitalism (VOC) approach, which emphasizes how national institutional arrangements and national institutional complementarities structure the behavior of firms in forging distinctive forms of national capitalism, either "liberal" or "coordinated" (Hall and Soskice 2001). However, a broader comparative perspective on banking behavior reveals problems with VOC's emphasis on institutional conditioning and complementarity. There is a basic institutional determinism in this approach, the assumption being that firms within the same kind of institutional complexes will behave in similar ways. Yet similar banking crises have occurred of late in different types of capitalist systems ("liberal" and "coordinated"), suggesting that the approach might be overplaying arguments about national institutional conditioning (Crouch 2005). Furthermore, if we compare what happened in Australia, Canada, the United States, and the United Kingdom, it is clear that "liberal" market systems actually exhibit different institutional histories and differing market and regulatory conditions. For example, Australia and Canada, while notionally "liberal market economies" (Hall and Gingerich 2009, 453), in fact have highly structured banking markets and relatively strong regulation. This degree of comparative hybridity or diversity is not captured in the VOC approach (Deeg and Jackson 2007). This suggests that approaches that give greater scope to agency and that emphasize how national institutional complexes often feature diversity and scope for institutional innovation might be more useful. Agent-centered forms of historical institutionalism can explain such outcomes. The rational actor model and the broad "system" rationality that underpins the VOC approach may thus need revising. In the Australian and Canadian cases, the substantial level of institutional complementarity was not the product of rational design, but arose more through happenstance and the impact of historical experience and policy legacies. Indeed, conscious design was quickly subverted in the case of the four pillars policy, for example, which was designed to uphold banking competition but ended up supporting a banking oligopoly.

9

Bank Reform

Winning Battles but Losing the War?

Prior to the financial crisis, the prevailing view was that banking and finance had entered a new era, one in which financial innovation in general and securitization in particular had tamed risk. The efficient markets hypothesis was taken as an article of faith, bank executives were trusted to protect the long-term financial interests of their organizations, and financial regulation was suitably "light-touch."

Major crises often shatter conventional wisdoms, and so it was in this case. The crisis produced a "fairly complete train wreck of a predominant theory of economics and finance" (Turner 2009a) and encouraged "a fundamental reconsideration of financial regulation" (Goodhart 2010, 173). Influential free market gurus such as Alan Greenspan were discredited, and financial markets are now widely seen as risk prone and unstable.

Driven in part by "the still seething public anger" (Economist 2011) over the crisis and the subsequent bailouts, governments have responded with new regulatory measures. Yet a procession of postcrisis revelations about exorbitant bankers' bonuses and about bank misbehavior—including JP Morgan's so-called London Whale trading losses of almost $6 billion, the LIBOR interbank interest rate fixing scandal, errors made by a number of banks in relation to customer interest rate hedging, and revelations about bank involvement in international money laundering—have only further outraged governments and the public (Elliot 2012; C. Ferguson 2012; Hutton 2012; Johnson 2012).

The reforms that have been rolled out thus far would have been unthinkable prior to the crisis and promise substantially more state intervention in banking and financial affairs. Primarily, they have included raising the levels of bank capital, new forms of system-wide macroprudential financial regulation, and structural reforms aimed at shielding retail or commercial banking from riskier investment or trader banking activities. We briefly outline these reforms in this chapter. We also argue that the reforms have confronted substantial resistance and that there is already evidence that specific reform measures are being diluted as a result of successful lobbying by powerful banking and financial interests. This is in part because many decisions, especially about implementation, are being taken within the cloistered world of expert technical committees away from the public gaze. This is an arena that suits banking and finance because of its preponderant expertise, resources, and networks. That reform has already been partially blunted in the immediate wake of the crisis, when popular and government resentment regarding banking has been high, bodes poorly for the capacity of legislators and regulators to fight off further dilution or evasion of the reforms amid what will inevitably be the next financial boom.

We also argue that the reform measures so far do not squarely address the original source of the crisis—a combination of liberalization, which promoted a frenetic search for ever-higher profits, with financialization, which led to the emergence of a banking sector that is too large to fail, too complex to manage, and riddled with systemic risk. The new reforms try to buffer or shield the major banks from such threats. But they are limited institutional responses to entrenched structural phenomena.

At a technical and political level, the reforms will be difficult to implement and will be the subject of intense lobbying and attempted evasion. Migration of risky activities to the shadow banking sector as a result of regulatory arbitrage also remains a key challenge that is likely to become more manifest. The financial system is like a balloon: squeeze one part and another expands. Under the current reform approach, the sheer size, complexity, and rapidly evolving nature of modern finance will also see regulators in a game of catch-up with financial innovators, placing regulators at a distinct disadvantage. Just as sports antidoping authorities are endlessly chasing the next generation of drugs and evasion strategies, banking regulators will face a similar challenge, one where their administrative capacities, resources, and expertise will be severely tested.

More fundamentally, the continuance of strong interdependencies between governments and finance means that the scope and scale of the current system of big finance has not been effectively challenged. Risk-taking incentives and systemic risk, a central structural characteristic of the financial system, are still key threats. The problem here is that governments and reformers in the major economies have not fundamentally questioned or challenged the scope and scale of their financial sectors. This means that big finance will remain big and powerful.

It is true that governments have won some of the initial reform battles, especially in legislating substantial structural reforms and, up to a point, in raising capital levels. But the power, scale, and adaptiveness of finance suggest that governments are likely to lose the wider war over bank reform. Some leading reformers, such as Adair Turner (2009a) in the United Kingdom, have depicted a good deal of finance as a "socially useless" speculative activity. Yet governments in the United Kingdom and the United States are still wedded to the notion of having a large financial sector as a key part of the economy. The power and capacity of governments and state leaders are not just the products of particular fixed attributes but are also the outcome of political *relations* with key interlocutors. The main problem impeding thoroughgoing bank reform is that governments have become materially dependent on big finance and ideationally aligned with the notion of supporting a large financial sector. The productive or cooperative interaction between state and societal actors, where it occurs, is assumed in the literature on "state capacity" to provide a basis for state authority and the legitimate exercise of state power. Evans (1995) has coined the term "embedded autonomy" to describe this, while Weiss (1998) refers to "governed interdependence" to convey a similar notion. The problem with the state-finance nexus in the major economies such as those of the United States and the United Kingdom is that the relationship has not been productive but dysfunctional. The power of private interests also raises tough questions about responsibility for governance. Taming finance will thus require a fundamental rethink of the entire system and a new "theory" of reform. The financial system needs to be much smaller and much simpler, focused primarily on serving the real economy. Whether governments are up to this task is an important question.

In the first part of this chapter we briefly outline the reforms thus far. We then show how revised ideas held by state elites helped strengthen their hand in specific power contests with the banks during the postcrisis reform period. The ideational shift that has occurred in politicians' minds since the crisis, although real, is, however, limited. State elites, especially government leaders, have persisted with a mind-set that still values the economic centrality of a large and complex banking sector. Government leaders may have been able to win high-profile policy victories over the banking sector in the postcrisis period, but in accepting a large, complex, and constantly evolving financial system with high levels of systemic risk, they have unwittingly placed themselves at a continuing disadvantage in the regulatory arena.

The Reforms

In his 2009 Mansion House speech to bankers and financiers in the City of London, the chancellor of the Exchequer, Alistair Darling (2009), told his audience: "We cannot go back to business as usual. If there is anyone in this room, or in the industry, who thinks that they can carry on as if nothing has happened, they need to think again." Echoing this assessment, the deputy US Treasury secretary, Neil Wolin (2009), told the Independent Community Bankers Association that "in the wake of this financial crisis, one thing is clear: we cannot go back to business as usual." President Obama entered office in January 2009 with a mandate to reform Wall Street and a determination, in the words of his chief of staff, Rahm Emanuel, quoting Churchill, to "never let a serious crisis go to waste."

In the United Kingdom, however, the close political relationship between New Labour and the City initially retarded reform. Labour's prime minister, Gordon Brown, publicly lambasted the banks for causing the crisis but eschewed substantial reform. The former governor of the Bank of England, Mervyn King (2009b, 3), subsequently complained in 2009 that "never in the field of financial endeavour has so much money been owed by so few to so many. And, one might add, so far with little real reform." The government's 2009 White Paper and the subsequent Banking Act of

2010 drew heavily upon two reports by City grandees, Robert Wigley and former Citi chairman Sir Win Bischoff, to reaffirm the "pivotal" role of finance in the British economy, and rejected calls to formally separate retail and investment banking. Alistair Darling (2009) expressed his "determination" to work with the banking sector to "maintain the UK's position as the world centre for financial services." Despite its lamentable performance prior to the crisis, the government confirmed that the Financial Services Authority (FSA) would remain the lead regulator. The government also shied away from introducing regulatory rules limiting the size of bankers' bonuses.

Since 2010, the Conservative and Liberal Democrat coalition government led by David Cameron has been more active. The government has endorsed the new Basel III rules promulgated by the Basel Committee on Banking Standards. The limitations of the Basel II approach, which was being rolled out and implemented at the national level in the years immediately prior to the financial crisis, have been clearly exposed. Not only did it fail to mitigate risk and avert the crisis: its specific risk methodologies and approach worsened them. Basel II had focused narrowly on the soundness of individual institutions, overlaid by a regulatory philosophy that largely assumed efficient markets, rational bankers, and the benefits of market competition. All that was required in this view was market transparency and effective risk management in individual institutions. The reality, of course, as the Turner Review (2009b, 45) concluded, is that "the events of the last five years have illustrated the inadequacy of market discipline." Light-touch regulation did not address market irrationality, deeply flawed investment strategies, procyclical dynamics, and complex interconnections among financial institutions. As a result, in the run-up to the crisis, many risk indicators looked benign at precisely the point when systemic risks were mounting. Basel II's other problems were its loose definitions of what counted as capital and the limited quality and size of its capital buffers, which in some cases had been eroded prior to the crisis and which proved woefully inadequate during it. More seriously, as we have already argued, the Basel approach gave low risk weightings to mortgage-backed securities (MBSs) and encouraged off–balance sheet activities in the shadow banking sector. Basel also devolved risk management to banks and to ratings agencies, with disastrous results.

Unfortunately, the Basel III approach is not a radical departure from Basel II, although it does require higher and more detailed capital levels within banks. Basel III requires that at least 75% of bank capital be high-quality tier 1 capital, of which at least 4.5% must be common equity capital (up from 2% under Basel II). Basel III also introduces new additional capital buffers, including a capital conservation buffer of 2.5% and a further macroprudential-style countercyclical capital buffer of up to 2.5%, the latter to be used in periods of excessive aggregate credit growth. These new capital levels need to be phased in by 2019. Basel III also insists on a new leverage ratio that requires 3% of equity to be held against a bank's total assets. In the UK the government has resolved that systemically important banks should hold more capital than recommended under the new Basel III capital adequacy rules, with the 2012 Treasury White Paper committing to a primary loss-absorbing capacity of 17% of risk-weighted assets for large, systemically important institutions, comprised of 4.5% minimum equity capital, topped up by further equity and nonequity capital buffers (HM Treasury 2012, 35). The government also endorsed the idea of resolution authorities having a statutory bail-in power to involve creditors and assist bank resolution "without the use of state resources." The government's White Paper argued that a bail-in strategy would "expose holders of unsecured liabilities to the costs of resolving a bank" and thus "re-align risk and reward in the banking sector" (HM Treasury 2012, 40). "By improving the authorities' ability to deal with the failure of financial institutions in an orderly manner, the government is substantially reducing the perceived implicit guarantee that benefits large incumbents" (HM Treasury 2012, 51).

In the United Kingdom, the charge to go beyond the limited prescripts of the Basel III agreement has been led by the Financial Policy Committee (FPC) and the Prudential Regulatory Authority (PRA), which were established within the Bank of England in a shadow form in February 2011 prior to their statutory creation in April 2013. The ten-member FPC—which is modeled on the Monetary Policy Committee—is charged with the "identification of, monitoring of, and taking of action to remove or reduce systemic risks with a view to protecting and enhancing the resilience of the UK financial system" (HM Treasury 2011b, 7). Prior to the establishment of this new committee, Bank of England officials had publicly expressed concerns about the adequacy of Basel III. In October 2010, for example, Mervyn King (2010) described Basel III as a "step in the right direction" but warned that "on its own it will not prevent another crisis." Since then, the FPC has, in its own words, taken a "conservative and comprehensive view of capital adequacy" (FPC 2013b, 5). In March 2013, for example, the FPC asked the PRA—which is responsible for the day-to-day supervision of banks and other financial bodies—to conduct an additional capital-adequacy audit to ensure that banks were using appropriate risk weights and had factored in the potential costs of future interest rate rises and conduct charges. As a result, UK banks were required to raise an additional £27 billion in capital. The FPC (2013b) had indicated that, as the economy recovers, it will conduct additional stress tests to ensure continued capital adequacy and introduce specific "sectoral" capital requirements to control specific forms of lending or trading activity.

The government also endorsed institutionally separating, that is, "ring-fencing," normal High Street or retail banking from riskier investment banking activities, as proposed in 2011 by the Independent Commission on Banking (ICB) chaired by Sir John Vickers. Under this arrangement, ring-fenced banks will have their own capital and a separate board of directors and be constituted as a distinct legal entity. The commercial or retail entity will thus be required to be operationally separate from the other entities within a banking group to ensure that it will be able to continue providing services irrespective of the financial health of the rest of the group. The *Financial Times* argued that this proposal constituted the "biggest shake-up of British banking in a generation" (Goff 2011). Finally, in June 2010 the UK government announced that it planned to introduce a bank levy to raise additional revenue and discourage wholesale borrowing by taxing liabilities at a variable rate depending upon the duration of the debt incurred. In 2013 the chancellor pledged to raise the overall size of the levy and to use it to raise £2.7 billion in 2014–2015 and £2.9 billion in subsequent years.

In the United States, the government and the regulatory authorities have also signed onto the Basel III framework and in June 2012 proposed new rules to guide its implementation. House of Representatives and Senate banking reform proposals were also distilled into the omnibus Dodd-Frank Wall Street Reform and Consumer Protection Act, passed in July 2010.

This is a vast piece of legislation containing new prudential and macro-prudential regulation, structural reforms, and a range of other measures. The Collins Amendment to Dodd-Frank tightens up the definition of capital, contains minimal capital and liquidity standards for banks and other institutions where required, and establishes a shorter phase-in period than envisaged under the Basel III framework. The act requires enhanced prudential requirements for larger banks and financial entities, including relevant systemically important nonbanks, with assets of more than $50 billion. The act also requires financial institutions engaged in significant volumes of securitization, derivatives trading, repo deals, and other potentially risky or disruptive transactions to hold additional capital. Dodd-Frank also requires the regular stress testing of institutions. Section 616 of Frank-Dodd requires the development of a countercyclical capital buffer similar to the requirement proposed under Basel III. Section 165 of Dodd-Frank requires a tighter leverage ratio than Basel III, specifying a debt-to-equity ratio of no more than 15:1. Under Dodd-Frank, regulatory authorities have also been given the legal capacity to proscribe risky trading activities or restructure financial entities deemed to pose a systemic risk (Richardson, Smith, and Walter 2011, 197). There are also new provisions to bring substantial parts of the former largely unmonitored and unregulated over-the-counter (OTC) derivatives markets into more structured and transparent trading arenas.

In a clear rebuke to the credit ratings agencies, Section 939 of the legislation also removes reference to credit ratings agencies when evaluating creditworthiness and instead asks regulators to find other appropriate means by which to establish financial risk. The act also tries to tackle the "too big to fail problem" by insisting on living wills or resolution plans for systemically important financial institutions to be administered by the FDIC. The plan rules out taxpayer support and instead proposes bails-ins for shareholders and creditors and ex post levies on large surviving financial firms to assist with any bailouts. In commenting on the new rule, President Obama stated: "The American people will never again be asked to foot the bill for Wall Street's mistakes. There will be no taxpayer-funded bailouts. Period" (Quinn 2010). The act also calls for the possible use of contingent capital (sometimes called CoCo bonds), a form of financing whereby debt can be converted to equity under given circumstances—essentially a bail-in mechanism in times of crisis. Dodd-Frank will also require the establishment of a central clearinghouse for standardized derivatives trading, reforms to mortgage lending, greater disclosure from hedge funds, and requirements that securitizers retain a stake in the assets they trade, as well as the establishment of a Bureau of Consumer Financial Protection (to be housed within the Federal Reserve).

In terms of regulatory architecture, Dodd-Frank has established a ten-member Financial Stability Oversight Council (FSOC) that will include the main regulators and be chaired by the Treasury secretary. Its actions will be subject to appeal in the courts. In contrast to the neglect of systemic stability issues prior to the crisis, the new council will be explicitly charged with monitoring and dealing with systemic risk. It will also have the power to identify large nonbank financial institutions as systemically important and be able to direct subsidiary agencies, such as the Federal Reserve, to closely monitor the activities of any financial institution deemed to pose a systemic risk. In theory, such arrangements will help focus the regulatory effort, although the FSOC will not be a "front-line" regulator and will need to rely on information flowing up from subsidiary regulatory agencies and the new Office of Financial Research. The Federal Reserve nevertheless emerges as the biggest winner from the postcrisis reassignment of responsibilities and will be charged with regulatory responsibility for the largest banks. However, the Federal Reserve will also attract new restrictions and greater oversight, notably in terms of restrictions on its ability to lend and provide liquidity during a crisis, especially to nonbank entities. The authorities will instead rely on a new set of regulatory and crisis resolution mechanisms, which are as yet untested. Notwithstanding this greater centralization of regulatory authority, the array of regulatory agencies that existed prior to the crisis will nevertheless continue to operate, potentially with at least some of the problems of institutional fragmentation that have long existed.

The Dodd-Frank Act also contains an amended version of the so-called Volcker rule, which aims to restrict US banks from making certain kinds of speculative proprietary trading investments that do not benefit customers but generate systemic risk. This is a structural reform of the banking system that bears certain similarities to the proposed ring-fencing of High Street banks in the United Kingdom. The original version of the Volcker rule accepted that large, systemically important banks could engage in commercial and investment banking activities but attempted to restrict the scope of the latter, specifically by banning proprietary trading, hedge fund activity, commodity speculation, and private equity fund management from the activities of federally insured deposit–taking banks. These banned activities would need to move to *separate* institutions with which the main banks could not have holdings or links, a move not too dissimilar to the original Glass-Steagall intent of separating commercial from investment banking.

One key feature of the reform process in the United States and the United Kingdom is that politicians, central bank officials, and regulators have endorsed the need for a macroprudential approach to regulation. Prior to the crisis, prudential regulation in each country was focused upon capital buffers within and the general financial well-being of individual banks. In the United Kingdom a tripartite division of the regulatory system, whereby the Treasury, the Bank of England, and the FSA pursued fiscal policy, monetary policy, and microprudential regulation, respectively, but meant that "no single institution had the responsibility, authority or powers to oversee the financial system as a whole" (HM Treasury 2011a, 12). As Lord Turner (2009a) puts it, "The big picture got lost; the overall trends in credit extension across the economy and in asset prices were not put together with certain business developments to sound a warning." Macroprudential regulation takes a broader view of the financial system and focuses on capital buffers and other regulatory controls in relation to systemic risk in the financial system as a whole, as well as across the economic cycle. Macroprudential policy aims to build up buffers in good times at the height of the cycle, partly to constrain market actors, with buffers to be used if needed during a subsequent downturn. Key policy tools that can be used within such an approach include countercyclical capital requirements; dynamic loan loss provisioning; countercyclical liquidity requirements; administrative caps on aggregate lending; reserve requirements; limits on leverage in asset purchases; loan-to-value ratios for mortgages; loan-to-income ratios; minimum margins on secured lending; transaction taxes; and capital controls (Baker 2013). Macroprudential thinking derives many of its working assumptions from theories of financial instability and behavioral finance (outlined in Chapter 2), which emphasize market irrationality, herding, procyclicality, and network externalities. Paul Tucker (2011, 3–4), a former deputy governor at the Bank of England, argues that the shift from a "default assumption that core markets are more or less efficient most of the time" to "thinking of markets as inefficient, riddled with preferred habits, imperfect arbitrage, herding and inhabited by agents with less than idealised rationality" constitutes a substantial "gestalt flip." Macroprudential thinking had been sidelined prior to the crisis because it challenged then-prevailing market-based ideologies and theories. Since the crisis, macroprudential regulation has rapidly become the new orthodoxy, especially in the official policy community (Borio 2009, 32; Baker 2013). Andrew Haldane (2009, 1) of the Bank of England describes macroprudential policy as "a new ideology and a big idea."

Winning Battles

The former US Treasury secretary, Tim Geithner (2012a), has complained in exasperation that the banking industry is suffering from a form of "financial crisis amnesia," pointing to the way in which bankers and financiers have resisted reforms. Yet it would be a mistake to think that bankers have been able to exercise a veto over reform efforts. In the political arena the banks have lobbied fiercely and have also attempted to exert "structural power" by emphasizing the economic costs of reform and by threatening to disinvest or move offshore (Lindblom 1977). The banks' most explicit attempts to exert structural power have, however, been challenged by governments, especially in high-profile contests over structural reforms.

Structures do not come with an "instruction sheet" (Blyth 2003): the meaning and ramifications of structural power need to be interpreted and worked out on the ground by key agents. These agents can mediate structural power relations, either increasing or decreasing the salience of such power (Bell 2013; Bell and Hindmoor 2013). This underlines an important factor in the politics of bank reform. The scale and costs of the banking crisis have chastened politicians, and public anger over the banking crisis has given them a strong incentive to promulgate reform measures in the immediate postcrisis period. Indeed, the banks have met with only modest success in attacking the reforms head-on in high-profile political contests. One lesson here is that the arenas in which political battles are fought matter.

Culpepper (2011) argues that business power varies depending upon the context of interaction between business and government. On the one hand, "when governing parties . . . know that political issues are debated in the media—and that people are watching—they have powerful electoral incentives to respond to the dictates of public opinion" (Culpepper 2011, xv). On the other hand, in arenas of "quiet" politics, away from the public and media gaze, business interests can bargain directly with government over time and deploy their key resources of networks, expertise, and knowledge of the "facts on the ground" (Culpepper 2011, 189). The high-stakes politics of structural reform in the United Kingdom illustrates this power dynamic. As noted earlier, after the 2010 election, the coalition government adopted a more aggressive reform stance. This was an electoral contingency that opened up the traditional cloistered world of British finance to public scrutiny and political intervention (Engelen et al. 2011). Shortly after taking office, the government established the ICB, which recommended ring-fencing commercial banking. The banks argued that this would threaten UK banking and the City's role as a global financial center. The lobbying was also fueled by analysts' reports that ring-fencing would jeopardize the profitability of the banks and lead to job losses. Barclays argued in a submission to the ICB that "a major and unilateral change to the structure of UK banks would simply lead to a reduction in the competitiveness of the UK banking industry." Lloyds Banking Group (2010) similarly argued that the proposed changes "would lead to a much-reduced availability of credit to households and small businesses." At this time, newspapers carried stories that, fearful of their future profitability, HSBC and Standard Chartered were considering moving their headquarters and stock market listings from the United Kingdom to, respectively, Hong Kong and Singapore, and that Barclays was also planning to move parts of its operations offshore (Jenkins, Goff, and Parker 2011). Similarly, in the United States, "banks and Wall Street have argued that over-regulation will drive the financial services industry overseas" (Borak 2011, 1).

During the financial boom, threats by the banks to cut investment or move abroad would have been politically very powerful. As we saw in Chapter 1, the typical starting point of policy deliberations at this time was the question asked by Economic Secretary Ed Balls (2006): "What more can I do . . . to support and enhance the critical role that the Banking

Industry plays in our economy?" Yet in the postcrisis context, threats by the banks were reinterpreted by government leaders to produce less challenging assessments, modifying the threat perceptions normally associated with structural power or investment veto threats. For example, calls to delay banking reforms because of the Eurocrisis were rejected. Business Secretary Vince Cable thought that the "uncertainty and instability in the markets makes it all the more necessary that we press ahead and make our banks safe and reform them" (quoted in Wachman and Curtis 2011). Clearly, the scale of the crisis had weakened the structural bargaining position of the banks, casting them in part as an economic liability. As Deputy Prime Minister Nick Clegg put it, "We cannot ever again allow the banking system to blow up in our face in the way that it did before" (quoted in Mulholland and Quinn 2011). The credibility of the banks' threats to exit the United Kingdom was also questioned. Critics pointed out that if major UK banks were to move to Asia they would be just as heavily regulated, and that if HSBC moved to Hong Kong it would be required to undertake delicate regulatory negotiations with the Chinese government. As the *Financial Times* (2011) put it amid the showdown with the UK banks, "Threats [to exit] should be faced down, not just because they are unreasonable but because they are of questionable credibility." The paper went on:

> It is not clear what "moving abroad" actually means. Were a bank such as Barclays to shift its headquarters, the impact on the UK would surely be minimal as it would still do much of its business and pay taxes in the country. What is more likely anyway is rather than upping sticks altogether, some banks may reduce their new investments in Britain. This might make the City slightly less of a hot spot, but it would not be a disaster. And were it to be the price of financial stability, this would be a price worth paying. It is hardly as if Britain has an under-developed banking sector.

Clearly, the crisis and the way it has catapulted the earlier closed world of finance into a hostile public arena has changed the politics of banking. Yet the shift in power has also occurred because the mind-set of key policy makers has shifted to a position that is critical of the banks, highly aware of their actual and potential costs, and in part dismissive of their threats. In this revised view, reform is *good* for the banks, and potentially for taxpayers too. As the *Financial Times* (2011) puts it, "There is no value in an unstable financial system."

Losing the War: Governments Are Still Committed to Big Finance

Despite some success in high-profile battles over bank reform, the far more fundamental problem that impedes reform is that governments still remain closely aligned with the interests of big finance, especially the notion of preserving large, complex financial sectors as a core part of the economy. Reform debates on both sides of the Atlantic have been peppered with caveats by government leaders that the reforms should not be allowed to undermine the strength or the competitiveness of domestic financial markets. A key reason is that heavily indebted governments have come to rely on banks and financial markets as sources of much-needed funding. Government leaders also continue to support the idea of having "internationally competitive" financial systems. Government leaders in countries such as France, Germany, and Japan have been particularly active in attempting to water down reforms in efforts to protect their banks (Admati and Hellwig 2013, 193; Rixen 2013). As Rixen (2013, 20) argues, in a world of mobile capital,

> regulation is hampered by intensive jurisdictional competition. Governments fear losing internationally mobile financial activity to competitor states. They are not able to solve collective action problems to curb or ease competition amongst each other because they are influenced, even captured, by domestic financial interest groups . . . Subject to these different pressures governments can only agree on incremental and ineffective reforms, which are symbolically potent enough to soothe popular concerns.

Policy makers, especially politicians, also continue to see financial innovation as a good thing, despite critics such as former Federal Reserve chair Paul Volcker arguing that the most useful financial innovation in recent decades has been the ATM. Despite complaints from certain politicians and policy makers that the financial sector has become outsized, governments have shied away from trying to shrink the sector. The big banks have not been broken up in the United States or the United Kingdom because of fears of undermining New York's and London's status as global trading centers. Even critics such as Lord Turner (2009a) in the United Kingdom think that "London will continue to be a major financial centre," despite agreeing that "the whole financial system has grown bigger than is socially optimal." The only direct attempt at size restraint comes under a proposed Dodd-Frank rule that aims to limit the size of the largest banks to no more than 10% of total consolidated liabilities of all financial firms in the United States. However, even if this were followed through on, it would not necessarily reduce the size of the banking sector relative to GDP (Haldane 2012c, 11).

Although governments have become more skeptical about banks, they have not taken the next step and questioned the system as whole, mainly because they value the economic resources the sector generates. President Obama (2010) has stressed the value of financial innovation and the importance of Wall Street to the US economy. The UK 2012 White Paper on bank reform insists on the need to "enhance the UK's reputation as the world's leading financial centre," pointing out that "the financial services sector is an important part of the UK economy, employing around 1.4 million people and, in 2010/11, contributing £63 billion in tax" (HM Treasury 2012, 3). David Cameron (2012) has argued that "pursuing a modern industrial strategy doesn't mean being anti-finance . . . Those who think the answer is just to trash the banks would end up trashing Britain. I say—recognise the enormous strength and potential of our financial sector—regulate it properly and get behind it." The chancellor of the Exchequer, George Osborne (2010), has encapsulated the problem of bank reform as the "British Dilemma": the need to "preserve the stability and prosperity of the nation's entire economy" while also protecting London's status as a "global financial centre that generates hundreds of thousands of jobs."

The result of such state support, as well as crisis-driven banking consolidation, is that the big banks are now bigger and remain "too large to effectively risk-manage" (Mervyn King, quoted in HM Treasury 2013, 333). Major banking groups in the United States and the United Kingdom are now larger than they were prior to 2007 (IMF 2012, 99). In a wave of consolidation during and after the crisis, Lloyds took over HBOS; Barclays acquired substantial assets from Lehman Brothers; JP Morgan took over Bear Stearns; Bank of America acquired Merrill Lynch; and Wells Fargo acquired Wachovia. Total assets at JP Morgan rose from $1.351 trillion in 2006 to $2.415 trillion in 2013, while total assets at Bank of America rose from $1.459 trillion in 2006 to $2.102 trillion in 2013. On the other hand, Goldman's total assets rose slightly, from $838 billion in 2006 to $938 billion in 2012, while at a group level Citibank's assets fell slightly, from $1.884 trillion in 2006 to $1.88 trillion in 2013. In the United Kingdom, Barclays' assets rose from £996 billion to £1.490 trillion between 2006 and 2012, and Lloyds' assets increased dramatically, from £343 billion in 2006 to £924 billion in 2012. Finally, HSBC has also grown, from £1.186 trillion total assets in 2006 to £2.692 trillion in 2012. Such is the level of bank consolidation that by 2009 the world's five largest wholesale banks originated nearly 60% of all capital market transactions. In the United Kingdom, Switzerland, and Germany, the largest three banks accounted for between half and three-quarters of total banking assets (IMF 2012, 100, figure 3.4). The IMF (2012, 101) also reports that "domestic inter-connectedness among financial institutions within an economy—as represented by interbank assets, interbank liabilities and the wholesale funding ratio—has not fallen in general for the advanced economies."

Losing the War: Market Competition and Financial Trading

State support for large-scale finance and banking means that the original drivers of the crisis have not been adequately addressed. This is particularly so in terms of the sheer scale of the financial industry and the intensity of the competitive profit pressures within it that drove baroque forms of financial innovation and risky investment behavior in the main banks and the expanding shadow banking sector. Haldane and Madouros (2012, 22) argue that "cross-system complexity has exploded over recent decades due to the growth in opaque, intra-financial system chains of exposure . . . complexity that is currently largely unrecognizd and un-priced by regulatory rules." The loss of internal control apparent in JP Morgan's London

Whale derivatives trading scandal underlines the difficulties bank executives, risk officers, and regulators face. A senior investigative officer from JP Morgan, Mike Cavanagh, told investors he had uncovered "numerous embedded risks that this team did not understand and were not equipped to manage" (Observer 2012). As a ratings agency analyst has commented, "Finance is continuously evolving, so you have highly niche financial areas that fewer and fewer understand" (Luyendijk 2012). In a freewheeling system, complex new financial instruments will inevitably arise, posing poorly understood risks. Individual balance sheet risks will be linked through market transactions and then compounded into new forms of systemic risk involving complex externalities and knock-on effects. Reforms such as Basel III remain focused on the behavior of individual institutions, not on systemic risk; indeed, a firm's capital requirements under the new rules do not depend on interactions with other financial firms (Acharya, Kulkarni, and Richardson 2011, 144). It is also the case that new regulatory rules in relation to capital as well as the structural reforms may encourage banks to take more risks to compensate for the costs of regulation. According to a senior Fitch analyst, "Since it is impossible for regulators to perfectly align capital requirements with risk exposure, some banks might seek to increase returns on equity through riskier activities that maximise yield on a given unit of Basel III capital, including new forms of regulatory arbitrage" (Treanor 2012a). Similarly, the IMF (2012, 103) warns that "Basel capital and liquidity rules could be promoting a greater intermediation of new financial products as financial institutions use other avenues to make up for the higher expenses imposed by the Basel rules." Another industry analyst has argued that new rules on capping investment in private equity funds under Dodd-Frank in the United States have "forced fund-managers to target higher returns on an annualised basis to compensate" for the limits imposed by the regulation (Chipman 2012).

Market pressures on managers to boost bottom-line returns thus persist. Earnings pressures initially saw banks resort to digging into already low capital buffers in order to support dividend payments at roughly pre-crisis levels, a practice "at odds with the objective to reduce bank credit risk," according to the Bank for International Settlements (BIS) (2012, 70). The BIS (2012, 64) reports that depressed equity prices, collateral demands, and depressed conditions in lending markets suggest that general conditions in banking remain difficult. Ominously, major banks are still heavily engaged in risky lending and trading activities. The BIS has reported that a key driver of income growth for banks has been "trading income, which the crisis exposed as unreliable" (2012, 66). The BIS (2013, 6) points to the "persistent search for yield" and argues that "historically low yields in core bond markets" have been an important underlying factor "drawing investors towards the higher returns of riskier assets." The IMF (2012, 99) warns that "developments in newer types of financial products need careful monitoring." It notes that a number of banks have been securitizing derivative counterparty risk to get around Basel III credit value adjustment capital charges. The IMF also warns that banking interconnectedness—as measured by interbank assets and liabilities and wholesale funding—has not fallen since the crisis. As the IMF (2012, 101–104) concludes:

> Overall, banking systems are generally more concentrated and are as reliant on wholesale funding today as they were before the crisis. Although some countries, notably the United States, have reduced their dependence on short-term funding, the bulk of the evidence suggests that the structure of the system has not changed in healthier directions and could reflect the lack of deep restructuring that should have occurred . . . Financial systems are not safer than before the crisis . . . Of particular concern are the larger size of financial institutions, the greater concentration and domestic interconnectedness of financial systems, and the continued importance of non-banks in overall-intermediation. The potential future use of structured and some new derivative products could add to complexity and a mispricing of risk.

It is true, however, as Timothy Geithner (2012b) argues, that some of the earlier forms of risk taking have "been forced out of the financial system," especially in securitization markets. Equity markets recognize these dangers, as reflected in the depressed equity prices within the sector. Haldane and Madouros (2012, 23) hope the current situation may see equity market pressures support a separation of retail from riskier trader banking: "Bankers today, cursed and condemned, could make a virtue of necessity. The market could lead where regulators have feared to tread." Several banks have rationalized their portfolios and engaged in asset divestitures. Two large international banks have divested their fixed-income, currencies, and commodities trading business in efforts aimed at balance sheet rationalization (IMF 2012, 85). In the United States, the residential and commercial MBS markets have all but collapsed, and the market in outstanding derivatives has also leveled off since the crisis (IMF 2012, 98). OSIRIS data shows that some of the largest banks have reduced their trading exposures and increased their capital buffers. At JP Morgan trading securities as a proportion of total assets fell by 40% between 2006 and 2013 while tier 1 regulatory capital rose from 8.7% to 12.5%. At Citigroup the value of trading securities as a proportion of total assets fell by 22% over the same period while capital rose from 8.5% to 14%. At RBS the value of trading securities as a proportion of total assets fell by 46% between 2006 and 2012 while tier 1 capital rose from 7.5% to 12.4%. At Barclays the value of trading securities fell by 38% while capital rose from 7.7% to 13.3%. HSBC and Lloyds have also reduced their exposures to trading securities while increasing capital. The largest commercial banks have also gone some way to reducing their dependence upon wholesale funding and have increased their reliance on customer deposits. At JP Morgan, for example, total customer deposits were the equivalent of 51% of total assets in 2012 (up from 47% in 2006). And at Citibank total deposits were the equivalent of 50% of assets in 2012 (up from 38% in 2006). Some banks have also pulled back somewhat from trading and lending markets and have instead invested heavily in government securities that have been used to fund government budget deficits swollen by bank bailouts and reduced taxation revenue.

Nevertheless, as Geithner admits, "these gains will erode over time" as new investment opportunities and new forms of risk taking become more pronounced during the next upswing. As JP Morgan's 2012 London trading woes make clear, new forms of risky financial trading are already being developed. The recent banking scandals noted earlier also suggest that old habits die hard. Only the next upswing, however, can fully test the hypothesis that markets and equity investors may be able to restrain risky behavior. Past experience with booms suggests, however, that this could be a forlorn hope, especially since competitive dynamics and the quest to beat market leaders remain prevalent motives. Morgan Stanley's CEO during the crisis, John Mack (2010), has admitted that the intensity of such pressures means that "I don't think we can control ourselves." Haldane (2012a, 8) notes that "there is some evidence recently of return on equity targets having become a less important determinant of some banks' portfolio allocation and executive pay decisions." But he also suggests that "returns remain hardwired into both to some degree"; that "many global banks continue to publish return on equity targets"; and that this "attachment to counter-productive performance metrics . . . raises questions about whether the lessons from the crisis have truly been learnt." The fact that the largest banks have become larger and that key markets have become more concentrated does not therefore mean that banking is now less competitive. In order to maintain their share price, jobs, and bonuses, bank executives remain under intense pressure to sustain their market share and return on equity. Banks continue to be judged not simply by their absolute level of performance but also by their relative performance. No doubt the next major financial boom will be supported by some widely shared version of reality purporting to argue that "this time is different": that risk has been calibrated and minimized, that markets are efficient, and that increasing asset prices are not evidence of a bubble. The reality is more likely to mirror the findings of behavioral finance theory that emphasize myopia, irrational exuberance, and market herding. Indeed, we have shown in detail how in many cases senior managers can be outwitted by the scale of their firms and lose touch with the complexities and risks of leveraged trading.

Losing the War: Regulatory Complexity and Evasion

The notion of "embeddedness" within the state capacity literature as well as Mann's (1990) notion of "infrastructural power" points to cooperative relations between the state and key societal interlocutors as one of the foundations for "state capacity." Yet the state-finance nexus prior to the crisis in the United States and the United Kingdom produced a dysfunctional form of embeddedness and permissive forms of regulation that were one ingredient of the crisis. Now, with more forceful regulation, bankers have no incentive to cooperate and every incentive to instead push to dilute or sidestep the new reforms. Bankers and financiers are skilled at this. Mervyn King (2009b) has warned about the "sheer creative imagination of the financial sector in dreaming up new ways of taking risks," leading him to conclude that "the belief that appropriate regulation can ensure that speculative activities do not result in failures is a delusion." As Richardson, Smith, and Walter (2011, 192) similarly argue, "The idea that Large Complex Financial Institutions can or will regulate themselves prudently has been shown to be distorted by the industry's competitive dynamics, embedded agency conflicts, and ever present moral hazard." Market competition and the pressure for profits are structural factors that helped drive the crisis in the first place. These same pressures now encourage regulatory evasion.

Higher capital requirements and other new forms of regulation may even encourage banks to take more risks in chasing higher profits to compensate for the costs of regulation. A report by Fitch estimates that the costs of the new capital regime for the twenty-nine largest international banks could be in the order of $566 billion. According to a senior Fitch analyst, "Since it is impossible for regulators to perfectly align capital requirements with risk exposure, some banks might seek to increase returns on equity through riskier activities that maximise yield on a given unit of Basel III capital, including new forms of regulatory arbitrage" (Treanor 2012a). Similarly, the IMF (2012, 103) warns that "Basel capital and liquidity rules could be promoting a greater intermediation of new financial products as financial institutions use other avenues to make up for the higher expenses imposed by the Basel rules." Another industry analyst has argued that new Dodd-Frank rules on capping investment in private equity funds have "forced fund-managers to target higher returns on an annualised basis to compensate" for the limits imposed by the regulation (Chipman 2012). Reform measures are thus vulnerable to ongoing lobbying and evasion efforts. As one banker told the *Economist* (2011), the "banks don't think the war is over yet."

Traditionally, the politics of banking was a "quiet" arena where rules were written and enforced in a cloistered world well beyond the public gaze, where the supposedly expert judgments, technical acumen, and market efficiency of bankers were largely accepted by the authorities, and where the latter trusted the former to be prudent. Olson's (1965) logic of collective action theory also supports the view that concentrated sectors such as banking and finance with much at stake will more effectively mobilize to support their aims than the more general and diffuse electorate (Rixen 2013,

7). This cloistered relationship between government and bankers was disturbed by the crisis and the high politics that ensued, but it is now returning as regulatory authorities, reflecting the competing objectives of reform measures, come under strong and continuing pressure from the banks to revise their interpretations and guidance. Bankers and financiers are trying to push the politics of bank reform policy toward arenas characterized by low political visibility and technical work by expert committees. As Young (2013, 2) argues, the "increased salience of financial regulation and the more strained policy network [have] meant that financial industry groups have altered the stages at which they most actively intervene in the regulatory policymaking process. The capacity to 'veto' regulatory proposals at the stage of actual policy formulation has been significantly weakened since the crisis." The result has been that bankers and financiers have focused more on the implementation stage of the policy cycle (Young 2013).

Much of the work on definitions, standard setting, instrument selection, calibration, and other detailed aspects of implementation will proceed slowly and will involve the work of specialized expertise, committees, and agencies. Such processes provide ample opportunities for banking lobbyists to negotiate over rules and technical details and to search for or construct loopholes during implementation. Bart Naylor, a lobbyist for the consumer rights coalition Americans for Financial Reform, argues that debate about market-making and proprietorial trading is "the subject of a very quiet, closed-door battle right now, not just between us and Wall Street, but among the agencies as well" (LaCapra 2011). Mark Plotkin, at the large corporate law firm Covington & Burling, suggests that "during the run-up to the [Dodd-Frank] legislation, while it was very active, there was a limit to how much people could really influence the statute . . . The implementation phase is really industry's opportunity to influence what the final product looks like" (Becker 2010).

In the United Kingdom, the chair of the ICB, Sir John Vickers, and Mervyn King have warned that certain elements of the ICB reforms have been watered down due to lobbying (Treanor 2012d). For example, the ICB's proposed leverage ratio of 4% has been reduced to 3%; ring-fenced banks will now be allowed to engage in certain derivatives trades such as interest rate and currency swaps, whereas small banks will be exempt from ring-fencing requirements altogether. The government also proposes exempting the overseas operations of UK banks from new rules relating to capital adequacy. The lobbying will continue. The IMF (2012, 17) warns that "there is a need for a continued strong commitment to the regulatory reform agenda" and that "momentum to carry through the agenda, in full, should not be lost." Lord Turner (2009a, 6) worries that there is "a danger that after the crisis, everyone gives up, either because of finance sector lobbying or because it's all very exhausting."

In the United States, when he signed the Dodd-Frank Act into law, President Obama (2010) decried the "furious lobbying of an array of powerful interest groups" and argued that the "primary cause" of the "severe recession" was a "breakdown in our financial system . . . born of a failure of responsibility from certain corners of Wall Street to the halls of power in Washington," which resulted in "antiquated and poorly enforced rules that allowed some to game the system and take risks that endangered the entire economy." Yet in the United States, a highly fragmented and contested political system has given Wall Street ample opportunity to invest an estimated $2.3 billion in ongoing lobbying since the crisis (Schwartz 2011). For their part, bank executives have argued that the crisis was caused by poorly designed regulations that, for example, gave banks an incentive to hold securitized assets on their balance sheets. They argue that new regulations will be equally counterproductive.

According to the *Economist* (2012a), a banker close to the action in the United States has predicted "a decade of grind, with constant disputes in courts and legislatures, finally producing a regime riddled with exemptions and nuances that may, because of its complexity, exacerbate systemic risks rather than mitigate them." Pro-market Republicans in Congress blocked the appointment of the prominent reformer Elizabeth Warren to head the new Consumer Finance Protection Bureau. They have also delayed other prominent regulatory appointments and moved to cut the budgets of regulatory agencies (Wyatt 2011). For example, difficulties in Congress meant that it took the Treasury over seventeen months to appoint the head of the new Office of Financial Research (Alden 2012). The SEC was forced to suspend hiring 800 new staff to help cope with new regulatory demands and was forced to cancel much-needed technology upgrades (Sorkin 2011). Lobbying has also thwarted attempts to force banks to contribute to a bailout insurance fund. Several business associations successfully sued the SEC in 2011 over a Dodd-Frank–related rule on shareholder voting rights. It is clear already that reform will prove to be a long and difficult process. Moreover, the major rounds of reform-resisting litigation have only begun. As Richardson, Smith, and Walter (2011, 206) argue, the outcome will "depend on constant vigilance and the hard slog of effective enforcement by regulators pitted against the banks[,] their lawyers and lobbyists."

At the international level, Tsingou (2008) argues that major international banks and bank lobby groups such as the Institute for International Finance (IIF) have traditionally had substantial input into the Basel deliberations. We have already noted how banks argued during the formulation of Basel II that they should be allowed to use their own internal risk assessments for determining risk-weighted capital levels in a process Hellwig (2009, 190) describes as "regulatory capture by sophistication." Lall (2012) argues that even after the crisis the influence of bankers persists. He contends that the Basel Committee for Banking Supervision (BCBS) is a cloistered, technocratic arena generally shielded from public scrutiny and clear lines of accountability, especially in relation to governments and domestic stakeholders. Organizations like the IIF, the International Swaps and Derivatives Association, and the European Securitization Forum are all well-resourced lobby groups, and all have close contacts with the BCBS. Senior financial officials in government and in central banks have often ended up working for the IIF (Lall 2012, 627). During the Basel II negotiations, not only did banks argue successfully for internal risk assessment procedures, they also successfully lobbied for dropping a proposed capital surcharge on risks associated with credit derivatives, for the use of VaR-based methods in risk analysis, and for a light-touch approach to risks associated with securitization (Lall 2012). The financial crisis may have undermined the credibility of these approaches, but the banking industry soon mobilized postcrisis, gaining what Lall (2012) sees as "first-mover advantages" in the lobbying process.

Major international banks and bodies such as the IIF successfully argued for a reduction in the size of the proposed capital buffers, as well as for a long phase-in period out to 2019. The Basel III reforms, as noted, require banks to hold equity equivalent to at least 7% of risk-weighted assets (composed of a 4.5% tier 1 equity and a further 2.5% buffer) by the start of 2019. The reforms thus continue the path of earlier Basel rules that endorsed the efficacy of the risk-weighted approach. This requires capital to be held only against "risky" assets. Calibrating such risk weightings adds enormously to regulatory complexity and creates many loopholes. Moreover, making clear distinctions between risky and less risky assets can be problematic, especially in the midst of a banking crisis. The Basel rules have always meant that banks hold very low levels of equity against their *total* assets. Admati and Hellwig (2103, 176) show, for example, that Deutsche Bank's 14% equity holdings against its risk-weighted assets in late 2011 amounted to only 2 or 3% of equity against its *total* assets. A decline of a mere 2.5% in the value of the bank's total assets could wipe out equity, making the bank insolvent. In other words, the capital buffers under Basel III are still far too low. No wonder Martin Wolf (2010) at the *Financial Times* refers to the new Basel III capital rules as a "capital inadequacy ratio," suggesting that "this amount of equity is far below levels markets would impose if investors did not continue to expect governments to bail out creditors in a crisis." Under the Basel rules banks will be allowed to adjust to higher capital standards by raising equity or reducing the size of balance sheets, including shedding assets and limiting credit (IMF 2012, 83). Banks have threatened the latter in the face of what they see as "excessive regulation" (Baker 2012).

An innovation under the Basel III rules is to introduce a new leverage ratio that requires 3% of equity to be held against a bank's total assets. Admati and Hellwig (2013, 177, emphasis added) write that "if this looks outrageously low, it is because the number *is* outrageously low." The new ratio will allow banks to accumulate assets to thirty-three times tier 1 capital, similar to the levels in many banks prior to the crisis. There are also other weaknesses. A proposed capital surcharge on systematically important banks was watered down during Basel III negotiations, moving it to a "nonbinding" Pillar 2 status within the Basel framework. The BCBS also announced that the surcharge would be dropped from a proposed 7% of risk-weighted assets to a range of 1.5 to 3% (Lall 2012, 626–632). Lall argues that large international banks "enjoyed considerable success in watering down Basel III." Key provisions were relaxed, rendered nonbinding, or delayed, in some cases until 2019.

As we have already noted, the PRA in the United Kingdom has raised minimal bank capital requirements beyond those stipulated in Basel III.

In doing so, the Bank of England, along with a number of other European central banks, has resisted an attempt by the European Commission to interpret Basel III as stipulating both minimum and maximum capital levels (FPC 2013a). Yet, even here, while the FPC has reversed the momentum over the last few decades, it has not attempted to set capital ratios at a level investors would be likely to demand in the absence of an assurance that governments would bail out a failing bank. For much of the nineteenth and early twentieth centuries, when banks were not comprehensively backstopped by the state, market investors demanded equity holdings of between 30 and 50% of total assets before banks were deemed relatively safe (Haldane and Alessandri 2009). The growth of state support for banks since the 1930s in the form of deposit insurance and lender of last resort schemes has transferred risk to the state and emboldened bankers. They now claim, spuriously, that holding equity is too costly relative to debt. But the cost of the latter is now artificially low because of state support for banks. As we first noted in Chapter 2, Andy Haldane (2012c, 4) has calculated the taxpayer subsidy to the world's largest banks at $70 billion every year between 2002 and 2007: roughly half of the average posttax profits enjoyed by these banks over that period. From a societal perspective, the advantage of equity over debt as a source of bank financing is that equity means that investors themselves face risk and the costs of bank failure. More equity also implies less leverage. Therefore, having lots of equity on hand during a crisis means that banks are far more resilient. They would not be as reliant on high levels of leverage and fragile wholesale funding markets, the proximate cause of many bank failures during the 2007–2008 crisis. It also means that equity investors have substantial skin in the game and are thus more likely to be risk conscious. Admati and Hellwig (2013, 179) think that equity levels of around 20 to 30% would be appropriate as an adequate buffer against risk and as a way of privatizing risk. This would help make banks much safer and more resilient, thus substantially reducing systemic risk. It is crucial to set equity levels at this level, argue Admati and Hellwig (2013, 181), for a number of reasons:

> First, the equity levels of recent decades were artificially low because banks and their creditors had become used to the government safety net. Second, the increases in the intensity of competition in financial

> markets that we have seen since the 1970s have decreased the [banks'] ability to withstand shocks. Third, the high degree of interconnectedness in the system that has come with financial innovation and with globalization has magnified the potential fallout from the failure of a systemically important financial institution for the global economy. Moreover, institutions tend to be exposed to the same shocks and therefore run into trouble at the same time. All these concerns lead to the conclusion that the levels of equity banks have had in recent decades do not provide appropriate guidance as to what bank equity should be.

The question of bank equity is but one example of the broader situation in recent decades in which bankers and financial interests have been one jump ahead of governments and regulators. The endless game of regulatory arbitrage is another arena in which bankers appear to be winning. Here, bankers are in a strong position because of information asymmetries: they know more about their banks than politicians and regulators. They have also been able to outspend regulators in political and court battles and have often poached key regulators. Administrative capacity, including coherent policy, skilled officials, and effective policy tools and institutions, is a key element identified in the literature on "state capacity" (Bell and Hindmoor 2009). The issues of regulatory ineptitude and capture were major problems prior to the crisis (Baker 2010). Yet now, in the postcrisis era, heroic assumptions are being made about the capacity of regulators to stay ahead of the banks and the shadow banking sector. It is true that regulators have been chastened by the crisis and are now more likely than they once were to aggressively pursue banks that they believe are gaming or evading the rules. Nevertheless, the question of regulatory performance and capture has not attracted sufficient attention post the crisis (Baker 2010). In the United States the same regulatory agencies that failed before the crisis are still in charge and are now being assailed by antireform interests in the banks and the Republican Party. In testimony to Congress, the SEC's chairman, Elisse Walter (2013), has suggested that Dodd-Frank "cannot be handled appropriately with the agency's previous resource levels without undermining the agency's other core duties," that it has still not been given "all the resources necessary to fully implement the law," and that without "additional resources . . . many of the issues to which the Dodd-Frank Act is directed will not be adequately addressed."

In the United Kingdom, the FPC has been granted a considerable degree of autonomy from both elected politicians and business interests. In an exchange of letters with the chancellor of the Exchequer, it has been confirmed that the FPC's "members need to be, and be seen to be, independent of government and other influences" (FPC 2013a, 3). Importantly, the FPC has not been given a statutory responsibility to consult with financial interests prior to reaching decisions or, as was the case with the FSA, to "have regard" to "the international character of financial services and markets and the desirability of maintaining the competitive position of the UK" (Financial Services and Markets Act 2000). Yet the FPC has also warned that a "shortfall in the number of sufficient senior, experienced staff" poses a key risk to financial stability and that it has yet to develop a "good working model of the macro-financial system" (Barwell 2013, 201).

The fact that the new regulations are so appallingly voluminous and complex also poses significant problems for implementation and compliance. In the United States, the Glass-Steagall Act was only 37 pages long, but the Volcker rule within the Dodd-Frank Act span 300 pages, and the Dodd-Frank Act itself is over 800 pages. The reforms will require more than 400 new regulations to be formulated by eleven regulatory agencies. Sheila Blair, the former head of the FDIC, told Congress in late 2011 of her fear that the "recently proposed regulation to implement the Volcker rule is extraordinarily complex" (Economist, 2012a). As of late 2012, two years after being legislated, only about a third of the new rules and regulations stemming from Dodd-Frank had been finalized. Those completed have added more than 8,000 pages to the rulebook. Once finalized, the Dodd-Frank Act could run to over 30,000 pages of rules (Haldane and Madouros 2012, 10). Dennis Kelleher, who runs Better Markets, a financial regulatory reform group in the United States, argues that "most of the length, complexity and questions are in there because of industry lobbying." He describes the SEC rulebook as the "the bastard child of the lobbying industry . . . You can't demand and insist and lobby for all these rules and exemptions and then complain that it's too long and complex" (Eisinger 2012).

Questions have also been raised about regulatory complexity in relation to the new Basel III capital standards. The rules for Basel I with its basic risk weightings ran to thirty pages. Basel II, with its more complex risk weighting, had rules spanning 347 pages. Basel III now has over 600 pages of rules, and with domestic implementation provisions the rules have expanded to over 1,000 pages in countries such as the United States and the United Kingdom. Basel III's far more fine-grained system of assessing risk weightings greatly complicates regulation and raises serious questions about "regulatory robustness," the "near limitless scope for arbitrage," and "over-reliance on probably unreliable models" (Haldane and Madouros 2012, 10). These new standards follow the same basic approach as the older versions of the Basel rules, but with far more complex rules around capital standards.

Ongoing financial innovation and regulatory arbitrage are also likely to challenge regulatory capacity. The continuing amplification of and feedbacks between financial and regulatory complexity will make regulation contingent and vulnerable. For example, as we saw in Chapter 3, Lehman Brothers and some other banks exploited a loophole prior to the crisis through "Repo 105" transactions, aimed at reducing stated leverage. This involved treating repo transactions as "sales," the proceeds of which were used to temporarily pay down liabilities for reporting purposes. In the first two quarters of 2008 Lehman used this mechanism to reduce reported leverage by $50 billion. Firms can also reduce nominal leverage by overstating asset values or delaying the recognition of losses (Merced and Sorkin 2010; Acharya, Kulkarni, and Richardson 2011, 157). As Kenneth Rogoff (2012) argues: "As finance has become more complicated, regulators have tried to keep up by adopting ever more complicated rules. It's an arms race that underfunded regulatory agencies have no chance of winning." Information asymmetries and limited resources mean that regulators will almost inevitably lose such a contest.

In the case of the Volcker rule, concerns about the capacity of the largest banks to subvert the new rules have been raised. Lobbyists have already met with some success, with revisions allowing the main banks to hive off proprietary trading and investment banking activities to separately capitalized subsidiaries or affiliates, a move that raises questions about whether such offshoot entities can be effectively ring-fenced from the capital of the main bank in a crisis. The amended Volcker rule also allows the largest banks to engage in securities and derivatives trading if these are conducted for the "near term demands of clients, customers, or counterparties." The rule also allows large banks to trade in foreign exchange derivatives and high-grade credit default swaps (CDSs). Dodd-Frank allows banks to place trades when hedging risk, and they can also buy securities from clients with an eye to sales to other clients later, with the line becoming "fuzzy between that business and proprietary trading" (Protess 2011). Evasion will also occur through informal channels. As Richardson, Smith, and Walter (2011, 202), comment:

> Some large banks have already moved some of their proprietary traders to client desks that nevertheless use the firm's own capital. Equally troubling, traders in that position now have privileged insight into client trades and, by stretching the rules, can front-run them. It seems doubtful that highly compensated practitioners, backed by phalanxes of lawyers and lobbyists well versed in putting pressure on regulators, will take very long to find ways to erode the practical focus of the Volcker Rule's proprietary trading restrictions.

The IMF (2012, 86) comments that "implementation of the [Volcker] rule will be a challenge to prudential authorities; and an inability to clearly distinguish permissible activities (market making and underwriting) from prohibited ones (proprietary trading) may mitigate the impact of the rule." The *Economist* (2012a) similarly argues that the problem with regulatory complexity is that "it encourages efforts to game the system by exploiting the loopholes it inevitably creates . . . Anticipating the Volcker rule, bank departments that previously used the word 'proprietary' have been dropped, renamed or quietly shifted to sheltered corners." David Viniar (2010), the CFO at Goldman Sachs, has commented that market inefficiencies related to the Volcker rule could even make trading more profitable.

Lobbyists working on behalf of the banks have also ensured that Dodd-Frank's structural reform clauses will now be subject to judicial review. Importantly, lobbyists have also helped ensure the passage of an amendment that requires regulators to take account of the international competitiveness of the US financial services industry, a large loophole that will allow firms to lobby and even litigate on the basis of perceived threats to their "global competitiveness" (Richardson, Smith, and Walter 2011, 198). There have also been disputes about the definition of what constitutes "customer-driven" forms of trading in relation the Volcker rule. Wall Street lobbyists have also fought to exempt mutual funds and insurers and trusts from the Volcker bans on proprietary trading and have also won exemptions for banks to trade up to 3% of their capital, a potentially large amount for the biggest banks. In 2011 the SEC published a draft set of rules in relation to the Dodd-Frank Act. These were then the subject of over 18,000 public comments and detailed hearings within the House of Representatives and the Senate. One of the most contentious issues related to securities and derivatives trading. Here, opponents wanted regulators to expand the definition of activity, which could be said to constitute market making of benefit to consumers and, conversely, narrow further the definition of what counts as proprietary trading. UBS (2012) has argued that Dodd-Frank charged regulators with "drafting regulations that ensure vibrant and liquid markets so that investors continue to have access to a broad range of transactions" and that, in a number of technical respects, the proposed draft did not meet this obligation. Similarly, lawyers representing Deutsche Bank and Bank of America sought to remind the SEC that "in implementing the Volcker rule" it must "give effect to legislative intent" and that draft rules "ignore Congress's intent to exempt market making and underwriting activities" (Cleary, Gottlieb, Steen, and Hamilton LLP 2012). JP Morgan, for its part, argued that "in some areas [the SEC's draft rules] turned the statute's narrow prohibition [on proprietary trading] into a more general prohibition on risk-taking" (Zubrow 2012). The SEC was unable to dismiss these arguments out of hand because its own draft proposals were, in the words of its chair, Mary Schapiro (2012), "intended to . . . strike an appropriate balance between preserving important market functions and preventing proprietary trading unrelated to such functions."

Profit pressures and regulatory arbitrage suggest that new arenas of risk taking are likely to migrate to the most shadowy sectors of finance or emerge in new institutional settings (Goodhart 2010, 166; Acharya, Kulkarni, and Richardson 2011, 144; IMF 2012, 77). This is especially so since nonbank entities face less stringent capital standards and do not face anything like the regulation that is currently being imposed on the main banks.

In the aftermath of the crisis, the G20 (Group of Twenty 2009a) pledged to "extend regulation and oversight to all systemically important financial institutions, instruments and markets." The FSB was subsequently tasked with assessing countries' compliance records with regulatory standards. This has generated new information about the extent and nature of the offshore shadow banking system (FSB 2012a). It has not, however, resulted in new regulations to limit its growth. Basel III has increased the risk weightings for securitization exposure and off–balance-sheet vehicles. In general, however, international regulators still lack any "hard means of enforcement" (Rixen 2013, 11). As the *Economist* (2012a) argues, "The shadow banking system existed before the crisis, but it is expected to grow as some financiers decamp to companies that evade Dodd-Frank's definitions." The IMF (2012, 77) agrees: "Tighter regulation and more intense supervision may push bank-like activities into some less-regulated non-bank financial institutions (the shadow banking system)." Regulators may have new (if untested) powers in relation to the main banking system, but investment migration will pose significant challenges for regulators and supervisors. At this stage in relation to the shadow banking sector "a firm consensus has yet to emerge on what, if any, regulatory action is needed" (IMF 2012, 91). The Financial Stability Board (FSB 2011) has also argued that "although Basel III closes a number of identified shortcomings, both the incentives for, and the risks associated with, regulatory arbitrage will likely increase as Basel III raises the rigor of bank regulation." Indeed, in its Global Shadow Banking Monitoring Report, the FSB (2012a, 3) found that the assets of the shadow banking system, which had reached $62 trillion in 2007 before then declining, had increased to $67 trillion by the end of 2011.

The constant surveillance and catch-up challenge for regulators will be never ending as they attempt to keep abreast of complexity and the evolving minutiae and innovations in the financial world. Tim Geithner (2012a) defends the current approach by arguing that the regulations are "no more complex than the problems they are designed to solve." Yet the problems generated by the current structure and dynamics of the financial system are so complex that attempts to mirror and chase such complexity through regulation are likely to fail. All the while, investors will be seeking and finding new loopholes in the regulatory net.

More fundamentally, the game of catch-up means that the authorities are not squarely addressing the key problems that caused the crisis—excessive competition and the way in which this drives financialization, leveraged trading, and systemic risk. The reforms to banking focus mainly on the balance sheets of the large banking entities and on limiting trading activities. But the reforms do not focus squarely on competition and trading per se, especially in relation to the shadow banking system. The banking crisis arose because the banks and shadow banks had become too big, too profit-oriented, too complex, too risky, and too debt-ridden and interconnected. In such a context, substantial balance sheet problems in individual banks wreaked havoc on the entire financial system and then the real economy. Yet the reforms have not changed the basic dynamics of this system. In relation to the issue of systemic risk, Turner (2011, 14) argues, "risks could exist even if we were able to resolve all banks, or even indeed if we broke up large banks into smaller ones. A system of multiple interconnected players could be as risky as one with large specific institutions." Even ring-fenced commercial banks could face significant counterparty risks. The impact of major collapses within the shadow banking system could still impact on the main banks in complex and unpredictable ways. As Alastair Darling has argued, "I have always thought to separate banks doesn't deal with the real problem . . . It is the connections between institutions that cause problems" (Treanor 2012e). Risky trading will inevitably increase, and it is not clear that the proposed structural ring-fencing designed to shield the main banks from such risks will work. The ICB final report (2011, 11) argues that ring-fencing would "achieve the principal benefits of full separation but at a lower cost to the economy," and that ring-fencing would allow a banking group to use profits from its investment banking arm to support a failing retail division while preventing a bank from using money from its retail division to bail out a failed investment arm (ICB 2011, 26). Goodhart (2010) counters by arguing that efforts to screen off activity create a "boundary problem" where attempts to enforce the rules will generate incentives to climb over or evade the boundary. Haldane (2012c, 10–11) similarly argues that current attempts to ring-fence or quarantine the effects of risky banking within commercial banks are likely to be problematic:

> The Volcker rule separates only a fairly limited range of potentially risky investment banking activities, in the form of proprietary trading. The Vickers proposals mandate only a limited range of basic banking activities to lie within the ring-fence, namely deposit taking

> and overdrafts . . . As the history of the Glass-Steagall Act demonstrates, today's loophole can become tomorrow's bolt hole . . . In the go-go years, will these reforms be sufficient to prevent the grass always looking greener on the riskier side of the (ring)-fence?

Martin Wolf (2012), who sat on the ICB, is also worried: "I fear this blurred line will be breached repeatedly under pressure from banks until the ring-fence is almost totally permeable." Paul Volcker has similarly warned of such maneuverers. In testimony to the Parliamentary Committee on Banking Standards in the United Kingdom in 2012, he stated that "when you adopt a ring-fence, pressure from inside the organisation tends to weaken the restrictions . . . I'm not saying it will be totally ineffective, but the Vickers Report says it's going to have a ring-fence with exceptions, and once you go down that road of having exceptions the organisation is going to push for more exceptions and widen the limits" (Inman 2012). The ring-fence is also limited because it applies only to activities within the United Kingdom. As the IMF (2012, 88) comments, "As retail ring-fencing is limited to the United Kingdom, it may have little, if any, effect on the cross-border activity of internationally active UK banks." In other words, risky activities could simply migrate to another jurisdiction. Speaking in the House of Lords, the economist Lord Eatwell (2013) also raised concerns about "regulatory arbitrage and the possibility of European banks in the UK undermining ring-fencing."

Such concerns have seen reformers attempt to buttress the ring fence. In late 2012, the chair of the Parliamentary Commission on Banking Standards, the Conservative MP Andrew Tyrie, argued that "over time the ring fence will be tested and challenged by the banks" (Treanor 2012c). Tyrie argued that reforms needed to go further and called for "electrification" of the ring fence by adding new legislation that could invoke reserve powers for full separation if needed. Haldane (2012c, 11) agrees, arguing for a modern-day Glass-Steagall Act: "The main benefit this would bring, relative to structural ring-fencing, is that it would eliminate loopholes from the ring-fence and better insure the distinct cultures of retail and investment banking were not cross-contaminated . . . Full separation may also be operationally simpler to implement than the existing structural proposals." Even Sandy Weill, Citigroup's former CEO, who lobbied successfully to repeal the Glass-Steagall Act, has now argued that reformers should "split up investment banking from [commercial] banking" (Treanor 2012b). After initially expressing some skepticism, Chancellor George Osborne (2013) announced in February 2013 that the "government will go further than previously announced and that if a bank flouts the rules, the regulator and the Treasury will have the power to break it up altogether—full separation, not just a ring fence." In July 2013, in response to the high-profile publication of the Banking Commission's final report, the government also announced that it would introduce a criminal offence for reckless misconduct for senior bankers; would work with regulators to ensure that bankers' pay is aligned with their performance; and would reverse the burden of proof so that bank bosses are held accountable for breaches within their areas of responsibility (HM Treasury 2013). Yet the government resisted a recommendation that the Treasury be given the reserve authority to impose a full separation of all commercial and investment banks across the UK industry rather than simply the authority to separate the activities of particular banks (Deighton 2013).

Problems will also arise because new regulatory concepts and approaches, such as macroprudential regulation, as well as how to measure systemic risk over the cycle, are still largely at the concept stage. The details of how to measure systemic risk over the cycle have yet to be worked out, and the metrics here can be fraught (Bell and Quiggin 2006). The development, implementation, and operation of countercyclical policy instruments are also in their infancy and will take years of research and trial and error (Giustiniani and Thornton 2011, 327; Baker 2013). This is what happened with the refinement of inflation-targeting approaches within monetary policy, a process that took several decades to work through. Bank of England officials argue that "the state of macroprudential policy resembles the state of monetary policy just after the second world war, with patchy data, incomplete theory and negligible experience, meaning that macroprudential regulation will be conducted by trial and error" (Aikman, Haldane, and Nelson 2010). A recent report to the G20 is very clear on these technical problems, describing systemic risk identification as a

> nascent field, that requires fundamental applied research, so as to inform the collection of analysis and data, to fill data gaps and to lead

> to the development of better models . . . There is no widely agreed and comprehensive theoretical framework for the optimal choice and calibration of macroprudential tools. It is still too early to provide a definite assessment of the set of macroprudential tools that will prove] most useful further down the road, in part because financial innovation and change within the financial system will give rise to new risks in due course. (FSB, IMF, and BIS 2011, 9–10)

Similar calibration and implementation issues will also affect the implementation of Basel III's capital and liquidity controls, the design and maintenance of ring-fences, the definition and regulation of proprietary trading, and the definition of systemically important financial institutions, as well as bank resolution strategies and associated private sector bail-in mechanisms. The IMF (2012, 86) comments that "implementation of the [Volcker] rule will be a challenge to prudential authorities; and an inability to clearly distinguish permissible activities (market making and underwriting) from prohibited ones (proprietary trading) may mitigate the impact of the rule."

All this suggests that regulators and supervisors face serious implementation challenges and will be forced into an endless game of catch-up. The president and CEO of the Federal Reserve Bank of Dallas, Richard Fisher (2013), argues that "regulatory supervision, by definition, is always at least one step behind the actions taken by market participants. The more complex the rules, the more difficult it is to bridge the gap due to the complexities of financial markets. None of this is helpful for financial stability."

Finally, on the question of bank resolution, there are also concerns about whether the new resolution or bail-in mechanisms will work as planned, especially during a crisis. In the 2008 crisis governments bailed out the banks and simultaneously allowed them to make large dividend payouts to shareholders. This weakened the banks, making the public bailouts even more imperative. In the United States the private payouts to shareholders are estimated at about half the amount of the public bailouts (Admati and Hellwig 2013, 175). This is hardly a sound precedent for future private sector bail-ins. The best solution would be to have the banks establish a fund to cover such bailouts prior to the next crisis. But bank lobbying and threats that such measures will harm the banks and slow recovery have seen governments in both the United States and the United Kingdom shy away from setting up an ex ante resolution fund designed to draw on contributions from large financial entities and banks. Instead, the plan under Dodd-Frank, for example, as noted earlier, is to try to levy firms for such a contribution in the teeth of a crisis. As Acharya, Cooley, Richardson, et al. (2011, 10) argue, "It is highly incredible that in the midst of a significant crisis, there will be the political will to try and levy a discretionary charge on surviving financial firms to recoup losses inflicted by failed firms." Standard and Poor's argues that there is a good chance that governments would simply step in and bail firms out rather than attempting to use their new powers amid the challenges of a crisis (Braithwaite and van Duyn 2011). Attempts to do so would impose additional pressure on banks at the worst possible time and might well increase panic and uncertainty and further exacerbate systemic risk. Admati and Hellwig (2013, 139) state that "hardly anyone considers the no-bailout commitments credible." In the United Kingdom, Haldane (2102c) also doubts that private sector bail-ins will work during a crisis. The most likely scenario is that governments will, as usual, be drawn into bailouts, as happened in the 2008 crisis. If this is the case, it means that the largest banks still have unlimited implicit guarantees. The banks lobbied hard to head off ex ante resolution contributions, yet the proposed system is unlikely to work effectively, especially from the taxpayer's point of view. Bank resolution and attempted bail-ins also pose daunting administrative and legal challenges due to the global nature of operations in the major banks. Under existing arrangements there would need to be specific resolution procedures tailored to the legal jurisdictions and rules of each country in which large banks operated. Inevitably any such process would be lengthy and disruptive, hardly a procedure suitable amid a banking crisis and credit collapse (Admati and Hellwig 2013, 76).

A New Approach Is Needed

The scale of the problems just outlined suggests that a new approach to reform should be considered. Reformers should not aim to play cat and mouse games with bankers trying to chase the latest financial innovations and sources of risk taking. Nor should they aim to patch up and support the existing industry. Instead, they should seek to fundamentally change it. This book and many other studies have shown that modern, complex financial systems are prone to serial, large-scale crises. Our study has shown that most of the core financial institutions in the United States and the United Kingdom are too large and complex, driven to extremes by competitive pressures and typically run by agents prone to myopia, irrational exuberance, and herding behavior. In recent decades such dynamics have seen risky traders and investment bankers rise to the top of corporate hierarchies, displacing more traditional, conservative bankers. The interconnections, externalities, and knock-on effects among institutions, especially during a crisis, greatly amplify these basic problems.

If attempts at regulatory catch-up and external market discipline are problematic, then there are two other basic approaches to reform. The first is to insist that banks self-insure and hold more capital to create a stronger buffer against crisis, to reduce bank leverage, and to force investors to have more skin in the game. The latter might breed more caution, although this form of restraint could be offset by moral hazard incentives. Thus far, the moderate increases in capital that are proposed by Basel III are insufficient. As noted earlier, Admati and Hellwig propose capital levels of between 20 and 30% as the basis for adequate risk buffers. They argue, however, that bankers have successfully convinced politicians and the media that significantly increasing bank equity or capital is costly and will reduce lending and slow economic recovery post the crisis. In 2010, for example, the British Bankers Association frightened the government, arguing that the new regulations would force British banks to "hold an extra £600 billion of capital that might otherwise have been deployed as loans to businesses or households" (quoted in Admati and Hellwig 2013, 5). Barclays Bank made much the same argument more recently (Treanor 2013b), one seemingly believed by the British business secretary, Vince Cable (Pratley 2013). Arguments of this type essentially equate bank capital with "reserves" to be set aside by banks. Yet, to their credit, as Bank of England officials have recognized (Bailey 2013; King 2013), this is a spurious argument. Bank capital (or equity) is just another source of financing for banks, just like customer deposits or wholesale debt funding. Like the latter two, bank capital is a source of funds that banks lend out to borrowers. In principle, holding extra capital is not a cost to banks. In reality, however, bank equity or capital tends to be more expensive than wholesale funding, and this explains why banks (compared to other companies) use so much borrowed money and hold so little equity. To the extent that equity is more costly than wholesale debt for banks, this is, however, largely because of the distortion of debt markets due to artificial government support for banks through the various support measures already mentioned. In other words, debt is cheaper for banks than equity because "too big to fail" banks carry a lower risk premium in funding markets. In a more ideal world, private investors, not governments and taxpayers, would underwrite the banking sector, as should happen in a capitalist system. As the former president of the Federal Reserve Bank of Minneapolis, Gary Stern (2009), has argued: "Creditors will continue to underprice the risk-taking of these financial institutions, overfund them, and fail to provide effective market discipline. Facing prices that are two low, systemically important firms will take on too much risk."

In contrast to debt, capital can act as a mechanism to help reduce risk taking and absorb losses. The implication of the lack of fundamental reform to capital levels is that the high levels of bank dependence upon wholesale funding will continue, posing a major threat regarding systemic risk. This explains why Daniel Tarullo, a governor of the Federal Reserve, insists that "US and global regulators need to take a hard, comprehensive look at the systemic risks present in wholesale short-term funding markets" (Tarullo 2013). As noted above, the IMF (2012, 101–104) has warned that banking systems are "as reliant on wholesale funding today as they were before the crisis." The new Basel rules also remain focused on the behavior of individual institutions, not on systemic risk. Overall, the previous Basel system increased systemic risks, and the new system fails to adequately deal with this core issue.

There is a second, more radical, approach. Instead of seeing a large, complex banking and financial sector as a major plus for the economy and as a source of "international competitiveness," as governments in the United Kingdom and the United States still essentially do, a different view, which sees banking and finance as a basic utility function—an essential service, much like water supply—could be adopted. Such a perspective would aim to simplify and downsize the sector, suppressing or stripping out much of the risky, speculative, and casino-like activity. A stable banking and financial sector that serves the real economy should be the aim, much like the regime of financial regulation that was put in place during the post–World War II economic boom, an era that produced high and stable rates of economic growth.

As we have argued, the reforms above are not squarely addressing the key problems that caused the crisis—intense competition and subsequent risky trading and systemic risk. One approach here is to alter market structures to reduce competition and thus the profit and risk drivers that are built into the current core financial systems. As Gowan (2009, 9) argues, "Ensuring the safety of the system requires that competition between banks be suppressed." Yet policies still often endorse market competition as an efficiency stimulus. While it is true that exposing bond holders to greater risk can be a useful form of "market discipline," intense levels of market competition and the chase for yield can be very damaging, especially in prompting risky behavior. As Goodhart argues:

> How much competition within our banking systems do we actually want? Remember that the measures taken after the Great Depression in the United States were primarily and intentionally anti-competitive . . . One of the reasons why the Australian and Canadian banking systems have done so much better was . . . in part because the Australian and Canadian banking systems (at least domestically) were in some part protected from competition. (RBA 2010b)

In Australia and Canada banking competition is limited, market structures encourage banks to focus on domestic and business lending, and banks serve the credit needs of the real economy rather than engaging in trading and speculative activities primarily focused on relations with other financial firms.

A further solution is that potentially risky forms of trading within investment banking or indeed the wider shadow banking sector should be taxed or prohibited. Turner (2011, 14) argues that "policy tools (such as counterparty capital requirements or tax) should be used to lean against the proliferation of complex interconnectedness and the externalities it creates." First proposed by J. M. Keynes in the 1930s as a way of curbing speculation, a transaction tax on financial institutions would aim to tax those activities deemed to contribute to systemic risk. Acharya, Pedersen, et al.

(2011) argue that forcing firms to internalize the costs of corporate and systemic risk through the mechanism of taxing such risk exposures is the best solution. Similarly, the president of the Federal Reserve of Minneapolis has argued that

> taxes are a good response because they create incentives for firms to internalize the costs that would otherwise be external . . . A financial firm should be taxed for the amount of risk it creates that is borne by taxpayers . . . It seems to me that capital and liquidity requirements are intrinsically backwards-looking . . . We need forward-looking instruments . . . And that's a key reason why taxes, based on market-information, will work better. (Quoted in Acharya, Pedersen, et al. 2011, 122)

In recent years over forty countries have adopted some version of a financial transactions, which has raised $38 billion (Griffith-Jones and Persaud 2012). France, for example, introduced a financial transaction tax in 2012. Two other taxes were also introduced, one aimed at high-frequency trading and another aimed at taxing naked sovereign CDSs. At least eleven European countries are supporting or moving in the direction of imposing a financial transactions tax. One version of such a tax, a stamp duty on share trading, has been in place in the United Kingdom since 1694. It currently raises over £3 billion per annum. UK leaders say they favor a global form of a financial transactions tax but worry about investment flight if the United States fails to move in this direction (M. Lawson 2012). Current European taxes focus on shares, bonds, and derivatives where one of the parties to the trade is based in a country where the tax has been introduced. Taxation on computer-driven high-frequency trading strategies is also being deployed. From a European perspective this means that some of the trading in London will be subject to the tax. Ernst and Young estimate that the tax liability of City institutions (payable to European governments) could be in the order of £20 billion annually (M. Lawson 2012). This will impose an incentive for the United Kingdom to join the scheme and reap the tax benefits.

Conclusion

Charles Goodhart (2010, 153) argues that financial reform has always tended to be a pragmatic firefighting exercise reacting to the latest crisis, and so it is in this case. Although the financial crisis was severe and a reform push is now under way, many of the key underlying structural contours and pressures of the system remain in place and are impeding reform. First, competitive pressures remain intense. Second, in the context of weak lending markets, trading remains a key source of profit. Securitization markets have been decimated, but new markets and sources of risk are developing. Third, the interconnectedness of the system and potential for systemic risk remain. Finally, even after the financial crisis, the structural power of finance means that the nexus between finance and credit-dependent states remains strong in the United States and the United Kingdom. Postcrisis banking reform has subsequently seen bankers once again occupy a privileged position, as reformers seem unwilling to fundamentally overturn the institutions and structures created by bankers prior to the crisis.

In the wake of the crisis, governments have introduced wide-ranging reforms that would have been unthinkable prior to the crisis. They have also prevailed in overt power contests to institute banking reform. Yet wider questions about state capacity persist. We have argued that a significant limit on state capacity is ideational. Governments have not asked fundamental questions about what banks and finance are for. Governments still value the existing system and have simply tried to fix it. They have accepted the tenet that market-led financial innovation will drive and shape the system. Substantial authority therefore still remains with the private sector. Inevitably, under intense competition, this will mean the proliferation of ever more baroque forms of financial complexity. This will place regulators in a difficult if not impossible position in an endless game of catch-up, attempting to stay ahead of rapidly evolving markets.

New rules that focus squarely on and seek to restrain risky trading and systemic risk are thus required. These will require market restructuring to reduce competition and probably punitive transactions taxation on certain activities as well as outright bans on the riskiest and most socially useless financial activities. Overall, as Kay (2012) argues,

> we need instead smaller, simpler, financial institutions, which specialise in particular lines of provision of financial services to the non-financial economy, rather than trading with each other. The only sustainable answer to the issue of systemically important financial institutions is to limit the domain of systemic importance. Until politicians are prepared to face down the [City and] Wall St. titans on that issue, regulatory reform will not be serious.

It is now time to "go back to first principles," as Goodhart (2010, 153) puts it. Proper reform will require a fundamental rethink of the entire financial system. Politicians are likely to find this a terrifying prospect. Nevertheless, questions about reform should start with a few truisms: namely, that large, complex and interconnected financial systems are prone to serial, large-scale crises. Banking and financial systems in the heartlands of finance also remain massive and difficult, if not impossible, to manage effectively. At bottom, this is an issue about complexity and the limits of human control. Since the crisis, these issues have in some ways become more extreme, largely because the major banks have become larger and even more complex. Despite the above-noted criticisms, governments have largely accepted this state of affairs, mainly because they still see large financial systems as a key part of their economies and seem unwilling to fundamentally confront the status quo.

Conclusion

This book has tried to solve the puzzle of why some countries and their financial systems imploded in 2008 and why others did not. We have focused on the core crisis-hit banking and financial systems in the United States and the United Kingdom and on two countries that did not have a banking crisis, Australia and Canada. We have also examined why some banks in the crisis-hit countries largely resisted the temptation to borrow heavily on short-term wholesale markets, expand their balance sheets, and engage in securitized asset trading.

One of our key conclusions is that banking markets are extremely important in shaping banker behavior and banking outcomes. Intense competition within markets put CEOs under pressure to seek ever-higher market shares, return on equity, and share prices during the financial boom. Evolving financial markets also offered opportunities that channeled activity into what we now know were risky forms of leveraged trading. While many politicians and commentators continue to argue that the banking meltdown was caused by greed, the reality is that bankers who did not make strong profits were removed from their positions, while banks that were falling behind in the financial arms race were subject to takeover threats. Banks are extremely hierarchical institutions, and in the absence of any effective internal checks and balances, the pressure upon CEOs to outperform their rivals was also communicated to other executives, risk managers, and traders via the threat of unfavorable appraisals or termination. On the other hand, the bankers who performed well in such pressure-cooker markets won huge rewards through remuneration systems that rewarded risk taking. In contrast, in Australia and Canada, CEOs were under less pressure to maximize short-term profits while the market also offered strong profit opportunities in traditional lending activities. In Australia, for example, the Commonwealth Bank's gross loans constituted 76% of assets in 2007. At Barclays in the United Kingdom, gross loans constituted just 28% of total assets.

We used the imagery of "slaves of the market" to emphasize the impact of markets on banker behavior and choices. Our argument, however, is not determinist. Although the pressures were intense, not all bankers succumbed to the lure of highly leveraged trading, even in the financial heartlands of the United States and the United Kingdom. In the United States, for example, Wells Fargo and JP Morgan second-guessed the market and resisted pressures to significantly reengineer their balance sheets, while Goldman Sachs outwitted the market and successfully bet against it in 2007. Agents can sometimes swim against the tide, driven by alternative ideas and supported by niche institutional capacities and prudent bank cultures. There is, nevertheless, a key question about how long CEOs like Jamie Dimon at JP Morgan could have continued to impose a more cautious attitude at a time of apparently ever-rising profits. In 2005 Phil Purcell was sacked and John Mack appointed at Morgan Stanley when shareholders reached a view that the bank was forgoing profit opportunities.

Markets may have strongly encouraged risky leveraged trading in mortgaged-backed securities and other assets in the United States and the United Kingdom, but this is far from being the key cause of the 2007–2008 crisis. Indeed, the scale of the losses that occurred in the asset-backed securities markets was not that large, even when compared with the size of single bank balance sheets in 2007. The puzzle, then, is why subprime losses of around $500 billion triggered a far larger and more general financial meltdown, especially the failure of global wholesale credit markets. The answer is that the initial losses occurred in a context of systemic risk, in which relatively small perturbations in asset values were capable of triggering a much larger calamity. The slow-motion collapse of markets between August 2007 and October 2008 inexorably unfolded as agents in a range of different kinds of financial institutions panicked amid a complex system of payment interdependencies among banks that had very little capital and huge short-term debt liabilities. It was this panic, combined with the interdependencies and vulnerabilities, that mattered most. The scale of these structural effects overwhelmed many banks.

Very few bank executives, regulators, economists, or other commentators saw the crisis coming (Hindmoor and McConnell 2014). Over several decades, senior bank executives, along with supportive state elites, created a fragile financial system riddled with systemic risk that no one could fully understand or control. Lessons from earlier financial collapses were not transposed into the financial bonanza of the 2000s because the view formed that the markets were resilient and that "this time is different." Our Masters of the Universe were true believers, beguiled by the promise of originate-and-distribute securitization, liquid markets, high-tech risk management systems, and the reassurances of credit ratings agencies, auditors, investors, and regulators. At the behest of the Parliamentary Commission on Banking (Parliamentary Commission on Banking Standards 2013b), the UK government has promised to criminalize "reckless" behavior by bankers. Yet most bankers did not comprehend the risks they were taking. As we have documented, many senior bankers knew relatively little about key forms of securities trading, shadow bank exposures, or the collateral demands of the credit default swap market.

We have outlined a method for explaining the most recent major banking crisis. This primarily involves focusing on bankers as agents who hold beliefs about markets and who operate within powerful sets of corporate-based and market-based institutional incentives. Much of the time, especially amid a financial boom, prevailing ideas will spur the markets forward and incentivize risk taking. Broader structural dynamics will come into play if factors such as systemic risk lead to market panics and shutdowns and eventual financial collapse, as was the case in 2008. We believe our approach, based on historical institutionalism, can be more generally applied to other forms or cases of financial market dynamics and crises.

Agents operating in the context of bounded rationality, irrational exuberance, and systemic risk were central to what happened in the US banking crisis of the 1930s, for example. The same set of dynamics also pertained to the more recent banking meltdowns in the debt-fueled property bubble in Ireland, and also in Iceland, where bank debt grew to six times the national GDP prior to its banking meltdown. Analyzing agents and how they perceive and operate in the institutional and structural contexts they confront is the key to our approach. At the top of our list of factors that matter are ideas and markets. The ideas that agents hold are crucial in shaping their behavior, especially during financial booms. Ideas and perceptions about risk distinguished the more prudent banks in the United States and the United Kingdom from those that crashed during the crisis. The next financial boom will be supported by a claim that "this time is different": that finance has been transformed, that the economy is not caught in a bubble, and that profits can continue to rise. Markets will also exert strong pressures on agents. In particular, we have argued that the nature of banking markets and levels of market competition, together with profit opportunities, strongly shape banking outcomes. Reform measures that rely on assumptions that market competition is an effective discipline on bankers are thus misguided. Markets are also prone to create complex interdependencies and sources of systemic risk. This too will be central to the next crisis.

Ultimately, financial crises highlight the limits of human understanding in complex systems. The concept of bounded rationality and the findings of behavioral finance theory have never been more applicable, excepting in the few cases where bankers who did perceive unacceptable risks refused to join the herd or managed to exit just in time. The limits of human control in complex systems were also apparent when contagion and chain reaction effects wreaked havoc in a fragile structure that participants thought was built on solid foundations. This is a striking example of agency-structure interaction. The ideas held by agents about the safety of the system blinded them to mounting systemic risk prior to the crisis. Prevailing ideas and assumptions concealed the true nature of the structural system that confronted agents. Ideas and structures proved to be dangerously congruent. Only as the crisis was breaking did bankers finally come to recognize the true nature of the financial system they had helped create. Most bankers ceased being true believers at precisely the moment that it became too late to escape. Once the housing bubble in the United States burst and losses began to accumulate, bankers became caught in a downward spiral of collapsing confidence, falling asset values, and rising interest rates and credit freezes in wholesale funding markets. In this context, banks struggled to sell their assets, struggled to raise new capital to cover losses, and struggled to roll over their debts. Their collective agency was expressed in asset fire sales, loan refusals, and the freezing of credit markets driven by a structural context that made such behavior more or less the only choice available.

The net outcome was a banking collapse and the worst financial crisis in the history of capitalism. The 2008 crisis stymied wholesale credit markets, which brought down the banking system and plunged the major economies into deep recessions. Between the fourth quarter of 2007 and the third quarter of 2009, output fell by 8.6% in the United States; 8.6% in Canada; 7.2% in Germany; 9.8% in Italy; 8.9% in Japan; and 9.8% in the United Kingdom (Gorton 2012, 184–185). Bank failures necessitated massive government bailouts. This had the effect of transferring debt and the burden of fiscal adjustment from the private to the public sector. In 2010 the initial banking crisis centered upon the United Kingdom and the United States morphed into the Eurozone crisis (see Gamble 2014 for a careful exposition of crisis dynamics during and since 2007–2008). Although the economic logic of the European Monetary Union was central to this crisis, liberalization of the banking sector, high levels of leverage, and systemic risk constitute a point of common origin with the 2007–2008 crisis (Patomaki 2012, 9). The Greek debt crisis, which marked the start of the more general Eurozone crisis, can be traced back to the decision of executives within German and French banks operating in competitive markets to pursue additional yield by investing in Greek government debt rather than German debt at a time when interest rates were low and the prospect of any government defaulting on its debt seemed exceptionally low. When it became clear that the Greek government had, with the assistance of US investment banks, concealed the true extent of its debts, investors panicked and fled not only Greek but Spanish and Portuguese sovereign debt. As Blyth (2013) argues, austerity policies in Europe are now the mechanism by which the burden of the debts and the wider crisis are being transferred from the private to the public sector.

Bankers and supportive state elites have wrought havoc in the banking and financial systems in the major economies. But there is now a bigger problem. Unimpeded liberalization and financialization in the heartlands of finance have led to massive structural change, supercharging markets and creating a financial order that now appears as a new kind of financial

Frankenstein—one that is too big to fail, too complex to manage, too embedded in the wider economy, yet extremely fragile and crisis-prone. Despite this, the leaders of heavily indebted states have become closely associated with the banking and financial sector. American and British politicians still depend upon tax revenues and campaign contributions from the financial sector. If past experience is any guide, they are likely to want to ride the next financial boom, having convinced themselves of the merits of some new brand of financial innovation and that "this time is different." State leaders may have been chastened by the crisis, but they remain wedded to big finance and to ideas about internationally competitive financial markets. Most fundamentally, they have refused to countenance the idea of trying to substantially scale back the sector. Indeed, in the wake of the crisis the big banks are now bigger and the nexus between the state and finance has in some ways been strengthened. The massive bailouts in the teeth of the crisis and policies of quantitative easing since have flooded the system with extra money, much of which is funding financial trading and pumping up equity markets. The problem of moral hazard has become much worse. Bankers have recognized that they will be bailed out, come what may. The only potential constraint here is that the scale of the last set of bailouts now makes it almost impossible for states to incur the same level of expenditures on any new round of bank bailouts in the near to medium-term future. This is especially so in a context where state leaders in the United States and the United Kingdom have resisted proposals that would require banks to contribute to a bailout fund prior to the next crisis and where the crisis management and bank resolution schemes that have been put in place are unlikely to work effectively in the next crisis. It seems that state leaders cannot afford to live with big finance but cannot live without it. Bankers and financiers therefore do not lack agency, even in the wake of the crisis. In some ways they have become stronger: sitting atop more consolidated banking sectors, still highly influential, and busily undermining current reforms. Irrationally exuberant bankers ended up being the slaves of the markets they had created amid the last financial boom and bust. Now it looks increasingly like governments too are becoming slaves of the markets.

Our argument has important implications for banking reform. Because governments in the United States and the United Kingdom still see large financial sectors as a major economic asset, this has forced regulators into an endless game of writing complex rules in attempts to constrain bankers and risk taking as markets evolve. This game of cat and mouse does not favor regulators, as we argued in Chapter 9. By contrast, Australia and Canada have pioneered much safer banking models, featuring highly structured banking markets, limited competition among the main banks, and an emphasis on traditional banking. These banking markets are much smaller than those in the core economies and largely serve the needs of the real economy. This is the model that should be pursued in the United States and the United Kingdom. The catch is that because highly indebted governments in the United States and the United Kingdom have become closely aligned with finance, this is now a key problem limiting more substantial reform efforts. This means that the core financial markets are likely to experience repeated cycles of financial crisis, followed by yet more bailouts, if more fundamental reform is not pursued.

Finally, what does our study tell us about institutional theory and, in particular, historical institutionalism? We have argued that versions of institutional theory that emphasize or overemphasize the constraints that institutions place on agents need to be rethought. What is striking about financialization and the revolution in banking we have documented is that this was a major episode of institutional change spanning several decades that was wrought by agents. Clearly, there is something wrong with institutional accounts that excessively limit the scope for agency. Institutions are mutable, and it is the mutually shaping interactions between agents and institutions that are important in driving change and reshaping institutions. This is especially so if agents have authority. Our Masters of the Universe, especially CEOs and senior bankers, were powerful and authoritative and for a time seemed to have forged a new form of legitimacy based on financial wizardry. These actors could change institutional rules and norms; they could sideline opponents; they could strongly influence states and obtain the forms of regulation they required and transfer risk from themselves onto states.

The question then is, where is the institutional constraint? More particularly, why refer to bankers as "slaves of the markets," as we have done? It is true that the majority of bankers working in the majority of the major banks in the financial heartlands of the United States and the United

Kingdom confronted severe institutional pressures to conform. Traders who adopted conservative strategies or risk officers who refused to endorse aggressive trading strategies risked not only their bonuses but their future careers. As Andy Haldane observes, not only was it "very difficult for any firm individually to step back—to step out of the party," it was very difficult for individuals to do so given that their colleagues would say that they had "a friend who stopped two years ago and they're not in a job any more" (interview, 9 May 2013). Individual bankers were also operating within the context of a wider profit frenzy in which banks were continually reporting increased profits which, in turn, set new benchmarks for acceptable performance. To this extent, and within the context of the hierarchical authority relations banks displayed, individual bank employees were indeed slaves of the market.

Yet authority and hierarchy are important here. If functionaries within the banks had only limited agency, their bosses, especially imperious CEOs, had much more agency. After all, it was CEOs and other senior bankers who had created the banking revolution and aligned the state with their interests. But once they had created their new trading empires and fueled the financial boom, did they not also become slaves of the system they had created? Mark Blyth (2013, 21–22) argues that "you could have replaced all the actual bankers of 2007 with completely different individuals, and they would have behaved the same way during the meltdown: that's what incentives do." We disagree, because Blyth's argument is too "institutionalist": it goes too far in discounting agency. As we have shown, the way in which bankers behaved prior to the 2007–2008 crisis also depended on how they thought and how they understood the financial world. Those senior bankers who were best placed to exercise authority and discretion were ultimately guided by incentives *and* by their ideas. Those who believed that "this time was different" and that the financial boom could be managed extended their leverage and trading positions. Those executives who foresaw at least the possibility of a financial downturn acted more conservatively. As we have also argued, the wider culture of their banks and their capacity to exploit niche institutional capacities for making money, while also being more prudent, were important institutional supports in the more prudent banks.

Theoretically, then, agents *and* their ideas matter. This is in accord with recent versions of historical institutionalism that argue for an agent-centered approach to institutional analysis *and* that incorporate constructivist notions about how agents use ideas to make sense of the world in order to work out potential (though institutionally constrained) courses of action. We have been at pains to show that not all agents think alike, even when embedded in wider banking cultures where running with the herd seemed to be the norm. True, agents faced strong material incentives to ride the boom, whatever their views about the markets or the sustainability of the boom. But what also stands out are the views of those who dissented and thought and acted differently. This variability in thought and action suggests that the generalized accounts of behavior found in behavioral financial theory that point to irrational exuberance, herding, and the like are too universalist to be able to explain exactly what happened inside a number of banks operating in Wall Street and London during the boom. In other words, agents matter.

References

Acharya, Viral, Thomas Cooley, Matthew Richardson, Richard Sylla, and Ingo Walter. 2011. "Prologue: A Bird's Eye View: The Dodd-Frank Wall Street Reform and Consumer Protection Act." In Viral Acharya, Thomas Cooley, Matthew Richardson, and Ingo Walter (eds.), *Regulating Wall Street: The Frank-Dodd Act and the New Architecture of Global Finance.* Hoboken, NJ: John Wiley and Sons, 1–32.

Acharya, Viral, Thomas Cooley, Matthew Richardson, and Ingo Walter. 2009. "Manufacturing Tail Risk: A Perspective on the Financial Crisis of 2007–9." *Foundations and Trends in Finance* 4(4): 247–325.

Acharya, Viral, Nirumpama Kulkarni, and Matthew Richardson. 2011. "Capital, Contingent Capital, and Liquidity Requirements." In Viral Acharya, Thomas Cooley, Matthew Richardson, and Ingo Walter (eds.), *Regulating Wall Street: The Dodd-Frank Act and the New Architecture of Global Finance.* Hoboken, NJ: John Wiley and Sons, 143–180.

Acharya, Viral, Lasse Pedersen, Thomas Philippon, and Matthew Richardson. 2011. "Taxing Systemic Risk." In Viral Acharya, Thomas Cooley, Matthew Richardson, and Ingo Walter (eds.), *Regulating Wall Street: The Frank-Dodd Act and the New Architecture of Global Finance.* Hoboken, NJ: John Wiley and Sons, 121–142.

Acharya, Viral, and Matthew Richardson. 2009. "Causes of the Financial Crisis." *Critical Review* 21(2): 195–210.

Acharya, Viral, Matthew Richardson, Stijn Nieuwerburgh, and Lawrence White. 2011. *Guaranteed to Fail: Fannie Mae, Freddie Mac, and the Debacle of Mortgage Finance.* Princeton, NJ: Princeton University Press.

Acharya, Viral, and Philipp Schnabl. 2009. "How Banks Played the Leverage Game." In Viral Acharya and Matthew Richardson (eds.), *Restoring Financial Stability: How to Repair a Failed System.* Hoboken, NJ: John Wiley and Sons, 83–100.

Acharya, Viral, Paul Wachtel, and Ingo Walter. 2009. "International Alignment of Financial Sector Regulation." In Viral Acharya and Matthew Richardson (eds.), *Restoring Financial Stability: How to Repair a Failed System*. Hoboken, NJ: John Wiley and Sons, 365–376.

Ackermann, Josef. 2005a. Speech presented at the General Meeting of Deutsche Bank AG, Frankfurt, 18 May. Available at https://www.db.com/medien/en/downloads/RedeDrAckermannHV2005englisch.pdf.

———. 2005b. Statement at the Annual Press Conference of Deutsche Bank, 3 February. Available at https://www.db.com/medien/en/downloads/RedeENG.pdf.

Admati, Anat, and Martin Hellwig. 2013. *The Bankers' New Clothes: What's Wrong with Banking and What to Do about It*. Princeton, NJ: Princeton University Press.

Aikman, David, Andrew Haldane, and Benjamin Nelson. 2010. "Curbing the Credit Cycle." Speech presented to the Columbia University Center on Capitalism and Society Annual Conference, New York, 20 November. Available at http://www.bis.org/review/r101214e.pdf.

Alden, William. 2012. "For Wall Street Overseer, Progress Comes at a Crawl." *New York Times*, 3 January.

Aldrick, Philip. 2012. "Paul Tucker Warns Backlash to Another Bank Bailout Would Be 'Uncontainable.'" *Telegraph*, 12 October.

Allen, Franklin, Ana Babus, and Elena Carletti. 2009. "Financial Crises: Theory and Evidence." *Annual Review of Financial Economics* 1: 97–116.

Allen, Jason, and Walter Engert. 2007. "Efficiency and Competition in Canadian Banking." *Bank of Canada Review*, Summer: 33–45.

Anderson, Jenny, and Landon Thomas Jr. 2007. "Goldman Sachs Rakes in Profit in Credit Crisis." *New York Times*, 19 November.

Andrews, Edmund. 2008. "Greenspan Concedes Error on Regulation." *New York Times*, 23 October.

ANZ (Australia and New Zealand Banking Group). 2008. *Annual Report 2008*. Melbourne: ANZ.

APRA (Australian Prudential Regulation Authority). 2004. "APRA Releases Changes to Home Loan Risk-Weighting." Press release, 16 September. Available at http://www.apra.gov.au/MediaReleases/Pages/04_33.aspx.

———. 2009. "APRA's Risk-Rating Activity, Trends and Risk Outlook." *APRA Insight* 1: 2–9.

Archer, Margaret. 1995. *Realist Social Theory: The Morphogenetic Approach*. Cambridge: Cambridge University Press.

———. 2000. "For Structure: Its Reality, Properties and Powers: A Reply to Anthony King." *Sociological Review* 48(3): 464–472.

———. 2003. *Structure, Agency and the Internal Conversation*. Cambridge: Cambridge University Press.

ASIC (Australian Securities and Investment Commission). 2009. *Global Crisis: The Big Issues for Our Financial Markets*. ASIC Summer School, Sydney, 2–3 March.

———. 2010. *Securities and Investment Regulation: Beyond the Crisis.* ASIC Summer School, Melbourne, 1–3 March.

Augar, Philip. 2010. *Reckless: The Rise and Fall of the City.* London: Vintage Books.

Bacon, Kenneth. 2010. *Memorandum for the Record.* Interview of Kenneth Bacon by the Financial Crisis Inquiry Commission, 5 March. Available at http://fcic.law.stanford.edu/resource/interviews.

Bailey, Andrew. 2013. "Capital and Lending." *Sunday Times*, 5 May.

Baker, Andrew. 2010. "Restraining Regulatory Capture? Anglo-America, Crisis Politics and the Trajectories of Change in Global Financial Governance." *International Affairs* 86(3): 647–663.

———. 2012. "When New Ideas Meet Existing Institutions: Why Macroprudential Regulatory Change Is an Incremental Process." In Manuela Moschella and Eleni Tsingou (eds.), *Explaining Incremental Change in Global Financial Governance.* Colchester, UK: Routledge, 35–56.

———. 2013. "The New Political Economy of the Macroprudential Ideational Shift." *New Political Economy* 18: 112–139.

Bakir, Caner. 2003. "Who Needs a Review of the Financial System in Australia? The Case of the Wallis Inquiry." *Australian Journal of Political Science* 38(3): 511–534.

———. 2005. "The Exoteric Politics of Bank Mergers in Australia." *Australian Journal of Politics and History* 51(2): 235–256.

Balls, Ed. 2006. Speech to the British Bankers Association Industry Dinner, 11 October. Available at http://www.bba.org.uk/media/article/economic-secretary-ed-balls-mp-speaks-of-greater-government-support-for-the/speeches/.

Bank of America. 2006. *Annual Summary Report.* Charlotte, NC: Bank of America. Available at http://media.corporate-ir.net/media_files/irol/71/71595/reports/BAC_summaryAR.pdf.

———. 2007. *Annual Report.* Charlotte, NC: Bank of America. Available at http://media.corporate-ir.net/media_files/irol/71/71595/reports/2007_AR.pdf.

Bank of Canada. 2008. *Financial System Review—December 2008.* Toronto: Bank of Canada. Available at http://www.bankofcanada.ca/2008/12/publications/periodicals/fsr/december-2008/.

Bank of England. 2006. *Financial Stability Report, July.* London: Bank of England. Available at http://www.bankofengland.co.uk/publications/Documents/fsr/2006/fsrfull0606.pdf.

———. 2007. *Financial Stability Report, April.* London: Bank of England. Available at http://www.bankofengland.co.uk/publications/Documents/fsr/2007/fsrfull0704.pdf.

Banks, Eric. 2011. *See No Evil: Uncovering the Truth behind the Financial Crisis.* Basingstoke, UK: Palgrave Macmillan.

Barclays. 2007a. *Barclays 2006 Preliminary Results* (webcast). London: Barclays.

———. 2007b. *Barclays PLC Annual Report 2007.* London: Barclays. Available at http://group.barclays.com/about-barclays/investor-relations/annual-reports.

———. 2008. *Barclays PLC Annual Report 2008.* London: Barclays. Available at http://group.barclays.com/about-barclays/investor-relations/annual-reports.

Barnett, Michael, and Raymond Duvall. 2005. "Power in International Politics." *International Organization* 59(1): 39–75.

Barwell, Richard. 2013. *Macroprudential Policy.* London: Palgrave Macmillan.

Batchelor, Charles. 2006. "Victor Blank Set to Take Over at Lloyds Helm." *Financial Times,* 22 January.

Battellino, Ric. 2007. "Australia's Experience with Financial Deregulation." Address to the China Australia Governance Program, Melbourne, 16 July. Available at http://www.rba.gov.au/speeches/2007/sp-dg-160707.html.

Beales, Richard. 2006. "Banks Hope to Cash In on Rush to Hybrid Securities." *Financial Times,* 5 February.

Bear Stearns. 2007. *Annual Report to Shareholders.* Available at http://www.sec.gov/Archives/edgar/data/777001/000091412108000077/be11750956-ex13.txt.

Becker, Amanda. 2010. "Multitudes of Lobbyists Weigh In on Dodd-Frank Act." *Washington Post,* 22 November.

Bell, Stephen. 1997. *Ungoverning the Economy: The Political Economy of Australian Economic Policy.* Oxford: Oxford University Press.

———. 2004. *Australia's Money Mandarins: The Reserve Bank and the Politics of Money.* Melbourne: Cambridge University Press.

———. 2011. "Do We Really Need a New Constructivist Institutionalism to Explain Institutional Change?" *British Journal of Political Science* 41(4): 883–906.

———. 2013. "The Power of Ideas: The Ideational Shaping of the Structural Power of Business." *International Studies Quarterly* 56(4): 661–673.

Bell, Stephen, and Hui Feng. 2013. *The Rise of the People's Bank of China: The Politics of Institutional Development in China's Monetary and Financial Systems.* Cambridge, MA: Harvard University Press.

Bell, Stephen, and Andrew Hindmoor. 2009. *Rethinking Governance: The Centrality of the State in Modern Society.* Cambridge: Cambridge University Press.

———. 2013. "The Structural Power of Business and the Power of Ideas: The Strange Case of the Australian Mining Tax." *New Political Economy,* 30 May. Available at http://www.tandfonline.com/doi/abs/10.1080/13563467.2013.796452#.U_X7GPldVK.

———. 2014. "The Ideational Shaping of State Power and Capacity: Winning Battles but Losing the War over Bank Reform in the US and UK." *Government and Opposition* 49, special issue 03 (July): 342–368.

Bell, Stephen, and John Quiggin. 2006. "Asset Price Instability and Policy Responses: The Legacy of Liberalization." *Journal of Economic Issues* 60: 629–649.

Berkshire Hathaway. 2002. *Annual Report.* Omaha, NE: Berkshire Hathaway. Available at http://www.berkshirehathaway.com/2002ar/2002ar.pdf.

Bernanke, Ben. 2005. "The Global Saving Glut and the U.S. Current Account Deficit." Speech presented at the Sandridge Lecture, Virginia Association of Economists, Richmond, VA, 10 March. Available at http://www.federalreserve.gov/boarddocs/speeches/2005/200503102/.

———. 2006. "Modern Risk Management and Banking Supervision." Speech presented to the Stonier Graduate School of Banking, Washington, DC, 12 June.

Available at http://www.federalreserve.gov/newsevents/speech/bernanke20060612a.htm.

———. 2010. Statement by Ben S. Bernanke before the Financial Crisis Inquiry Commission (transcript), 2 September. Available at http://fcic-static.law.stanford.edu/cdn_media/fcic-testimony/2010-0902-Bernanke.pdf.

———. 2012. "Some Reflections on the Crisis and the Policy Response." Speech presented at the Russell Sage Foundation and the Century Foundation Conference on Rethinking Finance, New York, 13 April. Available at http://www.federalreserve.gov/newsevents/speech/bernanke20120413a.htm.

Besley, Tim, and Peter Hennessy. 2009. "Global Financial Crisis—Why Didn't Anybody Notice?" Letter from the British Academy to HM Queen Elizabeth II. Available at http://www.britac.ac.uk/events/archive/forum-economy.cfm.

Bezemer, Dirk. 2009. *No One Saw This Coming: Understanding Financial Crisis through Accounting Models*, research report no. 09002. Groningen: University of Groningen, SOM Research Institute.

Bhide, Amar. 2009. "An Accident Waiting to Happen." Centre on Capitalism and Society working paper no. 39. Available at http://capitalism.columbia.edu/files/ccs/CCSWP39_Bhide.pdf.

———. 2010. *A Call for Judgement: Sensible Finance for a Dynamic Economy.* Oxford: Oxford University Press.

BIS (Bank for International Settlements). 2009. *79th Annual Report.* Basel: BIS.

———. 2011. *Basel III: A Global Regulatory Framework for More Resilient Banks and Banking Systems.* Basel: BIS.

———. 2012. *82nd Annual Report, 1 April 2011–31 March 2012.* Basel: BIS. Available at http://www.bis.org/publ/arpdf/ar2012e.pdf.

———. 2013. *Quarterly Review*, September. Available at https://www.bis.org/publ/qtrpdf/r_qt1309.pdf.

Black, Julia. 2006. "Managing Regulatory Risks and Defining the Parameters of Blame: A Focus on the Australian Prudential Regulation Authority." *Law and Policy* 28(1): 1–30.

Blackmore, Vanessa, and Esther Jeapes. 2009. "The Global Financial Crisis: One Global Financial Regulator or Multiple Regulators?" *Capital Markets Law Journal* 4(3): S112–122.

Blair, Shelia. 2012. *Bull by the Horns: Fighting to Save Main Street from Wall Street and Wall Street from Itself.* New York: Free Press.

Blankfein, Lloyd. 2009. "Do Not Destroy the Essential Catalyst of Risk." *Financial Times*, 8 February.

———. 2010a. *Interview of Lloyd Blankfein by the Financial Crisis Inquiry Commission* (audio). Available at http://fcic.law.stanford.edu/resource/interviews.

———. 2010b. *Testimony by Lloyd C. Blankfein as Chairman and CEO of the Goldman Sachs Group, Inc., before the Financial Crisis Inquiry Commission*, 13 January. Available at http://fcic-static.law.stanford.edu/cdn_media/fcic-testimony/2010-0113-Blankfein.pdf.

Blinder, Alan. 2013. *After the Music Stopped: The Financial Crisis, the Response, and the Work Ahead.* New York: Penguin.

Blodget, Henry. 2008. "Bob Rubin: Citi (C) Collapse Was an Act of God." *Business Insider,* 29 November.

Bloomberg, Michael, and Charles Schumer. 2007. "Sustaining New York's and the US' Global Financial Services Leadership." New York: Office of the Mayor; Washington, DC: US Senate. Available at http://www.nyc.gov/html/om/pdf/ny_report_final.pdf.

Blundell-Wignall, Adrian, and Paul Atkinson. 2008. "The Sub-prime Crisis: Causal Distortions and Regulatory Reform." In Paul Bloxham and Christopher Kent (eds.), *Lessons from the Financial Turmoil of 2007 and 2008.* Sydney: Reserve Bank of Australia, 55–102.

Blundell-Wignall, Adrian, Paul Atkinson, and Se Hoon Lee. 2008. "Current Financial Crisis: Causes and Policy Issues." *Financial Market Trends,* 1–21. Paris: OECD. Available at http://www.oecd.org/finance/financial-markets/41942872.pdf.

Blyth, Mark. 1997. "'Any More Bright Ideas?' The Ideational Turn of Comparative Political Economy." *Comparative Politics* 29(2): 229–250.

———. 2002. *Great Transformations: Economic Ideas and Institutional Change in the Twentieth Century.* Cambridge: Cambridge University Press.

———. 2003. "Structures Do Not Come with an Instruction Sheet: Interests, Ideas and Progress in Political Science." *Perspectives on Politics* 1(4): 695–706.

———. 2007. "Beyond the Usual Suspects: Ideas, Uncertainty, and Building Institutional Orders." *International Studies Quarterly* 51(4): 761–777.

———. 2013. *Austerity: The History of a Dangerous Idea.* Oxford: Oxford University Press.

BMO (Bank of Montreal). 2008. *191st Annual Report 2008.* Available at http://www.bmo.com/ci/ar2008/downloads/bmo_ar2008.pdf.

Boone, Peter, and Simon Johnson. 2010. "Will the Politics of Global Moral Hazard Sink Us Again?" In Adair Turner et al. (eds.), *The Future of Finance: The LSE Report.* London: London School of Economics and Political Science, 247–288.

Booth, Lawrence. 2009. "The Secret of Canadian Banking: Common Sense?" *World Economics* 10(3): 1–7.

Borak, Donna. 2011. "Will Dodd-Frank Drive the Financial Industry Overseas?" *American Banker,* 22 July.

Bordo, Michael, Angela Redish, and Hugh Rockoff. 2011. "Why Didn't Canada Have a Banking Crisis in 2008 (or in 1930, or 1907, or . . .)?" National Bureau of Economic Research working paper no. 17312. Cambridge, MA: National Bureau of Economic Research.

Borio, Claudio. 2009. "Implementing the Macroprudential Approach to Financial Regulation and Supervision." *Banque de France, Financial Stability Review* 13: 31–41.

Borio, Claudio, Craig Furfine, and Phillip Lowe. 2001. "Procyclicality of the Financial System and Financial Stability: Issues and Policy Options." BIS working paper no. 1, March. Basel: BIS.

BNS (Bank of Nova Scotia). 2007. *Annual Report.* Toronto: BNS. Available at http://cgi.scotiabank.com/annrep2007/en/.

———. 2008. *Annual Report.* Toronto: BNS. Available at http://cgi.scotiabank.com/annrep2008/en/.

———. 2009. *Annual Report.* Toronto: BNS. Available at http://www.scotiabank.com/annrep2009/ARWeb/.

Brady, Dennis. 2009. "Bernanke Blasts AIG for 'Irresponsible Bets,' That Led to Bailouts." *Washington Post,* 4 March.

Braithwaite, John. 2005. *Markets in Vice, Markets in Virtue.* Annandale, NSW: Federation Press.

Braithwaite, Tom, and Francesco Guerrera. 2010. "Wall Street Titans Face the Flak." *Financial Times,* 13 January.

Braithwaite, Tom, and Aline van Duyn. 2011. "A Disappearing Act (US Financial Regulations)." *Financial Times,* 20 July.

Broadbent, Ben. 2012. 'Deleveraging'. Speech at Market News International, 15 March.

Brown, Gordon. 2007. Speech by the Chancellor of the Exchequer to Mansion House. London, 20 June. Available at http://webarchive.nationalarchives.gov.uk/20100407010852/http://www.hm-treasury.gov.uk/speech_chex_200607.htm.

———. 2010. *Beyond the Crash: Overcoming the First Crisis of Globalization.* New York: Free Press.

Bruner, Christopher, and Rawi Abdelal. 2005. "To Judge Leviathan: Sovereign Credit Ratings, National Law, and the World Economy." *Journal of Public Policy* 25(2): 191–217.

Brunnermeier, Markus. 2009. "Deciphering the Liquidity and Credit Crunch 2007–2008." *Journal of Economic Perspectives* 23(1): 77–100.

Buiter, Wilem. 2009. "Wilem Buiter's Maverecon." *Financial Times,* 15 April.

Bushnell, David. 2010. Interview of David Bushnell by the Financial Crisis Inquiry Commission, 1 April. Available at http://fcic.law.stanford.edu/resource/interviews#B.

Business Monitor International. 2010. *Canada Commercial Banking Report Q2 2010.* London: Business Monitor International.

Businessweek. 2006. "Inside Wall Street's Culture of Risk." *Bloomberg,* 11 June.

Butler, Ben. 2008. "Bad Debt Provisions Hit ANZ." *Herald-Sun* (Melbourne, Australia), 29 July.

Caballero, Ricardo, and Arvind Krishnamurthy. 2009. "Global Imbalances and Financial Fragility." *American Economic Review* 99(2): 584–588.

Cable, Vincent. 2009. *The Storm: The World Economic Crisis and What It Means.* London: Atlantic.

Cameron, David. 2012. Speech to the Lord Mayor's Banquet, London, 12 November. Available at http://www.telegraph.co.uk/finance/newsbysector/banksandfinance/9673847/David-Camerons-Lord-Mayors-Banquet-speech-in-full.html.

Campbell, John. 2004. *Institutional Change and Globalization.* Princeton, NJ: Princeton University Press.
———. 2011. "The U.S. Financial Crisis: Lessons for Theories of Institutional Complementarity." *Socio-economic Review* 9(2): 211–234.
Carew, Edna. 1997. *Westpac: The Bank That Broke the Bank.* Sydney: Doubleday.
Carney, John. 2011. "Hazing at Goldman Sachs." CNBC.com, 26 April.
CBA (Commonwealth Bank of Australia). 2008. *Annual Report 2008.* Sydney: CBA. Available at https://www.commbank.com.au/about-us/shareholders/pdfs/annual-reports/2008_Annual_report.pdf.
———. 2009. *Annual Report 2009.* Sydney: CBA. Available at https://www.commbank.com.au/about-us/shareholders/pdfs/annual-reports/2009_Annual_report.pdf.
Chipman, Derek. 2012. "How the Volcker Rule Influenced Morgan Stanley's Global Infrastructure Fund." *Seeking Alpha*, 15 October.
Christophers, Brett. 2013. *Banking across Boundaries: Placing Finance in Capitalism.* Oxford: Wiley-Blackwell.
CIBC (Canadian Imperial Bank of Commerce). 2006. *CIBC Annual Accountability Report.* Toronto: CIBC. Available at https://www.cibc.com/ca/pdf/about/aar06-en.pdf.
———. 2007. *CIBC Annual Accountability Report.* Toronto: CIBC. Available at https://www.cibc.com/ca/investor-relations/annual-reports.html.
———. 2008. *CIBC Annual Accountability Report.* Toronto: CIBC. Available at https://www.cibc.com/ca/investor-relations/annual-reports.html.
Cimilluca, Dana. 2007. "For BofA's Lewis, Investment Banking Is a 4-Letter Word." *Wall Street Journal*, 18 October.
Citigroup. 2007. *Annual Report 2007.* New York: Citigroup (USA). Available at http://www.citigroup.com/citi/investor/quarterly/2008/ar07c_en.pdf.
———. 2008. *Annual Report 2008.* New York: Citigroup (USA). Available at http://www.citigroup.com/citi/investor/quarterly/2009/ar08c_en.pdf.
CityUK, The. 2008. *Economic Contribution of UK Financial Services 2008.* London: The CityUK. Available at http://www.thecityuk.com/assets/Uploads/Economic-Contribution-of-UK-Financial-Services-2008.pdf.
Claessens, Stijn, Giovanni Dell'Ariccia, Deniz Igan, and Luc Laeven. 2009. "Lessons and Policy Implications from the Global Financial Crisis." International Monetary Fund working paper no. 10/44. Washington, DC: IMF. Available at http://www.imf.org/external/pubs/ft/wp/2010/wp1044.pdf.
Clark, Andrew. 2009. "Why We Are Different but Not Necessarily Safe." *Australian Financial Review*, 4 December.
Clark, Ed. 2007. Presentation to TD Bank Financial Group Scotia Capital Financials Summit 2007, 11 September. Available at http://www.td.com/document/PDF/investor/2007/td-investor-2007-scotia-summit-transcript.pdf.
Cleary, Gottlieb, Steen and Hamilton LLP. 2012. "Marketing Issues in the Volcker Rule Proposal" (SEC file no. S7-41-11) (letter), 13 February. Available at http://www.sec.gov/comments/s7-41-11/s74111-310.pdf.

Cleland, Carol. 2011. "Prediction and Explanation in Historical Natural Science." *British Journal for the Philosophy of Science* 62(3): 551–582.
Clementi, Gian, Thomas Cooley, Matthew Richardson, and Ingo Walter. 2009. "Rethinking Compensation in Financial Firms." In Viral Acharya and Matthew Richardson (eds.), *Restoring Financial Stability: How to Repair a Failed System*. Hoboken, NJ: John Wiley and Sons, 197–214.
Cohan, Peter. 2007. "Will the Subprime Fallout Snag Private Equity?" *Daily Finance*, 3 August.
Cohan, William. 2009. *House of Cards: A Tale of Hubris and Wretched Excess on Wall Street*. New York: Doubleday.
———. 2011. *Money and Power: How Goldman Sachs Came to Rule the World*. New York: Doubleday.
Colebatch, Tim. 2009. "How Australia Avoided the Global Financial Meltdown (Touch Wood)." *The Age*, 6 June.
Conlisk, John. 1996. "Why Bounded Rationality?" *Journal of Economic Literature* 34(2): 669–700.
Cornell, Andrew. 2009. "How Australia's Banks Dodged the Crisis." *Australian Financial Review*, 21 December.
Cortell, Andrew, and Susan Petersen. 1999. "Altered States: Explaining Domestic Institutional Change." *British Journal of Political Science* 29(1): 177–203.
Costello, Peter. 2009. "Parting Thoughts of a Political Party's Proud and Fortunate Son." *Sydney Morning Herald*, 8 October.
Crary, David. 1998. "Canada Bank Mergers Are Rejected." Associated Press, 14 December.
Croft, Jane. 2007. "Home Loan Slowdown Forecast." *Financial Times*, 3 October.
Croft, Jane, and Charles Pretzlik. 2003a. "HSBC Sees Its Profits Increase by 21%." *Financial Times*, 5 August.
———. 2003b. "Quiet American Ready with Charm Offensive." *Financial Times*, 16 April.
Croft, Jane, and Peter Thal Larsen. 2008. "'Old Fashioned' Banking Boosts Lloyds." *Financial Times*, 22 February.
Crosby, James. 2003. "High House Prices Rest on Solid Ground." *Financial Times*, 7 January.
Crotty, James. 2009. "Structural Causes of the Global Financial Crisis: A Critical Assessment of the 'New Financial Architecture.'" *Cambridge Journal of Economics* 33(4): 563–580.
Crouch, Colin. 2005. *Capitalist Diversity and Change: Recombinant Governance and Institutional Entrepreneurs*. Oxford: Oxford University Press.
———. 2007. "How to Do Post-Determinist Institutional Analysis." *Socio-Economic Review* 5: 527–567.
———. 2009. "Privatised Keynesianism: An Unacknowledged Policy Regime." *British Journal of Politics and International Relations* 11(3): 382–399.
Crouch, Colin, and Maarten Keune. 2005. "Changing Dominant Practice: Making Use of Institutional Diversity in Hungary and the United Kingdom." In

Wolfgang Streeck and Kathleen Thelen (eds.), *Beyond Continuity: Institutional Change in Advanced Political Economies.* Oxford: Oxford University Press, 83–102.

Culpepper, Pepper. 2011. *Quiet Politics and Business Power: Corporate Control in Europe and Japan.* Cambridge: Cambridge University Press.

Darling, Alastair. 2009. Speech by the Chancellor of the Exchequer, Mansion House, London, 17 June.

———. 2011. *Back from the Brink.* London: Atlantic Books.

Dash, Eric. 2011. "AAA Rating Is a Rarity in Business." *New York Times,* 2 August.

Dash, Eric, and Michael De la Merced. 2009. "Wachovia Acquisition Drags Down Wells Fargo." *New York Times,* 28 January.

Davies, Howard. 2010. *The Financial Crisis: Who Is to Blame?* Cambridge: Polity Press.

Dawson, Jo. 2012. "Banking Standards: Written Evidence from Jo Dawson." Parliamentary Commission on Banking Standards, Fifth Report, *Changing Banking for Good.* Available at http://www.publications.parliament.uk/pa/jt201314/jtselect/jtpcbs/27/27vii_we_b05.htm.

Debelle, Guy. 2009. "A Comparison of the US and Australian Housing Markets." Speech presented to the Sub-prime Mortgage Meltdown Symposium, Adelaide, 16 May.

deCarlo, Scott. 2011. "The World's Biggest Companies." *Forbes,* 20 April.

Deeg, Richard, and Gregory Jackson. 2007. "Towards a More Dynamic Theory of Capitalist Variety." *Socio-economic Review* 5: 149–179.

Deighton, Paul (House of Lords). 2013. *Financial Services (Banking Reform) Bill—Second Reading (Clmn. 1338)—Moved by Lord Deighton,* 24 July. Available at http://www.publications.parliament.uk/pa/ld201314/ldhansrd/text/130724-0001.htm.

Deogun, Nikhil. 2009. "The Future of Finance (a Special Report)—Is Wall Street Over?" *Wall Street Journal,* 30 March: pR4.

DeYoung, Robert, and Tara Rice. 2004. "How Do Banks Make Money? The Fallacies of Fee Income." *Economic Perspectives* 28(4): 34–51.

Diamond, Douglas, and Raghuram Rajan. 2009. "The Credit Crisis: Conjectures about Causes and Remedies." National Bureau of Economic Research working paper no. 14739. Washington, DC: National Bureau of Economic Research.

Dickson, Julie. 2009a. "Foundations of Effective Supervision and Regulation." Speech presented to the American Bar Association 2009 Spring Meeting, Vancouver, BC, 18 April. Available at http://www.osfi-bsif.gc.ca/app/DocRepository/1/eng/speeches/aba0409_e.pdf.

———. 2009b. "Economic and Financial Turmoil: Are There Lessons for Boards?" Speech presented to the 2009 Financial Services Invitational Forum, Cambridge, ON, 7 May. Available at http://www.osfi-bsif.gc.ca/Eng/Docs/fsif0509.pdf.

———. 2011. *Evidence Given to an Inquiry into the Present State of the Domestic and International Financial System.* Minutes of Proceedings of the Standing Senate Committee, issue no. 5, 23 November. Available at http://www.parl.gc.ca/content/sen/committee/411%5CBANC/05EVB-49195-e.HTM.

Dimon, Jamie. 2010. *Testimony of Jamie Dimon, CEO of JP Morgan Chase to the Financial Crisis Inquiry Commission* (interview), 20 October. Available at http://fcic.law.stanford.edu/resource/interviews#D.

Dodd, Randall, and Paul Mills. 2008. "Outbreak: US Subprime Contagion." *Finance and Development* 45(2): 14–18.

Dodge, David. 2005. "Reflections on the International Monetary and Economic Order." Speech presented to the Conférence de Montréal, Montreal, 30 May. Available at http://www.bankofcanada.ca/2005/05/publications/speeches/reflections-international-economic-monetary-order/.

———. 2006. "Global Imbalances and the Canadian Economy." Speech presented to the Barbados International Business Association, Bridgetown, Barbados, 6 February. Available at http://www.bankofcanada.ca/2006/02/publications/speeches/global-imbalances-canadian-economy/.

Dore, Ronald. 2008. "Financialization of the Global Economy." *Industrial and Corporate Change* 17(6): 1097–1112.

Drummond, Matthew. 2011. "NAB Accused of Failing Investors." *Australian Financial Review,* 18 March, 53.

Duncan, Richard. 2009. *The Corruption of Capitalism: A Strategy to Rebalance the Global Economy and Restore Sustainable Growth.* Hong Kong: CLSA Books.

Duquerroy, Anne, Nicholas Gauthier, and Mathieu Gex. 2009. "Credit Default Swaps and Financial Stability: Risks and Regulatory Issues." *Banque de France, Financial Stability Review* 13: 75–88.

Eatwell, John. 2013. *Financial Services (Banking Reform) Bill—Second Reading (Clmn. 1342)—Moved by Lord Deighton,* 24 July. Available at http://www.publications.parliament.uk/pa/ld201314/ldhansrd/text/130724-0001.htm.

Economics References Committee (Senate). 2011. *Competition within the Australian Banking System.* Canberra: Economic References Committee. Available at http://www.reia.com.au/userfiles/126O1025.pdf.

Economist. 2009. "Wall Street's New Shape: Rearranging the Towers of Gold." 10 September.

———. 2010a. "Cinderella's Moment." 11 February.

———. 2010b. "The Gods Strike Back." 11 February.

———. 2011. "Bank Reform: Commission Accomplished." 22 April.

———. 2012a. "The Dodd-Frank Act: Too Big Not to Fail." 18 February.

———. 2012b. "From Vanilla to Rocky Road." 25 February.

Edwards, John. 2008. "The Sub-prime Mortgage Meltdown: Origins, Trajectories and Regional Implications—Australia's Experience in the Sub-prime Crisis." Speech to the Flinders University International Expert Symposium, Adelaide, 16 May. Available at http://archive.treasury.gov.au/documents/1396/HTML/docshell.asp?URL=04_Sub-prime_paper.htm.

Eichengreen, Barry, Ashoka Mody, Milan Nedeljkovic, and Lucio Sarno. 2009. "How the Subprime Crisis Went Global: Evidence from Bank Credit Default Swap Spreads." National Bureau of Economic Research working paper no. 14904. Cambridge, MA: National Bureau of Economic Research.

Eisinger, Jesse. 2012. "The Volcker Rule, Made Bloated and Weak." *New York Times*, 22 February.
———. 2013. "Financial Crisis Suite Suggests Bad Behaviour at Morgan Stanley." *New York Times*, 23 January.
Elliott, Larry. 2012. "Barclays Libor Case Could Have Severe Consequences for Banks." *Guardian*, 28 October.
Ellul, Andrew, and Vijay Yerramilli. 2010. "Strong Risk Controls, Lower Risk: Evidence from U.S. Bank Holding Companies." National Bureau of Economic Research working paper no. 16178. Cambridge, MA: National Bureau of Economic Research.
Engelen, Ewald, Ismail Erturk, Julie Froud, Sukhdev Johal, Adam Leaver, Mick Moran, Adriana Nilsson, and Karel Williams. 2011. *After the Great Complacence: Financial Crisis and the Politics of Reform*. Oxford: Oxford University Press.
Epstein, Gerald (ed.). 2005. *Financialization and the World Economy*. Cheltenham: Edward Elgar.
Erturk, Ismail, and Stefano Solari. 2007. "Banks as Continuous Reinvention." *New Political Economy* 12(3): 369–388.
Estey, Willard. 1986. *Report of the Inquiry into the Collapse of the CCB and the Northland Bank*. Ottawa: Canada Government Publishing Centre. Available at http://epe.lac-bac.gc.ca/100/200/301/pco-bcp/commissions-ef/estey1986-eng/estey1986-part1-eng.pdf.
Evans, Peter. 1995. *Embedded Autonomy: States and Industrial Transformation*. Princeton, NJ: Princeton University Press.
Faber, David. 2010. *And Then the Roof Caved In: How Wall Street's Greed and Stupidity Brought Capitalism to Its Knees*. Hoboken, NJ: John Wiley and Sons.
Falcon, Armando. 2010. *Testimony of Armando Falcon before the Financial Crisis Inquiry Commission*, 9 April. Available at http://fcic-static.law.stanford.edu/cdn_media/fcic-testimony/2010-0409-Falcon.pdf.
Farlow, Andrew. 2013. *Crash and Beyond: Causes and Consequences of the Global Financial Crisis*. Oxford: Oxford University Press.
Farrell, Greg. 2010. *Crash of the Titans: Greed, Hubris, the Fall of Merrill Lynch, and the Near-Collapse of Bank of America*. New York: Crown Business.
FCIC (Financial Crisis Inquiry Commission). 2011. *The Financial Crisis Inquiry Report: Final Report of the National Commission on the Causes of the Financial and Economic Crisis in the United States*. New York: FCIC. Available at http://www.gpo.gov/fdsys/pkg/GPO-FCIC/pdf/GPO-FCIC.pdf.
Ferguson, Adele. 2008a. "Derivative Exposure Still Dogs Our Banks." *Australian*, 12 July.
———. 2008b. "Goode-bye: ANZ Chairman Must Go." *Australian*, 11 August.
———. 2008c. "Goode Time to Move On from ANZ." *Australian*, 21 April.
Ferguson, Charles. 2012. "Bare-Faced Bankers Should Be Treated as Criminals: Prosecuted and Imprisoned." *Guardian*, 20 July.
Ferguson, Niall. 2008. *The Ascent of Money: A Financial History of the World*. New York: Penguin.

———. 2010. *Civilization: The West and the Rest.* New York: Penguin.
Financial Times. 2008. "Lloyds TSB." 31 July.
———. 2011. "King Helps the Case for Banking Reform." 8 March.
Fisher, Richard. 2013. "Correcting 'Dodd-Frank' to Actually End 'Too Big to Fail.'" Statement before the Committee on Financial Services Hearing, *Examining How the Dodd-Frank Act Could Result in More Taxpayer-Funded Bailouts*, US House of Representatives, 26 June. Available at http://financialservices.house.gov/uploadedfiles/hhrg-113-ba00-wstate-rfisher-20130626.pdf.
Fishman, Steve. 2008. "Burning Down His House." *New York Magazine*, 30 November.
Fitch (Ratings). 2006. *Global Credit Derivatives Survey: Indices Dominate Growth as Banks' Risk Position Shifts.* New York: Fitch Ratings. Available at http://www.securitization.net/pdf/Fitch/Derivatives_21Sept06.pdf.
Fitzpatrick, Dan, Gregory Zuckerman, and Liz Rappaport. 2012. "J. P. Morgan's $2 Billion Blunder." *Wall Street Journal*, 11 May.
Foley, Stephen. 2003. "Worth Banking on Lloyds TSB." *Independent*, 29 May.
Foucault, Michel. 1991. *Discipline and Punish: The Birth of the Prison.* London: Penguin.
FPC (Financial Policy Committee). 2013a. Record of the Financial Policy Committee Meeting, 18 June. London: Bank of England.
———. 2013b. Record of the Financial Policy Committee Meeting, 20 November. London: Bank of England.
Freeland, Chrystia. 2009. "Transcript: View from the Top with Julie Dickson, Canadian Bank Regulator." *Financial Times*, 18 December.
———. 2010a. "Canada's Great Escape." *Financial Times*, 30 January.
———. 2010b. "What Toronto Can Teach New York and London." *Financial Times*, 29 January.
Friedman, Jeffrey. 2009. "A Crisis of Politics, Not Economics: Complexity, Ignorance and Policy Failure." *Critical Review* 21(2–3): 127–183.
Friedman, Milton, and Anna Schwartz. 1963. *A Monetary History of the United States, 1867–1960.* Princeton, NJ: Princeton University Press.
Friedman, Paul. 2010. *Testimony of Paul Friedman before the Financial Crisis Inquiry Commission* (transcript), 5 May. Available at http://fcic-static.law.stanford.edu/cdn_media/fcic-testimony/2010-0505-Friedman.pdf.
FSA (Financial Services Authority). 2006. *Financial Risk Outlook 2006.* London: FSA. Available at http://www.fsa.gov.uk/pubs/plan/financial_risk_outlook_2006.pdf.
———. 2007. *Financial Risk Outlook 2007.* London: FSA. Available at http://www.fsa.gov.uk/pubs/plan/financial_risk_outlook_2007.pdf.
———. 2011. *The Failure of the Royal Bank of Scotland: Financial Services Authority Board Report.* London: FSA. Available at http://www.fsa.gov.uk/pubs/other/rbs.pdf.
———. 2012a. *Final Notice to Peter Cummings.* 12 September. Available at http://www.fsa.gov.uk/static/pubs/final/peter-cummings.pdf.

———. 2012b. *Final Notice to the Bank of Scotland Plc regarding the Issuance of a Public Censure.* 9 March. Available at http://www.fsa.gov.uk/static/pubs/final/bankofscotlandplc.pdf.

FSB (Financial Stability Board). 2011. *Shadow Banking: Scoping the Issues.* Basel: FSB. Available at http://www.financialstabilityboard.org/publications/r_110412a.pdf.

———. 2012a. *Global Shadow Banking Monitoring Report 2012.* Basel: FSB. Available at http://www.financialstabilityboard.org/publications/r_121118c.pdf.

———. 2012b. *Peer Review of Canada: Review Report.* Basel: FSB. Available at http://www.financialstabilityboard.org/publications/r_120130.pdf.

FSB, IMF, and BIS. 2011. *Macroprudential Policy Tools and Frameworks: Progress Report to G20.* 27 October. Available at http://www.imf.org/external/np/g20/pdf/102711.pdf.

FSF (Financial Stability Forum). 2008. *Report of the Financial Stability Forum on Enhancing Market and Institutional Resilience.* Basel: FSF. Available at http://www.financialstabilityboard.org/publications/r_0804.pdf.

Gamble, Andrew. 2014. *Crisis Without End? The Unravelling of Western Prosperity.* Basingstoke, UK: Palgrave Macmillan.

Gapper, John. 2009. "Master of Risk Who Did God's Work but Won It Little Love." *Financial Times*, 23 December.

Garnaut, Ross, and David Llewellyn-Smith. 2009. *The Great Crash of 2008.* Melbourne: Melbourne University Press.

Geithner, Tim. 2009. Statement by Treasury Secretary Tim Geithner on Compensation (press release). Washington, DC, 10 June. Available at http://www.treasury.gov/press-center/press-releases/Pages/tg163.aspx.

———. 2012a. "Financial Crisis Amnesia." *Wall Street Journal*, 1 March. Available at http://online.wsj.com/news/articles/SB10001424052970203986604577253272042239982.

———. 2012b. Remarks by Treasury Secretary Tim Geithner on the State of Financial Reform. US Department of the Treasury (press release), 2 February. Available at http://www.treasury.gov/press-center/press-releases/Pages/tg1408.aspx.

Gieve, John. 2006a. "Financial System Risks in the UK—Issues and Challenges." Speech at the Centre for the Study of Financial Innovation Roundtable, London, 25 June. Available at http://www.bis.org/review/r060727e.pdf.

———. 2006b. "Pricing for Perfection." Speech at the Bank of England, London, 14 December. Available at http://www.bis.org/review/r061218d.pdf.

———. 2007. "The City's Growth—The Crest of a Wave or Swimming with the Stream?" Speech to the London Society of Chartered Accountants, Bank of England, London, 26 March. Available at http://www.bis.org/review/r070327c.pdf.

Giustiniani, Alessandro, and John Thornton. 2011. "Post-Crisis Financial Reform: Where Do We Stand?" *Journal of Financial Regulation and Compliance* 19(4): 323–336.

Gluyas, Richard. 2008. "Commonwealth Bank Faces Scrutiny by ASIC." *Australian*, 20 December.

———. 2009a. "CBA Chief Warns of Further Downturn, Despite $4.7bn Profit." *Australian*, 13 August.
———. 2009b. "Westpac's Optimist Outlook." *Australian*, 5 November.
Goff, Sharlene. 2011. "The Price of Protection." *Financial Times*, 11 September.
Goffman, Erving. 1961. *Asylums: Essays on the Social Situation of Mental Patients and Other Inmates*. New York: Doubleday.
Goldman Sachs. 2006. *Annual Report*. New York: Goldman Sachs. Available at http://www.goldmansachs.com/investor-relations/financials/archived/annual-reports/attachments/2006-gs-annual-report.pdf.
———. 2007. *Annual Report*. New York: Goldman Sachs. Available at http://www.goldmansachs.com/investor-relations/financials/archived/annual-reports/attachments/entire-2007-annual-report.pdf.
———. 2008. *Annual Report*. New York: Goldman Sachs. Available at http://www.goldmansachs.com/s/swf/2008-annual/pdfs/GS_2008_Annual_Report.pdf.
Goodfellow, Chris. 2011. "How Canada Slipped the Net of Financial Crisis." *Business and Finance*, 30 April, 48–49.
Goodhart, Charles. 2010. "How Should We Regulate the Financial Sector?" In Adair Turner et al. (eds.), *The Future of Finance: LSE Report*. London: London School of Economics and Political Science, 153–176.
Goodley, Simon. 2012. "Serious Fraud Office Investigating Barclays Payments to Qatar." *Guardian*, 30 August.
Gorton, Gary. 2009. "Slapped in the Face by the Invisible Hand: Banking and the Panic of 2007." Presented at the Federal Reserve Bank of Atlanta's Financial Market Conference, "Financial Innovation and Crisis," Jekyll Island, GA, 11–13 May. Atlanta: Federal Reserve Bank of Atlanta. Available at http://www.frbatlanta.org/news/Conferen/09fmc/gorton.pdf.
Gorton, Gary. 2012. *Misunderstanding Financial Crises: Why We Don't See Them Coming*. Oxford: Oxford University Press.
Gouvin, Eric. 2001. "The Political Economy of Canada's 'Widely Held' Rule for Large Banks." *Law and Policy in International Business* 32(2): 391–426.
Gow, David. 2009. "Swiss Bank UBS to Cut a Further 8,700 Jobs." *Guardian*, 15 April.
Gowan, Peter. 2009. "Crisis in the Heartland." *New Left Review* 55: 5–30.
Greenspan, Alan. 1997. "Government Regulation and Derivatives Contracts." Speech to the Financial Markets Conference of the Federal Reserve Bank of Atlanta, Coral Gables, FL, 21 February.
———. 1998. *The Regulation of OTC Derivatives: Testimony of Chairman Alan Greenspan before the Committee on Banking and Financial Services*, US House of Representatives, 24 July.
———. 2002. "Rethinking Stabilization Policy," opening remarks at symposium sponsored by the Federal Reserve Bank of Kansas City, Jackson Hole, WY, 29–31 August.
———. 2004. "Remarks by the Chairman." American Bankers Association Annual Convention. New York, 5 October.

———. 2005. "Risk Transfer and Financial Stability." Speech to the Federal Reserve Bank of Chicago, Forty-First Annual Conference on Bank Structure, Chicago, 5 May. Available at http://www.federalreserve.gov/boarddocs/speeches/2005/20050505/default.htm.

———. 2009. "We Need a Better Cushion against Risk." *Financial Times*, 26 March.

———. 2013. *The Map and the Territory: Risk, Human Nature, and the Future of Forecasting*. London: Allen Lane.

Griffith-Jones, Stephany, and Avinash Persaud. 2012. "Financial Transactions Taxes." Paper presented to the Committee on Economic and Monetary Affairs of the European Parliament, 6 February. Available at http://www.europarl.europa.eu/document/activities/cont/201202/20120208ATT37596/20120208ATT37596EN.pdf.

Griffiths, Katherine. 2011. "Ringfence Will Cost Britain's Banks Dear, Wall Street Says." *Times* (London), 1 September.

Group of Eight. 2005a. First Letter to the Board of Directors of Morgan Stanley, 3 March. Available at http://www.futureofms.com/letters_to_the_board.html.

———. 2005b. "Shareholders and Former Senior Executives of Morgan Stanley Release Letter to the Board of Directors." Press release, 29 March. Available at http://www.futureofms.com/press_releases.html.

Group of Thirty. 2009. *Financial Reform: A Framework for Financial Stability*. Washington, DC: G30. Available at http://www.group30.org/images/PDF/Financial_Reform-A_Framework_for_Financial_Stability.pdf.

Group of Twenty. 2009a. *Leader's Statement: London Summit*, London, 2 April. Available at http://www.treasury.gov/resource-center/international/g7-g20/Documents/London%20FM__CBG_Comm_-_Final%204-5%20Sept%202009.pdf.

———. 2009b. *Leaders Statement: Pittsburgh Summit*, Pittsburgh, PA, 24–25 September. Available at http://www.g20.utoronto.ca/2009/2009communique0925.html.

Guerrera, Francesco, and Charles Pretzlik. 2004. "HSBC Chairman Warns Price War Looms for World's Banks." *Financial Times*, 3 August.

Haldane, Andrew. 2009. "Small Lessons from a Big Crisis." Speech to the Federal Reserve Bank of Chicago, Forty-Fifth Annual Conference, "Reforming Financial Regulation," Chicago, 8 May. Available at http://www.bis.org/review/r090710e.pdf.

———. 2010. "The $100 Billion Question." Speech to the Institute of Regulation and Risk, Hong Kong, 30 March. Available at http://www.bankofengland.co.uk/publications/Documents/speeches/2010/speech433.pdf.

———. 2011. "Control Rights (and Wrongs)." Speech to the Wincott Annual Memorial Lecture, Westminster, London, 24 October. Available at http://www.bankofengland.co.uk/publications/Documents/speeches/2011/speech525.pdf.

———. 2012a. "Financial Arms Races." Based on a speech to the Institute for New Economic Thinking, Berlin, 14 April. Available at http://www.bankofengland.co.uk/publications/Documents/speeches/2012/speech565.pdf.

———. 2012b. "A Leaf Being Turned." Speech at Occupy Economics, "Socially Useful Banking," London, 29 October. Available at http://www.bankofengland.co.uk/publications/Documents/speeches/2012/speech616.pdf.

———. 2012c. "On Being the Right Size." The 2012 Beesley Lectures, Institute of Economic Affairs, London, 25 October. Available at http://www.bankofengland.co.uk/publications/Documents/speeches/2012/speech615.pdf.

Haldane, Andrew, and Piergiorgio Alessandri. 2009. "Banking on the State." Paper presented to the Federal Reserve Bank of Chicago, Twelfth Annual International Banking Conference, "The International Financial Crisis: Have the Rules of Finance Changed?" Chicago, 25 September. Available at http://www.bis.org/review/r091111e.pdf.

Haldane, Andrew, Simon Brennan, and Vasileios Madouros. 2010. "What Is the Contribution of the Financial Sector: Miracle or Mirage?" In Adair Turner et al. (eds.), *The Future of Finance: The LSE Report*. London: London School of Economics and Political Science, 87–120.

Haldane, Andrew, and Vasileius Madouros. 2012. "The Dog and the Frisbee." Speech to the Federal Reserve Bank of Kansas City, 366th Economic Policy Symposium, "The Changing Policy Landscape," Jackson Hole, WY, 31 August. Available at http://www.bis.org/review/r120905a.pdf.

Haldane, Andrew, and Robert May. 2011. "Systemic Risk in Banking Ecosystems." *Nature* 469 (20): 351–355.

Hall, Peter, and Daniel Gingerich. 2009. "Varieties of Capitalism and Institutional Complementarities in the Political Economy: An Empirical Analysis." *British Journal of Political Science* 39: 449–482.

Hall, Peter, and David Soskice. 2001. "An Introduction to Varieties of Capitalism." In Peter Hall and David Soskice (eds.), *Varieties of Capitalism: The Institutional Foundations of Comparative Advantage*. Oxford: Oxford University Press, 1–70.

Hall, Peter, and Rosemary Taylor. 1996. "Political Science and the Three New Institutionalisms." *Political Studies* 44(5): 936–957.

Hardie, Iain, and David Howarth. 2013a. "Framing Market-Based Banking and the Financial Crisis." In Iain Hardie and David Howarth (eds.), *Market-Based Banking and the International Financial Crisis*. Oxford: Oxford University Press, 22–55.

———. 2013b. "A Peculiar Kind of Devastation: German Market-Based Banking." In Iain Hardie and David Howarth (eds.), *Market-Based Banking and the International Financial Crisis*. Oxford: Oxford University Press, 103–127.

Hardie, Iain, and Sylvia Maxfield. 2013. "Market-Based Banking as the Worst of All Worlds: Illustrations from the United States and the United Kingdom." in Iain Hardie and David Howarth (eds.), *Market-Based Banking and the International Financial Crisis*. Oxford: Oxford University Press, 56–78.

Hawtrey, Kim. 2009. "The Global Credit Crisis: Why Have Australian Banks Been So Remarkably Resilient?" *Agenda: A Journal of Policy Analysis and Reform* 16: 95–114.

Hay, Colin. 2002. *Political Analysis*. Basingstoke, UK: Palgrave.

———. 2007. "Constructivist Institutionalism." In Rod Rhodes, Sarah Binder, and Bert Rockman (eds.), *The Oxford Handbook of Political Institutions*. Oxford: Oxford University Press, 56–74.

———. 2013. *The Failure of Anglo-Liberal Capitalism*. Basingstoke, UK: Palgrave.

Hay, Colin, and Ben Rosamond. 2002. "Globalisation, European Integration and the Discursive Construction of Economic Imperatives." *Journal of European Public Policy* 9(2): 147–167.

HBOS. 2001. *Annual Report and Accounts 2001*. London: HBOS. http://www.lloydsbankinggroup.com/media/pdfs/investors/2001/2001_HBOS_R&A.pdf.

———. 2003. *HBOS Results* (transcript). Available at http://www.lloydsbankinggroup.com/media/pdfs/investors/2003/2003_HBOS_Results_Transcript.pdf.

———. 2006. *Annual Report and Accounts 2006*. Edinburgh: HBOS. Available at http://www.lloydsbankinggroup.com/media/pdfs/investors/2006/2006_HBOS_R&A.pdf.

———. 2007a. *Annual Report and Accounts 2007*. Edinburgh: HBOS. Available at http://www.lloydsbankinggroup.com/media/pdfs/investors/2007/2007_HBOS_R&A.pdf.

———. 2007b. *Pre-close Trading Statement Conference Call*, 13 December. Edinburgh: HBOS. Available at http://www.lloydsbankinggroup.com/media/pdfs/investors/2007/2007Dec13_HBOS_Trading_Smt_Conf_Call_Transcript.pdf.

———. 2007c. *Preliminary Results 2006* (presentation), 28 February. Available at http://www.pres.investorrelations.lloydstsb.com/hbos/results/2006prelims/files/prelim06_transcript.pdf.

———. 2008a. *Interim Results 2008*. Edinburgh: HBOS. Available at http://www.lloydsbankinggroup.com/media/pdfs/investors/2008/2008_HBOS_Interim_Results_Transcript.pdf.

———. 2008b. *Preliminary Results 2007*. Edinburgh: HBOS. Available at http://www.pres.investorrelations.lloydstsb.com/hbos/results/2007prelims/files/prelims07_transcript.pdf.

Heinrich, Erik. 2008. "Why Canada's Banks Don't Need Help." *Time*, 10 November.

Hellwig, Martin. 2009. "Systemic Risk in the Financial Sector: An Analysis of the Subprime-Mortgage Financial Crisis." *De Economist* 157(2): 129–207.

Hermann, Margaret, and Thomas Preston. 2004. "Presidential Leadership Style and the Foreign Policy Advisor Process." In Eugene Wittkopf and James McCormick (eds.), *The Domestic Sources of American Foreign Policy: Insights and Evidence*, 4th ed. New York: Roman and Littlefield, 363–380.

HIH Royal Commission. 2003. *The Failure of HIH Insurance*. Volume 1, *A Corporate Collapse and Its Lessons*. Canberra: Commonwealth of Australia.

Hindmoor, Andrew, and Alan McConnell. 2013. "Why Didn't They See It Coming? Warning Signs, Acceptable Risks and the Global Financial Crisis." *Political Studies* 61(3): 543–560.

———. 2014. "Who Saw It Coming? The UK's Great Financial Crisis." Journal of Public Policy, Available at http://journals.cambridge.org/action/displayAbstract?fromPage=online&aid=9182220&fileId=S0143814X1400004X.

Hindmoor, Andrew, and Josh McGeechan. 2013. "Luck, Systematic Luck and Business Power: Lucky All the Way down or Trying Hard to Get What It Wants without Trying?" *Political Studies* 61(4): 834–849.

Hirschman, Albert. 1970. *Exit, Voice, and Loyalty: Responses to Decline in Firms, Organizations, and States.* Cambridge, MA: Harvard University Press.

HM Treasury. 2000. "Banking Competition to Deliver Benefits to Consumers: Government Responds to Cruikshank Report." Press release, 4 August.

———. 2010. *Financing a Private Sector Recovery.* Cmnd. 7923. London: HMSO.

HM Treasury. 2011a. *The Government Response to the Independent Commission on Banking.* London: HMSO. Available at https://www.gov.uk/government/uploads/system/uploads/attachment_data/file/31585/govt_response_to_icb_191211.pdf.

———. 2011b. *A New Approach to Financial Regulation: Building a Stronger System* Cmnd. 8012. London: HMSO.

———. 2012. *Banking Reform: Delivering Stability and Supporting a Sustainable Economy.* Cmnd. 8356. London: HMSO. Available at https://www.gov.uk/government/uploads/system/uploads/attachment_data/file/32556/whitepaper_banking_reform_140512.pdf.

———. 2013. *The Government's Response to the Parliamentary Commission on Banking Standards.* Cmnd. 8661. London: HMSO. Available at https://www.gov.uk/government/uploads/system/uploads/attachment_data/file/211047/gov_response_to_the_parliamentary_commission_on_banking_standards.pdf.

Howarth, David. 2012. "France and the International Financial Crisis: The Legacy of State-Led Finance." *Governance* 26: 369–395.

HSBC. 2002. *HSBC Holdings PLC, Annual Review.* London: HSBC. Available at http://www.hsbc.com/investor-relations/financial-results.

———. 2006. *HSBC Holdings PLC Pre-close Trading Update* (transcript of conference call), 5 December. Available at http://www.hsbc.com/investor-relations/financial-results.

———. 2008. *HSBC Holdings PLC, Annual Report and Accounts.* Available at http://www.hsbc.com/investor-relations/financial-results.

———. 2009. *HSBC Holdings PLC, Annual Report and Accounts.* Available at http://www.hsbc.com/investor-relations/financial-results.

———. 2010. *Response to Independent Commission on Banking Issues Paper.* 24 November. Available at http://bankingcommission.independent.gov.uk/responses/.

Huang, Rocco, and Lev Ratnovski. 2011. "The Dark Side of Bank Wholesale Funding." *Journal of Financial Intermediation* 20(2): 248–263. Available at http://www.imf.org/external/pubs/ft/wp/2010/wp10170.pdf.

Hughes, Chris, and Andrew Edgecliffe-Johnson. 2008. "Lack of Ambition Pays Off for Lloyds TSB." *Financial Times*, 6 May.

Hughes, Chris, and Jennifer Hughes. 2008. "Barclays Wins Market Backing for US Swoop." *Financial Times*, 18 September.

Hutton, Will. 2012. "Let's End This Rotten Culture That Only Rewards Rogues." *Guardian*, 30 June.

ICB (Independent Commission on Banking). 2011. *Final Report: Recommendations.* London: ICB. Available at https://www.gov.uk/government/news/independent-commission-on-banking-final-report.

IMF (International Monetary Fund). 2006. *Global Financial Stability Report: Market Developments and Issues (April).* Washington, DC: IMF.

———. 2008. *Canada: Financial System Stability Assessment—Update.* Washington, DC: IMF. Available at http://www.imf.org/external/pubs/ft/scr/2008/cr0859.pdf.

———. 2009a. "Fiscal Implications of the Global Economic and Financial Crisis." Staff position note no.09/13. Washington, DC: IMF. Available at http://www.imf.org/external/pubs/ft/spn/2009/spn0913.pdf.

———. 2009b. *Global Financial Stability Report: Responding to the Financial Crisis and Measuring Systemic Risk.* Washington, DC: IMF. Available at http://www.imf.org/External/Pubs/FT/GFSR/2009/01/pdf/text.pdf.

———. 2010. *Understanding Financial Interconnectedness.* Washington, DC: IMF. http://www.imf.org/external/np/pp/eng/2010/100410.pdf.

———. 2012. *Global Financial Stability Report: The Quest for Lasting Stability.* Washington, DC: IMF. Available at http://www.imf.org/external/pubs/ft/gfsr/2012/01/.

Independent. 2005. *Jeremy Warner's Outlook: A Few Signs of Progress, but Lloyds TSB's Strategic Bind Still Looks as Bad as Ever.* 13 December.

Inman, Phillip. 2012. "Volker Says Banking Ring-Fence Is Flawed." *Guardian*, 17 October.

Interactive Investor. 2007. "RBS H1 Profit Up 11 Pct." 3 August.

Irwin, Neil. 2013. *The Alchemists: Three Central Bankers and a World on Fire.* New York: Penguin.

Jain, Ankoor, and Cally Jordan. 2009. "Diversity and Resilience: Lessons from the Financial Crisis." *University of New South Wales Law Journal* 32(2): 416–446.

Jeffery, Christopher. 2003. "BarCap Chief Hits Back at Buffett's Derivatives 'Time Bomb' Comments." *Risk*, 5 March.

Jenkins, Patrick, Sharlene Goff, and George Parker. 2011. "Banks Hope Their Lobbying Pays Off." *Financial Times*, 10 April.

Jenkinson, Nigel. 2006. "Risks to the Commercial Property Market and Financial Stability." Speech at the IPD/IPF Property Investment Conference, Grand Hotel, Brighton, 30 November. Available at http://www.bankofengland.co.uk/publications/Documents/quarterlybulletin/qb070113.pdf.

———. 2007. "Promoting Financial System Resilience in Modern Global Capital Markets: Some Issues." Speech delivered at the conference "Law and Economics of Systemic Risk in Finance," University of St. Gallen, Switzerland, 29 June. Available at http://www.bis.org/review/r070705f.pdf.

Jervis, Robert. 1976. *Perception and Misperception in International Politics.* Princeton, NJ: Princeton University Press.

Jessop, Bob. 2007. *State Power: A Strategic-Relational Approach.* Cambridge: Polity Press.

Jimenez, Katherine. 2008. "ANZ Faces Biggest Credit Dangers." *Australian*, 18 July.

Johnson, Simon. 2009. "The Quiet Coup." *Atlantic*, 1 May.

———. 2012. "Bob Diamond and Banking's Crisis of Legitimacy." *Guardian*, 19 July.

Joyce, Christopher. 2009. "An Outsider's Perspective." *Griffith Review* 25. Available at http://griffithreview.com/edition-25-after-the-crisis/an-outsiders-perspective.

JP Morgan Chase. 2006. *Annual Report 2006.* New York: JP Morgan Chase. Available at http://investor.shareholder.com/jpmorganchase/annual.cfm.

———. 2007. *Annual Report 2007.* New York: JP Morgan Chase. Available at http://files.shareholder.com/downloads/ONE/2739968746x0x184756/31e544ec-a273-4228-8c2a-8e46127783f8/2007ARComplete.pdf.

———. 2009. *Annual Report 2009.* New York: JP Morgan Chase. Available at http://files.shareholder.com/downloads/ONE/920873948x0x362439/a51db960-bda2-4e30-aacd-3c761b81ba75/2009_AR.pdf.

———. 2010. "Global Banks—Too Big to Fail? Running the Numbers." JP Morgan Global Research, 17 February. Available at http://www.docin.com/p-44748772.html.

———. 2013. *Report of JP Morgan Chase & Co. Management Task Force regarding 2012 CIO Losses.* New York: JP Morgan Chase. Available at http://files.shareholder.com/downloads/ONE/2272984969x0x628656/4cb574a0-0bf5-4728-9582-625e4519b5ab/Task_Force_Report.pdf.

Kahneman, Daniel. 2011. *Thinking, Fast and Slow.* London: Allen Lane.

Kahneman, Daniel, and Amos Tversky. 1979. "Prospect Theory: An Analysis of Decision under Risk." *Econometrica* 47(2): 263–291.

———. 1984. "Choices, Values and Frames." *American Psychologist* 39(4): 341–350.

Kalemli-Ozcan, Sebnem, Bent Sorensen, and Sevcan Yesiltas. 2011. "Leverage across Firms, Banks and Countries." National Bureau of Economic Research working paper no. 17354. Washington, DC: National Bureau of Economic Research.

Kaufman, Henry. 2012. "Henry Kaufman: Big Banks Are Not the Future." *Wall Street Journal*, 5 June.

Kay, John. 2012. "Take on Wall St Titans if You Want Reform." *Financial Times*, 18 September.

Kelly, Kate, and Carrick Mollenkamp. 2007. "Barclays Spars over Its Losses at Bear Stearns." *Wall Street Journal*, 21 July.

Kelly, Paul. 1992. *The End of Certainty: The Story of the 1980s.* Sydney: Allen and Unwin.

Kiff, John. 2009. "Canadian Residential Mortgage Markets: Boring but Effective?" International Monetary Fund working paper no. 09/130. Washington,

DC: IMF. Available at http://www.imf.org/external/pubs/ft/wp/2009/wp09130.pdf.

Kim, Hun Joon, and Jason Sharman. 2014. "Accounts and Accountability: Corruption, Human Rights and Individual Accountability Norms." *International Organization* 68(2) (May): 417–448. (April).

Kindleberger, Charles. 1978. *Manias, Panics and Crashes: A History of Financial Crises.* Basingstoke, UK: Macmillan.

King, Mervyn. 2007. "Monetary Policy Developments." Speech to the Lord Mayor's Banquet for Bankers and Merchants of the City of London, London, 20 June. Available at http://www.bis.org/review/r070622b.pdf.

———. 2009a. "Finance—A Return from Risk." Speech to the Worshipful Company of International Bankers, London, 17 March. Available at http://www.bis.org/review/r090319a.pdf.

———. 2009b. "Monetary Policy Developments." Speech to Scottish business organizations, Edinburgh, 20 October. Available at http://www.bis.org/review/r091022a.pdf.

———. 2010. "Banking—From Bagehot to Basel, and Back Again." Speech at Buttonwood Gathering, New York, 25 October. Available at http://www.bis.org/review/r101028a.pdf

———. 2011. "Monetary Policy Development." Speech at the Lord Mayor's Banquet for Bankers and Merchants of the City of London, Mansion House, London, 15 June. Available at http://www.bis.org/review/r110617c.pdf.

———. 2012. Speech by the governor at the 2012 BBC Today Program Lecture, London, 2 May. Available at http://www.bankofengland.co.uk/publications/Pages/speeches/2012/567.aspx.

———. 2013. "A Governor Looks Back—And Forward." Speech at the Lord Mayor's Banquet for Bankers and Merchants of the City of London, Mansion House, London, 19 June. Available at http://www.bankofengland.co.uk/publications/Documents/speeches/2013/speech670.pdf.

Kirkup, James. 2009. "Mervyn King: Regulators Unable to Stop City Banks Taking Risks Due to Government." *Telegraph*, 26 February.

———. 2011. "Bob Diamond: Bankers Should Stop Apologising." *Telegraph*, 11 January.

Kovacevich, Richard. 2010. *Interview of Richard Kovacevich with the Financial Crisis Inquiry Commission* (audio), 24 August. Available at http://fcic.law.stanford.edu/resource/interviews.

Kravis, Marie-Josée. 2009. "Regulation Didn't Save Canada's Banks." *Wall Street Journal*, 7 May.

Krippner, Greta. 2011. *Capitalizing on Crisis: The Political Origins of the Rise of Finance.* Cambridge, MA: Harvard University Press.

Krugman, Paul. 2010. "Good and Boring." *New York Times*, 31 January.

Kwak, James, and Simon Johnson. 2010. *13 Bankers: The Wall Street Takeover and the Next Financial Meltdown.* New York: Pantheon Books.

Kynaston, David. 2011. *City of London: The History.* London: Chatto and Windus.

LaCapra, Lauren. 2011. "Goldman Lobbying Hard to Weaken Volcker Rule." Reuters, 4 May.

Laker, John. 2006. "Basel II—Observations from Down Under." Speech to the Second Annual Conference on the Future of Financial Regulation, London School of Economics, London, 6–7 April.

———. 2009. "The Regulatory Landscape 2009–2010." Speech to Finsia Financial Services Conference, Sydney, 28 October.

Lall, Ranjit. 2012. "From Failure to Failure: The Politics of International Banking Regulation." *Review of International Political Economy* 19(4): 609–638.

Lam, Eric. 2009. "CIBC Named World's 15th Worst Bank." *National Post*, 2 July.

Landy, Heather. 2013. "Why Regional Banks Are the Right Size Right Now." *American Banker Magazine*, April. Available at https://www.53.com/resources/pdf/accolades/accolades-american-banker.pdf.

Lane, Philip, and Gian Maria Milesi-Ferretti. 2010a. "Cross-Border Investment in Small International Financial Centers." International Monetary Fund working paper no. 10/38. Washington, DC: IMF. Available at http://www.imf.org/external/pubs/ft/wp/2010/wp1038.pdf.

———. 2010b. "The Cross-Country Incidence of the Global Crisis." International Monetary Fund working paper no. 10/171. Washington, DC: IMF. Available at http://www.imf.org/external/pubs/ft/wp/2010/wp10171.pdf.

Large, Andrew. 2003. "Financial Stability—Maintaining Confidence in a Complex World." Speech at the City of London Central Banking Conference, National Liberal Club, London, 17 November. Available at http://www.bis.org/review/r031121g.pdf.

———. 2004. "Financial Stability Oversight—Past and Present." Speech at the London School of Economics, London, 22 January. Available at http://www.bis.org/review/r040202g.pdf.

———. 2005. "A Framework for Financial Stability." Speech at the Istanbul International Conference on Financial System Stability and Implications of Basel II, Istanbul, 18 May. Available at http://www.bis.org/review/r050520d.pdf.

Lawder, David, and Rachelle Younglai. 2010. "Bear Stearns' Cayne Concedes Leverage Was Too High." Reuters, 5 May.

Lawson, Max. 2012. "Rejecting the Robin Hood Tax Would Be a Spectacular Own Goal." *Guardian*, 11 October.

Leahy, Joe, James Mackintosh, Charles Pretzlik, and Gary Silverman. 2002. "How Bond Laid Foundations for the World's 'Local Bank.'" *Financial Times*, 10 August.

Leblond, Patrick. "Cool Canada: A Case of Low Market-Based Banking in the Anglo-Saxon Worlds." In Iain Hardie and David Howarth (eds.), *Market-Based Banking and the International Financial Crisis*. Oxford: Oxford University Press, 201–217.

Lehman Brothers. 2007. *Form 10-K: Annual Report Pursuant to Section 13 or 15(d) of the Securities Exchange Act of 1934 for the Fiscal Year Ended November 30, 2007* (commission file no. 1-9466). Washington, DC: United States Securities and

Exchange Commission. Available at http://www.sec.gov/Archives/edgar/data/806085/000110465908005476/a08-3530_110k.htm.

Le Pan, Nicholas. 2005. "Economy and Efficiency in Financial Sector Regulation." Speech to the Ottawa Economics Association, Ottawa, 12 April.

Levin, Robert. 2010. *Written Statement of Robert J. Levin before the Financial Crisis Inquiry Commission*, 9 April. Available at http://fcic-static.law.stanford.edu/cdn_media/fcic-testimony/2010-0409-Levin.pdf.

Lewis, David. 2008. "Weathering the Storm: APRA's Role in Financial Crisis Management." Speech to Continuity Forum, Business Continuity Expo, Melbourne, 27 November.

Lewis, Michael. 2010. *The Big Short: Inside the Doomsday Machine*. London: Allen and Lane.

Lieberman, Robert. 2002. "Ideas, Institutions, and Political Order: Explaining Political Change." *American Political Science Review* 96(4): 697–712.

Lindblom, Charles. 1977. *Politics and Markets: The World's Political Economic Systems*. New York: Basic Books.

Littrell, Charles. 2011. "Responses to the Global Financial Crisis: The Australian Prudential Perspective." Speech to APEC Regional Symposium on Enhancing Financial Policy and Regulatory Co-operation—Responses to the Global Financial Crisis, Melbourne, 8 March. Available at http://www.apra.gov.au/Speeches/Documents/apec-sc-speech-cwl-2-0.pdf.

Lloyds Banking Group. 2010. "Response to the Independent Commission on Banking: Issues Paper." Available at http://bankingcommission.independent.gov.uk/responses/.

———. 2011. "Lloyds Banking Group Response to the Independent Commission on Banking: Issues Paper Response." Available at http://www.lloydsbankinggroup.com/media/pdfs/2011/ICB_Issues_Response.pdf.

Lloyds TSB. 2007. *Annual Report and Accounts 2007*. London: Lloyds TSB. Available at http://www.lloydsbankinggroup.com/media/pdfs/investors/2007/2007_LTSB_Group_R&A.pdf.

———. 2008. *Presentation of Interim Results 2008*. London: Lloyds TSB. Available at http://www.pres.investorrelations.lloydstsb.com/results/2008interims/files/Lloyds_TSB_Group_plc_-_Interims_2008_-_final.pdf.

Lockhart, James. 2010. *Memorandum for the Record*. Telephone interview between James B. Lockhart and the Financial Crisis Inquiry Commission, 19 March, 10:30. Available at http://fcic-static.law.stanford.edu/cdn_media/fcic-docs/2010-03-19%20FCIC%20memo%20of%20staff%20interview%20with%20James%20Lockhart,%20Federal%20Housing%20Finance%20Agency.pdf.

Longworth, David. 2013. "Strengths and Weaknesses of Canadian Financial Regulation before and after the Global Financial Crisis." Paper presented at the 2013 Banking Law Symposium "Who Wants Big Banks?," University of Ottawa, Ottawa, 26–27 June.

Lowenstein, Roger. 2010. *The End of Wall Street*. New York: Penguin.

Lowndes, Vivien. 2010. "The Institutionalist Approach." In David Marsh and Gerry Stoker (eds.), *Theory and Methods in Political Science*. London: Palgrave, 60–79.

Lucas, Robert. 2003. "Macroeconomic Priorities." *American Economic Review* 93: 1–14.

Lukes, Stephen. 1974. *Power: A Radical View.* London: Macmillan.

Luyendijk, Joris. 2012. "Former Rating Agency Worker: I'm Genuinely Frightened." *Business Insider*, 24 July.

Macfarlane, Ian. 2009. "The Crisis: Causes, Consequences and Lessons for the Future: The Australian Perspective." In *Global Crisis: The Big Issues for Our Financial Markets*, ASIC Summer School, 2–3 March. Sydney: ASIC.

Mack, John. 2010. *Interview of John Mack by the Financial Crisis Inquiry Commission*, 2 November (audio). Available at http://fcic.law.stanford.edu/resource/interviews#M.

MackIntosh, James. 2002. "The Art and Science of Bad Loans." *Financial Times*, 1 March.

Macquarie Bank. 2008. *Annual Report.* Sydney: Macquarie Bank. Available at http://static.macquarie.com/dafiles/Internet/mgl/au/about-macquarie-group/investor-relations/financial-disclosure/documents/2008/mbl-fy08-annual-report.pdf?v=1.

Maheras, Thomas. 2010. *Interview of Thomas Maheras by the Financial Crisis Inquiry Commission*, 10 March. Available via http://fcic.law.stanford.edu/resource/interviews.

Mahoney, James, and Kathleen Thelen. 2010. "A Theory of Gradual Institutional Change." In James Mahoney and Kathleen Thelen (eds.), *Explaining Institutional Change: Ambiguity, Agency and Power.* Cambridge: Cambridge University Press, 1–37.

Mallaby, Sebastian. 2010. *More Money Than God: Hedge Funds and the Making of a New Elite.* London: Bloomsbury.

Mann, Michael. 1990. *The Rise and Decline of the Nation-State.* Oxford: Blackwells.

Martin, Iain. 2013. *Making It Happen: Fred Goodwin, RBS and the Men Who Blew Up the British Economy.* London: Simon and Schuster UK.

Matthews, Kent, and John Thompson. 2005. *The Economics of Banking.* Chichester, UK: John Wiley and Sons.

McAnulla, Stuart. 2005. "Making Hay with Actualism? The Need for a Realist Concept of Structure." *Politics* 25(1): 31–38.

McCarty, Nolan, Poole, Keith and Rosenthal, Howard. 2013). *Political Bubbles: Financial Crises and the Failure of American Democracy.* Princeton, NJ: Princeton University Press.

McDonald, Duff. 2009. *Last Man Standing: The Ascent of Jamie Dimon and JP Morgan Chase.* New York: Simon and Schuster.

McDonald, Lawrence. 2009. *A Colossal Failure of Common Sense: The Inside Story of the Collapse of Lehman Brothers.* New York: Crown.

McGee, Suzanne. 2010. *Chasing Goldman Sachs: How the Masters of the Universe Melted Wall Street Down—and Why They'll Take Us to the Brink Again.* New York: Crown.

McIlroy, David. 2010. "The Regulatory Issues Raised by Credit Default Swaps." *Journal of Banking Regulation* 11(4): 303–318.

McLean, Bethany, and Joseph Nocera. 2010. *All the Devils Are Here: The Hidden History of the Financial Crisis.* New York: Penguin.

McMahon, Peter. 2008. "HBOS Chiefs Buy Up GBP 6m in Shares." *Scotsman,* 24 March.

McMahon, Richard. 2005. "Behavioural Finance: A Background Briefing." Flinders University, School of Commerce Research Paper Series, no. 05-9. Available at http://www.flinders.edu.au/sabs/business/research/papers/05-9.pdf.

McPhilemy, Samuel. 2013. "Formal Rules versus Informal Relationships: Prudential Banking at the FSA before the Crash." *New Political Economy* 81(5): 748–767.

Mehran, Hamid, Alan Morrison, and Joel Shapiro. 2011. *Corporate Governance and Banks: What Have We Learned from the Financial Crisis?* Federal Reserve of New York staff report no. 502. New York: Federal Reserve Bank.

Merced, Michael, and Andrew Sorkin. 2010. "Report Details How Lehman Hid Its Woes." *New York Times,* 11 March.

Merrill Lynch. 2006. *Annual Report.* New York: Merrill Lynch. Available at http://www.ml.com/annualmeetingmaterials/2006/ar/pdfs/annual_report_2006_complete.pdf.

———. 2007. *Annual Report.* New York: Merrill Lynch. Available at http://www.ml.com/annualmeetingmaterials/2007/ar/pdfs/annual_report_2007_complete.pdf.

Milne, Alistair. 2009. *The Fall of the House of Credit: What Went Wrong in Banking and What Can Be Done to Repair the Damage?* Cambridge: Cambridge University Press.

Minsky, Hyman. 1982. *Can It Happen Again? Essays on Instability and Finance.* New York: M. E. Sharpe.

Mishkin, Frederic. 2009. "Over the Cliff: From the Subprime to the Global Financial Crisis." National Bureau of Economic Research working paper no. 16609. Cambridge, MA: National Bureau of Economic Research.

Montier, James. 2002. *Behavioural Finance: Insights into Irrational Minds and Markets.* Chichester, UK: John Wiley and Sons.

Moore, Carter & Associates. 2010. *The RiskMinds 2009 Risk Managers' Survey: The Causes and Implications of the 2008 Banking Crisis.* Available at http://www.moorecarter.co.uk/RiskMinds%202009%20Risk%20Managers'%20Survey%20Report.19March2010.pdf.

Moore, James. 2008. "Helen Weir: From Marmite on Toast to a Budget Hotel, It's Back to Basics in High Finance." *Independent,* 12 January.

Moran, Michael. 2003. *The British Regulatory State: High Modernism and Hyper-innovation.* Oxford: Oxford University Press.

Morgan Stanley. 2007. *Annual Letter to Shareholders.* New York: Morgan Stanley. Available at http://www.morganstanley.com/about/ir/pdf/MS_Annual_2006.pdf.

———. 2008. *Form 10-K: Annual Report Pursuant to Section 13 or 15(d) of the Securities Exchange Act of 1934 for the Fiscal Year Ended November 30, 2008* (com-

mission file no. 1-11758). Washington, DC: United States Securities and Exchange Commission. Available at http://www.morganstanley.com/about/ir/shareholder/10k113008/10k1108.pdf.
———. 2010. *Form 10-K: Annual Report Pursuant to Section 13 or 15(d) of the Securities Exchange Act of 1934 for the Fiscal Year Ended December 31, 2010* (commission file no. 1-11758). Washington, DC: United States Securities and Exchange Commission. Available at http://www.morganstanley.com/about/ir/shareholder/10k2010/10k2010.pdf.

Moya, Elena. 2009. "UBS Reveals Investment Banking 'Revolution' to Regain Profits." *Guardian*, 17 November.

Mudd, Daniel. 2010. *Memorandum for the Record.* Interview by the Financial Crisis Inquiry Commission, 26 March. Available at http://fcic.law.stanford.edu/resource/interviews.

Mulholland, Hélène, and Ben Quinn. 2011. "Cable Claims Coalition Unity over Banking Reforms." *Guardian*, 31 August.

Munro, Ian. 2008. "Australia Faces 'Rocky Road,' Says Swan." *Age*, 10 October.

Murdoch, Scott. 2008. "NZ Warns of More Bad Debts." *Australian*, 19 December.

Myners, Paul. 2008. "Banking Reform Must Begin in Boardroom." *Financial Times*, 24 April.

NAB (National Australia Bank). 2008. *2008 Annual Financial Report.* Melbourne: NAB. Available at http://www.nab.com.au/content/dam/nab/about-us/shareholder-centre/Report-archive/Annual-Financial-Report-2008.pdf.

———. 2009. *2009 Annual Financial Report.* Melbourne: NAB. Available at http://www.nab.com.au/content/dam/nab/about-us/shareholder-centre/Report-archive/Annual-Financial-Report-2009.pdf.

National Audit Office (NAO). 2009. *The Nationalisation of Northern Rock.* London: NAO. Available at http://www.nao.org.uk/wp-content/uploads/2009/03/0809298.pdf.

North, Douglass. 1990. *Institutions, Institutional Change and Economic Performance.* New York: Cambridge University Press.

Northern Rock. 2006. *Annual Report and Accounts.* Newcastle upon Tyne: Northern Rock. Available at http://www.n-ram.co.uk/~/media/Files/N/NRAM-V2/corporate-reports/res2006pr-annualreportandaccounts.pdf.

Obama, Barack. 2010. Remarks by the President at Signing of Dodd-Frank Wall Street Reform and Consumer Protection Act, 21 July, Washington, DC. Available at http://www.whitehouse.gov/the-press-office/remarks-president-signing-dodd-frank-wall-street-reform-and-consumer-protection-act.

Observer. 2012. "Monsters Like the London Whale Swim in Waters Too Deep to Fathom." 15 July.

OECD. 2010. *Central Government Debt: Statistical Yearbook.* Paris: OECD.

———. 2011. *Income Statement and Balance Sheet Statistics.* Paris: OECD. Available at http://www.oecd-ilibrary.org/finance-and-investment/data/oecd-banking-statistics/income-statement-and-balance-sheet_data-00270-en?isPartOf=/content/datacollection/bank-data-en.

Olson, Mancur. 1965. *The Logic of Collective Action.* Cambridge, MA: Harvard University Press.

Oman, Mark. 2010. *Interview of Mark Oman by the Financial Crisis Inquiry Commission* (audio). Available at http://fcic.law.stanford.edu/resource/interviews.

Onaran, Yalman, and Dave Pierson. 2008. "Banks' Subprime Market-Related Losses, Capital Raised: Table." *Bloomberg*, 20 August.

Osborne, George. 2010. Speech by the Chancellor of the Exchequer to the Lord Mayor's Banquet for Bankers and Merchants of the City of London, Mansion House, London, 16 June. Available at http://www.telegraph.co.uk/finance/economics/8578168/Chancellor-George-Osbornes-Mansion-House-speech-in-full.html.

———. 2013. "Speech at JP Morgan." *Daily Telegraph*, 4 February. Available at http://www.telegraph.co.uk/finance/newsbysector/banksandfinance/9847127/George-Osbornes-speech-in-full.html.

OSFI (Office of the Superintendent of Financial Institutions Canada). 2009. *Prudential Regulation in Challenging Times: Annual Report 2008–2009.* Ottawa: OSFI.

———. 2013. *Financial Data: Banks.* Ottawa: OSFI. Available at http://www.osfi-bsif.gc.ca/osfi/index_e.aspx?ArticleID=554.

Palan, Ronen, Richard Murphy, and Christian Chavagneux. 2010. *Tax Havens: How Globalization Really Works.* Ithaca, NY: Cornell University Press.

Palmer, John. 2002. *Review of the Role Played by the Australian Prudential Regulation Authority and the Insurance and Superannuation Commission in the Collapse of the HIH Group of Companies.* Sydney: HIH Royal Commission.

Parliamentary Commission on Banking Standards (House of Commons). 2012. *Panel on HBOS: Oral Evidence Taken before the Parliamentary Commission on Banking Standards (HC 705-I, Sub-committee B)* (corrected transcript), 30 October. Available at http://www.publications.parliament.uk/pa/jt201213/jtselect/jtpcbs/c705-i/c70501.htm.

———. 2013a. *"An Accident Waiting to Happen": The Failure of HBOS.* HC 705, Fourth Report of Session 2012–13—Volume 1, *Report, together with Formal Minutes.* London: TSO. Available at http://www.publications.parliament.uk/pa/jt201213/jtselect/jtpcbs/144/144.pdf.

———. 2013b. *Changing Banking for Good.* HC 175-I, First Report of Session 2013–14—Volume 1, *Summary, and Conclusions and Recommendations.* London: TSO. Available at http://www.parliament.uk/documents/banking-commission/Banking-final-report-volume-i.pdf.

———. 2013c. *Changing Banking for Good.* HC 175-II, First Report of Session 2013–14—Volume 2, *Chapters 1 to 11 and Annexes, together with Formal Minutes.* London: TSO. Available at http://www.parliament.uk/documents/banking-commission/Banking-final-report-vol-ii.pdf.

———. 2013d. *Changing Banking for Good.* HC 175-III, First Report of Session 2013–14—Volume 3, *Oral Evidence Taken by the Commission (Minutes).* London: TSO. Available at http://www.publications.parliament.uk/pa/jt201314/jtselect/jtpcbs/27/121203.htm.

Patomaki, Heikki. 2012. *The Great Eurozone Disaster: From Crisis to Global New Deal.* London: Zed Books.
Perkins, Tara. 2008a. "BMO Burned by Subprime Mortgage Exposure." *Globe and Mail,* 27 August.
———. 2008b. "BMO Retreats to Its Low-Risk Roots." *Globe and Mail,* 5 March.
———. 2008c. "CIBC Vows to Harness Risk." *Globe and Mail,* 29 February.
———. 2009. "Gordon Nixon: Legacy at a Crossroads." *Globe and Mail,* 15 August.
Perman, Ray. 2013. *Hubris: How HBOS Wrecked the Best Bank in Britain.* Edinburgh: Birlinn.
Perrow, Charles. 2010. "The Meltdown Was Not an Accident." In Michael Lounsbury and Paul M. Hirsch (eds.), *Markets on Trial: The Economic Sociology of the U.S. Financial Crisis; Part A.* Bingley, UK: Emerald, 309–330.
Persaud, Avanish. 2003. *Liquidity Black Holes: Understanding, Quantifying and Managing Financial Liquidity Risk.* London: Risk Books.
Peston, Robert, and Laurence Knight. 2013. *How Do We Fix This Mess? The Economic Price of Having It All and the Route to Lasting Prosperity.* London: Hodder and Stoughton.
Phang, Stephanie, and Chia-Peck Wong. 2007. "HSBC to Shrink U.S. Mortgage Unit." *International Herald Tribune,* 30 March.
Pixley, Jocelyn. 2004. *Emotions in Finance: Distrust and Uncertainty in Global Markets.* Cambridge: Cambridge University Press.
Pontussen, Jonas. 1998. "From Comparative Public Policy to Political Economy: Putting Institutions in Their Place and Taking Interests Seriously." *Comparative Political Studies* 28(1): 117–147.
Pratley, Nils. 2013. "Vince Cable Has Swallowed the Bankers' Line on Capital." *Guardian,* 24 July.
Prince, Charles. 2010a. *Interview of Charles O. Prince by the Financial Crisis Inquiry Commission* (transcript), New York, 17 March. Available at http://fcic.law.stanford.edu/resource/interviews.
———. 2010b. *Testimony of Charles Prince before the Financial Crisis Inquiry Commission Hearing on Subprime Lending and Securitization and Government-Sponsored Enterprises* (Day 2, Session 1), 8 April. Available at http://fcic.law.stanford.edu/hearings/testimony/subprime-lending-and-securitization-and-enterprises.
Protess, Ben. 2011. "Wall Street and Washington React to Volker Rule." *New York Times,* 11 October.
———. 2012. "Wells Fargo Settles a Securities Case." *New York Times,* 15 August.
Pulliman, Susan, and Liz Rappaport. 2008. "Anatomy of the Morgan Stanley Panic." *Wall Street Journal,* 24 November.
Puri, Poonam. 2012. "Bank Bashing Is a Popular Sport." In Suzanne Konzelman and Marc Fovargue-Davies (eds.), *Banking Systems in Crisis: The Faces of Liberal Capitalism.* New York: Routledge, 155–185.
Quaglia, Lucia. 2009. "The 'British Plan' as a Pace-Setter: The Europeanization of Banking Rescue Plans in the EU?" *Journal of Common Market Studies* 47(5): 1063–1083.

Quiggin, John. 2010. *Zombie Economics: How Dead Ideas Still Walk among Us.* Princeton, NJ: Princeton University Press.

Quinn, James. 2010. "Obama Promises US Taxpayer Will Never Again Foot Bill for Banks." *Telegraph*, 21 July.

Quinn, James, and Sean Farrell. 2010. "London at Centre of Lehman Brothers' Accounting Gimmick." *Daily Telegraph*, 12 March.

Raghavan, Anita. 2007. "At Morgan Stanley, a Game of Catch-Up." *Wall Street Journal*, 29 May.

Ratnovski, Lev, and Rocco Huang. 2009. "Why Are Canadian Banks More Resilient?" International Monetary Fund working paper no. 09/152. Washington, DC: IMF. Available at http://www.imf.org/external/pubs/ft/wp/2009/wp09152.pdf.

RBA (Reserve Bank of Australia). 2006. *Financial Stability Review—September 2006.* Sydney: RBA. Available at http://www.rba.gov.au/publications/fsr/2006/sep/pdf/0906.pdf.

———. 2009. *Financial Stability Review—March.* Sydney: RBA. Available at http://www.rba.gov.au/publications/fsr/2009/mar/pdf/0309.pdf.

———. 2010a. *Financial Stability Review—March.* Sydney: RBA. Available at http://www.rba.gov.au/publications/fsr/2010/mar/html/aus-fin-sys.html.

———. 2010b. "Panel Discussion." In *Conference Volume 2010.* Sydney: RBA. Available at http://www.rba.gov.au/publications/confs/2010/caruana-disc.html.

———. 2011. *Financial Stability Review—March.* Sydney: RBA. Available at http://www.rba.gov.au/publications/fsr/2011/mar/pdf/0311.pdf.

———. 2013. *Financial Stability Review—September 2013.* Sydney: RBA. Available at http://www.rba.gov.au/publications/fsr/2013/sep/pdf/0913.pdf.

RBC (Royal Bank of Canada). 2008. *2008 Annual Report.* Toronto: RBC. Available at http://www.rbc.com/investorrelations/pdf/ar_2009_e.pdf.

———. 2009. *2009 Annual Report.* Toronto: RBC. Available at http://www.rbc.com/investorrelations/pdf/ar_2009_e.pdf.

RBS (Royal Bank of Scotland). 2005. *Presentation of RBS Interim Results for 2005* (transcript), 4 August. Available at http://www.investors.rbs.com/download/transcript/Interim-Aug05-Transcript.pdf.

———. 2006a. *Interim Results 2006.* Proceedings at an Analysts Conference, London, 4 August. Available at http://www.investors.rbs.com/download/transcript/RBS_06_Interims_Analysts_Briefing_Transcript.pdf.

———. 2006b. *Presentation of RBS Annual Results Conference for 2005* (transcript), 28 February. Available at http://www.investors.rbs.com/download/transcript/RBS_FY05_28_Feb_06_Transcript.pdf.

———. 2007a. *Annual Report and Accounts 2007.* Edinburgh: RBS. Available at http://www.investors.rbs.com/download/report/RBS_plc_Accounts_2007.pdf.

———. 2007b. *Presentation of Interim Results for 2007* (transcript), 3 August 2007. Available at http://www.investors.rbs.com/download/transcript/IterimResultsTranscript-3Aug2007.pdf.

———. 2009. *Annual Report and Accounts 2009.* Edinburgh: RBS.

Reinhart, Carmen, and Kenneth Rogoff. 2009. *This Time Is Different: Eight Centuries of Financial Folly.* Princeton, NJ: Princeton University Press.

Richardson, Matthew, Roy Smith, and Ingo Walter. 2011. "Large Banks and the Volker Rule." In Viral Acharya, Thomas Cooley, Matthew Richardson, and Ingo Walter (eds.), *Regulating Wall Street: The Frank-Dodd Act and the New Architecture of Global Finance.* Hoboken, NJ: John Wiley and Sons, 181–212.

Richardson, Matthew, and Lawrence White. 2009. "The Rating Agencies: Is Regulation the Answer?" In Viral Acharya and Matthew Richardson (eds.), *Restoring Financial Stability: How to Repair a Failed System.* Hoboken, NJ: John Wiley and Sons, 101–116.

Rigby, Elizabeth, and Lina Saigol. 2002. "HSBC's Prime Attraction." *Financial Times,* 15 November.

Rixen, Thomas. 2013. "Why Reregulation after the Crisis Is Feeble: Shadow Banking, Offshore Financial Centres, and Jurisdictional Competition." *Regulation and Governance* (online version available prior to publication). Available at http://onlinelibrary.wiley.com/doi/10.1111/rego.12024/full.

Robertson, Grant. 2010. "Lehman Brothers Suing CIBC for $1.3 Billion." *Globe and Mail,* 15 September.

Rogoff, Kenneth. 2012. "Financial Regulation Isn't Fixed, It's Just More Complicated." *Guardian,* 10 September.

Roubini, Nouriel, and Stephen Mihm. 2010. *Crisis Economics: A Crash Course in the Future of Finance.* New York: Penguin.

Royo, Sebastián. 2012. "How Did the Spanish Financial System Survive the First Stage of the Global Crisis?" *Governance* 26(4): 631–656.

Rutherford, Hamish. 2007. "HBOS Shares Slump on Mortgage Share." *Scotsman,* 13 June.

Ryan, Peter. 2008. "Top Staff Sacked over ANZ's Opes Failures." *ABC News,* 22 August.

Ryan, Stephen. 2009. "Fair Value Accountancy Policy Issued Raised by the Credit Crunch." In Viral Acharya and Matthew Richardson (eds.), *Restoring Financial Stability: How to Repair a Failed System.* Hoboken, NJ: John Wiley and Sons, 215–228.

Saigol, Lina. 2002. "HSBC Unperturbed by City Whispers." *Financial Times,* 21 May.

Salz, Anthony. 2013. *Salz Review: An Independent Review of Barclays Business Practices.* Available at http://online.wsj.com/public/resources/documents/SalzReview04032013.pdf.

Schapiro, Mary. 2012. *Examining the Impact of the Volcker Rule on Markets, Businesses, Investors and Job Creation.* Testimony to the Capital Markets and Government Sponsored Enterprises Subcommittee and Financial Institution and Consumer Credit Subcommittee of the US House of Representatives Committee on Financial Services, 18 January. Available at http://www.sec.gov/News/Testimony/Detail/Testimony/1365171489310#.UoD6o_msiFw.

Scharpf, Fritz. 1997. *Games Real Actors Play: Actor-Centered Institutionalism in Policy Research.* Boulder, CO: Westview Press.

Schleifer, Andrei. 1999. *Inefficient Markets: An Introduction to Behavioural Finance*. Oxford: Oxford University Press.

Schmidt, Vivien. 2008a. "Discursive Institutionalism: The Explanatory Power of Ideas and Discourse." *Annual Review of Political Science* 11(1): 303–326.

———. 2008b. "From Historical Institutionalism to Discursive Institutionalism: Explaining Change in Comparative Political Economy." Paper presented at the American Political Science Association Meetings, Boston, 28 August. Available at http://citation.allacademic.com/meta/p_mla_apa_research_citation/2/7/8/3/3/pages278339/p278339-1.php.

———. 2010. "Taking Ideas and Discourse Seriously: Explaining Change through Discursive Institutionalism as the Fourth 'New Institutionalism.'" *European Political Science Review* 2(1): 1–25.

Schwartz, Nelson. 2011 "Financial Leaders Expect Shift of Power after Election." *New York Times*, 2 November.

Scotsman. 2007. "Scottish Business Briefing." 12 June.

SEC (US Securities and Exchange Commission). 2005. *2005 Performance and Accountability Report*. Washington, DC: SEC. Available at http://www.sec.gov/about/secpar/secpar2005.pdf.

Senior Supervisors Group. 2009. *Risk Management Lessons from the Global Banking Crisis of 2008* (transmittal letter). Available at http://www.sec.gov/news/press/2009/report102109.pdf.

SFBC (Swiss Federal Banking Commission). 2008. *Subprime Crisis: SFBC Investigation into the Causes of the Write-Downs of UBS AG [SFBC-UBS Subprime Report]*. Berne: SFBC. Available at http://www.finma.ch/archiv/ebk/e/publik/medienmit/20081016/ubs-subprime-bericht-ebk-e.pdf.

Shaxon, Nicholas. 2011. "Tax Havens and the Financial Crisis." *May Day International*. Available at http://www.newleftproject.org/index.php/mayday/article/tax_havens_and_the_financial_crisis.

Shiller, Robert. 2000. *Irrational Exuberance*. Princeton, NJ: Princeton University Press.

Simon, Bernard. 2010. "Royal Bank of Canada Loses Top Credit Rating." *Financial Times*, 14 December.

Simon, Herbert. 1957. *Models of Man*. New York: John Wiley and Sons.

Smith, Randall. 2007. "O'Neal Out as Merrill Reels from Loss." *Wall Street Journal*, 29 October.

Smith, Peter, and Peter Thal Larsen. 2006. "Studzinski Plans to Quit HSBC." *Financial Times*, 18 May.

Sorkin, Andrew. 2009. *Too Big to Fail: Inside the Battle to Save Wall Street*. London: Allen Lane.

———. 2011. "Wall St. Aids S.E.C. Case for Budget." *New York Times*, 8 February.

Standard Chartered. 2007. *Annual Report and Accounts 2007*. London: Standard Chartered Bank. Available at http://www.standardchartered.com/sustainability-review-08/en/download/2007_ARA.pdf.

Standing Senate Committee on Banking, Trade and Commerce. 2008. *Evidence Given to an Inquiry into the Present State of the Domestic and International Fi-*

nancial System—Subject: The Bank of Canada Report. Minutes of Proceedings of the Standing Senate Committee, issue no. 18, 1 May. Available at http://www.parl.gc.ca/Content/SEN/Committee/392/bank/18ev-e.htm?Language=E&Parl=39&Ses=2&comm_id=3.

Steinmo, Sven, and Kathleen Thelen. 1992. "Historical Institutionalism in Comparative Perspective." In Sven Steinmo, Kathleen Thelen, and Frank Longstreth (eds.), *Structuring Politics: Historical Institutionalism in Comparative Analysis.* Cambridge: Cambridge University Press, 1–32.

Stern, Gary. 2009. "Addressing the Too Big to Fail Problem." Statement of Gary H. Stern before the Committee on Banking, Housing, and Urban Affairs, US Senate, Washington, DC, 6 May. Available at http://www.minneapolisfed.org/news_events/pres/sterntestimony05-06-09.cfm.

Stevens, Matthew. 2008a. "Kelly Leaves Doubters in Limbo over Value." *Australian,* 9 August.

———. 2008b. "We'll Have a Soft Landing, Says Westpac's Gail Kelly." *Australian,* 31 October.

———. 2009. "Kelly Green with Envy as Bernanke Calls the Bottom." *Australian,* 7 May.

Stevenson, Rachel. 2004. "Hampton Quits Lloyds TSB over Strategy Disagreements." *Independent,* 14 January.

Stiglitz, Joseph. 2009. "The Anatomy of a Murder: Who Killed America's Economy?" *Critical Review* 21(2–3): 329–339.

———. 2010. *Freefall: America, Free Markets, and the Sinking of the World Economy.* New York: W. W. Norton.

Straumann, Tobias. 2010. *The UBS Crisis in Historical Perspective.* Expert opinion presented to UBS AG, Zurich, 28 September. Available at http://www.static-ubs.com/global/en/about_ubs/transparencyreport/_jcr_content/rightpar/teaser/linklist/link_0.2098844921.file/bGluay9wYXRoPS9jb250ZW50L2RhbS91YnMvZ2xvYmFsL2Fib3V0X3Vicy90cmFuc3BhcmVuY3lyZXBvcnQvMTg0NjE4X1NocmF1bWFubl9lbi5wZGY=/184618_Straumann_en.pdf.

Streeck, Wolfgang. 2009. *Re-forming Capitalism: Institutional Change in the German Political Economy.* Oxford: Oxford University Press.

———. 2011. "The Crises of Democratic Capitalism." *New Left Review* 71 (September–October): 5–29.

Streeck, Wolfgang, and Kathleen Thelen (eds.). 2005. *Beyond Continuity: Institutional Change in Advanced Political Economies.* Oxford: Oxford University Press.

Strömqvist, Maria. 2009. "Hedge Funds and Financial Crises." *Economic Review* 1: 87–106.

Stumpf, John. 2010. Interview of John Stumpf by the Financial Crisis Inquiry Commission (audio), 23 September. Available at http://fcic.law.stanford.edu/resource/interviews.

Suárez, Sandra, and Robin Kolodny. 2011. "Paving the Road to "Too Big to Fail": Business Interests and the Politics of Financial Deregulation in the United States." *Politics and Society* 39(1): 74–102.

Syal, Rajeev, Jill Treanor, and Nick Mathiason. 2011. "City's Influence over Conservatives Laid Bare by Research into Donations." *Guardian*, 30 September.

Sydney Morning Herald. 2009. "Rudd Blasts Westpac over Banana Slip." 9 December.

Syron, Richard. 2010. Interview of Richard Syron by the Financial Crisis Inquiry Commission (audio), 31 August. Available at http://fcic.law.stanford.edu/resource/interviews.

Taibbi, Matt. 2009. "The Great American Bubble Machine." *Rolling Stone*, 9 July.

Takáts, Előd, and Patrizia Tumbarello. 2009. "Australian Bank and Corporate Sector Vulnerabilities—An International Perspective." International Monetary Fund working paper no. 09/223. Washington, DC: IMF. Available at http://www.imf.org/external/pubs/ft/wp/2009/wp09223.pdf.

Taleb, Nassim. 2007. *The Black Swan: The Impact of the Highly Improbable.* New York: Random House.

Tarullo, Daniel. 2013. *Dodd-Frank Act.* Testimony of Governor Daniel K. Tarullo before the Committee on Banking, Housing, and Urban Affairs, US Senate, Washington, DC, 14 February. Available at http://www.federalreserve.gov/newsevents/testimony/tarullo20130214a.htm.

Taylor, John. 2009. *Getting off Track: How Government Actions and Interventions Caused, Prolonged, and Worsened the Financial Crisis.* Stanford: Hoover Institution Press.

TD (Toronto-Dominion). 2007. *152nd Annual Report 2007.* Toronto: TD. Available at http://www.td.com/document/PDF/ar2007/td-ar2007-ar2007.pdf.

———. 2008. *Annual Report 2008.* Toronto: TD. Available at http://www.td.com/document/PDF/ar2008/td-ar2008-ar2008.pdf.

Teather, David. 2005. "JP Morgan Pays $1bn to Settle Enron Claim." *Guardian*, 17 August.

———. 2009. "HBOS's Gambler Deals Himself Out." *Guardian*, 11 January.

Telegraph. 2009. "HBOS Whistleblower Paul Moore: Evidence to House of Commons 'Banking Crisis' Hearing." 11 February.

Tett, Gillian. 2009. *Fool's Gold: How the Bold Dream of a Small Tribe at J.P. Morgan was Corrupted by Wall Street Greed and Unleashed a Catastrophe.* New York: Free Press.

———. 2010. "Silos and Silences: Why So Few People Spotted the Problems in Complex Credit and What That Implies for the Future." *Bank de France Financial Stability Review*, no. 14: 121–129.

Thaler, Richard (ed.). 1993. *Advances in Behavioral Finance.* New York: Russell Sage Foundation.

———. 2000. "From Homo Economicus to Homo Sapiens." *Journal of Economic Perspectives* 14(1): 133–141.

Thal Larsen, Peter. 2005. "HSBC Charges into the U.S." *Chief Executive*, 1 March.

———. 2006a. "Barclays' Cultural Revolution Leader." *Financial Times*, 15 May.

———. 2006b. "Sir John Leaves HSBC with Global Reach but Underperforming Shares." *Financial Times*, 7 March.

———. 2007a. "Barclays Bruised by Subprime Bout but Still in Fighting Spirit." *Financial Times*, 16 November.
———. 2007b. "Expensive Show of Confidence in Barclays." *Financial Times*, 10 November.
———. 2007c. "HSBC Closes Securities Operation." *Financial Times*, 9 November.
———. 2008a. "Barclays Unloads £6bn in Difficult Debt Assets as Sale Conditions Ease." *Financial Times*, 8 August.
———. 2008b. "HSBC Puts Resilience on Display." *Financial Times*, 13 May.
Thelen, Kathleen. 1999. "Historical Institutionalism in Comparative Perspective." *Annual Review of Political Science* 2(1): 369–404.
———. 2011. "Beyond Comparative Statics: Historical Institutional Approaches to Stability and Change in the Political Economy of Labor." In Glenn Morgan, John Campbell, Colin Crouch, Ove Pederson, and Richard Whiteley (eds.), *The Oxford Handbook of Comparative Institutional Analysis.* Oxford: Oxford University Press, 41–62.
Thompson, Helen. 2009. "The Political Origins of the Financial Crisis: The Domestic and International Politics of Fannie Mae and Freddie Mac." *Political Quarterly* 80(1): 17–24.
Thornton, Emily, David Henry, and Adrienne Carter. 2006. "Inside Wall Street's Culture of Risk." *Businessweek*, 11 June.
Tibman, Joseph. 2009. *The Murder of Lehman Brothers: An Insider's Look at the Global Meltdown.* New York: Brick Tower Press.
Treanor, Jill. 2007a. "Lloyds TSB Takes a £200m Hit but Attracts Nervous Savers." *Guardian*, 11 December.
———. 2007b. "When $24bn Profits Are Not Enough." *Guardian*, 10 January.
———. 2008. "Deutsche Stays in Black Despite Further £1.8bn Writedown." *Guardian*, 1 August.
———. 2012a. "Banking Rules May Encourage Riskier Trading, Warns Ratings Agency." *Guardian*, 17 May.
———. 2012b. "Citigroup's Sandy Weill Backs Separation of High Street and Investment Banking." *Guardian*, 25 July.
———. 2012c. "'Electrify' Bank Ringfence, Says Standards Commission." *Guardian*, 21 December.
———. 2012d. "John Vickers Says George Osborne's Banking Reforms Don't Go Far Enough." *Guardian*, 14 June.
———. 2012e. "To Break Up or Not Break Up the Banks, That Remains the Question." *Guardian*, 18 October.
———. 2013a. "Barclays Reveals Plans for £6bn Cash Call to Plug Capital Gap." *Guardian*, 30 July.
———. 2013b. "Barclays Warns on New Capital Rules." *Guardian*, 28 June.
Treasury Committee (House of Commons). 2008. *The Run on the Rock.* HC 56-1, Fifth Report of Session 2007–08)—Volume 1, *Report, together with Formal Minutes.* London: TSO (The Stationery Office).

———. 2009a. *Banking Crisis.* HC 144-I—Volume 1, *Oral Evidence.* London: TSO. Available at http://www.publications.parliament.uk/pa/cm200809/cmselect/cmtreasy/144/144i.pdf.

———. 2009b. *Banking Crisis.* HC 144-II—Volume 2, *Written Evidence.* London: TSO. Available at http://www.parliament.the-stationery-office.co.uk/pa/cm200809/cmselect/cmtreasy/144/144ii.pdf.

———. 2009c. *Banking Crisis: Dealing with the Failure of the UK Banks.* HC 416, Seventh Report of Session 2008–09—*Report, together with Formal Minutes.* London: TSO. Available at http://www.publications.parliament.uk/pa/cm200809/cmselect/cmtreasy/416/416.pdf.

———. 2009d. *Banking Crisis: The Impact of the Failure of the Icelandic Banks.* HC 402, Fifth Report of Sessions 2008–2009—*Report, together with Formal Minutes.* London: TSO. Available at http://www.publications.parliament.uk/pa/cm200809/cmselect/cmtreasy/402/402.pdf.

———. 2009e. *Banking Crisis: Reforming Corporate Governance and Pay in the City.* HC 519, Ninth Report of Session 2008–09—*Report, together with formal minutes.* London: TSO. Available at http://www.publications.parliament.uk/pa/cm200809/cmselect/cmtreasy/519/519.pdf.

———. 2011. *Competition and Choice in Retail Banking.* HC 612-I, Ninth Report of Session 2010–11—Volume 2, *Oral and Written Evidence.* London: TSO. Available at http://www.publications.parliament.uk/pa/cm201011/cmselect/cmtreasy/612/612ii.pdf.

———. 2012a. *Fixing LIBOR: Some Preliminary Findings.* HC 418-I, Second Report of Session 2012–13—Volume 1, *Report, together with Formal Minutes;* Volume 2, *Oral Evidence.* London: TSO.

———. 2012b. *The FSA's Report into the Failure of RBS.* HC 640, Fifth Report of the Session 2012–13—*Report, together with Formal Minutes, Oral and Written Evidence.* London: TSO.

Tsingou, Eleni. 2008. "Transnational Private Governance and the Basel Process." In Jean-Christophe Graz and Andreas Nölke (eds.), *Transnational Private Governance and Its Limits.* London: Routledge, 58–68.

Tucker, Paul. 2011. "Discussion of Lord Turner's Lecture, 'Reforming Finance—Are We Being Radical Enough?' " Speech at the Clare Distinguished Lecture in Economics, Cambridge, 18 February. Available at http://www.bis.org/review/r110308c.pdf.

Tucker, Robert. 1978. *The Marx-Engels Reader.* New York: W. W. Norton.

Tucker, Sundeep, Victor Mallet, and Peter Thal Larsen. 2007. "HSBC Warns of 'Tears' if Big Deal Goes Wrong." *Financial Times,* 27 June.

Turner, Adair. 2009a. "How to Tame Global Finance." *Prospect Magazine,* 27 August. Available at http://www.prospectmagazine.co.uk/magazine/how-to-tame-global-finance/#.UkQ7WYZmiFw.

——— 2009b. *The Turner Review: A Regulatory Response to the Global Banking Crisis.* London: FSA. Available at http://www.fsa.gov.uk/pubs/other/turner_review.pdf.

———. 2010. "What Do Banks Do? Why Do Credit Booms and Busts Occur and What Can Public Policy Do about It?" In Adair Turner et al. (eds.), *The Future of Finance: The LSE Report.* London: London School of Economics and Political Science, 5–86.

———. 2011. "Reforming Finance: Are We Being Radical Enough?" Speech at the 2011 Clare Distinguished Lecture in Economics and Public Policy, Clare College, Cambridge, 18 February. Available at http://www.fsa.gov.uk/library/communication/speeches/2011/0218_at.shtml.

Tversky, Amos, and Daniel Kahneman. 1974. "Judgment under Uncertainty: Heuristics and Biases." *Science* 185(4157): 1124–1131.

———. 1992. "Advances in Prospect Theory: Cumulative Representation of Uncertainty." *Journal of Risk and Uncertainty* 5(4): 297–323.

UBS. 2008a. *Annual Report 2008.* Zurich: UBS.

———. 2008b. *Shareholder Report on UBS's Write-Downs.* Zurich: UBS.

———. 2012. "Restrictions on Proprietary Trading and Certain Interests in, and Relationships with, Hedge Funds and Private Equity Funds" (letter to the SEC), 17 February. Available at http://www.sec.gov/comments/s7-41-11/s74111-414.pdf.

Urry, Maggie. 2007."Barclays £1.3bn Writedown Calms Market." *Financial Times,* 15 November.

US Federal Reserve. 2007a. *94th Annual Report.* Washington, DC: Board of Governors of the Federal Reserve System. Available at http://www.federalreserve.gov/boarddocs/rptcongress/annual07/pdf/AR07.pdf.

———. 2007b. *Structure Data for the U.S. Offices of Foreign Banking Organizations,* 31 March. Available at http://www.federalreserve.gov/releases/iba/200703/bycntry.htm.

Valukas, Anton. 2010. *Examiner Report: Lehman Brothers Holdings Inc., Chapter 11 Proceedings* (case no. 08-13555 JMP). Available at http://lehmanreport.jenner.com/.

Veverka, Mark. 2008. "Bank on Them." *Barrons,* 18 February.

Viniar, David. 2010. *Interview of David Viniar by the Financial Crisis Inquiry Commission* (audio). Available at http://fcic.law.stanford.edu/resource/interviews.

Vogel, Steven. 1996. *Freer Markets, More Rules: Regulatory Reform in Advanced Industrial Countries.* Ithaca, NY: Cornell University Press.

Wachman, Richard, and Polly Curtis. 2011. "City Hits Back at Vince Cable over Banking Reform Comments." *Guardian,* 31 August.

Wachovia. 2008. *Form 10-K: Annual Report Pursuant to Section 13 or 15(d) of the Securities Exchange Act of 1934 for the Fiscal Period Ending December 31, 2007* (commission file no. 1-10000). Washington, DC: United States Securities and Exchange Commission. Available at http://www.taxpayer.net/user_uploads/file/Bailout/BankBios/WellsFargo/Finance/WACHOVIACORP%2010K%202007.pdf.

Wade, Robert. 2009a. "From Global Imbalances to Global Reorganisations." *Cambridge Journal of Economics* 33(4): 539–562.

———. 2009b. "The Global Slump: Deeper Causes and Harder Lessons." *Challenge* 52(5): 5–24.

Walker, David. 2009. *A Review of Corporate Governance in UK Banks and Other Financial Industry Entities: Final Recommendations.* London: HMSO. Available at http://webarchive.nationalarchives.gov.uk/+/http:/www.hm-treasury.gov.uk/d/walker_review_261109.pdf.

Wallison, Peter. 2009. "Cause and Effect: Government Policies and the Financial Crisis." *Critical Review* 21(2–3): 365–376.

———. 2011. "Financial Crisis Commission Dissenting Statement." National Commission on the Causes of the Financial and Economic Crisis in the United States. *The Financial Crisis Inquiry Report.* New York: Public Affairs.

Walter, Elisse. 2013. *Wall Street Reform: Oversight of Financial Stability and Consumer and Investor Protections.* Testimony before the US Senate Committee on Banking, Housing, and Urban Affairs, 14 February. Available at http://www.sec.gov/News/Testimony/Detail/Testimony/1365171489582#.UoIF4vmsiFw.

Ward, Vicky. 2010. *The Devil's Casino: Friendship, Betrayal, and the High-Stakes Games Played inside Lehman Brothers.* Hoboken, NJ: John Wiley and Sons.

Warner, Jeremy. 2005. "Outlook: A Few Signs of Progress but Lloyds TSB's Strategic Bind Still Looks as Bad as Ever." *Independent*, 13 December.

Wearden, Graeme. 2008. "Lloyds TSB/HBOS: What the Analysts Say." *Guardian*, 18 September.

Weber, Max. 1946. "The Social Psychology of the World Religions." In Hans Heinrich Gerth and Charles Wright Mills (eds.), *From Max Weber: Essays in Sociology.* New York: Oxford University Press, 1991, 267–301.

Weihart, Louise. 2007. "Australian Government Says 'Four Pillars' Will Stay; Industry Disagrees, Says It Creates Threat of Foreign Ownership." *Financial Times*, 6 August.

Weiss, Linda. 1998. *The Myth of the Powerless State.* Ithaca, NY: Cornell University Press.

Wells Fargo. 2007. *Annual Report 2007.* San Francisco: Wells Fargo. Available at http://www.wellsfargohistory.com/archives/archives2.html.

———. 2008. *Annual Report 2008.* San Francisco: Wells Fargo. https://www.wellsfargo.com/downloads/pdf/invest_relations/wf2008annualreport.pdf.

———. 2009. *Annual Report 2009.* San Francisco: Wells Fargo. Available at https://www.wellsfargo.com/downloads/pdf/invest_relations/wf2009annualreport.pdf.

Wessel, David. 2010. *In the Fed We Trust: Ben Bernanke's War on the Great Panic.* New York: Three Rivers Press.

Westpac. 2007. *Annual Report 2007.* Sydney: Westpac. Available at http://www.westpac.com.au/docs/pdf/aw/ic/WAR2007_AnnualReport_optimi1.pdf.

———. 2008. *Annual Report 2008.* Sydney: Westpac. Available at http://www.westpac.com.au/docs/pdf/aw/ic/WAR2008_AnnualReport.pdf.

Weyland, Kurt. 2008. "Toward a New Theory of Institutional Change." *World Politics* 60(2): 281–314.

Williams, Mark. 2010. *Uncontrolled Risk: The Lessons of Lehman Brothers and How Systemic Risk Can Still Bring Down the World Financial System*. New York: McGraw-Hill.

Willis, Andrew. 2009. "RBC Write-Down Signals Caution Still Rules US Strategy." *Globe and Mail*, 21 April.

Wolf, Martin. 2009. *Fixing Global Finance: How to Curb Financial Crises in the 21st Century*. New Haven: Yale University Press.

———. 2010. "Basel: The Mouse That Did Not Roar." *Financial Times*, 14 September.

———. 2012. "Two Cheers for Britain's Bank Reform Plans." *Financial Times*, 14 June.

Wolin, Neal. 2009. Speech to the Independent Community Bankers Association's (ICBA) Washington Policy Summit, Washington, DC, 2 May. Available at http://www.treasury.gov/press-center/press-releases/Pages/tg1154.aspx.

Woll, Cornelia. 2014. *The Power of Collective Inaction: Bank Bailouts in Comparison*. Ithaca, NY: Cornell University Press.

Wyatt, Edward. 2011. "Dodd-Frank under Fire a Year Later." *New York Times*, 18 July.

Young, Kevin. 2013. "Financial Industry Groups' Adaption to the Post-Crisis Regulatory Environment: Changing Approaches to the Policy Cycle." *Regulation and Governnance* (online version). Available prior to publication at http://onlinelibrary.wiley.com/doi/10.1111/rego.12025/abstract.

Zubrow, Barry. 2010. *Interview of Barry Zubrow with the Financial Crisis Inquiry Commission* (audio). Available at http://fcic.law.stanford.edu/resource/interviews.

———. 2012. *JP Morgan Chase Comment Letter on the Notice of Proposed Rulemaking Implementing Section 619 of the Dodd-Frank Wall Street Reform and Consumer Protection Act*. Available at http://www.sec.gov/comments/s7-41-11/s74111-267.pdf.

Acknowledgments

In the course of writing this book we have accumulated a significant number of debts.

First and foremost we are very grateful to those bankers, regulators, and commentators who agreed to be interviewed on (and sometimes off) the record about their experiences before, during, and after the crisis. L. P. Hartley's novel *The Go-Between* opens with the famous line "The past is like a foreign country: they do things differently there." One of the difficulties in writing about the 2007–2008 crisis comes in trying to recover a sense of what it is that people thought they were doing. Hindsight is, in this case, beguiling. The flaws in the financial system now seem so obvious that it is tempting to leap to the conclusion that people did not spot them because they were exceptionally incompetent or remarkably greedy, or both. Against this we argue that one of the most important lessons of the crisis is that most bankers and regulators *genuinely* believed that risk had been calibrated and dispersed and that the financial system was stable. The reality was, as we show, quite different. The answers to our interview questions opened up new lines of research and led us to completely rewrite draft chapters. Most importantly, the interviews helped us to correct a hindsight bias.

Tony Payne, Pepper Culpepper, Mick Moran, Andrew Gamble, and William D. Cohan were kind enough to read an earlier draft of the book and to offer a judicious mixture of encouragement and constructive advice. We are very grateful for their help. Our research was supported through Australian Research Council Discovery grant DP110100612. Hugh Jorgensen ably assisted with the research. We also would like to thank John Donohue and Barbara Goodhouse of Westchester Publishing Services for their excellent copyediting work. Material in this book draws, with the publishers' permission, upon three articles we have written: "Masters of the Universe but Slaves of the Market: Bankers and the Great Financial Meltdown," *British Journal of Politics and International Relations* (20 May 2014), http://onlinelibrary.wiley.com/doi/10.1111/1467-856X.12044/abstract, used in Chapters 2,

3, and 10; "The Ideational Shaping of State Capacity: Winning Battles but Losing the War," *Government and Opposition* 49(3) (2014): 342–368, used in Chapter 10; and "Taming the City: Power, Structural Ideas and the Evolution of British Banking," *New Political Economy* (forthcoming 2015), also in Chapter 10.

Our families learned to live with our fascination with bank balance sheets, credit default swaps, and the intricacies of capital regulation, although, on occasions, we suspect that they sometimes have been humoring us in the hope that we would, eventually, finish. Which it now seems we have.

Index